LOST VICTORY

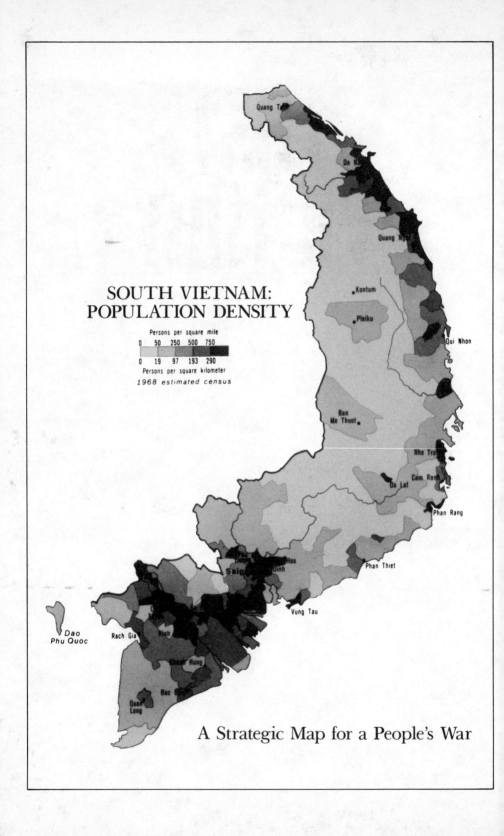

SOUTH VIETNAM: POPULATION DENSITY

Persons per square mile

| 0 | 50 | 250 | 500 | 750 |

| 0 | 19 | 97 | 193 | 290 |

Persons per square kilometer

1968 estimated census

A Strategic Map for a People's War

Quang T...

Da N...

Quang Ng...

Kontum

Pleiku

Qui Nhon

Ban Me Thuot

Nha Tra...

Cam Ranh

Da Lat

Phan Rang

Phan Thiet

Saigon

Vung Tau

Dao Phu Quoc

Rach Gia

Vinh

Khanh Hung

Bac Lieu

Quan Long

LOST VICTORY

A Firsthand Account of America's Sixteen-Year Involvement in Vietnam

William Colby

with James McCargar

CB

CONTEMPORARY
BOOKS

CHICAGO

Library of Congress Cataloging-in-Publication Data

Colby, William Egan, 1920–
    Lost victory / William Colby, with James McCargar.
      p.   cm.
    ISBN 0-8092-4509-4 (cloth)
        0-8092-4076-9 (paper)
    1. Vietnamese Conflict, 1961–1975—United States.
2. Vietnamese Conflict, 1961–1975—Personal narratives,
American.   3. Colby, William Egan, 1920–   .   I. McCargar,
James.   II. Title.
DS558.C66   1989
959.704′3373—dc20   89-17343
                                              CIP

Maps: The Center for Military History of the U.S. Army

Copyright © 1989 by William Colby
All rights reserved
Published by Contemporary Books, Inc.
180 North Michigan Avenue, Chicago, Illinois 60601
Manufactured in the United States of America
International Standard Book Number: 0-8092-4509-4 (cloth)
                                         0-8092-4076-9 (paper)

Contents

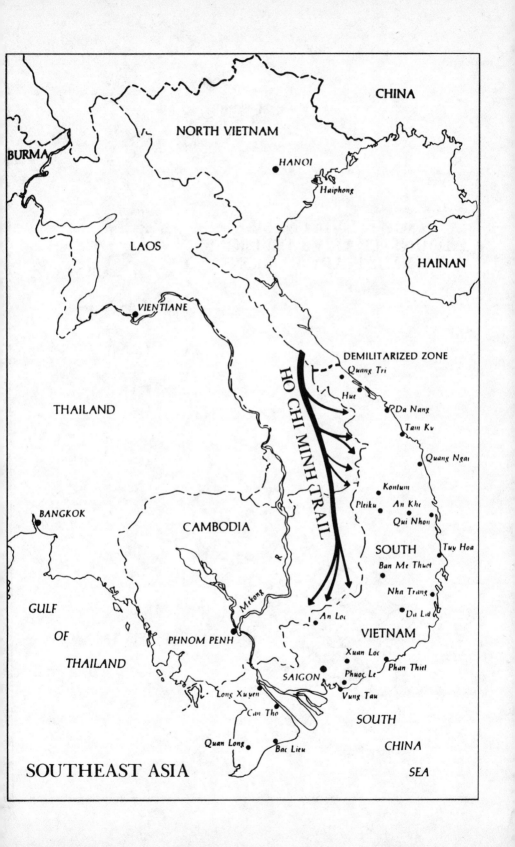

SOUTHEAST ASIA

CHINA

NORTH VIETNAM

BURMA

HANOI

Haiphong

HAINAN

LAOS

VIENTIANE

DEMILITARIZED ZONE

Quang Tri

Hue

Da Nang

Tam Ky

THAILAND

Quang Ngai

Kontum

Pleiku   An Khe

Qui Nhon

BANGKOK

CAMBODIA

SOUTH   Tuy Hoa

Ban Me Thuot

Nha Trang

Da Lat

GULF

Mekong

An Loc

VIETNAM

OF

PHNOM PENH

Xuan Loc

Phan Thiet

THAILAND

Phuoc Le

SAIGON

Vung Tau

Long Xuyen

Can Tho

SOUTH

Quan Long

Bac Lieu

CHINA

SEA

HO CHI MINH TRAIL

SOUTH VIETNAM:
ADMINISTRATIVE DIVISIONS
AND MILITARY REGIONS

Part One

THE DILEMMA
OF DEFEAT

THE LAST WEEK OF APRIL 1975, I went daily to the White House. They were long days. Congressional investigations charging that the CIA had engaged in illegal activities over the years since its founding and news leaks, especially the ultimately unsuccessful attempt to keep out of the papers—meaning from Russian knowledge—the fact that we were trying to lift a sunken Soviet submarine armed with nuclear weapons from the depths of the Pacific Ocean, were taking much of my time. But the White House meetings took priority over all other concerns, since it was plain that Saigon was facing total defeat.

On the morning of April 28, I again descended to the Situation Room in the basement of the West Wing. In that paneled room I joined Secretary of State (*and* National Security Adviser) Henry Kissinger, Secretary of Defense Jim Schlesinger, Deputy Secretary of Defense Bill Clements, Deputy Secretary of State Bob Ingersoll, Chairman of the Joint Chiefs of Staff General George Brown, and Deputy National Security Adviser Brent Scowcroft around the large conference table. Staff assistants were seated along the walls. This was the Washington Special Action Group—WSAG—the "crisis management" subcommittee of the United States National Security Council.

I gave the opening brief, as the Director of Central Intelligence traditionally does. North Vietnamese divisions were on the outskirts of Saigon and threatened its airport, Tan Son Nhut. Order was breaking down in the city as its inhabitants and refugees from outside Saigon, mixed with troops from South Vietnamese units that had dissolved, sought desperately to escape from the oncoming Communist forces.

The brief finished, we considered the major question before us: with North Vietnamese divisions on the outskirts of Saigon, at what point would we recommend to the President the evacuation of all Americans from Vietnam? True, the last of the 550,000 American forces who had been in Vietnam in mid-1968 had left two years earlier with the conclusion of the "Peace" Agreement that was supposed to have ended the long war in South Vietnam. But we still had hundreds of Americans in the Defense Attaché's Office, the Embassy, and other American agencies in Saigon. Our Ambassador, Graham Martin, had sought to stave off evacuation, first arguing that it would be interpreted as a sign of weakness and then hoping that at least a residual Embassy presence might be possible. Secretary Kissinger was not averse to delay, since he had continued to set store by the possibility of negotiating some nonviolent compromise through Moscow. Defense Secretary Schlesinger and I agreed: The Soviets had no control over their North Vietnamese allies, and the end was inevitable in the absence of American intervention. It was wrong to increase the risk of losing Americans to death or capture by delaying their evacuation.

The possibility of American intervention to save South Vietnam of course had vanished after Watergate with the resignation of the President who had promised air and logistical support to South Vietnam in the event of violations of the Peace Agreement by Hanoi. I had participated in briefing the Congress on a number of such violations during the previous two years as President Gerald Ford vainly tried to obtain full appropriations for the still threatened Saigon forces. Again and again I had explained to coldly unresponsive Congressmen how the North Vietnamese Army not only was still in Laos and Cambodia in violation of the Agreement but was also constructing an extensive network of full-scale roads—even pipelines—in those countries *and* in the western regions of South Vietnam to support the mechanized and armored forces they were maintaining on the borders of South Vietnam, ready to resume the attack.

The absence of any American reaction to these violations had set the tone. In January 1975 the North Vietnamese launched an attack against the isolated South Vietnamese province of Phuoc Long, north of Saigon, from the bases they had built up in Cambodia, to test the American reaction. Again there was none. The Congress declined any increase in aid to the South Vietnamese. The White House was unable to act on its own, even though this was the most openly flagrant violation to date of the Agreement the United States and North Vietnam had signed—and forced the South Vietnamese to sign on threat of stopping all aid—in January 1973.

Earlier, in December 1974, I had presented the CIA assessment—confirmed by the North Vietnamese after the War as having been their plan—that the North Vietnamese Communists would launch an attack in early 1975 aimed at victory by the end of 1976, i.e., after the next American Presidential elections. As their attack proved more effective than either they or we had anticipated, I had, in a mid-April meeting of the WSAG, modified this estimate. In a phrase I had inserted into the more careful prose provided me by the CIA analysts, I said that "South Vietnam faces total defeat—and soon."

My intelligence briefing for the April 28 meeting put the situation starkly:

> Communist forces are now on the outskirts of Saigon and clearly in a position to occupy it. The Minh government has been overtaken by events, and a complete military takeover in Saigon appears inevitable today or tomorrow.

The question was the same one we had faced all week: whether to order the evacuation of all remaining Americans from Saigon. Many had left during the past several weeks as the situation became grimmer in the northern and central parts of Vietnam and the South Vietnamese forces disintegrated. But Ambassador Martin, whom Kissinger supported as the "man on the spot," still hoped to arrange at least a peaceful surrender. The evacuation of many Americans and key Vietnamese by American aircraft from Tan Son Nhut Airport just outside Saigon had already begun.

Despite our feeling that collapse was only a matter of time, the meeting ended without a decision, in deference to

Martin's strong position. But the North Vietnamese decided for us. At 4:00 A.M. Saigon time (4:00 P.M. in Washington), their rockets and artillery opened up on Tan Son Nhut, wrecking many of the aircraft there, causing chaos among the Vietnamese waiting to leave, and putting the airport out of commission.

President Ford called an emergency meeting of the National Security Council for 7:30 P.M. The members assembled quickly: President Ford, Vice President Rockefeller, the Secretaries of State and Defense (with their deputies), the Chairman of the Joint Chiefs of Staff and myself as advisers, and Kissinger (in his additional role of National Security Adviser). It was clear that the evacuation had to take place—now by helicopters alone. The President wanted one last consultation with Ambassador Martin, which Kissinger arranged shortly thereafter. With the Ambassador's final acceptance of the inevitable, the President's order went out to remove all the remaining Americans and as many Vietnamese as could be taken out.

The helicopters then began the agonizing task of lifting evacuees off of rooftops and from improvised landing pads in the city. Crowds of Vietnamese frantically tried to be included in the escape. Although literally every American was removed, the confusion made it impossible to take the thousands of Vietnamese clamoring to go—including many who had been assured that they would be taken care of by the power that had dominated their lives, and that they had served and relied upon, for so many years. A few Vietnamese officers put bullets to their heads, some as a gesture of honor in defeat, others to escape the draconian punishment that they knew awaited them in Communist "reeducation" camps. In faraway Washington, there was literally nothing I could do at this point. But over that day's frustrations hung the tragedy of this waste of the lives and the years of effort of both Vietnamese and Americans who had hoped that Vietnam might develop in freedom.

In the early hours of the following morning, April 30, the last of a swarm of American helicopters, both military and the CIA's fleet—the CIA's Air America pilots had volunteered to work through the shot and shell of Saigon's last days—lifted off the rooftops of the American Embassy and other rendezvous points. They flew with their passengers to the *USS Coral Sea* and a powerful American fleet waiting offshore. In Saigon, and elsewhere in Vietnam, millions of Vietnamese began to consider how they would survive under a Communist regime or whether they could escape by taking to the sea on their own.

At the same moment—about 7:30 A.M.—the North Vietnamese Army's Russian-and Chinese-supplied T-54 tanks began their entrance into the city. Before the morning was out, one of the tanks had smashed through the gates of Independence Palace, the symbol of an independent South Vietnam. There General Duong Van Minh, leader of the 1963 coup against then-President Ngo Dinh Diem, accompanied by his "Foreign Minister," Vu Van Mau, whose last public act had been to shave his head in protest against Diem's policies toward the Buddhists in 1963, waited to surrender South Vietnam. The soldiers accompanying the tanks mounted the steps of the Presidential Palace and entered, revealing by their accents that they were all North Vietnamese—the disciplined and determined heirs of Ho Chi Minh. They refused to deal with Minh and his forlorn party and led them away as captives as the American armada disappeared over the eastern horizon. So began the General's and his aides' exposure to the harsh treatment that would be the lot of the South Vietnamese, whether they had fought for a South free of Northern and Communist domination or had been allies of the Communists of the North.

And thus ended the Second—or American—Indochinese War of 1959–1975, in a defeat for the United States as well as for South Vietnam. The victory for the Communist forces was manifestly greater and more complete than that they had achieved in the First—or French—Indochinese War of 1945–1954. The costs to all of the Second Indochinese War were immeasurably higher than those of the First. Millions of Vietnamese were killed, maimed, and displaced, as combatants on both sides, and as victims caught between American and South Vietnamese air or ground fire, or under the rockets, mortars, or terrorist grenades of the North Vietnamese Army or Southern guerrillas.

The American costs were 58,000 killed, some 300,000

wounded, and over $150 billion spent. To all this was added a deep disruption of American—and even world—social and cultural patterns. Protest against the war evolved into protest against society, in many cases envenoming the normal rift between generations. Escape into drugs and rejection of almost any authority marked the effective abdication of much of an entire generation. The flight from responsibility was followed by the "me" generation of concentrated self-interest and the refusal of commitment or sacrifice by all too many of our young citizens. As George Bush said on January 20, 1989, in his first address as President to his fellow citizens, the Vietnam War "cleaves us still."

The greatest question about the defeat, however, is how it could have occurred. The American armada of powerful aircraft carriers that sailed away to the east from fallen Saigon, with their supporting cruisers and destroyers, carried devastating firepower that could have blasted the North Vietnamese forces. Dozens of huge B-52 bombers of the Strategic Air Command were easily available from Guam to deliver hundreds of heavy "iron bombs," or even the ultimate nuclear weapons, onto the heads of America's enemies. American forces were still deployed around the world to support friends and deter foes. But all of this massive power had not changed the result in Vietnam. This contrast between potential power and actual defeat cries out for explanation. And what does this contrast presage for the future?

It is plain that this outcome did not result from any simple factor—a tactical failure on the battlefield, for example, such as Pearl Harbor's lack of readiness for the Japanese attack of December 7, 1941. Nor can one say that the American President could have changed it by some other decision in the last days. As with the fall of France before the Nazi legions in 1940, a host of factors stretched over many years produced the weaknesses that finally led to the collapse.

The question of American decline is broached at home and abroad. America's allies look anxiously about them, wondering to what extent they can count on American will—and wit—to help them fend off the challenges they see on their frontiers or subversive threats within their societies. It was not long after the fall of Saigon that hostile demagogues and religious and ethnic zealots asserted that

America is a muscle-bound "Great Satan" that can be reviled, and indignities wreaked upon its citizens and diplomats, without fear of reprisal.

In America itself, the reaction came in stages. Initially, the shame of the photos of Americans being lifted off of Saigon's rooftops hardly overcame the sense of relief that the war was finally over. The escape of all Americans left no concern for prisoners or hostages. The collapse of South Vietnam was so complete that it seemed beyond American capacity to have changed. The care, movement, and resettlement of the 130,000 Vietnamese who fled at the collapse, and the half million more who would take to leaky boats and brave the South China Sea in the ensuing months, provided an outlet for feelings of obligation to the South Vietnamese.

The United States turned to the celebration of its Bicentennial to rebuild its pride and confidence and to seek a new unity among its own people after the traumas of Vietnam and Watergate. The United States Army, which had borne the brunt of the battle in Vietnam over the years, turned firmly toward the more familiar tasks of propping up deterrence and preparing for a more understandable kind of war, should that be necessary, on the North German plain.

Time may not heal all wounds, but it does lessen the passions they engender. A new generation arises that seeks to understand the reasons for the intensity of those passions and to arrive at its own judgment. Participants separated by the intervening years from the heat of action seek explanations for their frenetic activity or try to justify their performance of their responsibilities and answer charges that their service was flawed. As the years pass, it becomes clear that history does not write itself but is influenced by the reflections and appreciations of those whose judgments and decisions made it happen.

Thus, the American experience in Vietnam has been coming out of the closet of rejection in which it was shut for so many years. The participants, aware that they played only a partial role in the sixteen-year experience, desire an explanation of where and how they fitted into the overall panorama, and whether their memories are of exceptional or typical events. New assessments of historical events—

such as Peter Braestrup's meticulous study of the Tet 1968 offensive showing that it was actually a Communist defeat hyped by the media into a decisive harbinger of inevitable Communist victory—challenge some of the accepted conclusions about key events. Debates over current policies, from Central America to the Philippines, are couched in terms of "another Vietnam," with different meanings for each advocate, heightening the need for some common perception of the experience for Americans.

That common perception has not yet been achieved. The proverbial blind men examining parts of the elephant and reaching conclusions about the whole animal therefrom come to mind: "A reptile," says the man holding the trunk; "Cousin to the whale," says he who is patting the side. Participants, observers, academics—all are producing quite different accounts of the Vietnam War.

In this situation I want to contribute my view, which includes a longer sweep of time than most, and some elements that are little known. Then, perhaps from my account and from those of others, we can see the whole of what we experienced rather than only parts. It is clear that we must do this as, even after the experience, the memorial to the American military who died in Vietnam, moving as it is with its healing intent, proved to be a dark and submerged wall of names, starkly ambiguous as to whether it signifies pride, pity, or shame.

It has long been true that a lieutenant's view of a war is that of a disaster. He is commanded to lead his troops into impossible situations, sometimes to certain death. The overall strategy is rarely explained to him, and his commanders often are less aware of the perils than he is. This was indeed the experience of American soldiers in Vietnam as they fought a faceless and shadowy enemy, amid a population they distrusted and feared, under the command of officers high above them in helicopters. The nature of the war deprived them of the satisfaction of seeing their lines advance against the enemy. Today's random search for the enemy to destroy him was repeated in the same area on the morrow. The obligation on those of us who bore major responsibility to explain to the "grunts"—and to the American people—what the leadership saw and intended, its successes and its failures, is therefore imperative. If it was not adequately explained at the time, it is even more important to do it now.

Three spectacular incidents dominate the ordinary American's view of Vietnam: Thich Quang Duc, a yellow-robed Buddhist monk, burning himself to death on a Saigon street in 1963 in protest against the South Vietnamese Government of President Ngo Dinh Diem, who ruled with support from the liberal Democratic Administration of John F. Kennedy; the Tet 1968 sapper assault within the very precincts of the American Embassy in Saigon, after assurances by the Johnson Administration that we had turned a corner in Vietnam, accompanied by the atrocity of the execution of a Communist saboteur-captive by the chief of Saigon's police, portrayed dramatically as on an American newsman's film; and the frantic rooftop evacuation by helicopter in 1975 of the last Americans from Saigon, they in crowded echelons on the ladder of a utility penthouse atop the Embassy, while below hundreds of Vietnamese left behind scrambled desperately—and futilely—to surmount the high Embassy walls, trying to reach that ladder, safety, and a future. The easy conclusion from these images was that the cause was hopeless and that the only proper lesson from the whole experience is not to repeat it.

But behind this surface impression, reality—as usual—is much more complex. The sixteen years of war in Vietnam offer an observer any image he seeks. Shadowy guerrilla, contented rice farmer, terrorist victim, bloated general, mystic monk, heroic mountain man, brave soldier, infuriating bureaucrat, dedicated reformer, sordid bargirl—all are there, on both sides among the Vietnamese. Nor can history deny a similar variety among the Americans involved.

The American debate over the Vietnam War selects among the available images to support the position of the advocate; very few seek any kind of middle ground. In recent years, however, the search for understanding has gained precedence over polemics; references to Vietnam have become more meaningful than mere repetition of the debate that characterized the era of America's involvement there.

This book is my contribution to the effort to achieve

understanding, and with it an appreciation of the vital lessons to be drawn from the suffering and agonies of the Second Vietnam War.

To this effort I bring experience of that War, through five American Presidencies, that few Americans have equaled. For the great majority of the millions of Americans who served in Vietnam, the standard tour of duty was one year (draftees had one year of training and one year in Vietnam). Even most Government officials in Washington or elsewhere had only a limited connection, lasting two or three years, to events in Vietnam. And most of the literature on the War essentially stops at 1968, a full seven years before the end (e.g., the "Pentagon Papers," Frances FitzGerald's *Fire in the Lake*, and Halberstam's *The Best and the Brightest*), or gives only cursory treatment to the period that followed (e.g., Stanley Karnow's *Vietnam*, only 100 of almost 700 pages; Neil Sheehan's *A Bright Shining Lie*, 70 of almost 800 pages). But my arrival in Vietnam on Tet (February 8), 1959, began an intense involvement with that country and its war that continued until April 29, 1975, when I sent from Washington the final message to close the CIA Saigon station.

My first tour lasted almost three-and-a-half years, until June 1962. In those years I traveled throughout all of South Vietnam, from the Demilitarized Zone at the 17th Parallel in the north to the swamps of the southern tip of Ca Mau. I became the principal American contact with President Ngo Dinh Diem's conspiratorial brother and closest adviser, Ngo Dinh Nhu. Then followed six years at the CIA's Washington headquarters as Chief of the Far East Division. These included briefing Presidents Kennedy and Johnson, visiting Vietnam with Secretary of Defense McNamara, and separate visits on my own several times each year. Again assigned to Vietnam just after Tet 1968, I spent the next three years as Ambassador and Deputy to the Commanding General, Military Assistance Command Vietnam, traveling to every province and sitting in on President Nguyen Van Thieu's Cabinet meetings as I directed American support of the rural pacification program. In June 1971, I returned to CIA headquarters in an administrative post handling the CIA's budget preparation and presentations to Congress, including activities in Vietnam. Two years later, in mid-1973, I became Director of Central Intelligence and, with our intelligence community, followed closely the final two years of the Vietnam War.

This intense involvement, extending over sixteen years and entailing varied assignments in senior capacities in both Vietnam and Washington, gave me a unique insight into the drama of the War. I was among the few Americans who knew the Vietnamese who fought their war at the village level and helped direct that local war at the national level. I sat with leaders of small communities and discussed their need for better weapons to meet the AK-47 submachine guns supplied by the Soviet Union and China through North Vietnam to their Communist enemies. I attended meetings in the Cabinet Room of the White House at which proposals were debated to move the bombing line one degree northward toward Hanoi to make clear American resolve and power to deter the Communist ambition to take over South Vietnam.

My intelligence responsibilities made me appreciate the hopes and failings of a long series of Vietnamese leaders trying to manage their country's struggle against the imposition of a Communist regime. They gave me insights into the relationships between Vietnamese leaders and Americans. On the one hand, I had abundant experience with the Vietnamese consciousness of their dependence upon the Americans, accompanied by their stubborn resistance to the status of a subordinate partner in determining how to fight what they thought was their war. On the other, I came to understand the effect on those relationships of the conviction widespread among the Americans that the failures of the various American formulas for success in Vietnam could be due only to the unwillingness or inability of the Vietnamese to perceive their validity—indeed, their brilliance—and apply them as indicated.

The result was that I came to look at the American involvement in Vietnam through Vietnamese as well as American eyes. My function was to understand President Thieu, as well as General Abrams, and the workings of both the American and the Vietnamese political processes. My intelligence responsibilities also required me to look at the contest from the viewpoint of the North Vietnamese Communist enemies and to appreciate their view of the situation they faced, including what they saw as American strengths and weaknesses.

From this special vantage point, it was abundantly clear that the continuing contrast between America's huge arsenal in Vietnam and its apparent inability to defeat the enemy caused Americans to question whether their leaders knew what they were doing. These doubts were certainly reinforced by the free—and critical—American media, but they stemmed from the fundamentals of the situation and were not the product of the media alone. In Vietnam, America's will was not overcome by superior enemy force. It eroded because of a conviction, which became a consensus, that the execution of the American intent was ineffectual— even counterproductive.

The American attention span is short. We insist on near-term results. The frequent American elections, during which American policy is subject to popular review and candidates are pressed to offer simple solutions to complex problems, reinforce this demand. Within the American political process, it is difficult to justify the small steps and gradual progress that frequently are necessary in the pursuit of long-term goals.

In the event, the American democratic process worked. American policy swung from support of the War to opposition, reflecting the change in judgment of the American people. Pragmatism is the ultimate test of American policy. If it does not work, it is firmly rejected. And so it was in Vietnam.

This is not to say that our processes are without their costs or that the pragmatism of the American people is necessarily just or right with respect to a particular problem and its solution. Our reluctance to face up to the threat Hitler posed to Western civilization made the inevitable contest with him harder and bloodier.

The boat people who endured unimaginable suffering at sea in their determination to escape today's Vietnam, the disappearance of the Southern Vietnamese Communists under Northern rule, the necessity for North Vietnamese divisions to remain, years later, in South Vietnam—all show that South Vietnam fell to an alien invasion from the North in a total triumph over the policies of several American Presidents committed to prevent exactly that result. The early fall of Cambodia and Laos and, later, American political failures in Angola, Iran, and Nicaragua were the consequence. Another was the hesitant and reluctant American response to later challenges as the cry of "Vietnam!" threatened to shut off discussion, and certainly deliberation, about what the United States should do when faced with new threats to its interests in Central America and the Middle East.

In 1980, the Presidential election was conducted largely around the questions of American morale and of confidence about the American role in the world's future. In somewhat simplistic terms, the issue was posed between the experience of the past few years and the image of a strong and self-confident America willing to use its forces and resources to press its values and interests, to support its friends, and to deny the ambitions of its enemies. The political debate shifted from the contemplation and discussion of whether America had pursued morally flawed policies—and ones that had, perhaps thereby, failed as well. The American people responded with enthusiasm to President Reagan's assertion of American will, of confidence that our cause is just and our actions proper, and his refusal to accept carping outside criticism of imperfection. This attitude was repeated—even reinforced—by the 1988 election, with its stress on the Pledge of Allegiance as a vehicle for a call to patriotism.

But the question of American will must be separated from the question of American wisdom. America's willingness to "bear any burden, fight any foe," the words with which President Kennedy stirred the nation, differs from our ability to choose the correct strategy and adopt the best tactics to attain our goals. This is why explanation and clarification of the Vietnam War are necessary—and become more necessary as time passes.

At this stage, we must dissect and examine the American experience in Vietnam in exquisite detail. We must exorcise the ghost of our agony there from the American psyche. We must identify what we did right there and what we did wrong. We must distinguish the strategy, or lack thereof, from the tactics and judge them separately to find which are worthy of adding to our national arsenal and which clearly were mistaken and should be rejected. We must sort out the optional from the inevitable aspects of our effort there, the choice of strategy and arms from the certain side effects of the presence of a large military force in an ethnically and culturally foreign community.

We must do this from the perspective of the War on the ground and in the villages, jungles, mountains, and rice paddies of South Vietnam. We must review the long span of years from 1959, when the Vietnamese Communists decided to open the "Second Indochinese War" against the "American-Diem" Government of South Vietnam, to their final victory in 1975. However important the factors of negotiations, the antiwar movement, logistics, or Saigon politics, their effects must be identified on the battleground contested by the two sides. We thus must examine the situation, the antagonists, and the basic strategies as they appeared at the start of the contest and as they changed over the years during which it was waged.

That is why this book appears now. As for its content, I can summarize it with a short story. After the end of the Vietnam War, an American Colonel, Harry G. Summers, engaged in a postmortem in Hanoi with a North Vietnamese Colonel. "You know," said the American, "you never defeated us on the battlefield." The Vietnamese agreed. "That may be so," he said. Then he added, "But it is also irrelevant."

This book is the story of why those purely military successes were, *indeed*, irrelevant.

It is also an answer to the question: was there a better way?

Part Two
THE TWAIN MEET

Oh, East is East, and West is West, and never
the twain shall meet,
Till Earth and Sky stand presently at God's
great judgment seat;
But there is neither East nor West, border,
nor breed, nor birth,
When two strong men stand face to face, though
they come from the ends of the earth!

Rudyard Kipling, "The Ballad of East and West"

1

Two-and-a-Half Cultures

MY BOYHOOD EXPERIENCES OF CHINA, when my father, an Army officer, was stationed in Tientsin, had prepared me for the exoticism of Asia. They had not prepared me for the blast of ovenlike heat as the Pan Am Stratocruiser's door opened at Saigon's Tan Son Nhut Airport. My family and I stepped out into the broiling sun of the Vietnamese capital's airport. It was Tet 1959—the Vietnamese name for the first day of the Chinese calendar's lunar year. The complexities and variations of the date—it is the first new moon falling between January 19 and February 19, February 8 in 1959—presaged those I would live through for the next sixteen years.

In the dusty, faded terminal we sought some relief in shade, if not in air-conditioning. Our passports, mine showing my assignment to the American Embassy to South Vietnam, were ritually stamped and our luggage waved on by customs inspectors much more interested in whether a Chinese-Vietnamese lady fellow passenger was trying to conceal some gold from Hong Kong among her silks and transistor radios. The heat, the ritualism, the suspicion of contraband were my introduction to my post as Deputy Chief of the CIA Station in South Vietnam.

From Tan Son Nhut to the city itself, the road led through the suburbs typical of a big Asian city—walled villas serving as islands of green and calm among squalid shanties teeming with life. The road was named Ngo Dinh Khoi, for the Vietnamese President's eldest brother murdered by the Communists in 1945. At the city line its name changed to Cong Ly, or "Justice." The city itself was shaded by tall trees spaced evenly along the streets, with gracious white and cream-colored tropical houses behind walls giving

19

both privacy and security. Their sight evoked memories of provincial towns in the south of France.

The names of Saigon's streets had been changed from those of the French colonial leaders who had conquered the country and designed the city a century ago to those of Vietnamese national heroes. But two French names remained: those of the famous Louis Pasteur and of Alexandre de Rhodes, a little-known Jesuit missionary. For the nine centuries from 111 B.C. to A.D. 939, Vietnam had been occupied and ruled by the Chinese. De Rhodes was still honored in Vietnam because in the 1640s, after a period in which the Vietnamese deliberately distanced themselves from classic Chinese language and literature, he successfully romanized written Vietnamese (followed by a flowering of their literature, which is a part of Vietnamese national pride).

Our route led past the Palace of the French Governor General—now Independence Palace, residence of the President of the Republic of Vietnam, and into a villa on a park facing the iron grilles of the front entrance of the Palace wall. The shaded scene gave no hint of the dramas to be enacted there—some before my family's and my own eyes.

It was a time of transition. The years of struggle between the Communist-led Viet Minh, fighting for Vietnamese freedom and revolution against the French colonists, had ended five years before in the French defeat at Dien Bien Phu, in the far-off mountains of North Vietnam. Reminders of that struggle were at hand: the prohibition of firecrackers during the celebration of Tet, even in Cholon, the Chinese section of Saigon; the grilles protecting the Arc-en-Ciel Restaurant—the best Chinese restaurant in Southeast Asia (and possibly the world)—from grenades; the presence in the South of some 900,000 refugees from North Vietnam, with their strong Catholic convictions and scorn for the softer Southerners.

But peace had returned to South Vietnam. The Communists had withdrawn some 90,000 of their cadres to the North, where they studied and trained for whatever future opportunity might arise to resume revolution in the South. Their networks there were dormant and skeletal, concerned chiefly with survival against periodic South Vietnamese

Government campaigns to wipe them out. Their leaders in the North gave them little attention. Ho Chi Minh and his colleagues were preoccupied with solidifying Communist authority in the North, where occasional flare-ups of opposition from Catholic and other opponents of their rule dictated their priorities. The Northern comrades' primary effort revolved around the land reform campaign. In order to collectivize land holdings and thus establish the basis for full Party control of the economy and the population, the emphasis was on punishing (and, in many cases, executing) landowners in "People's Courts," whose verdicts were never in doubt.

In the South, even those groups that had competed for power after the French withdrawal were quiescent. Despite the prevailing mythology, nourished by constant rumors, of wily French machinations still at work in South Vietnam, the French Embassy respected the Republic's sovereignty. The French colony concerned itself with its remaining rubber estates and commercial interests. Even the French "special services" restricted their activities to maintaining some useful contacts among the Vietnamese who could keep them well informed and serve as a base for future influence if French interests called for more vigorous action.

The Binh Xuyen bandit gang that had controlled Saigon for its own benefit had been forcefully suppressed. Its only relic was the walled "Grand Monde" complex on the edge of Cholon, which had provided a full service of prostitution, gambling, and opium but was now a youth center visited by tourists still titillated by its reputation. The private armies of the religious sects, the Cao Dai and the Hoa Hao, had been dissolved. Trade and commerce ran unimpeded through the regions where their religious appeal remained, but their temporal authority had been replaced by that of the fledgling Republic. The division of the city of Saigon between the French and Chinese sections was clear, but there were no inhibitions about circulating day or night, by car or by human- or motor-driven tri-shaws, in either one.

Life at the American Embassy reflected the generally relaxed atmosphere. We lived in high-ceilinged, French-style villas shaded by tall trees the French had planted years ago. Servants were plentiful, loyal, and friendly, freeing my

wife, Barbara, for a busy schedule of gatherings with wives
of senior Vietnamese and of other diplomats. Our three
sons—Jonathan, thirteen, Carl, nine, and Paul, five—attended the American Community School (after an abortive
experiment with a Catholic boys' school where the dominant language was a far too difficult Vietnamese rather
than the French we had expected). Our daughter, Catherine, ten, attended a Catholic girls' school in which French
was the language of instruction and communication among
the students. (Another daughter, Christine, was born in
Saigon the next year.) All enjoyed the sights and sounds of
Eastern civilization, from the dragon dance in Saigon's
Chinese quarter the day after we arrived to the tales of our
next-door neighbor, a professional hunter, as he explained
his capture of elephants in the mountains and their delivery
to zoos in Europe. The prevailing atmosphere of those days
raised no worries about their safety in our minds.

French was still the lingua franca of the foreign community, and all the Vietnamese we dealt with were comfortable
in it. The usual round of diplomatic receptions and dinners
occupied many evenings, made pleasant by the inclusion of
many sophisticated Vietnamese who fully held their own in
conversations on any subject. Noon frequently meant a
family gathering at the Cercle Sportif swimming pool,
where a fine French lunch was served during the two-hour
midday break. It was hot in the dry season and humid in the
wet, but one learned to reduce one's pace to limit the perspi-
ration, and air-conditioning in bedrooms permitted sleep.

The official pace also was sedate. The obvious stability of
the Government and the absence of challenge or conflict
meant that there were no crises. The substantial American
Agency for International Development (AID) program and
mission could concentrate on their longer-term objectives
and projects. The American military representatives could
maintain friendly relationships with their South Vietnamese counterparts and give full attention to the voluminous
reports required by Washington.

This surface calm covered a beehive of activity. The
intense and individualistic Vietnamese took advantage of
peace to launch their enterprises, large and small, in the
rice paddies and marketplaces. A vigorous economic and

social development program was under way, with new roads opening up jungle fastnesses, schools and teachers appearing in remote villages, light industries arising in urban suburbs, and motorized fishing boats proliferating along the coast. The South Vietnamese reveled in their free enterprise, continuing the dynamic drive that had brought their ancestors in their eight-centuries-long "March to the South," along the coast of Annam and into the Mekong River Delta—their energies and acquisitiveness thrusting the empires of the Chams and the Khmer aside and away.

Presiding over this busy scene, and indeed responsible for its creation, was a somewhat dumpy and certainly noncharismatic figure—President Ngo Dinh Diem. Born into a Mandarin and Catholic family in the imperial city of Hue in Central Vietnam, he was raised to a life of service to the Emperor and the community. He told me once how in his early years he and his brothers, standing in the muck and individually inserting the tender green rice shoots into the fertile mud, had thus taken part in the symbolic replanting of the shoots from their breeding beds to the paddies for their full growth into the staple of Vietnamese life.

Diem's real love was the community. He prepared himself to join the respected ranks of the minor officials who made Vietnamese authority function at the local level underneath the French colonial administrators. But after a promising beginning to his career, he found it impossible to serve both the French overlords and Vietnam. Leaving the French-controlled administration, he became one of the leading advocates of Vietnamese independence. In this role he acted as an individual, however, not as leader of a party or conspiracy, under a Mandarin's assumption that power would in due course devolve to him.

Diem's reputation grew to the point where in 1945, when the Japanese withdrew after their defeat, Ho Chi Minh sought his participation in a coalition effort to seize power from the discredited Vichy French authorities who had run Vietnam during World War II. Diem refused the offer. His was a deep-seated Catholic rejection of Communism, and he saw clearly that Ho would merely use him and other non-Communists as stepping stones to the acquisition of full power for the Communists.

During the next few years the French vainly tried to organize puppet governments under the "Emperor" Bao Dai, the last of the Nguyen dynasty. Diem refused every offer he received to join, and even one to lead, such a government because it was evident that it would merely be a nationalist facade behind which the French would retain every element of real power. In 1950 he went to the United States, where he stayed in several Maryknoll seminaries and spread his advocacy of an independent Vietnam among such figures as Francis Cardinal Spellman of New York and Senators Mike Mansfield and John F. Kennedy.

The collapse of the French effort in Indochina after the battle of Dien Bien Phu in 1954 and its formalization in the Geneva Accords that divided the nation into a Communist North and a non-Communist South (with both to hold elections after two years to reunify Vietnam) brought Diem, by then in France, a new opportunity. Bao Dai offered him the Prime Ministry with an assurance that Diem could be truly independent of French rule. Diem accepted. The prevailing wisdom of that day was that, over the following two years, Diem would merely preside over the collapse of South Vietnam and its absorption into a reunified Vietnam dominated by the more numerous, more regimented, and more dynamic North ruled by the disciplined cadres of the Communist revolutionary effort that had defeated the French. But Diem surprised the world.

His first priorities were to oust the pro-French leadership of the Army and to counter remaining French colonial hostility to his rule. In this his key card was American support. In announcing that henceforth all American assistance would be channeled through Diem's Government, the Eisenhower Administration reinforced the message by insisting that the American aid previously given to the French for distribution in Vietnam be given to Diem. The real dangers were many, and facing down a coup threatened by the Army commander that brought troops and tanks to surround Diem in the Palace was but one.

When, by dint of determination, presence of mind, and skillful maneuver, Diem had established authority over sufficient forces to protect him against the Army, he sent them into action against the bandit gang that ran the

Saigon police and operated the various cesspools of vice
that characterized the city—ignoring the mortar rounds
that fell on the Palace grounds in the process. His Saigon
base thus secured, he turned to a combination of guile,
intrigue, and force to divide, buy off, and suppress the
leaders and private armies of the Cao Dai and Hoa Hao
religious sects, which in effect were separate states within
the nation.

During these confusing and kaleidoscopic months, Diem
learned to depend on himself and his family, to hold hard
to a dangerous line, and to manipulate the corrupt and
devious figures he was dealing with. Even as he did so,
associates and supporters, including the official American
presence in Saigon, were abandoning him or concluding
that he had taken on too much and was doomed. However,
Diem's persistence and strength of conviction, plus his
tactical suppleness in using any means to advance his
cause, paid off.

This intense time of testing culminated when Diem
repudiated the hapless—and hostile—titular leadership of
Emperor Bao Dai. In October 1955, a bit over a year in
office, Diem presided over a referendum ousting Bao Dai
and electing himself President. To no one's surprise, or even
objection, the election was thoroughly stage-managed and
was in effect a ceremony, not a choice. In 1956, a Constitution having been approved, Diem established the Republic
of Vietnam and withdrew the Republic from the French
Union. Diem then used his new sovereignty to remove the
last danger to his regime. He announced that he was not
bound by the provisions of the Geneva Accords calling for
elections in both North and South Vietnam to reunify the
nation, since his Government had refused to sign the Accords and the outcome of the election was preordained by
the larger, regimented population of the Communist
North.

With this transformation in the prospects for South
Vietnam accomplished by 1956, Diem launched a campaign
to modernize and develop South Vietnam economically,
socially, and politically. By 1959, the campaign was well
under way. My briefings and discussions after my arrival
covered its concepts and statistics, while I traveled and

searched among Vietnamese of all types to understand its reality.

Part of this reality was American. In a preview of later American policymaking about Vietnam, Diem's very accession to power was marked by divisions among the Americans concerned.

By 1954, there was no vestige of the sentiment advanced in 1945 that America should support Ho Chi Minh's Communist-led movement against the French. This had been advocated by an Office of Strategic Services team that had worked with Ho in Vietnam when the enemies of both, the Japanese and the Vichy French, still held the country. That alternative had attracted practically no attention within the American Government at the time, not because Ho was a Communist, which his record clearly showed he was—but because the main focus of American policy then was the revival of Western Europe, in which France was a key factor. Franklin Roosevelt had died, and with him his impatience with the fact that the French "had been in Indochina for a hundred years, and the people were worse off than when they came." Roosevelt might have been able to translate his views into a period of tutelage in Vietnam leading to independence on the analogy of American policy in the Philippines. But without him that was not a practical possibility in 1945.

In Yugoslavia Tito had not yet declared his simultaneous loyalty to Communism and independence of Moscow (which brought him American support to maintain it), so a comparable Communist Vietnam independent of China was not foreseen (although Vietnam's history, if known then, and the traditional hostility of the Vietnamese toward China, revived in the 1980s, certainly could have suggested it). In the period 1945–1947, the question for American policymakers was, rather, whether the alliance with France, with its importance in the emergent confrontation with the Soviet Union in Europe, was more important than a faint hope for an independent Vietnam. And by 1954 there was no confidence that ex-colonial South Vietnam could muster the strength to stem the apparently inexorable tide of Communist expansion from China to Indochina and on to Malaya and Indonesia.

The collapse of French rule in Vietnam after the defeat at Dien Bien Phu led John Foster Dulles to turn to Diem and provide him with the political and economic support he needed to salvage what might be possible—at the least, to provide a decent interval before what was considered an inevitable Communist victory. But Diem did not agree with American doubts. He accepted such assistance as was made available, assurances of continued military assistance to his fledgling Army, and some political counsel and techniques offered by Colonel Edward Lansdale of the Central Intelligence Agency. Lansdale was posted to Vietnam to save what could be salvaged after a successful tour that had helped Ramón Magsaysay become the first honest and dynamic President of the Philippines.

Diem selected among the many, and sometimes contradictory, proposals made to him by eager Americans confident that their understanding of the challenges facing him exceeded his. Diem's spectacular success in establishing his rule convinced him of the validity of his technique: listening to all the American would-be counsel, taking from it what might be useful but not directly rejecting that which he thought wrong (useful and tangible aid might be made to flow even from sources and agencies whose advice he considered irrelevant), and always explaining in infinite detail the importance of continued American support for his Government. By 1959, this pattern in the relationship between Diem and the Americans had become fixed.

The leader of the Americans in Vietnam in 1959 was Ambassador Elbridge Durbrow. As the personal representative of the President of the United States, the American Ambassador to South Vietnam, as our other Chiefs of Mission around the world, presided, with varying success, over all the components of what we referred to as "the Mission"—embracing, when thus capitalized, all the local "missions" of the various Washington agencies—as often as we spoke of "the Embassy." (French is still the language of diplomacy, and "the Mission" comes from the French of the conventions making up diplomatic usage, which distinguish between an Ambassador who merely holds that rank, and an Ambassador who is a *Chef de Mission Diplomatique*.)

A career Foreign Service Officer, Durbrow was one of the Service's early specialists on the Soviet Union. Fluent in French from studies at the University of Dijon, Durbrow had honed his diplomatic skills as Clare Boothe Luce's deputy in Rome. There both she and he had fought off, and successfully delayed until Kennedy took over the White House, the "opening to the Left"—an Italian political development that I had vainly advocated from my position running the CIA's political operations there at the time, and that was designed to separate the Socialists from the Communists and bring the former into the national political spectrum. Durbrow had come to Saigon after an assignment as Consul General in the British Crown Colony of Singapore. Professional and peppery, he asserted his authority over the other American agencies already proliferating in Vietnam, while maintaining the detachment from the local scene and its personalities traditional to the diplomatic role of interpreting one nation to another.

Diem, perceiving this distance as reflecting less than the full commitment to his regime he thought necessary, made sure that Durbrow did not become the sole channel through whom his ideas were presented to Washington. For military matters, he turned to the chief of the Military Assistance Advisory Group (MAAG), Lieutenant-General "Hanging Sam" Williams, dapper of mustache and pleased with the nickname he had earned from the conviction and execution of a soldier for cowardice many years before. Insistent that his chain of command followed only military channels through Commander-in-Chief Pacific (CINCPAC) in Honolulu, Williams asserted his full authority over matters military and fiercely resisted Durbrow's efforts to have a voice in his dealings with Diem and his military officers. Durbrow reciprocated with a distinct distaste for Williams.

Another channel Diem turned to was Arthur Z. Gardiner, the thoughtful and gentle head of the local mission of AID, who presided over the flow of American assistance to Diem's economic development programs. Diem also made certain that he would have meetings with the stream of American visitors to Saigon, in those days primarily Government personalities involved in the management of the assistance programs in Washington. Diem's tactic was to

subject them to four-hour-long monologues about the perfidy of the Communists, his visions of the modern Vietnam
to be, and the venality of various opposition political
figures or of international neutralist personalities such as
Cambodia's Norodom Sihanouk.

Diem also maintained contact with a variety of Americans who had sympathized with him in previous times and
had admired his success in saving Vietnam from collapse.
They ranged from academic Wesley Fishel of Michigan
State University to Wolf Ladejinsky, initiator of the successful post–World War II land reform programs of Japan and
Taiwan, the Dulles brothers in the CIA and the State Department, Francis Cardinal Spellman of New York, then
effectively the leader of American Catholicism, and a rising
Catholic Senator from Massachusetts, John F. Kennedy.

But Diem had little time or patience for the press or
critical political figures at home or abroad, considering
them prejudiced and too shallow to comprehend the transformation of Vietnam into a modern nation that he was
directing. Diem's style was that of the traditional Mandarin, assuming the legitimacy of his position to be beyond
challenge and manipulating the currents of the distant
imperial court (now in Washington) to ensure the continued support necessary to his mission of modernization.

Critics of Diem existed, however, among Vietnamese and
Americans. Some Vietnamese harkened back to their suppressed religious sects and resented the prominence of Catholics in Diem's regime. Although Diem could prove numer-
ically the actual preponderance of non-Catholics among his
ministers, one hundred years of Catholic education under
the French had certainly given the small Catholic community a disproportionate role as the elite of the nation. The
resentment had been exacerbated by the advent of the energetic Northern Catholic refugees who chose freedom in
South Vietnam over a Communist future in North Vietnam.
Other critics of Diem focused on the differences between the
democratic regime outlined in the 1956 Constitution and
the reality of Diem's authoritarian rulings from the Palace
on all important matters.

Since these critics were particularly prevalent among the
more sophisticated intellectual circles of Saigon, their views

were readily available to Americans. They were a constant source of material for the Embassy's Political Section's officers, who thought they were reporting significant political developments, and for the CIA Station via its clandestine sources, who were deliberately cultivated among all political currents to provide warning of the unexpected.

The rotation of Americans contributed to the impact of the criticism. By 1960, there were literally no official Americans in Saigon who had experienced the chaotic days of Diem's accession to power. Accordingly, they judged events and individuals on the only scale they knew, today's measurement of Diem's apparent popularity and political support against the rumble of complaint against his rule. One subject of complaint was corruption, of course, but this was muted by the well-known monkish asceticism of Diem himself and the absence of flamboyant expenditure by his Ministers and other officials.

Saigon, center of power and governance in South Vietnam, was thus, as I found it in 1959–1960, a complex mixture of two cultures—the traditional Vietnamese (containing many Chinese elements), the bluff and assertive American—and the residue, the still-present half of another culture, imbued by a hundred years of French rule and favoritism for a brilliant Catholic minority who, like the English Catholics, had earlier survived centuries of recurrent persecution. But, as everywhere, the capital, dominant though it may be, was not the entire country. I was soon to find that out.

2

Court and Countryside

THE OPPORTUNITY SOON CAME TO MAKE my own judgments about the regime, as seen both in the capital and in the countryside. Stemming from Ed Lansdale's role as Diem's friend and confidant during the days of confusion in 1954-1955, the CIA Station had been established as an alternate channel for communication and influence between Diem and the American Government. In deference to Diem's rank as both Chief of State and Chief of Government (in the American fashion), the direct channel to and from the Americans went through Ambassador Durbrow. The CIA, however, maintained a separate link with Diem's brother and "Counselor to the President," Ngo Dinh Nhu. Shortly after my arrival in Saigon, the CIA Chief of Station (whom I would later replace on his transfer) left on home leave. Before departing, to maintain the channel of communication during his absence, he took me through the back gate of Independence Palace, turned to the left to the northern wing, and led me upstairs to the small office used by Nhu. Thin, dark, and intense, Nhu waved us to our seats, and we began the first of the long weekly meetings I would have with him over the next three years.

Papers and dossiers were piled on the desk and tables. There was a small table, for tea and ashtrays, next to three easy chairs. We spoke the French in which Nhu was most comfortable, its Cartesian logic and theoretics coming through clearly.

The contrast between us was striking. We Americans came with a set of subjects to discuss and tried methodically to tick them off one by one, informing Nhu of some activity we were undertaking with the Vietnamese services, trying to dissuade him from some activity we knew he was direct-

31

ing against Cambodia, or reinforcing some point Ambassador Durbrow was trying to make through the front door with Nhu's brother, the President. Nhu would listen quietly and make some noncommittal reply when he wanted to avoid the subject, but then he would be triggered by some remark into a long and complex exposition of the machinations of the French, the early days of his and Diem's struggle for power against various conspiratorial forces, or the importance of indoctrinating the Vietnamese bureaucracy into an ideology of service and commitment to replace their corrupt French practices. The cigarette smoke continually curled around him as hours passed and servants emptied the ashtrays and refilled the teacups.

In future meetings, I learned to sit patiently through these discussions as I sought to learn the style of Nhu's thought. I took to counting on an occasional Socratic question to cover points I had in mind, or to turn his thinking in directions I felt needed further exploration, or to stimulate some new activity on his part. Nhu's comments and train of thought were invariably intelligent and politically sophisticated. They were heavy with theory. At the same time, he was obviously fascinated by intrigue, whether in the opposition to the Diem regime, or in the moves he calculated would strengthen it against them.

Nhu had clearly been impressed by the Communist technique of manipulation of political movements by a disciplined core organization. It was his idea that the technique could be adapted, behind a facade of democracy, to manage the actions and political support of a regime determined to bring Vietnam into modernism and independence. In pursuit of this theory, he had formed a "secret" Can Lao (Labor) Party to provide the infrastructure through which to manage and manipulate the overt Government machinery. The motor behind this effort was Nhu's profound hostility to the French-trained—and influenced—Vietnamese elite who dominated the urban economic and social scene and what passed for a political opposition. They were especially prevalent among the Government bureaucracy. Nhu constantly referred to the need to replace them through an authentic Vietnamese revolution based on traditional community values.

In 1959 Nhu looked to the philosophy of "personalism," articulated by an obscure French Catholic philosopher, Emmanuel Mounier, which emphasized the value of each human being within his community, stressing equally the individual's integrity and his obligation to contribute to the community. Nhu saw this philosophy as a way to integrate the modern (in the East) Christian emphasis on the individual with the traditional Confucian stress on order and hierarchy. On occasion Nhu was quite critical of what he considered his brother's overemphasis on the tangible elements of modernization—Diem's programs of road building, resettlement of virgin wilderness areas, and economic development—when they lacked, in Nhu's view, the requisite political and revolutionary content.

For Nhu, the Communists were fundamental enemies of this needed moral revision of Vietnamese life—but not the sole ones. He also saw the colonial influence inherited from the French and the threat of its revival in another form by an overly dominant American role as equal dangers. It was but a short step for Nhu to see any political opposition as only corrupt and obstructionist advocates of these essentially foreign influences rather than as exponents in good faith of variations on how best to develop Vietnam to play its role in the modern world.

I believed my task was to understand Nhu's thinking rather than to debate it. But I could and did bring into our conversations the dimension of how the Government's policies appeared to the outside world, especially the Americans. Many were the times I had to stress that these factors were important to continued American support for the Diem Government, whether or not they were accurate perceptions of what Vietnam really needed. In general, however, I sympathized with Nhu's insistence that Vietnam needed to discover and develop a new political identity around which its people could rally if the competing Communist appeal for change and for nationalism was to be defeated. This identity had to find its roots in Vietnamese life and tradition, but it also had to promise a better material and social future.

Thus Diem's Government had to demonstrate its independence not only of the departed French but also of the Americans, whose assistance was nonetheless vital if the country was to develop the essential economic and social momentum. Diem's modernization of the Vietnamese economy and social structure from the colonial pattern was essential for the larger purpose. And it was, in the circumstances of the day, more important to the individual rural Vietnamese than were the subtleties of Western political practices appropriate for developed and pluralistic societies. The task in South Vietnam required strong leadership, and Diem's messianic dedication seemed more appropriate for it than did the confusion and indecision that could come from overly precise application of the American doctrine of the separation of powers.

My sympathy for and understanding of what Nhu was seeking was, of course, influenced by my own background. As a boy in China from 1929 to 1932, I had seen the old colonial regime there from the privileged vantage point of life in the foreign concession in Tientsin. I had had an opportunity to appreciate the ancient traditions of China and the vitality and energy of its people and to observe their suppression under a dying dynasty, brutal warlords, and foreign forces. My studies and summer in France in 1939 had enabled me to appreciate the pride of French nationalism and the tragedy of France's defeat—and collapse—before the dynamic and savage Nazis. My work with the French and Norwegian resistance forces in 1944 and 1945 had showed me what a few courageous people can accomplish even against an overpowering foe if they are moved to take risks for a cause in which they believe. My time in Sweden and Italy had educated me fully on the dangers the Communists posed to free peoples, but it also had shown that they could be defeated on the political and subversive levels that were their chosen battlegrounds, while being deterred on the military. Nhu's stress on the Vietnamese need for a cause around which they could rally was something I could agree with, despite the difficulty of articulating it in a nation so heavily burdened by its colonial past.

Nhu obviously reported his contacts with me to Diem, who decided, after an appropriate interval, that he wanted to meet this new player on the American team. With the approval of Ambassador Durbrow, who had grown confi-

dent that I operated under his leadership and had no false
ideas of becoming an alternate ambassador, I repaired to the
Palace to see the President. Entering, I turned to the left, as I
had before when entering to see Nhu. But this time, coming
in the front entrance, my left turn brought me to the southern, or Presidential, wing.

I was ushered into an office larger, neater, and altogether
more businesslike than Nhu's, to meet Diem. Talks with
him were to be repeated over the next three years, lasting
the same four or more hours as those with Nhu, and with
Diem consuming as many cigarettes (or at least the first
inch of each before impatiently stubbing it out), but they
were very different in character.

Instead of the involved theoretical examination in French
of the bases of Vietnamese society or of a real or suspected
conspiracy by some adversary of the regime, Diem led a
staccato review in English of the practical aspects of his
various development programs. He frequently turned to the
map to demonstrate the strategy of opening new roads into
isolated mountain regions and of planting agricultural
colonies of reliable refugees from North Vietnam there to
prevent those areas from becoming protected sanctuaries or
easy infiltration routes for Communists from the North.

Diem described with enthusiasm his new project of
building agricultural cities ("agrovilles") in the Mekong
Delta, where he could concentrate sufficient population to
support medical aid centers, high schools and primary
schools, and proper marketplaces for the peasants to exchange their rice and garden products for consumer goods.
The contrast he emphasized was with the actual tiny hamlet
life, isolated from any community, along the interminable
canals that characterized that rich, exploited, and disorgan-
ized region. He was equally excited over his programs to
introduce new cash crops such as kenaf for the local manu-
facture of rice bags, light industries such as textile plants in
the urban areas, and the National Institute of Administration to train a new corps of career Government officials
along American lines.

His missionary zeal was apparent in his determination to
produce practical improvements in the lives of the people.
Only once, some years later, did he advert to the Catholic

faith that motivated his monklike dedication. Commenting to me as a fellow Catholic, he remarked that the task of bringing progress is particularly difficult in the Eastern countries "in which the Holy Viaticum has only so recently arrived."

By chance, I was also able to meet and work with the third member of the "royal" family, Madame Nhu. Having heard from her husband that I was a lawyer, she asked that I help her translate into English the Vietnamese "family law" recently passed by the National Assembly. This legislation had been sponsored by Madame Nhu, and indeed it was she who had pressed it through the Assembly, of which she was an "elected" member. Proud of her accomplishment, she wanted to circulate the text internationally in women's circles. So on a series of afternoons I was ushered into one of the ornate Palace rooms, where she would join me at a gold-trimmed table on which rested the Vietnamese law and writing materials. In the course of our work, she gave me an historical account of the role of Vietnamese women in the family and society and, in her brusque and imperious manner, described how she was determined to change it.

One of her first assaults had been on the tight, high collar worn by Vietnamese women atop the flowing panels and tight bodice of the *ao-dai*, the national dress. She maintained that the collar was not authentically Vietnamese but had been imported from the Chinese *cheong-sam* during the past century. She had thus eliminated the collar from her own dresses, replacing it with a yokelike top, certainly making it more comfortable and, in her mind, more national. Her example was copied by a number of the ladies of the Government's "court," but others kept to the collar out of tradition, however short, and to demonstrate their independence from her direction.

The family law itself had equally ambiguous aspects. Many ascribed Madame Nhu's advocacy of it to the tangled affairs of her sister, whose marriage was ending because of her infidelities with a Frenchman. As the law proscribed divorce, the sister would be protected. Others saw in it a replacement of the traditional Vietnamese relationships by a strictly Roman Catholic regime, imposed on the overwhelmingly Buddhist and animist Vietnamese people by

the Catholic Ngo family. Madame Nhu termed it an attempt to provide basic rights to Vietnamese women, and, as
the details of the law emerged during our translation of it,
there was certainly much in support of her point.

The law did establish that the woman retained the rights
to her and her family's property after marriage instead of its
being shifted totally to her husband and remaining his
whatever happened to the marriage. It provided that the
children of the marriage would inherit the property of the
couple. It ended the unilateral right of the husband to
legitimate the child of an extramarital liaison, thus en-
abling that child to fully share in the inheritance with the
children of the marriage. In proscribing divorce, it ended
the custom under which the husband—but only the husband—could simply declare a divorce and send his wife
back to her family.

This translation was one of my first exposures to the
conflicting facts and opinions that permeated our experience in Vietnam. In the case of the family law, there was the
conflict between the merits of the arguments both for and
against it, between the benefits brought by modernization
and the resentment its changes wrought, and between the
facade of a democratic system and the reality of the Ngo
family's authoritarian regime.

Madame Nhu's attitude and personality heightened the
contrast. Hair meticulously coiffed and stiffened, nails
pointed and lacquered, fingers adorned with brilliant jew-
els, voice sharp and quick, she was the embodiment of real
and mythical Oriental empresses, and of Milton Caniff's
creation, "The Dragon Lady." The ambiguity persisted as I
got to know her better and saw her pride in and obvious love
for her children. I noticed that some of her sharpness reflected weaknesses in her command of English, coupled
with her determination to be outspoken in it in any case.
Some of Madame Nhu's more imperious characteristics
could be seen in her mother—though not in her mild father,
whom Diem had named as his Ambassador to Washington
in deference to his leading position among Vietnam's
wealthy landowning class.

Diem and Nhu had had four other brothers, but the eldest,
Khoi, was murdered by the Communists in 1945. Of the

other three surviving, Thuc, the next in line, had chosen the Catholic priesthood. He was the first native Vietnamese to be consecrated a bishop in the still French-dominated Church. Named Bishop of Vinh Long in 1938, he was to become Archbishop of Hue, the family home and the old imperial citadel, in 1961. Diem and Nhu were next, followed by Can, who lived a totally secluded life in the old family residence in Hue and cared for the aged mother of the family. In fact, however, he acted as Diem's eyes, ears, and representative for Central Vietnam, where all were awed by his power and fearful of his wrath. Can was a reasonably simple man, with few pretensions. He believed fully in the Mandarin style of governing and looked, in the Vietnamese national heritage, more to the primitive traditions of the land than to the intellectual pretensions of the French-trained elite. The youngest brother was Luyen, whose sole action of mark appears to have been to father six children. He had been sent off to London, where he held the title of Ambassador to the Court of St. James, but he played no role in developments in Vietnam or anywhere else as far as could be seen.

This well-nigh royal family was, of course, surrounded by a court. Most of its members also came from the bureaucratic and landowning elite who had risen to positions of prominence under the French and retained many of the habits and values absorbed at that time. Ho Chi Minh had swept this class away when he took over North Vietnam, but Diem had continued to use it since he had no alternative available. Those among it who had a commitment to their duties stressed competence in the physical and administrative tasks of building a modern and independent Vietnam; the others concentrated on their own privileges and powers. The political contest they saw predominantly in terms of a struggle with the Communists for the positions of authority and direction over the population, not a contest for its loyalties. They looked to Diem for decisions and devoted themselves to carrying out his concepts and programs.

They were puzzled by Nhu's flights of political theory. But they complied with the surface requirements of his various campaigns to produce a new basis for Vietnamese society, rationalizing their compliance much as they had earlier rationalized their support of French colonial rule notwithstanding the revolutionary rhetoric that clothed the French history they learned in their schooling. Like any medieval court, they thrived on rumor and myth about the doings of those near the throne, to the extent that the myth often became the reality on which fundamental attitudes were formed and decisions based.

Among the figures of this court nearest the throne was the Secretary of State for the Presidency, in effect Diem's chief of staff, Nguyen Dinh Thuan. Highly intelligent and personable, Thuan kept his fingers on all the major aspects of the Government's relationships with Americans—with all foreigners, for that matter. He was soft-spoken and fluent in English and listened more than he spoke, for which he was much appreciated among Americans who grew restive under Diem's compulsive discourses. Thuan was a master at communicating with the official American community. Circulating easily at one of the interminable diplomatic receptions, he would drop a tidbit into each senior official's ear so that at the next morning's meeting of the American "Country Team," each would have an exclusive item to report. American officialdom deemed him the man to do business with, although it was clear that, in his total loyalty to his President, Thuan's confidences were carefully gauged to produce American understanding and support of Diem's programs. As the American military presence in Vietnam grew, he was named Minister of Defense to continue his effective liaison in what was becoming the dominant field.

A figure of importance to me as a CIA officer was Tran Kim Tuyen, chief of the *Service d'Etudes Politiques et Sociales* (SEPES), the Palace's intelligence and security service. Entering the back gate of the Palace with a request to see "Doctor" Tuyen, one was directed to what clearly had been one of the French Governor General's servants' quarters. Confounding the expected image, Tuyen turned out to be one of the tiniest of men, less than five feet tall, his unbelievably thin body certainly weighing less than one hundred pounds. He projected the quiet and shy air of the Confucian scholar, the long and carefully tended nail on the little finger of his left hand certifying his status (this was an affectation from Chinese tradition, ostensibly to

assist reading the vertical lines of characters, but actually to
demonstrate abstention from physical labor).

Exchanges with Tuyen, who was less compulsive than the
Ngo brothers, were businesslike. He would carefully absorb
whatever message or request we had, with the understanding that the response would come at a later date after he had
obtained the reaction of Nhu. He then would inform us of
various developments or items of information he thought it
useful for us to know (even though we sometimes knew the
contrary from our own sources). His shadowy position and
its potential power made him the subject of constant stories
of his Machiavellian intrigues, but in fact he was one of
several "Young Turk" officials involved in foreign affairs
either in Vietnamese missions abroad or in the bureaucracy
in Saigon who, while following the Ngo brothers' orders,
were trying to open up the political processes to a greater
degree than the traditional colonial bureaucracy envisaged.
Tuyen later became disaffected with the Ngo brothers and
went into exile during the crisis of 1963. But in my early
days there, he contributed to my perception of the many
contradictions in Vietnam between surface appearances, the
accepted formulas describing them, and the great complexities beneath.

Two additional dimensions were essential to my learning
about this new country.

The historical could be learned from books about the
several-thousand-year history of the South Viets (*nam* being
the word for "south"), from their origins in China and their
migration to the Red River delta around Hanoi, then south
along the thin strip of coastal land on the edge of the
Annamite mountain chain, to spill out into the rich delta of
the Mekong River, fertile with the alluvial mud carried
from Tibet, through China, past Burma, Laos, Thailand,
and Cambodia to South Vietnam and into the South China
Sea. The warlike and xenophobic character of the Vietnamese was revealed in this long migration. The primitive,
indigenous peoples in their path were ruthlessly pushed
into remote mountain areas; and the Cham Empire, whose
few remnant temples in Central Vietnam offer mute testimony to the extent that Indian culture penetrated and then
was overcome by the Chinese element of "Indochina," was

demolished province by province. There is nothing new in Vietnamese at war in Laos and Cambodia. Nor was the conflict between North and South in Vietnam invented in the Geneva Accords of 1954. It was centuries old, northerners (Tonkin) and southerners (Annam and Cochin China) differing and fighting over dynasties and revolutionary movements.

In fact, there was little in terms of conflict that the Vietnam of the mid-twentieth century had not seen before. The expulsion of the French colonists equated to the expulsion of the Chinese overlords ten centuries before; the revolutionary attributes of Ho Chi Minh's cause found historical antecedents in the Tay-Son Rebellion of 1772; and the effort to create a strong and separate South Vietnam with American help bore strong similarities to the successful campaign of Nguyen Anh, with French help, to become the Emperor Gia Long over the opposition of the Tay-Son brothers in the North.

Madame Nhu found an historical antecedent in the story of the Truong sisters, who in A.D. 40 led a revolt against Chinese rule and committed suicide when defeated. As part of her campaign for better recognition of women, Madame Nhu had a statue erected to them, which, not surprisingly, had her features. Most remarkable to an American, accustomed from American history to think in terms of periods of "peace" interrupted by occasional periods of "war," was the realization that the Vietnamese grew up surrounded by the traditions and experience of constant conflict—civil, regional, ideological, and international—over centuries. Military and imperial heroes and heroics were as familiar to them as George Washington and Abraham Lincoln are to Americans.

A reading of the Vietnamese national epic, *Kim Van Kieu*, or the *Tale of Kieu*, teaches much about the people and the place. My rudimentary Vietnamese, laboriously learned during lunchtime sessions with a tutor (who, ten years later, confessed to having become a North Vietnamese spy—but that is another story), was inadequate to allow me to appreciate the poetry of the original text. But the English translation of the romantic and tragic vicissitudes of the girl Kieu fully evokes the travails of the South Vietnamese people under their Chinese and Western overlords over the centuries. One could appreciate how the Vietnamese revered this rather recently written fiction (early 1800s) as representing the way in which cruel fate imposed its burdens on Vietnam but its people steadfastly retained their integrity and loyalty to their dreams. The Chinese cultural heritage, the bluster of the warlords, the steel-like strength of women under adversity, the contest between revolution and order, and the contrast between sacrifice and corruption depicted in the story—all were repeated in daily life in Vietnam. It offered its readers hope that fulfillment could in the end come for Vietnam and its people as a whole, if not for the individuals lost in the struggles.

The second additional dimension of my learning process was geographical. Some of this orientation involved simple weekend picnics: to a rubber plantation to sit among the interminable, brooding rows of trees, each with its diagonal slit and small cup to catch the sap, the absence of undergrowth bespeaking the labor required to keep the jungle away; a four-hour trip to the mountain retreat of Dalat to breathe the five-thousand-foot-high, clear air and enjoy wearing a sweater; stopping at a stilled jungle clearing containing a small fort and listening to the cries of the jungle animals and birds; visits to the sparkling beaches on the coast north of Saigon for a climb onto the rusting hulk of a Japanese ship left from World War II or careful exploration of seaside villas gutted during the war against the French.

There was a visit to the Cao Dai sect's "Vatican" at Tay Ninh (past the roadside watchtowers in one of which Alden Pyle, Graham Greene's fictional "Quiet American," took refuge and fled from a Viet Minh attack). The polychromatic, swirled columns of the church there captured the Cao Dai effort to synthesize Chinese and Buddhist mysticism with Roman Catholic hierarchical order. But the stillness surrounding it confirmed its decline from a semi-autonomous temporal power tolerated by the French because it opposed Communist revolutionary authority to a powerless witness to President Diem's assertion of national sovereignty. On one trip up the coast to the town of Nha Trang, for a junk trip to the deserted island offshore to see the multicolored fish among the coral, the train jumped the track and we sat in the jungle for the night thinking of the tigers roaming around us.

My sons found adventure in accompanying me on trips such as a flight to Phu Quoc island in the Gulf of Thailand to examine (and smell) the fermentation of the Vietnamese staple fish sauce, *nuoc mam*, where, thumbing a ride from a passing fishing boat, we saw a shark longer than the boat. We also traveled the length of South Vietnam, by train to Hue and then by road to the Ben Hai River at the Demilitarized Zone, to see the North Vietnamese flag flying at the border, and then on Highway 9 along the DMZ, past Khe Sanh, to an old French border post and military prison tucked in the mountains on the border with Laos.

My trips to assess the work of the Diem regime in the countryside, and compare it on the ground with Diem's and Nhu's view from the Palace of their programs, provided more geographic orientation. In mid-1959, the main roads of the southernmost province of the Mekong Delta were filled with multicolored, rickety buses hurtling through bucolic villages to teeming market centers, where the peasants exchanged their agricultural products for tinseled consumer goods. An overnight stop in Bac Lieu produced the startling sight of a European in shorts sitting on a folding cot next to the diesel generator that powered the few lights in the center of town. When questioned, guttural German emerged from behind his gold teeth; we had stumbled upon a relic of the departed French Foreign Legion. The next day, a neighboring village brought us up to date with the inauguration of the primary school, teacher supplied by Saigon. This was only one part of the reestablishment of the village, which had been evacuated during the Viet Minh struggle against the French. The new school was only one of about thirty being opened in other rural areas of the province of An Xuyen.

Another trip to the jungles north of Saigon gave a glimpse of one of the new land development centers being carved out for refugees from North Vietnam. The land was being cleared and a village center and Catholic church erected. The new inhabitants were raising their tin-roofed huts and beginning to cultivate small vegetable gardens and a cash crop of kenaf, all under the fatherly control of the priest who had led them south from North Vietnam. Ceremonial openings of a textile factory and of a new main highway and bridge into Saigon from the north gave reality to the economic statistics of an increase in light industry and commercial activity.

In every region, in all these villages, everywhere the air was alive with bustling energy aimed at producing wealth.

Except in political life.

3

A Political Still Life

IN EARLY 1960 I WAS INVITED by a member of the National Assembly to accompany him and a delegation of other Assemblymen to spend a day examining a rural development project in the mountains. There the local officials met us and proudly displayed their plan to develop a new community to be occupied by refugees from the North then living in makeshift centers built for them near Saigon. We were given the usual briefing at the construction center, replete with charts and a map of the finished community. The plan included a community center with a market, church, school, medical aid center, administrative offices, and agricultural service center. A road was being cut through the jungle to link the village with a larger road in the area, and a bridge was already in place over the small stream that wound through the site and would provide its water. We then went out to watch the bulldozers clearing the huge jungle trees and see how the community was taking shape.

Two points about the experience particularly impressed me, aside from the image of pioneers opening up the jungle to homeless refugees. The first was the fact that the site was being prepared for people who were not yet there, and it was apparently being done without their participation. It was made clear in the briefing that the refugee community was anxious to move from its present location and that its elders and priests had been consulted about the plans. It was also clear that the new residents would be expected to construct their own homes on the plots allocated to them, provided they conformed to the overall plan.

But it all reminded me of somewhat similar projects I had seen in Italy in which the Government developed new

homes and communities on expropriated estates and provided day laborers with land—and homes. Physical improvements in the laborers' lives had indeed been provided—many had literally lived in caves—but no political
organizations into which the new community could fit
(except for the local parish) were offered. Soon Communist
activists rented a storefront. From there they sallied forth to
point out minor defects in the new homes and blame them
on corrupt officials of the faraway Government in Rome.
They were frequently successful in turning the attitude of
the new residents from appreciation for the change in their
lives to hostility toward the democratic Government and its
American ally that had brought it about.

In the Italian experience, I had recognized the technique
being used as the twin of one I had encountered one
summer during college when I had tried to organize Washington gas station workers for the Oil Workers' International Union. "Just talk about grievances—only grievances," my union chief had instructed me. Now, in
Vietnam, I thought about how Communist organizers in
this new rural community would concentrate on grievances, organizing the people against the Government that
had given them this new life, unless there were some positive political effort to supplement the physical improvements they would receive.

Plainly, the elements of this economic development program originated in Saigon Ministries and the Palace and
were being executed by the local officials without question.
It was these officials who decided where the roads would
run, how the land would be divided among the new settlers,
how the schools would be allocated and the curriculum set,
and what cash crop the community would grow. The sole
political function expected of the citizenry was to assemble
later in well-ordered lines in the hot sun to greet visiting
delegations of foreigners or officials from Saigon, to wave
the national flag with its three red stripes on a yellow field,
and to cheer *"Muon Nam!"* ("A Thousand Years!") at men-
tions of President Diem's leadership.

The second interesting point for me was the contrast
between the attitude of the visiting Assemblymen toward
the local officials and that of a typical American Congress-

man on a visit to an Embassy or AID Mission. The Assemblymen were uniformly deferential to the local authorities. They accepted the officials' briefings without doubts or probing questions, seeming anxious to display to the outside guest the success of the Government's program of development. They acted as members of the Government team rather than as independent representatives of their constituencies.

It was clear that, whatever the Constitutional provisions might say, political power in Vietnam flowed down from the Palace at the top, not up from the people. The result was visible in bustling markets and new communities, but it was also evident that political life was still, if not actually stagnant.

That this situation did not come merely from tradition and circumstances became clear during another trip, when I stopped to visit the school of "personalism" conducted by the Can Lao Party at a former rehabilitation center for the Grand Monde's prostitutes in Vinh Long province, in the Delta. To this copy of a Catholic retreat house came civil servants anxious to conform to the Ngo brothers' concepts of the philosophy they should follow as they carried out their mandarinate duties of directing the activities of the peasants in their charge. The highly abstract model of individual fulfillment through participation in the community fed—and, if anything, reinforced—the civil servant's conviction that his direction of the population of his community toward a better, modern life was just and proper. He would emerge reassured that his mission required little or no deference to potentially erroneous views of his subjects that might interfere with the process.

Strong, authoritarian leadership has forced other nations through the trauma of modernization and social revolution, from Ataturk in Turkey to Lenin in Russia. It has also generated such resistance that it ultimately failed, despite its positive contributions, as with the Shah of Iran, or been so flawed in its execution that it collapsed, as in Chiang Kai-Shek's China or Sukarno's Indonesia. But a major determinant in the fate of such an effort has often been the degree of outside involvement on the side of the proponent or his opponents. This was the case in American assistance to

Park's Korea and opposition to Allende's Chile. In South
Vietnam, it was already clear that the future would be
determined not only by the forces at work in the country but
also by the influences upon it from North Vietnam, and the
outside supporters of both North and South.

President Diem and his Government were all too aware of
this. More accurately, they were consumed by it. While
Diem constantly identified the three enemies of the new
Republic as colonialism, feudalism, and Communism, he
knew that essentially the first two had been defeated, but
that the third, based in the North, still posed a real threat.
More than intellectual conviction fueled his view: Diem had
lost a brother to Communist murder; his Catholic supporters from the North had suffered violence and had chosen
exile over subjection to a Communist regime; his own
nationalist credentials were under attack by Ho Chi Minh's
rivalry for leadership of Vietnam; and the bloody fate of the
elite and the landowner class in North Vietnam gave clear
promise of what would happen in the event of a Communist victory in South Vietnam.

Thus the dominant theme of Diem's monologues to visiting American officials, the strategy behind his location of
new communities in the trackless highlands, the purpose
behind the strident slogans festooned on banners across
Saigon streets or chanted by regimented peasants in rural
communities, was in each case the imperative to defeat
Communism. Its corollary was the denunciation of Communism's advocates or supporters. The Ministry of Information organized a "mass political organization," the National Revolutionary Movement, to serve as the vehicle for
exhortations of this kind. Lack of loyalty to the Movement
was viewed as treason to the nation and sympathy for the
Communists, in many cases resulting in incarceration or
ostracism. But like similar vehicles for the regimentation of
the citizenry in other authoritarian countries, the Movement had no life of its own and participation in its ceremonies was only one of the duties the Government imposed on
the people. It was like corvée labor or taxation—to be
endured because there was no alternative.

And there was no alternative within the South Vietnamese body politic. The political role that had been played

by the religious sects—the Hoa Hao in the Delta and the Cao Dai west and north of Saigon—had been eliminated by Diem's forceful and successful assertion of the supremacy of national sovereignty in 1955. The remnants of those organizations were fully penetrated by the Government's agents to ensure that they would not resume any active role.

During French times, there had been a number of underground parties other than the Communists. There were skeletal remnants of them, such as various factions of the Dai Viet ("Great Viets") and the Viet Nam Quoc Dan Dang, referred to as the VNQDD, which had a shadowy existence in Central Vietnam. These too were under close surveillance by the Government, which saw them as a threat to its monopoly of power and likely to produce friction in the modernization process.

Former leaders of these groups maintained their contacts with one another. They were also in touch with other Vietnamese who had been adversely affected by the Ngo family's monopoly of political power, or who believed that the democratic prescriptions written into the 1956 Constitution should be fulfilled rather than used as mere window dressing. Since all of these people were mostly of the educated—and indeed formerly wealthy—class, they had easy and natural access to foreign circles—official, commercial, journalistic, and private. Under these circumstances, a large part of political reporting from Vietnam reflected the views and complaints of those excluded from power. The truth was that almost all complainants had few if any roots in the population, urban or rural. The Government made certain they could not develop them.

Two real sources of political power were the military and the Catholic Church. Both were fully supportive of the regime. One of Diem's first acts had been to oust the military leadership that had served the French and resisted his coming to power. Holding himself the post of Minister of Defense, Diem kept a firm hand on promotions and the selection of commanders. He made certain that officers who might have had dreams or ambitions for themselves, such as General "Big" Minh, had no troops under their command. The Catholic Church, of course, fully supported the regime as a shield against the Communists. (Here too the Ngo

family was insured against dissent by the fact that the
President's older brother, Bishop Ngo Dinh Thuc at Vinh
Long, and later Archbishop at Hue, was the senior bishop
of Vietnam.)

These various combinations in the political life of the
country canceled one another out, and the result was a
political vacuum. The energies of the national leadership
were concentrated on economic development and declaim-
ing the iniquities of the Communist enemy. Nhu's Can Lao
Party controlled the behavior and attitudes of the bureaucracy. The agents he directed dogged the footsteps of any
possible sources of opposition to ensure that independent
initiatives from outside did not disturb the smooth flow of
control from the Palace throughout the echelons of the
Government. The few stirrings of independent political
thought among the urban intellectuals (even those asserting
their anti-Communism) were viewed by the Government as
essentially hostile to the main tasks—modernization and
solidarity against the Communists.

The real political contest—that with North Vietnam—
was dormant for the time being. The North Vietnamese
leadership was preoccupied with consolidating the power it
had won from the French in 1954. The doctrinaire advocate
of full revolution in the North, Truong Chinh (an assumed
name meaning "Long March"), copying Mao Tse-tung's
technique when the latter assumed power in China, led a
campaign of nationalization of the land and regimentation
of the peasantry under the banner of "land reform" as a way
of eliminating any challenge to the Communist Party's
authority in the countryside. Thousands of "landlords"
were executed. The urban elite, both dependents of the
French colonists and non-Communist nationalists, had
largely joined the exodus to the South, negating any significant challenge from that source. For the first several years
after 1954, the main thrust of Communist policy was thus
to bring the Northern society and economy under the control of the Party. The Geneva Accords, besides legitimating
that control, seemed to presage an almost automatic delivery of South Vietnam to the North in 1956. Both prudence
and confidence suggested that the Accords' provisions could
be allowed to work themselves out without interference, or
indeed much concern, by the Northern leaders.

The fact was that the Party in the North had more than enough to do to establish their authority and to impose the regimented society their doctrine called for. There were occasions on which they had to suppress flare-ups of revolt in rural communities, particularly among Catholics who had not escaped to the South. A peasant uprising in Ho Chi Minh's native Nghe An province was put down in blood by the 325th Division in November 1956—and ignored by the international media preoccupied with the Hungarian Revolution and the British and French assaults on Suez. Other such incidents were also passed over, the media appearing generally uninterested in the details of how the victors of Dien Bien Phu disposed of their spoils.

The result of Northern domestic preoccupations was that the Communists in the South were quiescent. Their cadres who had moved to the North in 1954 continued to train and prepare for their return home, but most of them thought this would involve little more than a triumphant entry over the prostrate and divided body of the Diem regime and its various sect and warlord opponents. Diem's rejection of the reunification elections in 1956 in fact eliminated that virtually automatic alternative. But to those watching in the North, it seemed for a time that the internal divisions and disputes in the South would certainly bring about a collapse of Diem's regime. The North could then easily take over, with general international acquiescence. So that they could assume power when the inevitable collapse came, the skeleton networks of Communist supporters left in South Vietnam concentrated on maintaining their existence in the face of Diem's campaigns to extirpate them.

The effect of this combination of internal and external factors added up to political stagnation in South Vietnam. The sects and other political forces were suppressed, the Communists were inactive, and the Diem regime was without a political dimension. Within this apparent vacuum, however, a certain political legitimacy of the Diem regime was growing. The development of a Constitutional form, the loyalty of the Army and the bureaucracy, the regime's success in extending its administrative writ throughout the countryside, growing international acceptance and support, and the visible progress of the economic and modernization programs were all roots feeding that growth.

Diem had successfully taken the political initiative against the divisive forces in South Vietnam while the North was diverted and not yet ready to contest him. By Tet of 1959, it was plain that a nationalist and non-Communist Vietnam was firmly established. It was also becoming apparent that its future was, if anything, more promising than the gray and regimented society in the North. The potentialities of this contrast did not escape the watchful men of Hanoi. But neither did the political stagnation of South Vietnam elude them. It was on this terrain that they would launch the Second Vietnamese War.

4

Hanoi Begins the War

IN 1958 LE DUAN, AN INTENSE but uninspiring personality who was to maneuver himself into succeeding Ho Chi Minh as leader of North Vietnam, paid a visit to South Vietnam. A Northerner born in the port city of Haiphong, Le Duan had spent many years during the war against the French as the North Vietnamese Lao Dong (Communist) Party's political commissar in Zone East of the South. His 1958 visit was to his old area. He returned to Hanoi with a significant report for his fellow Politburo members. While the Party's clandestine networks in the South still existed, and were able to carry out limited proselytizing and to attack—albeit rarely—isolated Government officials in the countryside, Le Duan reported, it was clear that the Diem regime was gaining authority and that its programs were having a major impact. Further, the regime was harshly but effectively eradicating the Communist structure in the countryside.

To the North Vietnamese leadership, it became plain that Diem's regime was not going to collapse, as earlier expected. In fact, the combination of Diem's modernization program, American assistance, and Diem's repression of the Communists pointed to the possibility that South Vietnam might in the foreseeable future achieve economic advances that would pose a major obstacle to the Party's ultimate aim since its formation by Ho Chi Minh in 1930: extension of its control throughout all of Indochina.

At its Fifteenth Plenum in May 1959, the North Vietnamese Party drew the consequences of Le Duan's analysis, by now espoused by the full leadership. They would revive the successful strategy of the "people's war" in the South, against the Diem regime and its American backers—against

53

those they viewed as the corrupt heirs of French colonialism in a new American version. They named the new foe "American-Diemists" (in Vietnamese *My-Diem*). The label was astute. In focusing on Diem's American supporters, it denied Diem's nationalist credentials.

The Fifteenth Plenum Resolution, which launched this enterprise, was not an official declaration of war. Nor was there a surprise attack across the 17th Parallel against South Vietnam, following the Korean model of 1950. The Vietnamese Communists had a more subtle, longer-term— and in the end more successful—strategy for their effort. The way in which they began the campaign broke the traditional mold of warfare. It showed that they intended to apply their own, novel approach, their confidence in it buttressed by its success in their long war against the French. Their determination to persevere in that approach, despite its costs, was reinforced by their conviction that its twin objectives, the defeat of "neocolonialism" and the triumph of Communist-led social revolution, were both just and inevitable.

In accordance with the Party strategists' reliance on spurring a revolution rather than starting an open war, the Resolution did not call for a conventional conquest (or even liberation) of the South. It called instead for a strong North Vietnam to become the base to help the South Vietnamese overthrow Diem and defeat the American overlords. Supported and strengthened from the North, the people of South Vietnam would be the principal force to conduct the war. The choice of strategy established the tactical priorities. If the South Vietnamese were to fight the battle, the first-priority task was the political organization and mobilization of the people of South Vietnam.

The leading elements of the attack would be the political cadres, those who would recruit the people of the rural villages to join a movement to overthrow the Diem regime. The initial ranks of these cadres were to be found in two places: first, among the cadres who had fought against the French in South Vietnam and had moved to the North— some 90,000 strong—in 1954, when the country was divided; second, among those who had remained in the South in dormant networks awaiting the day to resume the struggle for revolution.

In his exaltation of the victory against the French, General Vo Nguyen Giap, military chief of that long battle, had made the strategy of the "long-term revolutionary war" or "people's war" crystal clear: the stage of "contention" would lead to the stage of "equilibrium" and culminate in the stage of the "counteroffensive." The form of fighting was to be primarily guerrilla warfare. The basis of the strategy lay in the population. In Giap's words,

> The application of this strategy of long-term resistance required a whole system of education, a whole ideological struggle among the people and Party members, a gigantic effort of organization in both military and economic fields, extraordinary sacrifices and heroism from the army as well as from the people, at the front as well as in the rear. Sometimes erroneous tendencies appeared, trying either to bypass the stages to end the war earlier, or to throw important forces into military adventures. The Party rectified them by a stubborn struggle and persevered in the line it had fixed. . . . Political activities were more important than military activities, and fighting less important than propaganda (*People's War, People's Army*, Hanoi, 1961, pp. 47, 79).

That the beginnings of the war against the American-Diemists were barely perceptible, even to its target, was consistent with this long-term approach. Communists and their violence were a matter of course in the countryside, so a minor increment in such actions was hardly remarkable to outsiders—who included many of Diem's appointed officials.

But an important change *had* occurred. The decision to resume the people's war brought a number of actions, then secret and minor, whose importance is now evident. Thus, in May of 1959, the 559th Transportation Group was organized in North Vietnam to begin the arduous and critical process of establishing a communications and transportation link to the combatants in the South. (Even the numbers are revealing: five for the month, fifty-nine for the year.) Its first activities were to establish the way stations and paths through the Laotian side of the Annamite Mountains,

which in later years became the highways and pipelines of
the Ho Chi Minh Trail. The first passengers sent South on
the Trail were Southerners who had gone North in 1954 and
who could now put their training and dedication to work to
recruit fellow Southerners to join the new crusade against
the American colonialists and their Diemist puppets. Once
in the South, they returned to their home areas to persuade
their fellow former revolutionaries to resume enlisting the
rural population in secret networks and groups—the revolutionary political structure whose function was to contest
the Diem Government for control over the rural population
and countryside.

It is indicative of the failure to understand the nature of
the conflict, which would persist through the final collapse
in 1975, that American perception of this critical turning
point in 1959 was nil. Ironically, in May 1959, at the same
time the Lao Dong Party in Hanoi was reaching its conclusions after Le Duan's trip to the South, the American intelligence community produced a National Intelligence Estimate assessing the prospects for Vietnam. The scope of the
Estimate reflected the Americans' habitual preoccupation
with the Diem regime and its shortcomings. Seeming to
take as a constant North Vietnamese assistance to the guerrilla and subversive movements in the South, it focused its
evaluation on whether Diem could be expected to maintain
his authority through his military and police security
services. It forecast the lugubrious comments that would
characterize American attitudes toward Diem by noting the
presence of dissatisfaction among the educated elite and the
military and concluding that Diem's policies would inhibit
the "growth of popularity of the regime."

By tradition, such estimates were the work of the CIA's
Board of National Estimates, not the Operations element to
which the overseas stations belonged, so I had little connection with them. However, I probably would not have taken
great exception to them at the time, considering a test of
"popularity" essentially irrelevant to Diem's durability. My
own preoccupations were with trying to understand the
nature of the country and how the regime was carrying out
its self-imposed goals of modernization.

But in the countryside, the Hanoi decisions began to

show results. Once the decision to resume the people's war was made, the revived Communist apparatus began to show the peasantry the nature of the cause they were asked to join and to organize them. In the CIA Station, we began to receive from our Vietnamese intelligence and police contacts reports of increased incidents: the selective assassination of a village chief; a midnight attack on an isolated local security post in which the guards were killed and their weapons confiscated; the evening assembly of villagers for a discussion of the evils of the American-Diemist regime; the conscription of a group of village youths to augment the guerrilla unit in the nearby jungle, supplemented by the collection of taxes and contributions to help defray the costs of the campaign. The most important element of the activity was the least noticed: the appointment of a local resident as the secret chief of the revolutionary forces in the community and the recruitment of committees to support him—proselytizers, tax collectors, guerrilla liaison and recruitment, and other activities necessary to a clandestine government.

The Diem Government—and the Americans—concentrated on the incidents of violence. But neither the incidents themselves nor their evident increase was the basic problem. Their real importance lay in their indication of the underlying organizational campaign, designed to fill the political vacuum in the countryside and to build a political base for the struggle against the American-Diemists.

The sequence here was important and was barely discerned—if at all—by the Americans. In a "people's war," the first priority must be political. It is upon the political base that a paramilitary force of guerrillas to attack the enemy can be built. Thus the major purpose of "incidents" is less the tactical content of the incidents themselves than the need to impress the peasantry that the cause they are joining is having an impact on the regime. On the basis of a few incidents, those directing the enterprise seek to build momentum for the program of recruitment and further attack in order to exclude the regime from the countryside and replace its authority and programs there with those of the revolution. Once the rural base is well established, the war can be carried to the centers of government power, including the cities, and at this stage main force military units are added to the effort.

In the early stages, consequently, military forces are essentially irrelevant, as the revolution deliberately offers no targets for them. The concept is that when such targets finally do appear, the revolution should be in such a strong political position that it threatens the government's few remaining power bases through infiltration into the urban areas and subversion of the government's forces. Clearly, the answers to such a novel strategy of "war" must be found in its early stages—in the political contest in the countryside for the population's attachment to one side or the other. At this point, there obviously can be no military victory over a nonexistent military enemy. The Communists understood all this as an application of basic Leninism to rural Asia, laboriously developed by Mao Tse-tung in China and by Ho Chi Minh and his associates in their successful campaign against the French.

The Communists in Vietnam had another enemy besides the central Government. Thus, on July 8, 1959, a small American military advisory team to a Vietnamese Army division in Bien Hoa, some twenty miles north of Saigon, was interrupted during their evening movie diversion by a spray of automatic fire. Two were killed, the first American casualties of the Second Indochinese War.

Neither American nor Vietnamese intelligence had given any warning of the attack, and perhaps such a squad-sized operation could not have been predicted in specific terms. Probably this first inclusion of Americans as targets was not specifically decided upon at a high level by the enemy but was only a logical extension of the effort being made to impress the citizenry with the growing power of the revolution in the countryside. Such an extension was fully appropriate for the political message being sent; i.e., the revolution was being waged against the new colonialists and their puppets in a continuation of the earlier war against the French. The real intelligence failure of the Government and the Americans was to fail to appreciate the Hanoi decision to resume the war and to analyze correctly the tactics it would pursue.

Instead, the reaction to the Bien Hoa attack was to focus

on its military implications, to conclude that an increase in such guerrilla attacks could be anticipated and that military precautions should be undertaken to defend against them. It took almost two years for the Vietnamese and American establishments to devise a strategy to go behind such attacks, and for them to develop a political effort to remove the base on which they rested.

The structure of the American presence in Vietnam exacerbated the problem. The influence of General "Hanging Sam" Williams's Military Assistance Advisory Group (MAAG), with its chain of command to Honolulu's Commander-in-Chief Pacific (CINCPAC), was buttressed by the size of the military aid program it administered—some 75 percent of the overall American aid program. The MAAG and its leader received a great deal of deference from Diem and the rest of his Government, in which Williams reveled. His manner and position thoroughly irritated Ambassador Durbrow, whose influence with Diem was diluted by this independent American power center and who was obliged to cope with Diem's manipulation of the situation. At the weekly American "Country Team" meetings in the Ambassador's office, Williams regularly resisted Durbrow's inquiries about the advice and programs the military were providing the Vietnamese as not really matters to be discussed with mere civilians. The hostility between the two was often barely concealed. I tried to keep out of the line of fire between them, as I needed the support of both; but I sympathized with Durbrow, who was trying to carry out a consistent American policy with respect to Diem and who, after all, represented President Eisenhower.

The military dimension of Vietnam's security dominated much of the American liaison with Diem's Government. Assistance over the years since 1956 had been devoted to building the Vietnamese Army, Navy, and Air Force. The emphasis was on the Army, but for all three services the priority task was replacing the French model with the American model. The funds went not only for equipment and weapons but for training courses for officers in American service schools, support of the Vietnamese Government's budget for its forces, and for American advisers with the various Vietnamese units in the countryside.

For the several years preceding 1959, the stress had been
on creating an Army that could fight against a Korean-style
invasion from North Vietnam—a repeat of the American
military's last combat experience rather than of the previous great contest in Vietnam. Armored units therefore
were equipped with American tanks to use against Communist tanks, trucks were supplied to give mobility to meet
enemy units, and the command structure was built to include divisions, corps, and even a "field" headquarters
separate from that of the Vietnamese General Staff.

Diem happily went along with this program for its provision of an armed force for him to use for whatever purpose
he might need, for the muscle it gave his Government
against possible revival of armed sectarian or Communist
opposition, and for the physical and human infrastructure
it produced as a by-product of its military purpose. An
example of the last was a fine new road and bridge to serve
as the main entry to Saigon from the north. Its military
purpose was to enable rapid reinforcement in the event of
an attack on the capital, but in the interim it provided a
boon to the movement of traffic and commerce into and out
of Saigon and opened up an industrial zone for fledgling
industries.

The "field" headquarters also provided a providential
solution for what to do with one of the most senior officers
of the Vietnamese Army, Lieutenant-General Duong Van
Minh (called by Americans "Big Minh" to distinguish him
from a fellow General "Little Minh"), who had served Diem
well at a crucial moment in the struggles with the sects and
their armies but was distrusted and considered not very
bright by Diem and Nhu. Since as "field" commander he
had no troops under his permanent command, Minh
would be harmless and could divide his time between or-
chid-growing and tennis, which he loved, and grumbling
about the lack of a dynamic military campaign against the
enemy. I met him only at occasional receptions or ceremonies, but I found myself very much of Diem's and Nhu's
opinion, as I never heard him say anything the least bit
original or wise.

Lack of understanding of the nature of the Communist
strategy was also revealed in what was *not* done. Military

assistance in the form of weapons, equipment, and training
went exclusively to the Vietnamese Army, Navy, and Air
Force. None went to the local territorials of the "Self-
Defense Forces." These were village-level troops organized
in platoons to protect the local community, usually from
their mud fort near the village seat—a favorite, and generally easy, target of Communist guerrilla attacks. Nor was
military assistance given to the "Civil Guard"—also a
territorial unit but in company strength and used for local
operations and reinforcements by the Province or District
Chief.

These were the units at the very level at which the Communist offensive began. They were, in fact, the permanently located Government force and protection that the
Communists intended to remove, replacing their authority
over the villagers with their own. The reason these units
received no American military assistance in the turning-
point years of 1959 and 1960 was one that appeared logical
in Washington but was obvious nonsense in a faraway
Southeast Asian country facing a new style of warfare. In
Vietnam, these forces came under the Ministry of the Interior in Vietnam, not the Ministry of Defense. This made
them ineligible to receive American military assistance.

What in reality were the front-line forces therefore had to
make do with ancient weapons, without shoes, and without
communications even to advise when they were attacked, let
alone vainly request reinforcement. Little wonder that their
morale was abysmal, and that their nightly maneuver was
limited to closing the barbed wire around their pathetic fort
and waiting for morning in hopes that Communist guerrillas would ignore them as they went about the organization,
exhortation, and direction of their fellow villagers. The
contrast could not have been more stark between this real
level of the new war and the careful hierarchy of command
levels of the Vietnamese Army (including the "field" command of General Duong Van Minh), designed to permit
instant meshing with the levels of command of an American force sent to share the battle against a Korean-style
invasion from the North.

A vacuum rather than a defense also characterized the
political arena of the new struggle on the Government's

side. Some years before, the French had experimented with
a program to counter the Viet Minh's political and organizational campaign in the countryside. The same technique
had been tried in the early days of the Diem regime. Diem's
"civic action" program trained and sent small teams of civil
cadres to "eat, sleep, and work with the people," as advocated by his CIA adviser, Ed Lansdale. To emphasize their
identity with the rural population, they wore the black
pajamas traditional among the peasantry. They spent most
of their time building useful local projects such as schools,
village information halls, dispensaries, etc., while organizing the community by taking a census, holding meetings,
and helping the local officials.

The program ran into great difficulty when an effort at
expansion was made by assigning French-trained civil
servants to it. They viewed the very idea of rural work with
horror and disdain as a shameful demotion from the urban
paperwork world they considered their birthright. Others in
the Government thought the program interfered with Saigon's direction of regular ministerial projects. Also, it was
soon caught up in "anti-Communist denunciation campaigns," shifting its focus from helping the peasantry to
harassing them into accusing their neighbors of relations
with the Communists.

Perhaps providentially, the program's founder and dynamic spark plug, Kieu Cong Cung, died in 1957. The
residue of the program was then folded into Ngo Dinh
Nhu's Can Lao Party, where its original objectives were
replaced by Nhu's idea that the political situation could be
controlled by an internal and secret apparatus analogous to
a Communist party structure inside a society and its government. The result was to leave the rural areas of South
Vietnam subject only to heavy-handed Government administration, control, and propaganda exercises and without a
positive political program.

The political vacuum in the South Vietnamese countryside was soon to be complemented by developments in the
nation as a whole. The Fifteenth Plenum's May 1959 decision in Hanoi to launch the Second Indochinese War was
not the only critical turning point in Vietnamese history
that year. There were also elections in South Vietnam.

These presented a dramatic and disturbing contrast to the careful Communist organizational campaign afoot at the same time.

The National Assembly had been elected in 1956 as a Constituent Assembly to produce the Constitution and had automatically become the first National Assembly under it. On August 30, 1959, the first full elections for the Assembly were held throughout the country, and a great deal of the Government's political energies went into making it a success, or at least a success by the Government's lights. The National Revolutionary Movement, the Government's mass party, was mobilized to organize assemblies throughout the country, to put posters and banners in the streets and on the walls, and to urge that all citizens register and vote—for the Movement's candidates, of course. Support and discipline were the watchwords to counter the nefarious Communists.

As in most underdeveloped countries, the very idea of representative government was only vaguely perceived. The concept of a legislature in the Western sense as a forum for the development of a consensus of its own, or at least a vehicle for the determination of majority opinion, was little understood in a Vietnamese society that had experienced Chinese and French overlords. In the peasant's (and Diem's) mind, a legislature lay closer to a council advising the Emperor, modestly submitting its thoughts for him to consider, as he exerted his wisdom on behalf of the community.

Two more sophisticated groups took another view of the elections. A few of the non-Communist political elements, primarily urban and intellectual in character, looked forward to the prospect that the Assembly might play a real political role and be the vehicle by which they could gradually supplant the Mandarin rule that Diem represented and eventually participate in building the democratic regime suggested by the wording of the Constitution.

One of these groups was led by a Harvard-trained physician, Phan Quang Dan ("Doctor Dan"), who had participated in the struggle against the French and the Communists earlier, and who had built an effective practice serving the population of the Saigon suburb of Gia Dinh. Short, stocky, direct, and intense, he was a breed of political leader different from the rather wispy, elderly intellectuals who dominated the non-Communist political circles of Saigon. Perhaps influenced by his years at Harvard—in the shadow of Mayor Curley's Boston—he built an effective political organization. He also made his candidacy for a seat in the National Assembly something different from the traditional Vietnamese reliance on voter discipline or revolutionary conspiracy. I met him many years later, but in 1959 I was already impressed with his dedication, in both medicine and politics, to the Vietnamese people.

The other group was the Communists in the countryside. Both from the Vietnamese security services and from some of the CIA's independent operations, we received a number of Communist documents and propaganda leaflets exhorting the peasants to register for the upcoming vote. They called for support for the more liberally inclined—not Communist—candidates. The objective was the election of at least a few delegates who might support programs and policies reflecting the interests and needs of the rural communities and thus of the Communist activists, who were confident they could lead those communities. The tactic was to take advantage of the electoral process initiated by the Diem regime in order to get a foothold for the Communist political machine in the legitimate institutions of the new Republic. From those bases they hoped to expand their influence and power, and perhaps overcome the setback they had suffered in Diem's rejection of the Geneva-mandated elections of 1956.

When I first read some of these reports, I had some questions about their authenticity. They could have reflected the Vietnamese officials' view of wily Communist tactics and have been given to us to convince us that the Diem regime should be uncritically supported. They could even have been fabricated for this purpose. On reflection, however, and after checking into how we had acquired them, I decided they made sense for a Communist apparatus convinced that they could manipulate the South Vietnamese political process if they could just get access to it, eventually if not immediately. The time frame for the people's war in which the Communists were engaged was not only long term, it was undefined; their schedule was tied to developments, not to dates.

The Diem regime read many of these same reports and concluded that the Communist plan had to be defeated. The regime's conviction that the Communists would seek to exploit any opening to achieve power and then impose their rule was deep. It was not in fact unreasonable, based on experience in Vietnam and elsewhere with "national fronts." The resulting directives that emerged were clear: The Communist plots must be soundly defeated, or the nation would fall. To the sycophantic bureaucrats down the line, this meant that the Government party's candidates had to win—and win big. So in addition to the normal pressures for conformity in the countryside, the central Government's apparatus provided an extra stimulus to demonstrate local—and their own—loyalty to the regime. The posters urging the population to vote were supplemented by influential local advice to vote right, in the best Chicago tradition.

To these Government pressures was added Diem's and Nhu's disdain for the non-Communist opposition who ventured to run. The Ngo brothers considered them uniformly to be relics of the colonial regime, or erratic intellectuals with impractical and divisive ideas for a nation in the process of rapid modernization and facing a mortal enemy in the North.

The result was familiar in the developing world. The Government's candidates won smashing "victories" in the rural provinces and ran up large winning margins in the few cities outside Saigon. The returns were posted on a huge billboard in central Saigon, but they attracted little notice as they contained nothing unexpected. In the Saigon metropolitan area, the margins were lower, but substantial, and promptly explained by omnipresent critics as the result of troops trucked to significant districts to provide the necessary additional votes. Doctor Dan, however, proved irresistible. The voters, impressed with his sincerity and record of service to his community, gave him a six-to-one endorsement. Overreacting, the Government brought charges of electoral law violations against Doctor Dan to ensure that he would not take his seat in the Assembly and sent him to jail. The new Assembly would be totally subservient to the Palace: not content with having barred Communist influence, any opposition was also excluded.

Though little noticed, the 1959 South Vietnamese election thus became another turning point in the history of Vietnam. The responsibility must be laid at the door of Diem and Nhu despite—or perhaps because of—the excessive zeal displayed by their underlings in their desire to impress the inhabitants of the Palace. What was most significant for the long term was that the results of the election showed the Communists that the legal path to power was closed to them; their only course was to resume the people's war they had successfully waged against the French.

Meanwhile, various non-Communist nationalists in South Vietnam saw that they would have little or no role in a Diem regime. Diem and Nhu concluded that they could manipulate the forms of democratic government sufficiently to maintain control and carry out the forced draft modernization program as the long-term solution to Vietnam's problems. And the Americans in Vietnam divided between those who basically agreed with Diem that the priority task was modernization and growth to outpace the North and those who believed that the democratic principles of the South Vietnamese Constitution were being violated, thus weakening the cause against the Communists and negating the purpose of American assistance.

Part Three
A
SELF-INFLICTED
WOUND

5

A Mandarin and His Critics

BY EARLY 1960, SOUTH VIETNAM WAS beginning to feel—
and show—the results of the Communist organizational
and proselytizing campaign and its associated attacks. The
last four months of 1959 had seen 119 assassinations of local
government leaders. Tension was growing in the countryside, with direct effects on the Government's programs.

One such casualty was Diem's five-year effort, begun with
American aid, to eradicate malaria. A similar campaign
conducted in Italy after World War II had effectively wiped
out the disease. Periodic dusting of rural communities with
DDT was required (this was prior to the later discovery of
the counterproductive effects of applying DDT in this fashion). The teams of Government workers sent into the rural
areas to carry out the program were welcomed by the local
residents in the hope that this ancient scourge could be
lifted from them. But the Communists, identifying the
program as one that would help the Government's relations
with the rural communities, targeted it for termination.
They murdered the members of a number of teams and
passed the word that the same fate awaited others. The
result was that the teams charged with follow-up treatments
of DDT found it better not to go to remote areas. The
program thus collapsed, and the Communists achieved
their aim of keeping this Government service from the
population. The population, of course, resigned themselves
to the end of the program, perceiving in this result the
greater power of the Communists in the countryside, to
which they would have to adapt, as they had to others in the
past.

Diem's "agrovilles" program, launched in mid-1959 to
create large concentrations of rural population in the Me-

kong Delta, was another failure. A number of these "agricultural cities" were laid out, the inhabitants moved to their new homes, and the first steps taken to develop their schools, medical centers, and marketplaces. The plan provided each family with a small garden plot around the house they erected where they could grow their vegetables while raising their cash crop of rice in the outlying paddies. The scheme had a fatal flaw. The garden plots meant that the houses were separated by a considerable distance from one another. Spread over a large area, the community was difficult to defend against penetration by visiting Communist guerrilla and organizing teams. An idea that might have had promise in a peaceful atmosphere proved impossible in the face of Hanoi's campaign. The executors of the program, the local officials, also failed to build a political base for the program by explaining its purposes. Instead they simply dragooned peasants out of their existing homes and moved them to the new sites selected by the officials. In time the agrovilles, and their promise, simply eroded as the peasants moved back to their bamboo houses along the canals.

Tension in the countryside began to have its inevitable effect in the cities. Unease spread as indications of greater Communist activity filtered in from the villages. The result was increased pressures on the Diem regime. In the tea shops and intellectual centers, criticism that the Government was not meeting the new challenge mounted. CIA agents and contacts in the urban political community reported growing concern over the authoritarian attitude and arbitrary actions of the regime. The critics were uniformly reported as holding that only a more democratic approach to governing could rally the public support necessary to surmount the Communist pressure and manifestos. CIA and Embassy officers enthusiastically reported these comments. This was particularly the case when the comments came from those holding positions in the Government or in the Government party in the National Assembly. They were cited as indicating the real attitude of the politically knowledgeable, in contrast to the dreary recital of favorable statistics by the Government or to Diem's long harangues to visiting American officials.

In these encounters, a better appreciation of Vietnamese culture and traditions might have clarified the weight to be attached to the messages conveyed. The Vietnamese side in such conversations, seeking an agreeable outcome to the meeting and responding to the obvious search by the American questioner for desired answers, invariably responded affirmatively to the American's query about whether there was a degree of concern and unhappiness over the centralization of power in the Palace. The absence of free discussion and communication in Vietnamese political circles also played a role. In the absence of authoritative correctives, rumor and speculation replaced solid information as the basis for political discourse.

Part of the Americans' difficulty in dealing with urban and intellectual Vietnamese lay in the conception they shared that the democratic provisions of the 1956 Constitution should be taken seriously. This was at variance with the outlook of the rural Vietnamese, who lived in a more tradition-oriented world. For them Government officials were always exploiters of power, whether imperial or French. Rural hopes were largely limited to the family and the village community. Here also lay a partial explanation of the differences between the American military and civilians on these questions. Professionally trained and personally molded in the kind of hierarchical system they saw in Vietnam, the military valued the order and discipline they believed it produced.

Vietnamese civil servants, out of their long experience during French rule, which most of them had served, were especially prolific contributors to the rumors and speculation. They sat on the fringe of the power whose decisions they would be expected to implement. If starved of real information—which they largely were—their curiosity about what transpired at Court, now Vietnamese rather than French, was consuming. The Vietnamese Civil Service's experience in implementing policies imposed by French colonialists was not irrelevant, of course, to its duties under Diem's Mandarin-style regime. Nevertheless, Diem's decision, even though for lack of any real alternative, to continue to use the Civil Service that had served the French, was a fundamental weakness of his regime. Diem had

established a National Institute for Administration, conducted by the University of Michigan, to form a new, Amer-
ican-style Civil Service, but it had had little time to produce
results.

In the matter of public administration, the Communists
in the North provided a sharp contrast to the situation in
the South. They had little residue of the colonial regime and
used the cadres they had raised during the war. Besides
those cadres' loyalty, forged in the long fight, they viewed
their tasks in terms of political leadership rather than mere
administration—in the best Communist tradition. In the
South, a detached, rather than engaged, attitude of the civil
servants characterized administration. It also underlay their
willingness to offer critical comments to inquiring American officials and journalists.

At bottom, the wide gulf separating the urbane, educated
society of Saigon from the reality of rural life and interests
caused the urban elite, preoccupied with their own special
perspectives, to simply ignore the very real moves the Government was making in its development programs. Those
programs were the main strategy for the contest the Government viewed as determinant—improvement of the lot of
the rural population through modernization in order to
offer a better future than the Communists could. Thus the
Government concentrated on development, and its critics
complained of the lack of democracy, both barely considering the need for a balance between the two.

The issue thus posed dominated American discussions of
the situation. To most American observers, the development
part of the equation was accepted as a given and the democracy element a missing but necessary ingredient; thus there
was no choice between the two, as the Vietnamese views
would have it, but a gap—and a strategic one. My own
inclination was to be more understanding of the requirements of development in the near term, with the belief that
democracy could follow in good time if the Communist
challenge could be defeated.

In January 1960, a Communist attack overran a Vietnamese Army regimental headquarters near Tay Ninh, only
about fifty miles from Saigon, killing twenty-three soldiers,
capturing hundreds of weapons for later use, and inspiring

fear in Saigon circles. In April, eighteen mostly elderly, non-Communist, nationalist political figures from the sects and old political parties gathered at Saigon's modern Caravelle Hotel. Their purpose was to issue a manifesto stating their concerns and calling upon President Diem to "liberalize the regime, promote democracy, guarantee minimum civil rights, recognize the opposition." By doing this, they asserted, the people, making the obvious comparisons with the North Vietnamese regime, would "appreciate the value of true liberty and authentic democracy" and make the efforts and sacrifices necessary to defend them.

Diem's and Nhu's reaction was predictably negative. They dismissed the protesters as relics of the old colonial regime, their very choice of the glittering surroundings of a modern downtown hotel to launch their manifesto reflecting their lack of contact with, or even appreciation of, the rural people and society Diem's programs were striving to modernize. Diem and Nhu were certainly correct on the specifics but tragically wrong on the true significance of the manifesto. While it was indeed unreal in its expression of what the rural Vietnamese thought was important, it did have impact on two groups vital to the success of a free Vietnam—the educated elite, upon whom the hope for fulfillment of Diem's programs rested until a new elite could be raised, and the Americans, whose support of Vietnam determined whether it would survive.

The manifesto, then, served as another milestone in the gradual centrifugal separation of the Vietnamese body politic. While the Communist pressures in the countryside reduced Government authority there, the urban elite and political elements distanced themselves from the Diem regime. In the South Vietnamese spectrum, Diem and Nhu in fact held a central position, but their strength was ebbing away on both sides.

In September, Ambassador Durbrow sent to Washington his assessment of American relations with South Vietnam and his recommendations for American support there. He correctly stated that Vietnam faced two dangers: the Communists in the countryside and demonstrations or attempted coups in Saigon that the Communists could exploit. He had previously submitted a series of recommendations with respect to the rural security problem, dealing mostly with improvements in the Government's procedures, such as an internal security council and my proposal (I had become Chief of the CIA Station in June) for a Central Intelligence Organization to integrate and centralize the work of the various Vietnamese intelligence agencies in combating the Communist threat. In his September message, Durbrow turned to the political and psychological steps he felt were needed. The list demonstrated the ambiguity of the American relationship with Diem even then.

First the Ambassador asserted the need for a "psychological shock effect" to demonstrate to Communists and non-Communists that the Government had taken the initiative. The measures to achieve this "shock" effect included making Vice President Nguyen Ngoc Tho, a Southerner totally subservient to Diem, Minister of the Interior; Diem giving up the Ministry of Defense and appointing a full-time Minister; sending Nhu to a foreign embassy together with his henchman Tuyen; and naming one or two members of the opposition to the Cabinet. These moves were to be supplemented by an announcement of the disbanding of Nhu's Can Lao Party and publication of its membership; lifting of controls on the press and publications; stimulation of National Assembly investigations, on the American model, into corruption and mismanagement, and a series of economic measures such as subsidies to farmers for their rice production.

Although Durbrow's combative and peppery nature did little for his relations with Diem, I liked and respected him even when I did not agree with him. He tried manfully to make a "team" of the autonomous baronies that constituted the American presence in Saigon. But I strongly disagreed with him and his Embassy subordinates when they advocated American political practices that would change the locus of power in Vietnam with no clear perception of what the results on the war in the countryside would be. However desirable the political structure and procedures they prescribed might have been in a developed nation, it was plain that they were essentially irrelevant to the nature of the Vietnamese situation and society, aside from being transparently hostile to Diem and his Mandarin mission.

What Durbrow's September 1960 message was suggesting was the adoption by a Southeast Asian developing nation of the system of legislative controls and checks and balances that characterize the United States Government. What is more, it was being suggested in the confident belief that this would simultaneously be enthusiastically welcomed as an alternative to the national and social revolution propagated by the Communists in the countryside, and overcome the criticisms of the sophisticated urban intellectuals unhappy with Diem's Mandarin regime. The final paragraph of Durbrow's telegram was prophetic:

> U.S. should at this time support Diem as best available Vietnamese leader, but should recognize that overriding U.S. objective is strongly anti-Communist Vietnamese Government which can command loyal and enthusiastic support of widest possible segments of Vietnamese people, and is able to carry an effective fight against Communist guerrillas. If Diem's position in country continues deteriorate as result failure to adopt proper political, psychological, economic and security measures, it may become necessary for U.S. Government to begin consideration alternative courses of action and leaders in order achieve our objective.

In other words, we defined the necessary "psychological shock" in terms totally counter to Diem's personality and the realities of the Vietnamese power structure and society (and, in retrospect, of dubious value in themselves in any case—National Assembly investigating committees?). Then followed the suggestion that we might have to look for "other leaders" if Diem did not take our advice as to what was "proper" for him to do. The confrontation with Diem had begun.

Durbrow's cable reflected another problem: disagreement among the Americans. The increase in rural incidents had led the Military Assistance Advisory Group under "Hanging Sam" Williams and his successor, Lieutenant-General Lionel McGarr, to call for an increase in American assistance to the Vietnamese military—specifically, to provide the funds necessary to raise the Army from 150,000 to 170,000 men. The civilian side of the American "team" knew Diem would welcome this and wanted to use it as a lever to get Diem to make the kinds of political changes they sought. The American military rejected this flatly, saying that the forces were needed to hold off the enemy and should not be delayed for such unrealistic bargaining. I tried to keep out of this line of fire, as I found both positions missed the main point—how to meet a people's war in the countryside. More regular soldiers would not do it, but neither would the irrelevant political suggestions aimed at the urban elite. One immediate result of this impasse was that Durbrow's relations with the Palace deteriorated as Diem became aware of the Ambassador's role in blocking the additional military assistance Diem believed was needed. I began to look for a better answer.

Even as I did so, the struggles escalated even further. On November 10, 1960, the United States Marine contingent responsible for guarding the Saigon Embassy held their traditional Marine Birthday Ball. Dress uniforms, black tie, and formal gowns marked those fortunate enough to have been invited by the tiny unit to share its pride in the long history of the Corps, with the youngest and oldest Marine present slicing the cake in a ceremony repeated around the world that evening wherever Marines served. After the party, my wife and I and the Durbrows stopped at a restaurant barge on the Saigon River to enjoy the tropical evening a bit before turning in. When we did so, it was with an agreeable sense of relaxation. The tranquil atmosphere was interrupted about three o'clock in the morning by a series of sharp noises in the street below our home facing the Presidential Palace. It soon became clear that the noises were not the usual thunderstorm as tracer bullets crossed the night sky and thudded into our bedroom.

I activated the voice radio I kept in the closet for such an emergency and began to report at first hand to the Embassy the initiation of a paratrooper attack on the Palace. During the rest of the night, I moved my wife and children into a makeshift redoubt of bookcases and armed my weapons in case any of the fighting came into our house. By dawn, the situation had stabilized into a standoff. An Army parachute unit surrounded the Palace, and the Presidential Guard held them outside the gates. This gave me the opportunity to evacuate my family to friends whose house was farther from the center of the action (our places at home being taken by Vietnamese Marines as the Palace reinforced its defenses) and to slip away to the Embassy.

Over the next day, our independent reporting sources and our officers who had been invited to join their carefully cultivated friends among the dissidents informed us by telephone and over our radio net that the parachutists wanted to convince Diem to make substantial changes in the Government and military structure to better confront the Communist attack against South Vietnam. The paratroop commanders rather naively had not thought the matter through to any kinds of specific actions they wanted Diem to take. This vacuum, however, was soon filled by the arrival of several volunteer political leaders from the Caravelle group and its supporters, led by the charismatic Doctor Dan (who had abstained from the Caravelle manifesto). In short order they established a council and began issuing the appropriate political declarations to give form to the paratroopers' revolt.

But Diem was not idle. Helped by his Military Aide, General Nguyen Khanh (also a paratrooper, incidentally, but risen higher), who had climbed the rear wall of the Palace when he heard the gunfire indicating that it was under attack, Diem used the independent radio networks available at the Palace to contact field units of the Army in the provinces around Saigon. Among them was the commander of the Fifth Division at My Tho to the South, Colonel Nguyen Van Thieu. These officers saw the futility of the paratrooper outburst without broader planning or supporting forces and assembled their troops to move to the relief of the Palace. The Ambassador moved down to join me in the CIA Office for the night to be handy to the Station's radio network, which immediately reported the developments at the Palace, the parachute headquarters, the General Staff, and the dissident political center. At one moment we went onto the balcony to see the tracers from a short exchange of fire, and I urged Durbrow to go inside. It was just in time: a stray bullet came in a few seconds later and gave my deputy a flesh wound in the shoulder.

The following morning, we saw the deliberate movements of lines of Vietnamese soldiers along the streets of Saigon, each with a colored scarf to indicate his unit (and to distinguish him from fellow Army paratroopers), until the paratroopers were themselves surrounded and outnumbered. Significantly, Saigon's population stayed indoors, joining neither side, leaving the fight to the soldiers. The attempted coup collapsed with the departure of its leaders for Cambodia in a transport aircraft made available to fellow officers and friends by the head of the Air Force Transport Command, Colonel Nguyen Cao Ky (which he later assured the Palace had been commandeered by force).

The political figures who had joined the coup and tried to give it political content saw their base of support vanish, exposing them to the secret police of the Palace. They were rounded up and incarcerated in the Chi Hoa prison, which had housed several generations of their compatriots who had similarly risen against the French. Doctor Dan remained in prison until the end of the Diem regime in 1963, as did many of the signers of the Caravelle manifesto. The major conclusion of the coup attempt was the clear lesson that such a move against the Ngo brothers would have to be carefully planned to include the whole of the Army, not just a part.

A second conclusion was that American support of the Diem regime was less than total. Durbrow had plainly indicated to Diem through phone calls during the crisis that the U.S. position was not to take sides. The brothers soon also found out that the CIA's reactions had indicated ambivalence, its officers having been seen at paratrooper headquarters with their radios in contact with the Station. The commander of the coup was a carefully cultivated friend of one of the Station's officers and had welcomed him when he arrived to check developments on that side. Another officer had sat in on the opposition political council discussions and been overheard telephoning "Bill" about their problems. Others, however, were in touch with Dr. Tuyen at the Palace, and I had agreed with Nhu's telephoned request that I go to the front gate of the Palace to be an American presence during discussions there seeking a resolution of the confrontation (which never took place, as the coup collapsed in the face of the arriving loyal troops).

In several conversations following the coup attempt, Nhu made it clear that he was aware of the Station's presence on both sides, which I justified as merely reflecting our responsibility to know what was going on. Nhu commented, "All nations conduct espionage, and this is not a matter to get upset about." Clearly annoyed, he went on, "But what no nation can accept, and our Government no less, is interference with its political authority and processes." He made a particular point about the officer who had been at the political deliberations, saying that he had gone beyond reporting to encourage the politicians in their effort against the regime. I knew that he had not, as I had been in close touch with and control of him during the affair, and held him faithfully to the Ambassador's policy of nonsupport of either side (although to do so, I had had to word my directives very strongly). Thus I stuck to his "cover story" that he was only a junior officer of the Mission and not a CIA officer at all, which Nhu clearly did not believe. Nhu responded that the officer would have to leave the country because of his activities and asked that I send him away. I replied that we had no reason on our side to order him out, bringing us to an impasse.

This was soon subtly and cleanly solved by the appearance of a note in the officer's letter box, ostensibly from some of the dissidents, berating him for his encouragement of them and his assurances of American support whether or not the coup succeeded. It said they now needed that support as they hid from the regime's wrath, and it was not forthcoming. It added a threat of retribution against the officer and his family. Recognizing the ploy—and even the typing from Dr. Tuyen's office—I took the note to Nhu and stated that we had to protect the officer and his family from the possibility of any harm stemming from this false charge, so we were arranging that he leave the country. Nhu gravely agreed and arranged a police guard for the officer's house until he and his family were escorted to the airport by protective jeeps full of armed police. Face was saved on both sides.

One political dissident, who had been one of our agents,

did in fact land on the doorstep of one of our officers and asked for help. Since his fate would be sealed if we did not accept him, I arranged that he be moved to one of our temporarily empty houses, where he hid silently for several days. We then brought in an aircraft for an "air shipment" and put him aboard inside a large mail sack. He was later resettled in Europe with instructions to say nothing about how he had left Vietnam. We had protected our source.

A much more important political event took place elsewhere during this period. In the war against the French, the chosen vehicle was the Viet Minh (a short version of a longer name meaning "League for the Independence of Vietnam"), a front group formed by Ho Chi Minh's Indochinese Communist Party to assemble non-Communists in support of the rebellion—under firm Communist control. In the Second Indochinese War, the Communists never used the name *Viet Cong*, although it translates literally as "Vietnamese Communist." In fact, the Vietnamese Communists never used the term "Communist" after 1945, turning instead to such terms as "revolutionary," "workers," or "Marxist." "Viet Cong," though, was the term used by the Government and the Americans. It was essentially accurate in its reflection of the fact that the true leadership of the revolution was indeed Communist with its direction in the North. Its simplicity, however, delayed the development of a full picture of the political structures through which the Communists actually carried on their priority effort of mobilizing as much of the population as possible.

By 1960, a grouping similar to the Viet Minh was needed for the war in the South, one that could present itself as only a grouping of organizations, Communist and non-Communist, to unify the efforts of all who opposed the American-Diemists, and which the Communists would control from within. The long, patient work of organization and political construction undertaken by the Communist cadres infiltrated from the North and recruited in the South now bore fruit. A patchwork of associations and front groups for youth, women, intellectuals, non-Communists, farmers, and others, in the best Communist style, was assembled under which the war against the American-Diemists could be conducted. It was time to integrate them all into a disciplined structure that could serve as the symbol of the overall revolt against Diem and the Americans.

In its best conspiratorial style, a clandestine radio station announced on December 12 the formation in a South Vietnamese jungle of a "National Front for the Liberation of South Vietnam," which was finally confirmed in a Hanoi broadcast of January 29, 1961. Hanoi reported that the National Liberation Front had been "recently formed in South Vietnam by various forces opposing the fascist Ngo Dinh Diem regime," and asserted that these "various forces" had issued a political program and manifesto on December 20, 1960—now generally accepted as the effective date of the formation of the National Liberation Front.

In order to dilute the Communist identity of what purported to be a South Vietnamese all-party movement, the Communist participants in the Front in 1962 changed their own organizational name from the "Lao Dong (Workers') Party," the name of the Party in North Vietnam, to the "People's Revolutionary Party" (a literal translation), ostensibly only a South Vietnamese grouping. Its function as the vanguard of the National Liberation Front, meaning providing control and direction, remained. The Southerners whose names as leaders of the National Liberation Front were internationally trumpeted had no more control over the group's activities than their earlier non-Communist nationalist counterparts had over the Viet Minh front of fighters against the French. The true significance of the formation of the Front was that the political structure that Ho Chi Minh needed to fight a people's war was now in place. Both broader political organizational work and local guerrilla offensives could proceed apace.

6

Roads to Strategic Hamlets

AMBASSADOR DURBROW'S SEPTEMBER 1960 cabled recommendations to Washington for American support of the South Vietnamese Government were one aspect of the development, which took a good part of that year, of a comprehensive Counterinsurgency Plan, an American bureaucratic exercise involving a minimum of discussion with the Vietnamese. The final result was in the main a consolidation of the preferred ideas of each American agency in Vietnam for its own activities. There was a minimum of integration into an overall strategy. It related minimally to the reality of the Communist efforts at organizing the peasantry and undermining the Government's presence in the countryside at its most exposed points.

The military component of the Plan essentially consisted of the 20,000-man increase in the Vietnamese Army and American military support for 32,000 of the 68,000-man Civil Guard, the provincial-level territorial forces. In retrospect, I confess bafflement at the reason for this numerical subtlety.

The Military Assistance Advisory Group advocated a "net and spear" strategy of sending patrols into the back country to locate Communist units, whereupon the Army could "spear" them with mobile forces—a traditional military tactic to find, fix, and fight the enemy. One of the preoccupations of the American military was to use the territorials to relieve the Army of "static" defensive missions on bridges, public works, and other potential targets so that the regular soldiers could take the offensive in the best American spirit. Another preoccupation was to bring the territorials under a single military chain of command, taking them from the province chiefs who, it was asserted, used them too much for "defensive" tasks.

The civilian side of the Counterinsurgency Plan followed the Embassy's September recommendations: that opposition elements be brought into Diem's Government (not just the Legislature) and that the Legislature undertake investigations of the Executive Branch to root out mismanagement and corruption in the best Washington tradition. For the rural peasantry, the prescription was "civic action" by the military forces (handing out goodies and constructing public works) to generate appreciation. But nowhere in the Plan was there a program for pure political action—organizing the population into political groups, articulating a cause that would attract their participation and support, developing leadership and cohesion at the local rural community level, etc.—in other words, a direct counter to the program the Communists were carrying out in the countryside. Americans consider these activities part of individual and group initiative in political life, not something organized by the government. The concept of a battle between a government and a hostile force on this terrain is foreign to American experience. Any such measures therefore were left out of the American Plan in 1961. But they were the core of the Communist plan.

The major CIA feature of the Plan was my suggestion for a Vietnamese Central Intelligence Organization to coordinate the work of the various intelligence agencies against the Communists. This useful but prosaic contribution was in keeping with the posture of the CIA Station at the time. In the cease-fire atmosphere that characterized South Vietnam from 1956 to 1959, and in recognition that the major interest and effort of the Government and the American mission lay in economic development programs, the CIA Station had kept a low profile. It had worked with the Vietnamese civilian intelligence service and with the Special Branch of the National Police, providing training and occasional special equipment in return for their reports of developments in the countryside.

Of course, the Vietnamese conducted their own independent operations outside our cooperation, such as their bumbling efforts to unseat Prince Sihanouk in neighboring Cambodia. When the Cambodians became aware of these activities, they naturally blamed the United States and the CIA. They could not conceive that Vietnamese operations were conducted without our participation. Since we also knew of these operations from our internal sources, we tried to argue against them with Diem and Nhu, with a conspicuous lack of success. Then Sihanouk wrapped up one of the would-be coup leaders and found the man's aide in possession of a CIA radio we had provided so that he could secretly keep us informed of his chief's plans. Understandably, Sihanouk believed he had firm evidence of our involvement in the Vietnamese efforts against him, which he then came to call his "War with the CIA."

The Station also developed a number of independent sources among the civilian politicians who perpetually sought a change in the Diem regime's authoritarian ways, if not the regime itself, and were happy to be in confidential contact with a sympathetic American who could pass their views along to American decision makers. We also had some independent sources both within and outside the Government, so that for our assessments we would not be dependent only on what the regime and its services chose to tell us. To me the surprising aspect of the Station's posture when I arrived was the complete absence of any kind of political or paramilitary action program—something beyond the mere collection of information that would use the CIA's techniques and talents to advance American policies and interests. The basic American policy of supporting the Diem Government made it obvious that we would not be supporting its opponents, but I was concerned that we seemed to be doing little or nothing to strengthen it, aside from our connections with the intelligence services. My surprise was in part due to the fact that I had come to Vietnam from Italy, where, apart from our cooperation with the Italian intelligence services, the CIA had conducted major programs to support the Italian center democratic parties against the Communist effort to subvert Italy through political means.

Less surprising was the absence of any meaningful coverage of North Vietnam and the Southern Communists, except for what we obtained through the uncertain channels the Vietnamese services offered. This was understandable in light of the almost total lack of communication between South and North, the draconian Communist security practices, and the clandestine nature of the Communist apparatus in the South.

As the war in the South began, however, we in the CIA began to look for ways to improve our coverage, help the Vietnamese learn more about the Communists in their midst, and strengthen their defenses against hostile penetrations and pressures. On the professional intelligence side, this was the genesis of the suggestion to provide better pooling and analysis of the intelligence available to the different Vietnamese civilian and military services through the establishment of a Central Intelligence Organization, fashioned on the CIA model (as had been done in a number of other nations), in addition to training courses in intelligence techniques for Vietnamese officers.

But we also began to contemplate the nature of the Communist efforts and the best ways for the Government and its American ally to combat them. I had, of course, operated as a guerrilla myself during World War II in France and in Norway, and the CIA had been involved in many operations, both political and paramilitary, in support either of insurgents against a hostile government (Indonesia, Guatemala) or of a government against such a challenge (Philippines, Laos). Uniquely in the American bureaucracy, the CIA understood the necessity to combine political, psychological, and paramilitary tools to carry out a strategic concept of pressure on an enemy or to strengthen an incumbent. In my weekly meetings with Nhu, therefore, we frequently went into long discussions of the nature of the Communist "people's war" and their political warfare in Europe, China, and elsewhere.

Nhu and I also covered the various programs the French had tried in Vietnam or those applied in other countries, such as Malaya or Algeria, in a search for a strategy that could meet the Communists in Vietnam on their own ground and build strength in the countryside to combat them. As these conversations proceeded, Nhu gradually moved from his initial fascination with the Leninist technique of the controlling party apparatus (his own Can Lao) to an acceptance of the necessity that the ordinary citizen not only be directed but also be motivated to resist the incursions of the enemy and be confident that in doing so he would be supported and protected in his choice.

These concepts were consistent with Nhu's contempt for the urban elite who ran Vietnam and his belief that their values were more foreign than Vietnamese. An approach that offered the hope of new leaders and a new base for the Vietnamese nation therefore appealed to him, especially one that directly combatted the Communist efforts of the same type. Nhu was also stimulated by the fact that our discussions were of political strategies, leaving to the side the military class, in which he had no great confidence. The germ of the "strategic hamlets," program had been born, but it took many hours of discussion for Nhu to develop the idea and become convinced of its validity.

These problems—and indeed the fate of far-off Vietnam—of course hardly played a role in the transcendentally important 1960 American contest for the succession to Dwight Eisenhower. The contention that a "missile gap" between the Soviet Union and the United States had been opened, the challenges of the neutralist Spirit of Bandung and of Castro's Cuba in the developing world, and the unfinished business of equal rights in the United States were of far more immediate concern to the people's choice of future political leadership than was Vietnam. John Kennedy's narrow victory over Richard Nixon, with its imagery of the young dynamic leader and his stunning wife and family, typified the hope of Americans for dramatic world leadership against the forces of darkness and complacency that seemed so strong at the end of the 1950s.

Kennedy had earlier visited South Vietnam and expressed his full support for its independence. He had met Diem and was enthusiastic about the man and his leadership. (Kennedy's inaugural address had an immense effect on Diem's chief of staff, Nguyen Dinh Thuan, who joined me at dinner to read the first USIS text received at the Embassy.) But the principal problem facing Kennedy in Southeast Asia when he took office was not Vietnam but Laos. There Soviet aircraft supplied North Vietnamese and Lao Communist forces, and American Army Special Forces teams and CIA operatives supported the Government's forces and some of the tribal groups in the mountains fighting to keep the North Vietnamese out of their homelands. The Communists were clearly winning the contest. The collapse of the Lao Army, coups, and countercoups accompanied the steady spread of Communist-controlled areas across the map.

Kennedy met the situation with a major call to action, including the commitment of American forces if necessary, stressing the likely roll of Communism southward unless it was stopped in Laos. But he also offered to negotiate a solution at Geneva if a cease-fire could be arranged. Soviet leader Nikita Khrushchev had much more important subjects on his mind, such as Berlin, and no desire for a confrontation in the faraway land of Laos. At Vienna in June 1961, the two met. Despite their differences in other areas, they agreed to set Laos aside as an issue between them and settle for its neutrality. The details were finally resolved at a meeting of fourteen nations at Geneva in July 1962.

But Vietnam could not be set aside. There the Soviet Union was only a supporter of ambitions defined, motivated, and led by the conviction of Ho Chi Minh and the North Vietnamese that Vietnam—and indeed all of Indochina—should be unified under their rule. It was plain that Vietnam would be a test of the new President's inaugural pledge to "pay any price, bear any burden, meet any hardship, support any friend, oppose any foe to assure the survival and success of liberty." Kennedy regarded the problem of Vietnam as part and parcel of the threat of Communist expansion on a world scale. In that view, the Soviet Union and China were standing behind the North Vietnamese in a firm alliance to spread *their* control southward in Southeast Asia. In fact, the Sino-Soviet alliance was coming apart just at this time, although intelligence analysts differed vehemently on whether the split was genuine or only a massive disinformation scheme to confuse the world. And thinking of Ho Chi Minh and the Vietnamese Communists as only an extension of Soviet and Chinese expansionist hopes certainly did not reflect Hanoi's insistence on its autonomous control of its actions.

But as support for a global view of the Communist threat in Vietnam, Kennedy did have Khrushchev's explicit statement in January 1961, just prior to the President's Inauguration, in which Khrushchev propounded the duty of Com-

munist countries to support revolutions or "wars of
national liberation" in present or former colonial territo-
ries, specifically including Vietnam. At the same time,
Kennedy was grasping for a better way for the United States
to meet these threats than reliance on military power alone.
While still President-elect, Kennedy sent old Vietnam hand
Edward Lansdale, now a General, to Vietnam to survey the
situation and report to him. Lansdale was the prototype for
the fictional "Ugly American" who developed warm and
personal relations with Asians and sought to understand
their cultures and yearnings, not just the texts of their
political and propaganda statements. His achievements in
the Philippines with President Ramón Magsaysay were
legendary, and his experience there in meeting the rural
Communist threat of the Hukbalahaps was particularly
relevant to what was now going on in Vietnam. His previous successful association with Diem during the critical
1954–1955 period was, of course, a major qualification to
advise the new American President on Vietnam.

In early 1961, there were rumors that Kennedy was considering naming Lansdale his Ambassador to Vietnam, so
on his visit he was naturally treated very delicately by the
Americans working in Vietnam, especially by us in the
CIA. At a dinner I organized to let him meet the officers of
the Station conducting our operations, he listened carefully
and presented a perfect poker face as to his reactions and
views. He did not limit himself to the American briefings
but traveled to the countryside, talking with Vietnamese to
get their side of the story. His conclusions on his return to
Washington were not earth-shaking: the situation was indeed deteriorating, and the friction between the Embassy—
especially Ambassador Durbrow—and Diem was stalling
needed action as Durbrow continued to delay a "green
light" for the increase in the Vietnamese Army urged by the
American military in an effort to extract his recommended
political concessions from Diem. Lansdale said that the
appointment of a new Ambassador was necessary to revive
Diem's confidence in working with the Americans.

As the tension in the countryside increased and the
Kennedy Administration's excitement stimulated us all to
look for new ideas with which to meet the rising Commu-

nist challenge, we in the CIA Station began to experiment with programs to contribute to the contest in a practical sense, not merely to report on what was happening. The Station still had a section descended from Lansdale's mission of 1954 and 1955 and now led by a gruff CIA paramilitary specialist. One of the contacts he had made was a young American working for the International Voluntary Service, a private charitable organization that was a precursor of Kennedy's Peace Corps. This young volunteer lived and worked among the Rhade tribe of highlanders. Observing that the Vietnamese Government and military pretty much ignored the highlanders, when they did not actually oppress them, rather in the manner we in the United States had handled Native Americans, he had become concerned about their vulnerability to Communist penetration and pressures.

The two came to me with the idea that the Rhade could protect themselves if they were armed and organized. The aim was sound. Highlanders who could defend themselves would deprive the Communists of the bases and assistance they needed and hoped to count on in the mountain areas. It was clear, however, that any such program would have to be approached very carefully so as not to arouse official Vietnamese suspicion and resistance. For this reason it could not be handled through the normal Vietnamese Government structure and channels or through the American AID program. In other words, it was a typical case for the CIA to handle: it required political sophistication and liaison at high levels of the Vietnamese Government, flexibility of management, finances, and logistics, plus the ability to adjust the program to fit the varying realities on the ground rather than to impose the same model uniformly. It was also obvious that the program would have to be delicately handled on the American side, since it would cut across the jurisdictional jealousies of the AID mission and the Military Assistance Advisory Group.

We thus decided that we should start small and make the case for a program by a successful experiment, rather than try to sell a massive panacea and arouse all possible objections before we had any experience with the idea. We looked for a few Vietnamese who could be convinced that the idea

was worth a try and could vouch to their Government that
they would keep a sharp eye on it to see that it did not go
awry. With these located, I went to Nhu and explained that
we had come across an opportunity to experiment with the
problem of generating local security in the critical highland region. As the Vietnamese officials we had briefed were
fully in the operation and able to report to Nhu on it, I got
his permission to proceed. With this in hand, I was then
able to get the Ambassador's approval for this small experiment as an item separate from the major AID and military
programs. Finally, we were able to arouse the interest and
enlist the participation of a few American Special Forces
members to provide the needed paramilitary training and
advisory functions.

Only after completing all these preliminaries could we
actually go to work with the elders and people of the little
community of Buon Enao, some ten kilometers outside Ban
Me Thuot in the highlands north of Saigon. As we had
hoped, they welcomed the idea, dug ditches for their families and foxholes for the defenders, put sharpened sticks in
the areas off the defended routes of access to the community,
quickly learned to handle and shoot the few ancient weapons we provided, and were delighted with the walkie-talkie
radio they could use to tell the local district headquarters
that they were under attack and needed help. In deference to
Vietnamese sensibilities, the Vietnamese flag was prominently displayed, and Vietnamese Special Forces shared the
training and leadership function with the big-nosed Americans. While it was clear to all that the real initiative lay
with the Americans, we met this potential problem with
the careful explanation that the American and Vietnamese
trainers would be moving on to another community to
repeat the process as soon as Buon Enao was ready to stand
on its own feet with its own leaders and had been integrated
into the defense scheme of the area.

The experiment did work and attracted leaders from
other communities in the neighborhood, who asked that
they be subjects of the same process. Admittedly, one of the
reasons it worked was that we knew that Buon Enao was
not especially exposed, so the chances of a devastating
attack and defeat during the confidence-building process

were not great. But this was precisely the point. As a political tactic it had been advocated a half-century previously by Marshal Lyautey, redoubtable Resident-General of Morocco in 1912–1925 (and member of the French Academy), under the concept of the "ink spot" (in French, *tache d'huile* or "oil spot"). The greater security provided by organized and armed communities should begin in the safer area and spread outward to the less secure area like ink on a blotter (or oil on cloth). Amoebalike, the process would add strength to strength in a strategic offensive conducted by a series of simple tactical defensive measures.

Totally absent from the concept was the idea of attack against the enemy. This was far beyond the simple capabilities of the villagers and, in any case, tangential to the real target of the people's war—the organization and mobilization of the people themselves by one side or the other. Nor were there any illusions that the villagers' participation and support were heroic or altruistic; it was clear that the medical aid program, the agricultural advice and assistance, and the other physical benefits of participation in the program were a substantial element in its appeal to them, and that they contrasted with the slim benefits the enemy could offer.

As the Buon Enao experiment prospered and was repeated in other communities in the Ban Me Thuot area in order to gradually establish a defensive belt around it, the Station looked for other areas where the technique could be applied. Several Catholic communities were first in line, wanting to revive the long-standing self-protection they had had in North Vietnam before moving as communities to the South in 1954. One of them lay at the southern tip of Vietnam, barely afloat in the marshes the Mekong River had built up there over the centuries. This community had followed their dynamic Pastor from the North, through Laos, to this last toehold President Diem offered them in an effort to people the area with a reliable (Catholic) element. The Station had provided the Pastor with the weapons he needed for self-defense (with Diem's full approval). During Lansdale's pre-Inauguration survey for Kennedy, Diem's skilled chief of staff, Thuan, took him to this watery refuge. Lansdale returned greatly impressed with the enthusiasm and strength of the Pastor, the Diem regime's willingness to move in this self-reliant direction, and, not at all unwelcome, the CIA Station's support of it.

The process was repeated in a number of other Catholic communities and, in some cases as a result of our specific search, non-Catholic ones, in the Delta, the highlands, and along the coast toward the North. A further step forward was made when the Station agreed to train, arm, and pay a sustaining wage to some of the members of the community defense units to allow them to operate full-time as reinforcement and patrolling forces for a group of defended communities. In this way, cries for help in the night were certain to be responded to by young men of the area rather than ignored by distant Vietnamese military forces. This involved no change in the basic strategy, however. The mission of these "strike forces" was still fundamentally defensive. We carefully gave them a name that we hoped would show their purpose—Citizens' Irregular Defense Groups, the first three words of which described their operations exactly.

At this stage some interesting initiatives came from the Vietnamese Government, launched by enterprising and imaginative local or national officials. I arose at 4:00 A.M. one morning to meet National Assemblywoman Pauline Nguyen Van Tho, a graduate of Bowdoin College in Maine, and drive south with her to her constituency in Kien Hoa province, historically a redoubt of the Communists in the war against the French and once again beginning to stir with revolutionary fever. We were met there by the new province chief, Colonel Pham Ngoc Thao, who combined strong Catholic credentials with an active role in the Viet Minh rebellion against the French. He had been assigned to the province by Diem and Nhu to experiment with his ideas on how to organize the rural countryside to preempt the Communists. After describing the benefits of concentrated economic and social development programs in building up the villages, and then providing these viable communities with local security forces, he took us on a tour by motorboat. We went through the canals to an arm of the Mekong, meandering through the Delta on its way to the sea, and stopped at a small village. The inhabitants greeted Colonel

Thao as a frequent visitor, and I was further impressed by the fact that he needed no guards for himself or his Saigon visitors.

On another occasion I returned to the deeper Delta in the company of Civic Action Minister Ngo Truong Huu, an ebullient and enthusiastic organizer of "civic action teams" of young Vietnamese sent to live with the villagers. The teams' functions were to help the villagers establish the elements of local government in their communities and to put them in touch with the national programs that could assist them. Later I realized that these teams were a revival of the program inspired by Edward Lansdale during the early Diem years to bring the new Government to former Viet Minh areas. The death of its first leader in 1957 had meant the death of the program as well, for its functions changed from bringing services to the population to strong-arm propaganda. However, the aim of the new teams, dressed in the traditional peasant black pajamas to identify them with the rural population, was to revive the original program.

The Station's repertoire did have a variation on all this defensive strategy. The CIA in Asia, inheriting the experience of the Office of Strategic Services in World War II, was familiar with penetrations behind enemy lines in an effort to generate guerrilla forces and resistance there; for example, the OSS mission parachuted into North Vietnam in 1945 to work with and support Ho Chi Minh. Lansdale had made some rudimentary efforts to leave a few nets or assets in North Vietnam in 1954, but they had all been suppressed or simply faded away. As the Communist offensive took shape in South Vietnam, the obvious point was raised that we should do in North Vietnam what it was doing in the South.

There were certainly assets that could be used for such a program. The 900,000 Northerners who had come South in 1954 offered a pool of volunteers who were willing to go back and had relatives known to be in the North for points of contact. There were also Catholic communities there, a few of which had already revolted against the Communist rule. Access by parachute drop, sea landing, or mountain crossing seemed feasible enough. The Vietnamese Army had

developed a Special Forces unit that could be used as the
nucleus of the activity. Its leadership was in close contact
with and under the direct control of the Palace, guarantee-
ing its reliability and ensuring the necessary Government
support of its activities. We began to work with the Vietnamese Special Forces (and Air Force) on the long process
of recruiting the potential agents, equipping and training
them, and working out the intelligence and planning requirements so that they could be sent to areas where they
might evoke a response from the population in the North.

It was a period of experimentation and innovation. Thus
one military region commander had the idea of using
selected highlanders to conduct long-range patrols through
the mountains to locate the Communist infiltration routes
and report them so that the military could arrange ambushes, attacks, or interdiction operations against them.
This called for weapons, a training camp, simple voice
radios for communications, and other special support outside the normal military aid program that went to the
regular units only. It was another task that called for the
informal and flexible logistics, finance, and program channels of the CIA.

In the separate fiefdom of Diem's brother Can, who essentially operated autonomously in Central Vietnam, small
teams of black-clad peasants (and only peasants, as Can
distrusted any form of bureaucrat or city dweller) were
specially trained to enter a rural community and, as fellow
peasants, help it to organize local community services and
defenses, then move on to another community to repeat the
process. Again the flexibility of the CIA allowed us to
furnish the needed weapons and training facilities—even
the black pajamas—but make the entire activity appear to
be purely Vietnamese in origin, direction, and character,
with minimal visibility of Americans (as Can insisted).

These experiments went on against the backdrop of
extensive American Governmental discussions of what
needed to be done to shore up Vietnam against the growing
Communist attack. The comprehensive Counterinsurgency
Plan, which had taken so much of everyone's attention
during 1960, was sent to Washington. It landed in the
White House almost simultaneously with the arrival of the

new President. Kennedy quickly approved it—one suspects
to get something moving as much as for what it provided.
Having done so, however, the new Administration called
for an interdepartmental "Program of Action for Vietnam."
Basic to its formulation were those of General Lansdale's
recommendations that had been adopted in the White
House. Chief among these was the appointment of a new
Ambassador. While Lansdale, in so recommending, may
have had himself in mind, the Pentagon considered him an
unguided missile whose appointment would cut across the
carefully arranged military lines of command. He was left
to languish in a desk job in Washington, his productive
imagination denied its useful place in Vietnam.

Instead of Lansdale, Kennedy named Frederick E. Nolting, Jr., a career Foreign Service Officer and a true Virginia
gentleman, to replace Durbrow as Ambassador, instructing
him to reverse Durbrow's prickly relations with Diem and
to try for sincere cooperation with the South Vietnamese
Government. The "Program of Action for Vietnam" was
approved by President Kennedy in May 1961. Its principal
provisions were for the military's recommended increase of
Vietnamese Army effectives from 150,000 to 170,000 and of
an additional 100 personnel for the American military
training mission, plus a border radar surveillance capability against Communist overflights (never before or later
detected), a "long-range economic development program,"
and acceleration of the Vietnamese public information program.

However much we in the CIA were convinced that our
activities were significant moves to strengthen South Vietnam against the Communist attack, it is clear in retrospect
that they were essentially marginal in scope and in impact,
especially in comparison with the major thrust of the
United States programs at the time. The 1961 "Program of
Action for Vietnam," for example, put these activities in a
general annex to the major points of the Program, according only a modest increase in the Station's strength to step
up its operations.

My own view that this modest increase was pushing the
machinery about as far as I dared at the time is both a
reflection of a lack of vision on my and my colleagues' part,

and an accurate reflection of the general attitude that the CIA's activities were perhaps useful on the margins but essentially secondary to a proper military approach to the problem of protecting South Vietnam. Part of this attitude stemmed, of course, from the disastrous Bay of Pigs failure just at this time. It cast doubt on the CIA's capabilities and even on its continued existence, as Kennedy mused that he would like "to scatter it to the winds." Even the redoubtable Lansdale proved unable to swim against this perception (and the institutional interests of the military and civilian bureaucracies) when his proposal for an unstructured advisory force of sympathetic ("Ugly") Americans spread throughout the countryside, with ample direct support for any activity that seemed useful in the local circumstances, was turned down.

In 1961 the situation in Laos deteriorated. There was an increase in Communist aggression and a fragmentation of the non-Communist defenders. This heightened concern in Vietnam and in Washington as to Vietnam's future. Diem's reaction was to call for a greater American commitment. He was especially concerned about American military support and broached the idea of a formal defense treaty, additional American advisers and support personnel, and more technology. He also asked for the American reaction as to whether he should accept a Nationalist Chinese offer from Taiwan of a division of troops to help the fight, to be based in the southern Delta far from the North Vietnamese (and, of course, the Chinese) border. (The Nationalist Chinese division did not come to Vietnam.) Diem maintained his earlier distaste for putting American troops into combat, but he was receptive to the arrival of American units to train and support the Vietnamese Army.

In May 1961, the American community in Saigon braced itself for a whirlwind—Vice President Lyndon B. Johnson would arrive to demonstrate the commitment of the United States Government to the cause of a free and non-Communist South Vietnam. In his raw Texas style, Johnson thrust aside the careful subtleties urged on him by local American officials to stress their concern over Diem's less than democratic rule. Exuberantly he referred to Diem as "the Winston Churchill of Southeast Asia," essential to American policy and to keeping the United States from having to fight "on the beaches of Hawaii."

I had only one exposure to Lyndon Johnson at that time (though others later). In the Ambassador's office late one hot evening, Johnson held temporary court to hear the briefings for his conversations with Diem. Seated at one end of the office, he was plainly more interested in attempts to get a telephone to work than in listening to the cacophony of advice thrown at him. He obviously had decided that the American interest was to support Diem, whatever Diem's failings, and that his visit would make that clear. In Johnson's attitude, as much as in his words, was evident his full confidence that if powerful America put its strength behind South Vietnam, we would prevail.

Diem took from Johnson's visit just what Johnson intended: the United States would back him at the highest level, and he could discount the antagonisms of the Embassy and the press.

But none of these steps really eliminated the tensions in the American community between the civilian critics of Diem, who believed it essential to press him to adopt democratic "reforms" by conditioning support upon such moves, and the military. The latter insisted on the primacy of strengthening the Vietnamese regular forces, meaning their constant recommendations to establish a single chain of command for all armed elements in Vietnam, to bring the local territorial forces into the military hierarchy, thus removing them from direction by local province and district officials.

In October 1961 another important visit to Vietnam took place. General Maxwell Taylor, who commanded the 101st Airborne Division when it parachuted into Normandy on D-Day 1944 and later rose to the position of Chief of Staff of the United States Army, had been selected by President Kennedy to be his Special Adviser for Military Affairs. In part this was because Taylor had resigned from the Army in protest against the Eisenhower Administration's overemphasis on nuclear forces at the expense of the regular forces ("a bigger bang for the buck"). President Kennedy sent him to make yet another survey of Vietnam and what would be needed there. He was accompanied by Walt Rostow, a vigorous and independent thinker on the National Security Council staff.

I missed most of their visit despite its importance, as I had been convoked to a meeting of CIA Chiefs of Station in the Far East to be presented to our newly appointed Director, John McCone. To McCone I had described how the Station was experimenting with various rural security programs and received his full support. On my return to Saigon, I had the chance for no more than a hurried exchange with Taylor and Rostow at the end of their visit, certainly not enough to give the rationale for our approach and to interest them in its potential.

Taylor himself had well-founded doubts about the CIA in any case, as he had chaired the committee President Kennedy had named to investigate the Bay of Pigs disaster only a few months before. Taylor's conclusion then had been that the CIA was not adequately staffed or organized to undertake paramilitary operations of larger than totally clandestine size. On his return to Washington from Saigon, Taylor's report thus focused primarily on how to make the military programs work better, especially with a substantially augmented advisory presence to stimulate the Vietnamese forces into better performance.

The question of strategy, adapting the Vietnamese structure and forces to the nature of the battle being waged by the Communists, was hardly addressed. The approach to this problem is perhaps best indicated by the bizarre Taylor recommendation that an American combat unit be deployed to the Delta region south of Saigon, under the pretense that it would be engaged in flood relief, to reassure the South Vietnamese that the United States stood steadfastly with them. A simultaneous expression of the Pentagon's thinking occurred in a memorandum by Chairman of the Joint Chiefs of Staff General Lyman Lemnitzer, generated by President Diem's invitation to the British to provide as an adviser Sir Robert Thompson, former Deputy Secretary and then Secretary of Defense of the Federation of Malaya during that nation's ultimately successful defeat of the Communist insurgency. Lemnitzer drew the obvious distinctions between the two situations, but he put his main stress on the importance of keeping the structure in Viet-

nam a military one and not allowing the police approach
the British favored to be adopted, even for local forces.

But one Vietnamese did begin to rethink the strategy of
the war—Ngo Dinh Nhu. In my weekly meetings with
him, we laboriously thought our way through the Communist strategy, and success, in organizing the rural population and building a "people's army" from local defense
forces to guerrilla units to local and main force battalions.
It was clear that the Vietnamese Army, however well
equipped with helicopters, artillery, and bombers, was not
going to arrest this process. Nhu was also convinced that
the Ministerial bureaucracies, with the development programs they planned in infinite detail in Saigon offices and
then sent to the provinces for implementation, would not be
able to stem the flow either. Nhu also began to realize that
his Can Lao Party apparatus had no roots in the rural
communities where the contest with the Communists was
taking place.

We thus began to discuss how a community could be
inspired and stimulated to organize itself under its own
local leaders and set up at least rudimentary defenses that
would be effective against the infiltration of recruiting and
proselytizing squads. A determined military or guerrilla
attack would, of course, require help from the nearby territorial forces. I had stressed to Nhu the obvious point that a
very few armed Communists could not only enter but totally
dominate a village whose local security unit had buttoned
itself into its fort for the night. Even a few armed villagers
who gave the alarm and fired a few shots at them, however,
would make it impossible for them to carry out their program of assembling the villagers for speeches, recruiting,
and—a vital item—collection of taxes.

As I described developments at Buon Enao and some of
the other experiments we were conducting, Nhu looked
beyond their potential contribution to defense against the
Communists to how they could constitute the basis for a
new Vietnamese social and political community, built up
from the rural areas to replace the elites left over from
French colonial times. He was concerned that too great an
American role in such a program could corrupt this process, tempting the peasants to become dependent on Ameri-

can economic aid programs and other tangibles, instead of developing self-reliance. All of this was long on theory and short on practicalities, but it was exciting to watch Nhu's mind work and gradually formulate elements of what I thought could be a basic strategy for the Government to follow to build a real political foundation of new and locally based rural leaders. From them could develop the leadership of a free and authentic Vietnam, neither Communist nor Western in culture or character.

Eventually I was able to persuade Nhu to leave the Palace to see on the ground some of our experiments and confirm the positive reports he and Diem were receiving from those involved in them. Granted, I made it more convenient for him by suggesting such a visit as a short detour from one of his visits to the mountains to hunt tigers (the tactics of which we had also discussed in our long sessions together). The result of Nhu's sorties, in which the CIA and Special Forces personnel made plain that their role was purely supportive, not dominant, was that we received the green light to continue to support these projects. By the end of 1961, Nhu was sufficiently convinced of the validity of the approach—and his own concepts had matured enough—that he was able to convince Diem to make a major national program of the technique, under the name of "strategic hamlets."

Sir Robert Thompson of the British Advisory Mission (whatever General Lemnitzer's view back in Washington of the adaptability of Thompson's successful techniques in Malaya to an American-supported Vietnam) certainly influenced the process, but Nhu stressed that the security of the hamlet should begin within it and gradually build the necessary defenses around that essentially political core. Thompson's Malayan experience suggested essentially an administrative action, surrounding the community with security so that its inhabitants could be controlled and their links to the guerrillas outside severed. I shared Nhu's view, of course, having argued its advantages with him, so this difference between Thompson and myself persisted for years. We so closely agreed on the necessity of a village-based approach, however, over the military one that we remained the closest of friends and collaborators.

Nhu himself took public and formal leadership and responsibility for the program. To launch it, he convoked the various levels of officialdom, administrative and military, to hear his explanations of the political and intangible fundamentals of the concept in seminars that lasted several hours. The quivering officials, well aware that their careers could depend on pleasing the brother of the President, anxiously tried to ascertain from Nhu's convoluted discourses what exactly it was that they were expected to do to carry out the program. Their bewilderment at everything beyond a few practical steps like digging a protective ditch, throwing up a fence, conducting an accurate community census, and asserting control over the inhabitants was often evident. Determined to show their zeal, they returned to their rural posts, insisting that the local communities erect the defenses, displaying their control of the peasants by moving homes within a perimeter fence if they were spread out too far, and calling for other community or private projects to be displaced by this priority.

Those local officials who had a CIA-sponsored project in their area (and by 1962 there were some 30,000 armed members of such projects throughout the country) had an advantage, of course, as they could—and did—simply fold these projects into the strategic hamlets program, giving them an instant accomplishment to report. And despite some grumbling from the Station about the loss of our direct influence over the experimental communities we had armed, I saw their incorporation into the strategic hamlets program as a means by which the approach they represented could become the much-needed fundamental strategy of the Diem Government to fight the people's war it faced. I thus welcomed this as a step taking us beyond the limited capabilities of the CIA to a national effort.

As Nhu put more and more pressure on the system for rapid progress, reports proliferated that it was being achieved, whether or not that was so on the ground. The Americans were somewhat bewildered by the sudden appearance of a major activity that had not been processed through their complex coordinating staffs. Under the leadership of Ambassador Nolting, however, they subordinated their injured pride and swung into support of what appeared to be a genuinely Vietnamese initiative. But neither the Vietnamese nor the American bureaucracies could keep up with the pace Nhu demanded, so there were many cases of promised materiel for new hamlets that did not arrive, and the essential exclusion of the military from the program by Nhu exposed some hamlets to enemy attack without arrangements for reinforcement. The urban elite focused on the failures in the program and transmitted their complaints to the foreign civilian and media communities, stressing particularly that the relocations produced peasant resistance to leaving ancestral lands—and tombs.

With all its drawbacks, however, the program achieved two major goals: it provided a basic strategy for the conduct of the war at the level of the enemy's attack, the rural communities, and it generated a major national and coordinated focus on its fulfillment, in place of each Ministry and service being absorbed in its own business-as-usual. Any major program, particularly one thrust onto a bureaucracy from above, is bound to have growing pains, and this one did. But the real test was its impact on the Communist enemy—and that qualified witness took it seriously.

The strategic hamlets program seized the initiative in the contest with the Communists for the first time. It began, in its halting and chaotic way, to reverse the tide of Communist progress in the countryside. As it took hold, the Communists recognized it as a major threat to their plans. They called for concentrated attacks upon the hamlets and destruction of their defenses, and denounced the mobilization of the peasantry. But the program gathered steam, and its obvious failures and fakeries were gradually identified and remedied. By early 1963, even that longtime Australian apologist for the Communists in Korea and Vietnam, Wilfred G. Burchett, reflected as usual his Communist friends when he wrote that "1962 must be largely credited to Saigon." He could have added that the main credit could properly have gone to Nhu.

Many years later, I heard from a former senior South Vietnamese general, a leader of the later coup against Diem and Nhu, a report that is stunning in its affirmation of the significance of the strategic hamlets program. This general claims to have heard, although not present himself at the encounter, that Nhu actually met in 1963 with Pham Hung, the leader of the Communist effort in the South. The meeting reportedly took place during the period when Diem and Nhu, facing major differences with the Americans, were desperately seeking some way out of the impasse they were caught in between the Communists and the Americans. My friend's account is that Pham Hung greeted Nhu with the statement that he was impressed to meet the author of the strategic hamlets program, whose effects had been devastating to the Communist efforts. The story may be apocryphal, but it is certainly consistent with other Communist statements at the time.

7

Conflict in the Capitals

DURING THESE YEARS OF GROWTH of Communist power
and Diem's and the Americans' developing responses to it,
another battlefront was taking shape. This was the hostility
growing between the Americans and the Diem regime. As
this conflict emerged, Diem, who was aware of it and
deplored it, was nevertheless severely handicapped in ma-
neuvering in and around it. American attitudes were influenced by many factors about which he could do little or
nothing.

Among the American civilians in Saigon, there were few
who had experienced either the French regime or Diem's
early days at the helm when, against all odds, he fought off
the various tendencies to anarchy to form the Republic and
extend its writ. The quieter years that followed—which he
had in fact created—were also reflected in a more tranquil
life for the Americans, the vast majority of them resident in
Saigon and working in their air-conditioned offices on
economic assistance programs and other developments of
interest to Washington.

The representatives, even the chiefs, of the various American agencies in Saigon were career officers whose hopes
and futures lay in their agencies. An officer's success or
failure—that is, his subsequent assignments and professional progress—would be determined by his fulfillment of
the agenda of his own agency. In these estimations of
performance, there was a possible escape hatch: shortfalls
attributable to the failings of the local government could be
exempted from the officer's personal responsibility. Physical problems from the weather or geography could be engi-
neered around; human weaknesses could be attributed to
the Diem Government and its officials. Hard-driving

Americans frustrated by cultural differences or by a maddening lack of compliance with their formulae for the solution of Vietnamese problems, thus found the answer in Governmental fault or fecklessness rather than in the possible fallibility of their own prescriptions.

The multiplicity of American agencies, and the consequent tendency to spend many hours in coordination meetings among themselves, encouraged the Americans to think of the Diem Government in confrontational terms, the shadowy Viet Cong hardly counting in the balance sheet. Like the blind men around the elephant, the Foreign Service Officers of the State Department, the Agency for International Development, the United States Information Service, the CIA, and the comparatively large contingent of the American military—Army, Navy, Air Force, and Marines—gathered about the Diem Government, each dealing with different pieces and sections of its problems and defining the animal accordingly.

All marched to different drummers in their programs, with little or no central control or comprehensive direction of their disparate activities. In theory they were integrated through a "Country Team" meeting of the heads of each agency each week in the Ambassador's office, but he was more the chairman of the meeting than the director of a "team." As the Ambassador had no command authority over any of the agencies except the State Department, and each agency head reported to his own Washington headquarters, the various offices could conduct their work independently of what the Ambassador's cables might say. This is not the right way to run a government, but it is the way it was done at that time.

The *lingua franca* of the foreign community was French when English did not work. As few Americans learned more than isolated words of Vietnamese, the Vietnamese with whom they consorted were chiefly the French-era officials now serving Diem, or the urban intellectuals and landowners of the upper classes. Naturally—and understandably—the Americans absorbed the distaste these groups felt for the authoritarian nature of the regime; like those with whom they associated, they shared little of the Government's drive to establish land development centers in the highlands or push new roads into the jungles. The Americans also saw the false notes in the regime's violations of the democratic phraseology and institutions of the Constitutional structure, and they sympathized with those who looked for better alternatives. In the circles in which they moved, the Americans were inescapably subject to all the rumors and complaints, true, fanciful or simply exaggerated, that circulated orally through Saigon in the absence of open political communications channels. Consciously or not, these became a major contribution to the formation of their judgments about the regime.

Even I contributed to the spread of these adverse opinions. I felt obliged to forward to Washington the various reports of corruption, pretense, and political unrest that came to our CIA officers from their sources among the Vietnamese. My own belief, nonetheless, was that on balance the regime was doing a reasonably good job of modernizing a backward ex-colony and deserved support in doing so to strengthen it against its Communist enemy. I could not censor my officers' reports and forward only what I thought, but I did adopt the practice of sending along a monthly summary and assessment in which I tried to put some balance into the overall picture. Unfortunately, my summaries were not highly classified, and they went by diplomatic pouch instead of cable, all of which guaranteed them little attention at the Washington end.

The result of the imbalance among the Americans was the gradual growth of the double standard so familiar in our judgments of other allied regimes. Diem and Nhu were criticized for their failure to meet the standards we expected (most of which were, indeed, contained in the Vietnamese Constitution), while little or nothing was said of the alternative regime the Communists intended to install in South Vietnam—an omission that depended in large part on simply brushing aside the ample evidence of the North Vietnamese experience. Nor was attention paid to the qualities of alternative leadership of South Vietnam available among the civilian political figures (the propounders of the Caravelle Hotel manifesto) or among the military. Even less was any question raised as to the readiness of the Vietnamese social and political community to adopt procedures and practices developed over two centuries in North America by very different people in totally different circumstances.

I found it significant that none of the vigorous and widespread American official and media critics of Diem's dependence on his brother Nhu for counsel that he could trust was able to divine any parallel in the American President's unprecedented appointment of *his* brother as Attorney General in order to bolster both the official weight and propinquity of counsel the President could trust. I also found the questions about the vagaries of the Vietnamese voting process perhaps different in degree but not in kind from the situation in such American communities as Boston, Chicago, and substantial areas of the South. This is not to condone or to excuse the failure of the Diem regime to follow its protestations of democratic ideals but only a belief that American critiques should have been a bit less moralistic and intense. As they stood, those critiques ignored the standards of the "art of the possible," which, in diplomacy as in politics, is the true test of performance. A debate with the Diem regime conducted on this basis would have been more on the lines of what could be done within a realistic framework to maintain the regime against its (and our) Communist adversary and to deepen its political base in indigenous, not in alien, terms.

The sum of the American critiques was represented in an August 1960 CIA National Intelligence Estimate stating that if recent "adverse trends" continued, Diem's regime would "almost certainly in time . . . collapse." That December, Durbrow repeated his concern that Diem was faced with "widespread popular dissatisfaction" and that he must improve his method of conducting the war against the Communists and take "vigorous action to build greater popular support," repeating that if he did not do so, "we may well be forced, in not too distant future, to . . . identify and support alternate leadership."

Heavily influenced by Lansdale, the new Kennedy Administration took a different tack. The new President's earlier confidence in Diem, the need to take an innovative approach, and above all the new Administration's confidence that it could make the machinery work caused the Kennedy approach to be one of convincing Diem that

American support would be steadfast, and thus something to be relied upon and worked with.

There were two early and significant indications of the new approach. One was the May 1961 "Program of Action in Vietnam," which, besides dropping some of the more undesirable elements of the "Comprehensive Counterinsurgency Plan" approved pro forma as the Administration entered office (such as the introduction of opposition politicians into the Government, the assignment of Nhu and Tuyen to diplomatic posts abroad, and the appointment of legislative committees of investigation into Diem's conduct of the war). The program also gave the long-awaited "green light" to the 20,000-man increase for the Vietnamese Army and authorized support for a Civil Guard of 68,000 and a Self-Defense Corps (village-level troops) of 40,000. (It added a Vietnamese "Junk Force" to operate against maritime infiltration, thus giving the Navy an equal role with the Air Force's radar surveillance against the never-detected Communist overflights.)

The new "Program of Action" offered an opportunity to include, and to obtain firm policy approval for, some of the CIA Station's programs we had developed in the months the "Comprehensive Counterinsurgency Plan" had been assembled the previous year. In April 1961, therefore, I flew back to Washington on the first of many trans-Pacific trips I would make during the coming years to help put together the CIA "covert action annex" to the Program. When I arrived in the capital, I dove into a flurry of interagency meetings, drafting and redrafting papers for submission to the appropriate decision makers. I frankly gave more thought and effort to ensuring that the Station would receive permission to continue the small—but, I thought, promising—projects we had started than to outlining any fundamental strategy for Vietnam. Unfortunately, this was the attitude of most of the other participants in the process. The result, therefore, was more a laundry list of the desires of the individual agencies involved than a basic review of our situation in Vietnam and of the strategic direction we should take in the future. In my own case, another factor limited my appeals for support to the essentials of our new projects: I was particularly sensitive to the facts that the Bay of Pigs disaster had just taken place and the CIA consequently was far from a favorite of the Kennedy Administration.

The final result was that the CIA "covert action annex" authorized us to "expand present operations of the [Vietnamese Special Forces] in guerrilla areas in South Vietnam, under joint MAAG-CIA sponsorship and direction . . . in full operational collaboration with the Vietnamese, using Vietnamese civilians recruited with CIA aid." The Program also permitted us to expand our operations across the Laotian border and to launch operations into North Vietnam. This, in turn, justified the expansion of the CIA Station in Vietnam by a number so modest as to hardly constitute a strategic escalation.

I was not privileged to attend the decisive conferences with the President, but it was clear from the documents that issued from them that the President in essence had approved the recommendations of the swarm of subordinates he had set to work on the problem. He had not articulated any very solid expression of his own ideas or strategy. Consequently, we had produced an agglomeration of the preferences of all the agencies involved, devoid of any strategic concept or inspiration.

My own reaction was to take the authorization I had received for CIA projects and run with them, convinced that they would demonstrate effective approaches to the conflict. I had a lot to learn about how big government bureaucracies work and how hard they are to bend to a common effort. But I was delighted that the new Kennedy Administration seemed to want to work with Diem rather than natter with him over his failure to meet the standards of New England town-meeting democracy.

The second significant indication of the new approach was Frederick Nolting's appointment as Ambassador in the place of Durbrow. Soft-spoken but tough when necessary, Nolting came to Vietnam with no experience of Asia. But his work in postwar Europe, smoothing relations with sensitive allies just beginning to reassert themselves after the trauma of the Second World War, stood him in good stead. He was quick to grasp the greater complexity of the relationship with Vietnam. In developing close and effective relations with the Vietnamese leadership, Nolting exerted his influence by persuasion as a friend, not by pressure as an adversary. He adhered to the view that the United States should support the constituted authority that Diem represented.

The new Ambassador took upon himself the charge—which originated in the White House—of convincing Diem that the Americans would be a reliable support, of understanding the special problems Diem and Vietnam faced, and of creating a relationship of confidence on which, Nolting hoped, the two Governments together could forge a strategy and effort that would stop the Communist offensive. The approach owed a great deal to Lansdale (even if he did not become its instrument), and the May 1961 visit of Lyndon Johnson expressed it firmly (and, incidentally, convinced Johnson that the United States should support South Vietnam, specifically including Diem as its leader).

The South Vietnamese side of the relationship—Diem, Nhu, and subordinates—had their role as well. They, and most particularly Nhu, were highly sensitive to the fact that Ho Chi Minh's appeal to the rural population to revolt was couched in terms that branded Diem a lackey of the Americans and his regime "neocolonialist." The drumbeat in the countryside of *"My-Diem"* ("American-Diemists") was insistent. The Ngo brothers, their supporters, and their subordinates believed it essential, therefore, not only to demonstrate their sovereignty and independence to the Vietnamese people; for the demonstration to be convincing, to ensure that they really represented a nationalist cause, they had to demonstrate it to themselves as well.

Their need evidenced itself not only in the formalities of their actions, but in a tendency to unilateral, prior announcements of programs and actions. The American establishment would react with surprise (and frequently criticism—sometimes well founded) to the appearance of some new plan that would require American support but that Americans had no opportunity to mold. Since the military were in closer contact with their counterparts than the civilians, this was less a problem for them than for the Embassy, which had fewer working-level contacts in the field of political actions and initiatives. Thus, after the fact,

Embassy (and CIA) officers would report to Washington the detailed complaints and objections to the newly announced activity expressed by the opposition political figures and the Saigon critics.

In contrast to some other regimes dependent on American support (in Asia, most notably the Chinese Nationalists), Diem made little effort to cultivate and activate a supporting political force in the United States. He relied almost solely upon his compulsive, four-hour descriptions and defenses of his activities to senior American officials from Washington passing through Saigon on orientation or inspection tours. His Ambassador to Washington, the henpecked traditionalist whose appointment stemmed from his being the father of Madame Nhu, was of no help.

The Kennedy Administration's idea that fortifying Diem's confidence in the will of the United States to stand by South Vietnam would produce a close and effective working relationship began to encounter obstacles. On the one hand, subordinate Vietnamese officials rarely could make decisions on their own; on the other, Diem and Nhu insisted on their independence, keeping their distance from real or apparent subjection to American leadership. In a situation in which mutual understanding between two cultures was difficult enough, there were all too few channels of real communication. The blame could certainly be fairly distributed on both sides. If the Diem regime was overly prickly with respect to its prerogatives and communicated badly with its ally and sponsor, too many of the Americans with whom it was working lacked the patience requisite for dealing with the problems of Vietnam, and were not overly modest about the brilliance or surgical precision of the prescriptions concocted in American staff meetings to solve them.

Almost unnoticed in this early period of the Kennedy Administration was the fact that on April 9, 1961, Diem conducted and won an election for another five years. The result was, of course, preordained. Rural officials made very certain that their constituencies showed no laggardness in demonstrating support of the President on whom their own jobs depended. But the forms were generally observed. Diem was opposed by two slates. One was headed

by Nguyen Dinh Quat, who called for a cease-fire with the
Communists and elections for the reunification of Vietnam.
The second was headed by Ho Nhut Tan, another traditional politician who, like Quat, attacked family rule and
the Government's arbitrary methods, and demanded freedom of speech and the press, the release of all political
prisoners, and an end to corruption. (A third candidate,
Truong Dinh Dzu, earlier president of Southeast Asian
Rotary, had potential appeal for the electorate; under Government charges of financial irregularities, he withdrew
from the race.) Diem actually received less than half the
votes in Saigon, so that his final tally was "only" about 89
percent of the total votes cast nationally.

In sum, the election may have been more ritual than
reality, but it certainly was not uncharacteristic of many
other Asian nations. Diem's 89 percent majority was less
than the 98 percent he had received in 1956. In view of this
reduced margin, small as it was, plus the address by the
opposition of real issues, the election could be viewed as a
substantial step toward the establishment of a constitutional regime, albeit not its fulfillment. Perhaps one of the
reasons it attracted so little comment was the concentration
of all American eyes a few days later on the Bay of Pigs
disaster in Cuba, so much closer to home.

With the rise in Communist activity in the countryside
and the Kennedy Administration's identification of Vietnam
as the place at which it had to meet the test of American
counterinsurgency against Communist insurgency, a new
American actor entered the scene—the media. The role of
the free press (and its modern technological heir, television)
in American society is that of the Fourth Estate—independent observer of the established authorities providing the
sovereign public with comment and criticism on how their
servants are serving their interests (or failing to do so).
Competition for the American public's attention is fierce,
not only among different purveyors of news and comment,
but between news and entertainment. Since for the most
part the public's attention span is limited, the press must
arouse its interest. One result is a premium on more colorful
and critical comment, on pointing up events involving
conflict or failings. During the quieter days in Vietnam

from 1956 to 1960, the American press gave little attention
to Diem's programs of economic and social modernization
(except for one enterprising reporter, whose name I have
long since forgotten, who visited in 1959 and produced a
criticism of the American aid program and the comfortable
lives of the American officials.) But as the War began
heating up in the rural areas and tension rose in political
circles in Saigon, visits by regional reporters from Tokyo or
Hong Kong became more frequent and the resident press
corps grew.

As with the American civilian officials, the reporters'
natural contacts were with Saigon officials and members of
the intellectual and political elite fluent in French or English. Their rounds in Saigon were only occasionally varied
by trips to the countryside or laboriously translated ques-
tion-and-answer sessions with rural or working class Vietnamese with whom the cultural gap was even greater than
the linguistic. Professionally, they sought out the flaws in
the Government's or the American Embassy's bland over-
statements of "progress," tranquillity, and public satisfaction. With the Communists inaccessible in their clandestin-
ity, the focus was on the Government and its American
support structure. Their failures made excellent copy in the
best American journalistic tradition. For some years the
Saigon assignment was a relatively secondary story base,
professional opportunities hardly compensating for physical inconveniences. Since most of the correspondents who
showed up in Vietnam were young and hopeful of launching their careers, there was a consequent tendency to come
up with the story or the picture which could make the front
page or the evening news. The wiser (and sometimes older)
heads at the editorial desks an ocean away could only rarely
filter through the products of their Saigon representatives
in search of a more balanced picture of developments as a
whole.

Certainly there was no conspiracy by the press to present
a false picture of Vietnam to the American people. But there
is an inherent problem of accurate perception of faraway
and exotic situations and cultures. Readers understand a
story in an American community that "man bites dog" as
recounting an exceptional event, and they understand as

well that there is no news value in a report that a dog bit a man. But reports of events in a distant country reach a reader who has no basis for judging whether the event is exceptional, or typical; indeed, the report of an exceptional event may well carry with it an inference that it describes one of the normal aspects of life in a very different culture. The cumulative effect of such impressions can be significant: it is the American readers and their elected representatives who in the end accept or reject our Government's policies toward that country.

Recurrent proposals by developing nations for a "New World Information Order" based on greater control over journalists and their product and advertised as producing a "balanced flow of information" (the governments doing the balancing) offer no solutions to this problem. Their interference with the free flow of information would only make things worse. The problem must be understood, however, and met with more extensive efforts to present the full picture by responsible officials, the governments concerned, and serious journalists. In Vietnam that process took many years, and misperceptions played major roles in American attitudes, policies, and actions throughout the war years.

In Vietnam, the impinging of past on present, the contrasting cultures, the clashes of pride, timing, and technique, the divisions in both societies, the differences over the "how" among the leadership of both countries, the increasingly evident preoccupation of prominent Americans, the turning of world attention to the struggle in Indochina, and the growth of American military involvement (including the first American helicopters in 1962) all combined during 1961 and 1962 to raise the level of tension in Saigon in conjunction with the rise of the Communist danger in the countryside. Vietnam began to fill headlines in the United States. The growth in general attention heightened the pressures among the various factions and forces involved in the situation. On the American side, the differences grew between those who saw the problem as chiefly one requiring a strong effort in the countryside, military and paramilitary, and those who believed the effort was doomed unless Diem changed his authoritarian regime to attract popular support and include oppositionists in a national effort.

During this period, I was directing the CIA Station as it grew in size to manage the various programs we had developed. The experimental village and hamlet development centers we had established, such as Buon Enao and the priest-led communities in the Mekong Delta, were folded into the overall strategic hamlets program. Ambassador Nolting understood the need and agreed with the strategy. He pushed the American establishment into full support of Nhu's program, despite lingering American criticism of Nhu, and the AID Mission established a special division for its support in terms of the needed barbed wire and other materiel for community efforts. It was led by an energetic and effective AID officer, Rufus Phillips of Virginia, who fully appreciated the political aim of the program. He nevertheless felt real concern that it was being overextended by Nhu's demands for fast action and the local officials' anxiety to placate him with positive statistics and the forms rather than the reality. A report to the Palace of progress in organization and deliveries of equipment could not take the place of new communities actually protecting themselves.

The Military Assistance Advisory Group had grown with the Kennedy Administration's approval of more support, and in February 1962 it was upgraded from a "Group" to the Military Assistance Command Vietnam (MACV), commanded by a four-star General, Paul D. Harkins. MACV still reported to Washington, however, through the Pacific Command in Honolulu, rather foolishly imposing that level of military hierarchy halfway between the action in Vietnam and the policy in Washington. But that was the way World War II and Korea had been fought, so Vietnam would have to be handled the same way. Harkins himself was no swashbuckler but a cavalry officer of the old school, and General Maxwell Taylor's own choice for the Vietnam Command. He saw his job as one of helping the Vietnamese Army strengthen itself to meet the Communist enemy and, in the classic American tradition, to stay out of politics, particularly Vietnamese politics. He had little sympathy for the American civilians who agonized over Diem's failings, and in fact had great sympathy for the Vietnamese leader. Nevertheless, Harkins maintained throughout his stay in Vietnam a private "military" channel for communication with Taylor, thus ensuring that the American Government spoke with a variety of tongues and produced frequently garbled messages.

Despite these organizational defects, the new commander and the new Ambassador meant a new start in American civilian-military relationships and an end to the tensions that had marked Durbrow's relations with "Hanging Sam" Williams and his successor. The "Country Team" meetings became pleasant sessions in which all tried to work together.

My own contribution was to continue my regular meetings with Nhu and try to translate his plans and hopes for the strategic hamlets program into terms understandable to the Americans responsible for its support, despite Nhu's frequent public exhortations that the program should be carried out by the communities themselves free of Government direction or support. I also looked for other programs we could conduct to help the war effort. We embarked on helping to build a central intelligence organization (CIO, not CIA) to pull together the many Vietnamese intelligence services, military and civilian. The aim was to provide the Palace with sensible summaries of the situation in the countryside and to improve coverage of the political apparatus the Communists were establishing there. The latter objective in particular required careful and sensible interrogations of Communist captives and defectors. The "mountain scout" program earlier suggested by the Vietnamese General commanding in the highlands—Ton That Dinh, volatile and erractic but talented—received a training center, weapons, and communications. Dinh's teams of mountain people could thus effectively infiltrate the jungles and mountains along the Lao border to report on Communist movements and installations on the Ho Chi Minh Trail.

As for North Vietnam itself, experienced Chinese Nationalist pilots trained Vietnamese pilots for night missions (on one or two occasions I wondered, as I stood behind the student pilots, whether their minimum altitude in the darkness over South Vietnamese mountains corresponded to the careful timing of their flight plans). On one occasion Colonel Nguyen Cao Ky, the colorful commander of the Vietnamese Air Force Transport Command, took me on a

low-level flight over water while I observed from the vantage point of the rear door, where I had also stood years
before in the early, only partially successful World War II
days of the American parachute field artillery. (For a long
time the guns were dropped in six pieces, to be assembled
by the parachutists on the ground if we could find all six
pieces—an infrequent achievement. After the war we
learned how to drop the guns in one piece.) Ky flew, as was
proper and intended, so close to the water that on landing I
commented to him that next time I would bring a fishing
pole.

But sometimes these flights did not work. On one occasion I took William Trueheart, Nolting's Deputy Chief of
Mission, on a several-day tour to show him what the Station
was doing. We visited a number of villages armed and
trained by the CIA and the U.S. Army Special Forces assigned to us for the program, several priests with their self-
defended communities, a training center for maritime landings and operations against North Vietnam, and the main
base we had set up outside Danang in Central Vietnam to
train Diem's brother Can's Popular Force teams to live in the
villages and develop their governing structures and defenses. I skipped one stop, though. We were trying to make
a landing near Hue in dense fog. Turning in from a swing
out to sea to descend to wave-top level, the Chinese pilots
headed toward the coast and the nearby mountains. They
controlled our approach only by the time delay on their
watches. As the time ticked by, I finally told them to abort
the landing and climb back to a safe altitude. Trueheart was
as relieved as I was.

The solid atmosphere of progress accompanying all this
activity was interrupted by only one incident. Early one
morning in February, while I was preparing to go to the
office, I heard the roar of an aircraft just above the roof of
the house, followed by an explosion at the Palace across the
street. I quickly went to the porch to see another airplane
coming in low and aimed at us. I saw its rockets release. I
ducked into the house and herded the family and servants
into a protected area under the stairs while some of the
rockets detonated in the trees in front of the house. The
planes made another pass, dropping napalm into the park

in front of us and bombs that blew out our windows and the plaster from the walls. I got on the phone to the Embassy and reported that there seemed to be only two planes and urged that others be sent up to knock them down. I could see that the Palace had received some hits on the Nhu wing. I learned later that the President had not been hurt, nor had the Nhus, but one of the nurses of the Nhu children had been killed. After the planes flew off to Cambodia, I learned they had been two fighter pilots who, like the parachutists in 1960, thought they could improve the war effort by eliminating the President and his brother. The incident quickly passed, however, as the pace of the Government's activity in the countryside grew.

In the spring, my chief in Washington and good friend, Desmond FitzGerald, then Chief of the Far East Division, told me he wanted me to return to Washington to become his Deputy. It was a great compliment, and certainly would be promising for my future career, but I asked him to delay the move for another year. I had the clear feeling that the Government and the Americans had finally captured the initiative in the war with the Communists and that there was much to do to carry out the programs we had started in order to make them really work. Since I knew them, and indeed had conceived many of them, I thought it would be best for me to stay to make sure they moved into high gear. Des demurred, however, saying he needed me for other areas. Accordingly, I arranged for a leisurely return home through India, Jerusalem, and the Greek Islands, and in May turned the Saigon Station over to my successor.

The new Station Chief was John Richardson, well experienced in Asia. I made a special effort to introduce him not only to the people he would be working with, but also to the ideas we had developed over the past three years. I was relieved when he wholeheartedly agreed with them and moved energetically to build on them.

In a final assessment of the situation just before my departure, I looked ahead to a possible successor to Diem if he, like President Magsaysay of the Philippines, hit a mountain flying in bad weather (e.g., landing near Hue in a dense fog) or an attempt at assassination succeeded. I thought Nhu might try to succeed him, but it seemed to me that his conspiratorial nature, and the simple fact that he was thoroughly disliked by the military as well as by many of the Vietnamese elite (for whom, obviously, he himself had no high regard), eliminated him as a possibility. There were the generals. The leading figure among them was generally considered to be General Duong Van "Big" Minh, senior in rank despite Diem's having selected another to head the Army because he did not really trust—and certainly did not respect—Minh. I dismissed him, notwithstanding the possibilities his rank offered, as personally unable to grasp and exercise power even if he had an initial chance at it. None of the other generals seemed to understand the nature of guerrilla war, and most were personally lacking or flawed in ways that would eliminate them.

There was one exception, I reported. I cited Nguyen Khanh, the President's Military Aide, who had shown courage and decisiveness by climbing over the rear wall of the Palace during the paratroopers' attempted coup of November 1960 to come to the President's aid, while others waited to see which way the wind would blow. I knew him quite well, exchanging with him the banter fellow parachutists can understand. He had told me of his days as a junior officer learning the parachutist mystique at the French school at Pau near the Pyrenees in Southern France. I saw that he had successfully maneuvered among the antagonisms of the General Staff, Ngo Dinh Nhu, and President Diem's direct interventions into the command structure. I also saw him as understanding the need for both unconventional and strictly military ways of fighting the Communists: he had convinced me during a tour we made just before my departure to the Danang area, including a stop at an isolated outpost on the Lao border in the A Shau Valley, where so much action later occurred. He had the necessary moral and physical courage, plus experience at the Palace of the problems and pressures of power. He seemed to me sufficiently forceful, and ambitious, to run the country and assert his authority over his military colleagues.

When written this was, of course, a roster of hypotheses, not a forecast of events.

My move to Washington now changed my focus from the

particular operations the Station conducted to a larger
stage embracing policy, Congressional relations, and interagency negotiations. My family and I settled into a pleasant
Washington suburb. We engaged in the station-wagon life
of families during that period, with the children scattered
among a series of high schools and primary schools. They
were pleased to be back in the United States, but we had
many mementos of our time in Vietnam, and my professional responsibilities ensured that we would be in touch
with developments there.

The move also put me in the midst of the principal actors
on the American side of the drama. While I knew most of
them from encounters of greater or lesser length, Des Fitz-
Gerald's departure for another job in January 1963 and my
succession to his post as Chief of the Far East Division of
the CIA threw me, by the force of coming events, among
them as a player on the Washington stage.

My closest connection with the principal actors was, of
course, with my boss, John McCone, Director of Central
Intelligence. McCone had made a fortune during World War
II building ships, and the drive and managerial toughness
that brought him that success had never left him. A Republican, he had been an Assistant Secretary of the Air Force
and a member of the Atomic Energy Commission under
President Eisenhower. When President Kennedy cast
around for someone to replace Allen Dulles as Director of
the CIA after the Bay of Pigs disaster, he turned to McCone
as a prominent Republican in order to indicate that the post
would not be a partisan one—and to protect himself from
such further problems as might arise with the Agency.

While McCone had a few foibles, such as his love affair
with a long Cadillac that came with the Director's job (later
dispensed with by Dick Helms), he was all business in his
direction of the Agency. He had a particularly demanding
tactic of giving his staff a set of specific questions about the
likely developments in world affairs and insisting on carefully thought-out answers by 8:00 the next morning so that
he could review and critique them before going to the
White House. The staff, of course, loved the challenge and
never grumbled about the hours involved; the tactic allowed
them to feel they were playing a real role in making policy.
His greatest accomplishment was his insistence, while hon-

eymooning in Southern France, that the U-2 reconnoiter Cuba in October 1962, after the Board of National Estimates had concluded that the Soviets had never—and consequently would never—put nuclear missiles outside the Soviet Union. The ensuing Cuban missile crisis was perhaps CIA's finest hour.

McCone was firm in his direction of the Agency, but he could be argued out of his own ideas—such as moving some of Taiwan's troops to Vietnam—if they didn't stand up to the analysts' scrutiny. He left the actual management of the Agency machinery to subordinates but insisted on effective performance by all hands. On one occasion, I told him I was trying to arrange a rotation system so that the dangers and unpleasantness of some of Vietnam's more difficult assignments could be shared more evenly among the Agency's officers. McCone turned on me sharply, fixed his steely eyes on mine, and said, "Mr. Colby, Vietnam is the most difficult and important problem the President faces. You will send the very best men there and keep them there, and I want to hear no more of rotation."

McCone used me frequently as his assistant in White House and other meetings on the subject of Indochina, especially as the tension over relations with Diem grew. But he made maximum use of his own status to impress his colleagues at the policy level that he was a major player, pushing into the President's office when necessary—to push his ideas, not the CIA's bureaucratic influence.

Technically, Dick Helms, as the Agency's Deputy Director for Plans—a euphemism that hid his real role as director of its operations—was my direct boss during this period. I made sure that I respected this chain of command by keeping him informed of all my doings, but McCone was inclined to come directly to me. Helms was most understanding of the relationship, however, so what could have become a problem did not. Helms's preference was truly in the area of professional intelligence operations—espionage and counterintelligence—rather than in the political and paramilitary tactics I was inclined to emphasize, so he left those activities in Vietnam pretty much to me. We got along very well, and he invariably supported what I was trying to do to stimulate rural programs in Vietnam.

During this period, there was something sad in watching

Secretary of Defense McNamara intensely trying to produce policy and carry out programs by the numbers. In so many briefings I saw him furiously scribbling notes about the number of weapons, trainees, and equipment being supplied to Vietnam rather than standing aside and considering how to adjust our style of war to the one being conducted from the North. He really believed that the intangibles and the fog of war could be brought under control if only they could be reduced to numbers, preferably in columns showing clear comparisons. The "bottom line" approach favored by an American industrial leader, which he had been, hardly fitted the kind of people's war of minimum investment, avoidance of confrontation, and targeting of intangibles that were the essence of the North Vietnamese strategy.

McNamara's appetite for figures had the natural result of stimulating his subordinates to supply them. Thus briefings and conferences were dominated by slides and graphics in the best military manner, and little time was devoted to trying to deal with the more intangible aspects of the conflict. Later the numbers of air sorties and bombs used on the Ho Chi Minh Trail were assumed to speak for themselves, with no measure of the intensity of the North Vietnamese leaders' and people's persistence at whatever cost in blood and effort. Even the CIA's intelligence estimates, which said plainly that the supplies the Communists in the South needed were only in small quantities, which would get through no matter how many large transports were stopped, did not dissuade McNamara and the military from their obsessive desire to interdict by air attack.

One of the saddest tales of all was told by my old friend from the Office of Strategic Services' operations into France, Stewart Alsop, recounting a visit to McNamara by Des FitzGerald, who countered the Secretary's figures by gently saying that in a war there is something more important than numbers—"spirit." Des spoke from experience; he had served with the Chinese Nationalists in World War II. But he was never invited to brief McNamara again.

McNamara's intellectual brilliance also left him somewhat uneasy when faced with the grubby realities of South Vietnam in a time of confusion. His intellectual approach also led him into the classic error in military conflict of escalating by increment instead of by overpowering force. This was true of both the buildup of American forces in South Vietnam and the exquisitely conceived targeting of the air attack on North Vietnam, moving it one degree north at a time. McNamara's purpose was to convince what he considered must be a rational enemy in Hanoi that he should concede the contest in the face of the inevitable further devastation these steps presaged. The result, however, was to enable the leaders in Hanoi to adjust to escalation before the next increment hit. The fault of the strategy lay in its totally ignoring the iron determination those leaders in Hanoi had displayed against the French and were exerting against the Americans. They could only be stopped, while McNamara—and later Kissinger—thought they could be convinced. Eventually, of course, McNamara concluded that his approach had not worked and resigned, but the tragedy of his mistake lived with him long afterward.

When in January 1963 I succeeded to Des FitzGerald's job as Chief of the Far East Division of the CIA, I also succeeded to the duty of a weekly meeting with Averell Harriman, then Assistant Secretary of State for Far Eastern Affairs. Harriman had taken the post after a brilliant career of dealing with almost everyone of prominence in recent history, from Churchill (as Lend-Lease Expediter, 1941–1943) and Stalin (as Lend-Lease Expediter, 1941–1942, then Ambassador to the Soviet Union, 1943–1945) to the postwar European leaders as head of the Marshall Plan in Europe. He had been friend, supporter, and adviser to Franklin Roosevelt and Harry Truman and was now in the same relationship to John Kennedy. By his own preference, Harriman was always addressed as "Governor," whatever post he held, in a bow to his election and service as Governor of New York State in the 1950s. While he was an ardent Democrat, his major focus was on how American power should be utilized in the world, most particularly how it should be applied in response to Stalin's hegemonic pretensions.

The purpose of my weekly meetings with Harriman was to brief him on what the CIA was doing in that part of the world and to assure him that we were following the policies the State Department and the White House decreed. Although FitzGerald and some of the Foreign Service staff working for Harriman had replied positively to the sharp questions Harriman posed as to who this new fellow was, he put me directly to the test. His method was simple, and he used it on others as well. He would sharply—sometimes almost insultingly—jab questions at me, scarcely leaving me time to reply. He insisted on direct answers, some impossible to give, and then turned away and ignored the answers. If a subject I was reporting on struck him as not that important, he would ostentatiously turn off his hearing aid and leave the matter to his aides to follow. On more than one occasion, he baited me sufficiently to cause me to shout my answers in apparent anger at him. But I saw through his technique as probing me to see if I could stand up to him or would fade away before his status as a close associate of the President, as well as to make clear that I would indeed report to him and follow his policies.

In this latter respect, Harriman considered me and the whole of the CIA as quite suspect. He had an abiding contempt for authoritarian leaders in East Asia—as did many in Washington—and knew that the Agency maintained good relations with most of them. He particularly despised Chiang in Taiwan, Park in Korea, Sarit in Thailand, Phoumi in Laos, and, by extension, Diem in Saigon. It could never be more than a guess whether Harriman's attitude stemmed from his New York Democratic liberalism, a belief that such leaders, especially Chiang, would inevitably harm the United States and a Democratic Administration (as in the case of Truman's "loss" of China), or from Harriman's own autocratic tendencies, arising from possession of important economic power from youth, which could not abide intransigence or assertions of independence from those so dependent on American support. I suspected the latter was a substantial factor, since Harriman dealt most effectively with equally authoritarian leaders, such as Stalin, who were not dependent.

One of Harriman's special concerns was whether the CIA would respect the provisions of the Geneva Accords of 1962, which he had negotiated to get the Soviet Union and the

United States out of Laos and leave it a neutral state. He knew of the CIA's connections with and support of right-wing military elements within Laos, as well as of tribal forces opposed to the North Vietnamese. He insisted that the Agency support to the Hmong tribal elements in Northern Laos be suspended when the Treaty came into effect, and I arranged that this be done. To his credit, Harriman accepted our urging that we keep two American CIA officers in Northern Laos to report on developments there, especially whether the North Vietnamese were complying with the Treaty as we were. In working all this out with Harriman, his toughness was a major asset, and I grew to enjoy our sessions, even those in which I had to fight hard to get his approval for some new step.

The other major actor in Washington with whom I became involved after my return there in 1962 was McGeorge Bundy, Assistant to President Kennedy for National Security Affairs—an exemplar of the Harvard establishment with a passion for public service, but appointed rather than elected. Invariably polite, restrained, and meticulous, he marshaled the views of the President's subordinates through EXCOM (meetings in the basement of the West Wing without the President present, to permit more open discussion and differences than if he were there) into neat packages that represented all views but seldom indicated any intense opinion of his own. His triumph was the management of the Cuban missile crisis in October 1962. Then his steady hand permitted the most delicate manipulation of diplomatic, military, and intelligence factors and relationships to take the United States to the edge of war with the Soviet Union, but not over it.

Bundy managed the growing Vietnam crisis in the same fashion, scheduling regular EXCOM meetings to review the situation and define the options for action, following these with full National Security Council meetings in the Cabinet Room to brief the President and outline the alternatives he faced. I generally attended these as McCone's backup man. On several occasions I gave the opening intelligence summary and assessment, one of which generated a compliment by the President to McCone about my performance (which was then passed by McCone to my superior, Dick Helms, and thence to me). Bundy's cool, rarified attitude and careful articulation of the alternatives certainly influenced the decision-making process in the White House. The result was a tendency to discount vigorous and immediate action decisions in favor of seeking more information, or to stress a rational and carefully coordinated program of "signals" to Hanoi in place of a direct and immediate attack or response. Later, in the rough-and-tumble world of faraway Vietnam itself, when an attack took place while he was there, Bundy reacted differently. A major rocket and ground attack on Pleiku airfield in the highlands shook the American command structure and was interpreted as a major escalation of the conflict by the Communists. Bundy sent a strong telegram to Washington calling for sharp retaliation against North Vietnam itself. Proximity to the reality of war presents great challenges to cool, intellectual analysis.

There were other figures playing supporting roles—and sometimes intervening substantially in the progress of events. Attorney General Robert Kennedy was, of course, a close adviser to his brother. On the one occasion I was sent to his cavernous office in the Justice Department to brief him, I was much amused by the gallery of children's drawings that festooned the walls. Dean Rusk presided over the State Department with exemplary loyalty to the President but with amazingly slight active involvement in the policy struggles that swirled about him, and in which his subordinates played major roles. Under Secretary of State George Ball, who was negative from the beginning about our military involvement in Vietnam, stands as one of the first to predict that the whole affair would be costly and fruitless. Michael Forrestal, an intelligent New York lawyer totally dedicated to President Kennedy, served as the Vietnam officer on the National Security Council. He maintained frequent contact with all the agencies and individuals involved and plainly showed his (and perhaps the President's) deeper doubts about supporting Diem. Vice President Johnson duly attended the meetings of the National Security Council, of which he was a statutory member, and, powerless to affect the outcome, watched with increasing distaste as the atmosphere turned against Diem.

These, then, were President Kennedy's principal official advisers. It was they who would provide the backdrop to those six months in 1963 that would alter the setting and cast of the high drama of Vietnam.

8

Major Missteps

AMONG THE COMPLAINTS AGAINST DIEM by his South
Vietnamese and American critics, mention was often made
of his religion. About 10 percent of Vietnamese were Catholic. But the Church's teaching effort under sympathetic
French rule had given it such predominance among the
bureaucratic, landowning, and commercial elite of the
nation that the omnipresence of Catholics in leading and
urban circles was a reflection of the country's history. In
addition, Catholics were predominant among the 900,000
refugees who fled from North Vietnam in 1954 when the
country was divided to escape Communist rule there. Diem
certainly favored these refugee communities in his land
development schemes in the highlands, both because he
considered them a reliable bulwark against Communism
there and because they certainly had to be resettled somewhere. But Diem's Vice President was not a Catholic, and he
did include non-Catholics among his Ministers (at times
they even were in the majority), so it could not be said that
they were excluded from his Government.

Diem had suppressed the political pretensions of the
religious sects in the South, the Cao Dai and the Hoa Hao,
which had in effect autonomously controlled large sectors of
the South in 1954 and 1955. He allowed them to continue to
act as purely religious bodies—without their private armies—conducting their services and gathering their faith-
ful without hindrance. The Buddhists were divided between
two versions: the Mahayana ("Greater Vehicle") persuasion,
which had crossed the Himalayas from India to Tibet and
thence to China, where it had taken on some of the attributes of Chinese culture—even of Taoism—giving it a ritualistic tradition and organized structure; and the Hinayana (a

pejorative description, since it means "Lesser Vehicle"),
properly referred to as Theravada ("Way of the Elders"),
which reflected the purer philosophy and lack of institu-
tionalism and had spread across Burma, Thailand, and
Cambodia. The meeting of the two in Vietnam gave reality
to the name "Indochina," but neither the saffron-robed
Theravada nor the purple-robed Mahayana had undertaken
a political role in the turbulence of the 1950s, and they
seemed to have neither the inclination nor the structure
with which to do so.

What the Buddhists did have was a close relationship
with the nonmodernized mass of the population. They
were certainly not sympathetic to the efforts of Communist
activists to mobilize those masses into the disciplined ranks
that characterized North Vietnam. But they were disturbed
at the destabilizing effects of the Diem regime's changes in
the traditional way of life wreaked by its educational, social, and economic programs. Those programs were identified by traditionalists—and certainly by the Buddhists—as
stemming from the essentially foreign influence of Diem's
Catholicism, his links with Occidentals (the Americans),
and the secular state he seemed to be creating.

The turmoil and tensions created in Vietnamese life at
this juncture by the simultaneous Communist drive in the
countryside, the turbulence of the strategic hamlets program, and the increasing presence of the Americans produced a superheated mixture. Into this volatile atmosphere
a spark of Buddhist protest ignited an explosion almost
immediately magnified to the status of a world-scale event
by the fact that Vietnam had become such a focus of American and Kennedy Administration concern. The ignition
occurred in May 1963 in the Central Vietnamese capital of
Hue. This bastion of traditional Vietnam housed a Buddhist center with strong leadership, the remnants of several
political conspiracies and associations, and Diem's politically rigid brother Can in a Byzantine (if the word is strong
enough to reflect the reality of Hue) conjuncture of competing ambitions and convictions.

On May 5, 1963, the ancient capital was festooned with
flags and garlands in celebration of the anniversary of the
ordination as Archbishop of Hue of the elder brother of

Diem and Can, Thuc—a festive occasion for Vietnamese Catholics as an indication of the Vatican's recognition of their national and religious identity, replacing their former representation only through the French. Among the flags was the gold and white of the Vatican, with the Pope's coat of arms.

On May 8, the Buddhists planned their annual celebration of the birthday of the Lord Buddha, but the local Government authorities decreed that the five-colored Buddhist flag could not be flown, reflecting old French restrictions on Buddhist demonstrations and the Diem Government's rules to prevent political activity by the suppressed sects. A crowd gathered to protest this ruling, and in the course of the confrontation a bomb—or perhaps a grenade—exploded. The troops who had been summoned opened fire, killing nine people and wounding twenty others. The Government stupidly blamed the incident on "Communists," while the Buddhists, under the leadership of their bonzes, demanded compensation for the victims, punishment of those responsible, and freedom for Buddhism and its flag.

Diem, perhaps influenced by his brothers Thuc and Can, who were anxious that no weakness be shown in their Hue, handled the whole affair with little understanding of its impact within Vietnam or abroad. He asserted that the 1956 Constitution already provided for freedom of religion, but that political activities by religious groups could not be countenanced. Nhu, and especially his wife, added to the problem by shrilly stating that Communists were at the root of the impasse and growing demonstrations that had now developed in Hue. Eventually, on June 13, a settlement was belatedly reached that provided for compensation and an investigation to determine who was responsible, freedom for Buddhist preaching, equality with Catholics for the Buddhist clergy (especially as chaplains in the Army), and permission for the Buddhist flag to be flown with the Vietnamese national flag. By then the damage had already been done, and the agreement did not defuse the antagonisms created by the incident and the Government's heavy-handed reaction to it.

But the continued tensions in Vietnam paled in comparison with the impact in the United States of the first of the stunning photographs that were to dominate American impressions of Vietnam—and decisions about it. On June 11, a press spokesman for the Buddhists alerted the resident American journalists that "something important" would happen that morning at a particular intersection in downtown Saigon. At the appointed time, before the assembled journalists and their cameras, a saffron-robed Buddhist monk, Thich Quang Duc, sat gravely while his fellows poured gasoline over his head and robe, whereupon he lit a match to immolate himself before the photographers. It was explained as a protest against the Diem regime. The horrifying color photos on the front pages of American newspapers and magazines confronted the liberal Kennedy Administration with the necessity to distance itself from a regime which could generate such protest. The arguments within the American Government over whether and how to support South Vietnam rose to a fever pitch.

Coincidentally, Ambassador Nolting was on leave in Greece, so communications with Diem were handled by the Deputy Chief of Mission, William Trueheart, whose sympathies were more with the need to assert a tough American line with Diem than to maintain his confidence in American steadfastness—the previous Kennedy line. As a result, Diem was the subject of a series of strong demands generated in the State Department that he take steps to conciliate the Buddhists. On his side, Diem was pressed by Nhu and his wife (Madame Nhu had the bad taste to refer to the monks' suicides—now several—as "barbecues") to maintain a hard line against the Buddhists and their "Communist" influences. Diem fluctuated between assurances to the Americans that he would be conciliatory, making some limited public statements in this direction, and procrastination in acting on them. Public protest demonstrations spread and intensified. Even members of the Government and the military expressed concern that Diem was not handling the matter correctly. Rumors and CIA reports of possible coup planning against the regime grew in number and credibility.

On June 27, yet another new factor was added to the situation. President Kennedy, obviously attempting to depoliticize the Vietnam issue in the United States, announced that Frederick Nolting would be replaced as Ambassador by Henry Cabot Lodge. A thoroughly patrician Boston Brahmin, Lodge had been the Republican Vice Presidential candidate in the 1960 election and had had a successful tour as Ambassador to the United Nations under Eisenhower. Nolting, the career officer, had fought for his policies from Saigon to Washington—and against some of the towering figures of the Kennedy Administration. In the end he lost the battle, but his story is among the more useful, prescient, and honorable of the American role in the Second Indochinese War.

Nolting made a last visit to Vietnam, where he faced a sharply divided American Embassy and Mission. During this final stay, almost as a parting gift from the Vietnamese President, Nolting secured a statement from Diem that he had always sought conciliation with the Buddhists and that this policy was "irreversible," a direct contradiction of Nhu's and his wife's calls for "crushing" the Buddhists. The tensions continued, nonetheless, among the various Vietnamese and American factions: those seeking to ignore the political dissidence and get on with the war in the countryside and those calling for political appeasement of the Buddhists and removing the Nhus from the scene and from the country. The Buddhist leaders escalated their demands at each step, and many in the regime believed their political role and ambitions should be suppressed as forcefully as Diem put down the political pretensions of the sects in 1955.

By July, there was debate among the Americans as to what would happen if a coup against the regime, presumably by the military, took place. Meetings occurred throughout Washington as the different agencies prepared the positions they would take in meetings of the National Security Council with the President in the chair. John McCone energized the analytical talents of the CIA to give periodic estimates of the situation of the Diem regime and of the war it was waging in the countryside. He was hardheaded in his demands for objectivity and direct in presenting the Agency's views in the interagency debates. He had other arrows in his quiver, however, in the operational role the CIA played, and in the possibilities offered by the many CIA connections throughout the country and with the Vietnamese political and military leaders. To back himself up with direct knowledge of these matters, McCone took me with him to the White House meetings, where I could use that knowledge to suggest actions that might help us solve the dilemma we faced.

The divisions among the participants in these meetings sharpened. For the State Department, Roger Hilsman had succeeded venerable and crusty Averell Harriman as Assistant Secretary of State for the Far East, Harriman having become Under Secretary of State for Political Affairs. A West Pointer, Hilsman had been with a guerrilla force in Northern Burma during World War II and, with some justice, considered himself an expert on the subject. He continually pressed me for more effective operations, especially in Laos, and I happily endured his war reminiscences in return for the welcome support at the policy level he gave our efforts. At this early stage, he was not yet disillusioned with Diem. He advised President Kennedy that the chances of chaos were considerably less than they were a year before, as the military seemed to be continuing the war despite the political turmoil and would probably continue to do so. From Saigon Nolting, in what can now be seen as a far more prescient judgment, predicted that if a revolution grew out of the Buddhist situation, the country would be split among feuding factions, the Americans would have to withdraw, and the country might be lost to the Communists. Only his prediction about the Americans was wrong.

What was particularly fascinating about the discussions in Washington of a possible end to the Diem regime was that, as in similar discussions among Americans in Saigon, there was an almost total absence of consideration and evaluation of the personalities who might succeed Diem beyond generalized references to "the military." This gap in forward thinking was to persist throughout the succeeding months.

On August 15 Nolting left Saigon, following the tradition that successive Ambassadors not be simultaneously present at a post. Lodge was in Honolulu being briefed by the Pacific military command, and Nolting went there so they could have some time to discuss Lodge's new responsibilities. I was attending for the CIA, and was anxious that Lodge get a good briefing on our programs and their contribution to the effort in Vietnam. Into this sparkling setting came the news that on August 21, in the middle of the night, a series of raids on the principal Buddhist pagodas of Vietnam had taken place. There were some 1,400 arrests and an undetermined number (although rumored figures were plentiful) of injured or wounded. The August 21 action was, of course, a direct repudiation of Diem's assurances to Nolting, during the latter's final days in Saigon, of his intent to effect conciliation with the Buddhists. Needless to say, Nolting, trying to counsel Lodge, felt betrayed by Diem as, earlier that godforsaken year, he had felt betrayed by his Deputy when, in his absence during the initial Buddhist outbreak in May, Trueheart, neglecting to communicate with his absent chief, took an anti-Diem line.

The Americans' sense of betrayal was compounded as the details of the affair became known. Initially it was reported that the raiding forces were regular Vietnamese military acting under a declaration of martial law recommended to Diem by the Vietnamese generals. It turned out instead that the raiders were police and Special Forces under Nhu's direct control. Clearly, Nhu had taken advantage of the military "cover" the generals had provided in acquiescing in a martial law decree to eliminate the Buddhist problem. If Lodge could thus be greeted on his arrival with a *fait accompli*, the dispute over how to deal with the Buddhists would no longer have to be a subject for discussions with the new American Ambassador. In this calculation, however, Nhu did not reckon with the character or the style of the Bostonian. Lodge's initial reserve with respect to the regime was changed by the raids on the Buddhists into a thinly disguised antagonism.

At one of the first ceremonies Lodge attended, his reaction to Diem's affectation of the traditional dress of the Vietnamese Mandarin rather than the white sharkskin suits of the French colonial regime was to suggest that the affair had all the trappings of a medieval court rather than the republic the Constitution called for. Befitting his standing as heir of an illustrious family and a national figure, Lodge was the antithesis of the careful bureaucrat. He considered his role in Vietnam to be one of general observation and the broadest of decision making, far above any concerns over the details of programs. His personal messages to Washington frequently reflected this detachment from the labored conclusions of the Mission. His independence of the Mission was matched by his knowledge of his independence of the Kennedy Administration stemming from his Republican credentials. The result was an attitude of personal but far from institutional responsibility baffling to the various career officers and services subordinate to him.

Kennedy responded by treating Lodge with the proverbial kid gloves. The last thing he needed at that stage was a possible resignation by the Republican he had engaged to be hostage to his policies in Vietnam. Deference to Lodge protected the President from any future charge that he had "lost" Vietnam as President Harry Truman and his fellow Democrats had "lost" China. American communications with Vietnam thus proceeded through a variety of channels and at many different levels. Those working at the military and rural levels were supporting the regime's programs to organize the countryside into a defensive framework against the Communist organizational efforts. In Saigon, the American agencies provided the necessary financial assistance, supplies, and equipment. Simultaneously an increasingly hostile political confrontation was taking place at the political level—which was, of course, the level that became the most important as Vietnamese-American relationships polarized over the summer of 1963.

The August 21 defiance of the new American Ambassador had its effect in Washington as well. The following August weekend found many of the leading Americans far from Washington: Kennedy was at Hyannisport on Cape Cod, Secretary of State Dean Rusk was in New York, and Secretary of Defense Robert McNamara and CIA Director John McCone were both away on vacation. At the State Department, however, a crisis atmosphere prevailed. There it was clear that the pagoda raids were the work of Nhu and his wife, not the Vietnamese military, and that they posed a direct challenge to American support of Vietnam. If not given the proper response, their effect would be to reduce the American Government to the role of blind supporter of whatever the Ngo regime chose to do, however reprehensible the regime's choices might appear in the eyes of the American public.

A Saturday morning in Washington is special: the telephones do not ring, senior officials are able to catch up on the week's work, and they are able to think about some of the larger questions that during supercharged weekdays are pushed off onto subordinates with instructions to draft the necessary cables, memoranda, or background papers. On this August Saturday, Roger Hilsman, Averell Harriman, George Ball, and National Security Council adviser Michael Forrestal were concerned that the United States not supinely accept Nhu's defiant *fait accompli.* They reviewed Lodge's first report of the situation after he arrived in Saigon, reporting the comments by senior generals and Diem civilian aides that the Nhus simply had to be removed from their role in the Diem Government if the battle against the Communists was to continue. Lodge, however, felt that the lack of clear-cut leadership among the generals and the presence of considerable troop strength in the Saigon area loyal to the regime would make a move against the Nhus only a "shot in the dark."

The four, with Harriman clearly the driving figure, then drafted a cable to Lodge that would start the American Government on the course of its first great mistake of the Vietnam War—the overthrow of the Diem Government. The key words of the cable were:

> The US Government cannot tolerate situation in which power lies in Nhu's hands. Diem must be given chance to rid himself of Nhu and his coterie. . . . If, in spite of all your efforts, Diem remains obdurate and refuses, then we must face the possibility that Diem himself cannot be preserved. . . .

To execute this policy, the key military leaders were to be informed that continued American military and economic support would be impossible unless the Nhus were removed and that if Diem refused, the United States was prepared to support Diem no longer. In the consequent interim period of breakdown of the central Government mechanism, the military would be provided directly with American support. As a final, pious hope, Lodge was instructed to look for possible alternative leadership and to make detailed plans of how to bring about Diem's replacement.

Such a major expression of American policy could not be sent off without obtaining the agreement or advice of the President's principal assistants and of the President himself. A summer Saturday hardly offered the occasion to convoke them for the full discussion that would have been natural during the workweek. Washington was equipped to act in emergencies, however, as each principal adviser had a deputy or duty officer able to give his institution's "clearance" of a message if the principal could not be reached, or to get in touch with him if necessary. The easiest was the President, who had secure communications wherever he went. His approval was quickly obtained. We do not know how the other approvals were obtained except for that of Rusk, who used the secure communications at the United States Mission to the U.N. in New York and thus saw the full text. General Maxwell Taylor, who was at a restaurant, was eventually contacted by telephone and given some kind of summary. McNamara and McCone were not contacted, Deputy Secretary of Defense Roswell Gilpatric accepting for McNamara and Richard Helms being notified for John McCone. While the technicalities of coordination had been complied with, it was plain that the substance had been the object of a bureaucratic end run. The principals obviously had had no opportunity for the kind of serious debate that should precede a major policy move.

When copies of this August 24 cable circulated among the agencies the next morning, the officers most closely involved with Vietnam realized that a major decision had been taken and that their absent chiefs needed a quick briefing on what had happened. Since I had been acting as one of McCone's principal assistants on the Vietnam problem and did not know that the cable had been passed to Helms, I got in touch with McCone to let him know about it. He well knew my own views that Diem might be difficult but that he was the best—and only—leader South Vietnam had; he had endorsed that position and supported me in it, and he knew that any direct action against Diem would entail the greatest dangers to American interests in a free South Vietnam.

At McCone's request, I flew that day to California to brief him in his splendid home there, using one of the White House's small jets, which McGeorge Bundy made available. When I showed McCone the text and explained that no one at the staff levels of the various departments had been consulted before it was sent, he was furious. He was, as always, outwardly calm, but his calm was now exceptionally icy. His brief vacation was abandoned. "I'll return to Washington with you tonight," he said.

Maxwell Taylor reacted in somewhat the same way and sent a message through his personal communications channel with General Harkins in Saigon to let him know that some second thoughts were developing in Washington on the course of action the cable launched.

On Monday the principals assembled with the President, in the usual Kennedy-style meeting, with twenty to thirty assistants present either at the Cabinet table or—where I was—along the walls. The President cut through the second thoughts by going around the table to ask each man if he wanted to back away from the cable. No one did. It is difficult indeed to tell a President to his face that something he has approved is wrong and to do so without something positive to offer in its place. Although none of the principals spoke up then, it became clear from later differences that several did have the "second thoughts" Taylor had mentioned to Harkins. But the next day Nolting, who was in Washington awaiting a new assignment and was invited to attend the White House meeting, spoke up, telling the President that we should not jump until we had some place to jump to, and meanwhile just take our lumps for the Vietnamese behavior.

Nolting's remarks brought George Ball to predict that the war could not be won. Averell Harriman, who earlier had expressed his impatience with Diem in many a meeting, now dramatically—even viciously—attacked Nolting. He said that Nolting's policy of going along with Diem (which, of course, had been the Kennedy Administration's policy) had been wrong all along and harshly denounced Nolting as having totally failed in his dealings with Diem—with the implication that Nolting's views were not worthy of the President's consideration. (Although I was outraged at this brutal treatment of a fine public servant, the incident was vintage Harriman, totally devoted to his view of what would benefit the President and the United States, and riding roughshod over anyone who dared to challenge him.) Secretary of Defense McNamara, Chairman of the Joint Chiefs of Staff Maxwell Taylor, and the CIA's John McCone clearly did not agree, but they muted their differences in this quasi-public forum. The assistants seated along the wall, including myself, were not included in the debate.

In an action that would typify much of the handling of the affair over the next few months, the President did not make a clear decision. He did force his principal officers to concur with his sending of the August 24 cable and expressed his annoyance with the divisions among them. But he did not clarify just where his policy was going; he merely authorized a cable to Lodge and Harkins to report whether they thought the political turmoil would spread from the cities to the countryside and affect the war effort—hoping that the answers to the question might solve the problem of deciding the policy. I had the impression that Kennedy was quite content to give Lodge his head in deciding how far to go against Diem, because Lodge's involvement and Republican credentials would protect him from recriminations whatever developed. And Kennedy was certainly being pushed by his main team—Rusk, Harriman, Hilsman, and Forrestal—to move forcefully, while the opponents—McNamara, Taylor, and McCone—seemed to have no particular plan to substitute.

Lodge, on the ground in Saigon, responded with vigor and enthusiasm to the policy expounded in the cable but judged that there was no point in giving Diem an opportunity to rid himself of the Nhus, as the chances that he would do so were "virtually nil." Thus he recommended that the generals be approached directly, bypassing Diem and leaving it up to them whether to "keep" Diem without the Nhus. Incongruously, he added that he would be presenting his credentials as Ambassador to Diem the next day, passing over the inconsistency of the two moves.

In Saigon, Lodge convoked his advisers and decided that
the process of informing the generals should be conducted
so that the "American official hand" would not show—in
accordance with the prevailing fiction that CIA operations
were not attributable to the American Government. There
was a clear inconsistency between John McCone's and my
opposition to the move against Diem and Lodge's use of our
subordinates to carry out the action we opposed. But the
CIA was not supposed to be a policymaking agency, and in
its covert actions was expected to implement the decisions
made by the President—who, in this case, had passed the
ball to Lodge. The Agency had had enough trouble with
accusations, already publicized, that it was an "invisible
government." We wanted to make it clear that the policies
we followed at the Agency were not ours but they were set by
the President and his policy advisers. The Kennedy Administration had emphasized this in a 1961 letter to all American Ambassadors stating that they were to maintain policy
authority over the CIA activities in their country. I fully
agreed with the Administration's insistence that American
missions abroad have one, and only one, chief—the Ambassador, in his capacity as the President's personal representative.

Consequently, John Richardson, at the head of the CIA
Station, following my very specific and insistent instructions that he take his direction from the Ambassador,
thereupon sent his officers to their carefully cultivated
Vietnamese military contacts to determine whether and how
they could conduct the coup that Lodge had decided Washington wanted.

The generals reacted with great caution, and even concern, as they knew that Richardson had maintained the
customary close contact with Nhu and they feared that what
they said might well get back to Nhu. They trusted the CIA
officers who had convinced them of the sincerity of their
friendship over the years, but they were afraid that the
reports of their conversations would nonetheless get out.
They had also not finished the careful plotting that they
knew would be necessary for a successful—and safe—coup.
In particular they had not brought into their councils
General Ton That Dinh, my friend whose "Mountain

Scouts" we had supported and who now controlled some of the key units in the Saigon area that would be essential to an attack on the Palace.

Over the next few days, a furious exchange of cables took place between the Embassy in Saigon and the political leadership in Washington recounting conversations with Vietnamese generals, deliberations in the White House, and fine-tuning of the tactics for handling the tensions with the Diem regime, the Buddhist protests, and the American journalists and their sensational reporting direct to the American people. Despite Washington's doubts and questions, usually contained in yet another message seeking clarification of some new facet of the situation, Lodge held firmly to his position: "We are launched on a course from which there is no respectable turning back: the overthrow of the Diem Government." Lodge's position had the virtue of frankness, which most of Washington's communications managed to obscure under the pretense that any coup would be the work of the Vietnamese generals, not the United States.

The striking omission in these exchanges, as in earlier discussions of the Vietnamese problem, was any real consideration of who and what would follow Diem and his regime. All attention was transfixed by the necessity and the details of eliminating him, as though that would solve the problems of dealing with him and his family and thereby automatically usher in an effective war effort. On only one occasion was any reference made to what might become of Diem and his family personally. In response to a casual reference by General "Big" Minh to the possibility of Diem's assassination, John McCone instructed me to send a harsh message to the Station to have my old colleague Lucien Conein, the principal point of contact with the senior generals, tell Minh in no uncertain terms that the United States would have no truck with any such discussion. Minh complied by not mentioning the subject again.

But the end result of the frenzied week of meetings and cables was summed up by John Richardson in a message to me that "this coup is dead." The generals decided they were not sufficiently united and lacked the necessary force to accomplish a coup, as well as being concerned over Ri-

chardson's relationship with Nhu. One of the generals told
his friend Conein, however, that if they did decide to move,
they would contact the Americans for the promised support, but that the moment was not opportune.

The pause in plotting in Vietnam did not slow the momentum in Washington. The contest between the two
points of view about Diem continued, with State and the
White House staff for his ouster and the Pentagon and the
CIA urging caution. The President continued to vacillate
under the intense differences among his principal lieutenants. Again decision was postponed by seeking yet another
assessment, this time from representatives of the two contesting points of view. Thus Foreign Service Officer Joseph
Mendenhall, who had served in Vietnam under Durbrow
and had drafted many of his cables calling for political
"reforms" as the key to progress there, was teamed with
Marine General Victor "Brute" Krulak (the nickname coming from his Annapolis midshipman days, when he was a
ferocious wrestler despite his diminutive size). The General
was a thorough believer in the precedence of the war in the
countryside over political machinations in Saigon. The two
were to make a one-week visit to Vietnam and return to brief
the President on the situation.

Each looked for, and found, what he wanted. Krulak
traveled throughout the provinces and reported that the
military was doing its job essentially unaffected by the
political turmoil and that the contest with the Communists
was going reasonably well. Mendenhall went to the urban
areas and talked to a number of his old contacts, concluding
that civil government was breaking down, a religious civil
war threatened, and the war against the Communists could
not be won with the Diem regime. President Kennedy's
response to their joint briefing was "You two did visit the
same country, didn't you?"

The quip was amusing, but it evaded the central question: whether each, having visited Vietnam and reported his
impressions accurately, had in fact seen quite different
aspects of the same situation, in the manner of the great
Japanese film *Rashomon*. The choice was not between their
versions of reality in Vietnam; rather, the issue was which
Vietnam was more relevant to United States interests there,

and which Vietnam, therefore, should receive American support as it struggled for its objectives.

Both versions were presented, of course, in light of the need for an effective war effort. Both were inevitably tangled in the web of political implications for the Kennedy Administration accompanying any decision giving direction to American policy. The one free agent in the picture was Henry Cabot Lodge. Having made up his mind that Diem must be ousted, he saw no downside for himself or his party in advocating this to the Democratic Administration, which had the responsibility of decision and would bear the brunt of the results. On the ground he maintained a studied detachment from the regime, waiting for it to come to him. His cables to Washington pressed for action to suspend nonmilitary assistance to the Government to show American displeasure.

Lodge had his way. To show its displeasure, Washington suspended the Commercial Import Program, which produced the local funds to pay the Vietnamese Government's budget, after President Kennedy said to Walter Cronkite on national TV on September 2 that the Vietnamese Government had "gotten out of touch with the people" there, but that "with changes of policy and perhaps with personnel," it might regain the people's support.

The verbal formulation that evolved to describe American policy at the time was that it would include "pressures and persuasion," but it was plain from the lack of contact between Lodge and the Palace that "persuasion" was conspicuously lacking. Lodge was waiting imperiously for Diem to "come to him" with concessions that would meet the American demands for changes in the Government's policies and programs. Diem did not budge—in part out of his prickly pride as a nationalist, in part out of resistance to what he thought would only weaken him in the struggle in which he was engaged within Vietnam.

Somewhat exasperated at this lack of communication and at the potentially dangerous consequences bound to follow if the Americans and the Vietnamese Government could not even discuss their differences while the war continued in the countryside, I drafted a note to McCone stressing the importance of bringing the two sides together. I offered to go out to Vietnam myself to do it, working fully under Lodge. McCone passed the note around a meeting in the White House basement of the key figures in the Washington debate (minus the President), but it evoked nothing beyond a shrug of the shoulders as unrealistic. In this situation, the Kennedy Administration took the all too familiar action of avoiding real decision by seeking additional information in the vain hope that this would provide an answer to the frustrating questions it faced.

Once again, therefore, Secretary McNamara and General Taylor, with a collection of representatives of the other agencies concerned, including me for the CIA, were bundled into the windowless KC-135 jet for the familiar leap from Andrews Air Force Base outside Washington to Anchorage, Alaska, to Tan Son Nhut airport in Saigon. The procedure was as always: diving upon arrival into a series of briefings in hot, stuffy rooms and a succession of conferences with American and Vietnamese officials (in that order) to try to determine what was happening "on the ground."

My own fact-finding efforts met a sudden and unexpected obstacle. Ambassador Lodge, knowing of my close contacts in the past with Ngo Dinh Nhu and the President, informed me that I was not to contact them, since he did not want the Palace to gain any false impression that I offered a potential way around his declared policy of waiting for Diem to come to him with the concessions Lodge thought necessary. Privately I was outraged at this prohibition, coming after a trip halfway around the world, but I knew I had no option but to comply. Lodge was the Ambassador, and I knew how he was being handled by Washington. When I informed McNamara of Lodge's prohibition, I sensed that he was far from happy about it himself, but I also knew that he could not afford to make an issue of it with Lodge. But I did quickly decide that any contacts with Vietnamese by me without also visiting Nhu (or Diem, if he asked me; I never initiated a request to see him even in the earlier days) would only be interpreted as a firm American decision to move against them, so I neither saw nor spoke with any Vietnamese at all. I did not want to be the vehicle for any such signal.

My survey of the situation was confined to the comments of the CIA Station officers about the attitudes and concerns of their contacts—Government officials, oppositionists, and military chiefs. The visit did expose me, however, to the intensely polarized attitudes of the American official community in Saigon, and to the total absence of communication between Lodge and the Embassy on the one hand, and the Palace and the President still in charge of the Vietnamese Government on the other.

The atmospherics of the city and the contacts I did have, however, suggested to me that Diem and Nhu might actually have achieved what they sought in the raids on the pagodas: the suppression of the Buddhist challenge to the authority of the Government—in short, a repetition of their success against the politicized sects in 1955. Since I had little confidence in what the Buddhists offered for the future of a modern Vietnam (I did not then have the basis of comparison offered by Iran's Ayatollah Khomeini and his brand of fundamentalist obscurantism, but I suspected something of the sort from the Buddhists' unworldly rhetoric), I thought that the reality of the situation might have allowed the Palace to get back to prosecuting the strategic hamlets program and the war—if the American reaction to the suppression could be contained.

On the way home in the same windowless KC-135, we drafted the report of the visit for the President, McNamara and his staff appropriately taking the leading role in the process. As it evolved from the series of draft sections that we put together on the plane, it came to continue the schizophrenic approach to Vietnam that had characterized the past several months. The war in the countryside was doing reasonably well—well enough, in fact, that the conclusion was inserted, "It should be possible to withdraw the bulk of U.S. military personnel" by the end of 1965. At the same time, the report recommended that several U.S. assistance programs be suspended "to impress upon Diem our disapproval of his political program," although it did say that "no initiative should be taken to encourage actively a change in government."

With the last phrase, I felt I could go along with the report as a whole. I did, however, make a somewhat forlorn

effort to point to the need for some real communication
with the Palace by resorting to the bureaucratic device
known as "taking a footnote," that is, taking exception to a
particular part of the otherwise agreed text of the official
report. Where the report called for a continuation of the
"purely 'correct' " relations with the leadership of the Vietnamese Government, I added a personal footnote that these
limited relations should be supplemented by some unoffi-
cial and personal relationships in which "persuasion"
could be fruitful. One of my traveling companions teased
me that "my slip was showing" in this comment, i.e., that I
was protesting my exclusion from meeting with my old
contacts during the visit. I felt a bit lonely during the rest of
the trip, but decided to stick to the position my footnote
stated.

What I was really concerned about were the political and
bureaucratic forces driving our policies toward Vietnam.
Lodge was beyond control by the Democratic Administration as he continued his lone-wolf vendetta against the
Diem regime, communicating with it, and Washington,
largely by leaks to journalists who shared his distaste for the
Diem regime. The programs of the CIA and AID were made
hostage to his policies, while the military programs and
contacts continued unaffected. American policy had become inherently contradictory. We were to continue to
support the South Vietnamese war effort but were to take a
detached—even hostile—position toward the Government
that was waging it. The basis for the contradiction was the
assumption that we Americans understood better than
Diem the kinds of policies and programs he should be
conducting in order to win the struggle against the Communists.

In concocting this witches' brew, the American journalists in Saigon had a big role. Eager to make the front page or
the evening news, they reported the evolving story in the
most dramatic and confrontational fashion they could. The
intensity of the dispute between the Buddhists and the Diem
Government made spectacular copy—and was a surrogate
for the equally intense struggle within the American Government over whether the United States should support or
overthrow Diem. A few journalists were frank in acknowl-

edging that their objective was to do away with Diem—in part from revulsion at his Mandarin rule, in part from the conviction that his leadership was hopeless—but all in the best journalistic tradition of detachment from responsibility for the consequences to follow.

In essence, the Mendenhall conclusions that political turmoil in the cities would bring collapse before the enemy were accepted, and the Krulak conclusions that the actual war in the countryside was going reasonably well were ignored. As earlier, the American thought process at the time almost totally lacked discussion, or even consideration, of what regime would follow Diem if he were replaced. In all the meetings on Vietnam over those many months, I recall no discussion whatsover of who might assume Diem's Leadership function beyond vague references to "the generals."

9

The Coup That "Succeeded"

IN EARLY OCTOBER, THE AMERICAN squeeze of Diem began. AID was instructed to continue the unannounced suspension of its commercial import program; it paid the dollar costs of many of Vietnam's imports and from their sale on the markets provided the local currency for much of the Government's budget. The CIA was told to stop its payments for the Vietnamese Special Forces, which it had supported in their irregular projects in the countryside and mountains, as well as their operations against North Vietnam, unless the Forces were reassigned under the Joint General Staff. That staff had been restive at the independence of the Special Forces, and particularly at their direct line of command from Nhu in the Palace, so this was both a gesture against Nhu and a favor to "the generals." A number of other AID projects were held up to carry out Lodge's effort to force the Government to come to him and to accept our terms to settle his differences with the Palace.

In an unmistakably direct stroke, John Richardson, the CIA Station Chief, who had carried out the established liaison with Nhu to supplement the Ambassador's dealings with Diem, was sent home by Lodge. The Ambassador, notwithstanding Richardson's full loyalty and support—notably in pressing the August effort to find a general to lead the coup despite his personal misgivings—saw Richardson as less than enthusiastic about the project. Lodge also saw that the Palace would correctly consider Richardson's departure as a clear sign of displeasure over the continued role and presence of Nhu, and as the elimination of what might have been a sympathetic channel for the Ngo brothers to communicate with the United States Government. It was perhaps the first time that the departure of a

CIA Chief of Station was announced in a Presidential press conference. McCone and I received the decision with annoyance, but we realized that it was pure Lodge and that the Kennedy team could not gainsay him—and did not particularly want to. The CIA was a tool easily used to pass a message: it would follow orders, and its programs were not so large that their termination would have the major effect on the war that suspension of military aid would.

Richardson's removal not only terminated the liaison with Nhu; it took out of the American deliberations another voice that urged that we combine our pressures with some degree of persuasion through contact and communication with Diem's Government, instead of merely standing aloof waiting for Diem to come to Lodge—a step that Diem's pride and anticolonialism made unlikely.

But Diem finally did come to Lodge through an invitation to spend a day together at Diem's Camp David–like hill retreat on October 27. Lodge dutifully reiterated the American ideas for resolving the tensions in the country, such as releasing arrested Buddhists and students, reopening the schools and universities, and "eliminating" anti-Buddhist discrimination. He voiced a complaint about the press and public criticism to which Diem's policies were subjecting President Kennedy, who, he said, was unavoidably associated by the American public with responsibility for supporting a regime that acted as it had, and had even beat up American newspeople when they took photos at the immolation of a Buddhist bonze (carefully scheduled). Lodge also mentioned Madame Nhu's inflammatory remarks during a trip she was making in the United States: she referred to the bonzes' immolations as "barbecues" deliberately arranged by the Buddhists at which she had "gaily clapped her hands" and offered to furnish the gasoline and a match if some of the American correspondents would follow the Buddhist example.

Diem did not "come to" Lodge on any of these points, returning only a "blank stare" when Lodge asked him for some action that would favorably impress American opinion. The encounter was a classic case of noncommunication between the Americans desperately searching for some act that would solve their public opinion problem and proud and prickly Diem determined to uphold the authority of his Government against disorder so that it could prosecute the main threat from the Communists.

Lodge did get across the American message of hostility, however. Nhu thereupon began an intense publicity campaign against American policy, especially the reduced assistance to Vietnam, supplemented by his wife's increasingly outrageous comments in the United States. (Some of the sting was taken out of Madame Nhu's outbursts by her father's resignation as Vietnamese Ambassador to Washington in public protest at Diem's policies and by statements he and his wife—who also resigned her official posts—then made countering those of their own daughter.) The regime began to tighten its belt and knuckle down for a long struggle with the United States and its aid reductions. On a separate track, Nhu also made several tentative approaches through other nations to North Vietnam, considering that these might be a way to obtain a resolution of the struggle between Vietnamese that could circumvent the Americans if they turned actively hostile to South Vietnam. (As these came partially to light, they were viewed by Nhu's American opponents as further evidence of his perfidy.)

At the same time, reports began to flow into the CIA of officers in the Vietnamese military considering, if not actually plotting, a coup. Some of these were in the mainstream of the military, and some were mavericks pursuing their own political or conspiratorial dreams. One of the latter was Pham Ngoc Thao, whom I had met several years earlier when Assemblywoman Pauline Nguyen Van Tho took me to Kien Hoa province in the Delta, where Thao had been assigned as chief by Diem and Nhu. Thao, who was to be heard from again later, was plotting with the encouragement of Tran Kim Tuyen from abroad, where this former chief of the Palace's intelligence and security service was languishing in exile decreed by Diem in a futile effort to mollify the Americans. This was a group of modern-minded Catholics who, having determined that the Diem regime had lost the mandate of Heaven (or, more practically, the United States), were looking for ways to supplant him.

But on a more important level, "the generals" began to

coalesce and seek assurances of American support if they moved against the regime. Again Lucien Conein was approached, this time by General Tran Van Don, to meet with "Big" Minh, who wanted to know the American reaction if the leading generals brought about a change in government. Having learned how the Americans liked to discuss such subjects, Minh carefully said the generals did not need American support but only assurances that the United States would not thwart them. This near-subtlety coincided with a warning sent from Washington that President Kennedy wanted no American initiative to encourage a coup, but that a covert effort should be made to build contact with possible "alternative leadership" in a "fully deniable" manner. Lodge cut through such sophistry in his own recommendation to Washington that the generals be told that the United States would not "thwart" them, would review their plans to give its counsel, and would continue American aid to "a government which gives promise of gaining the support of the people and winning the war against the Communists."

The last assurance was the critical one—that American aid would be given to the generals if they succeeded in a coup. All hands could, of course and notwithstanding, sanctimoniously maintain that the Americans had had no hand in the actual coup action, "however unjustifiably" the United States might be blamed for it by public opinion. This exquisite intellectualizing certainly kept dissension under control among the Americans. But a cable from the senior American General on the scene, Paul Harkins of the Military Assistance Command, showed that there was less than full agreement on the course of action being followed. It was remarkably prescient in its evaluation of likely consequences:

> I'm not opposed to a change in government, no indeed, but I'm inclined to feel that at this time the change should be in methods of governing rather than complete change in personnel. . . . In my contacts here I have seen no one with the strength of character of Diem, at least in fighting Communists. Certainly there are no Generals qualified to take over in my opinion.

> I am not a Diem man per se. I certainly see the
> faults in his character. I am here to back 14 million
> SVN people in their leader at this time. . . .
> After all, rightly or wrongly, we have backed Diem
> for eight long hard years. To me it seems incongru-
> ous now to get him down, kick him around, and get
> rid of him.

Up to the last moment, discussion between Lodge and
Washington over whether the United States could halt a
coup continued, Lodge maintaining that the generals were
acting on their own and that what they were doing was
essential to America's interests. Washington remained fearful that the coup would not succeed and asked that we in
the capital, or at least Lodge, have the opportunity to
review the plan in detail to determine whether the generals
should be dissuaded from it. The specific instructions given
to Lodge as to the United States posture limited direct
American help to the coup, though they concluded,

> But once a coup under responsible leadership has
> begun, . . . it is in the interest of the US Government
> that it should succeed.

This exchange encapsulates the entire affair: Lodge out
in front in a buccaneering project to overthrow Diem with
some quarters in Washington egging him on, various second thoughts and qualms arising in other Washington
circles hoping to have some control over events, the pretense
that "the generals" were acting on their own, and the
President not taking a firm position. And in the background lay the fact that Lodge had been the Republican
Vice Presidential candidate in 1960 (and McCone at the
head of the CIA was a strong Republican), so that Kennedy
was protected against right-wing opposition to what was
happening, while the left-wing pushed him against Mandarin Diem.

On November 1, 1963, Lodge accompanied visiting Admiral Harry Felt, the American Commander-in-Chief Pacific, on the latter's courtesy call on Diem at the Palace.
Diem recited his compulsive monologue denouncing his
opponents and calling for continued assistance to the war
effort. At the end of the meeting, however, he called Lodge

aside for a short private talk, saying that he wanted to have a discussion with Lodge about what Lodge wanted him to do. He also asked for greater understanding of his position, and particularly suggested that Nolting and I be consulted as we understood best how much he needed the assistance of his brother Nhu. But the moment for such talk had passed. As the two parted, the generals had already begun the execution of their plans to overthrow Diem, and Conein was with them at Joint General Staff Headquarters to serve as their communications link to Lodge. Diem had finally "come to" Lodge—tragically, too late.

The generals had planned their coup carefully and included all the necessary forces. The regional commanders were aboard, and the vital units around Saigon had been successfully brought along by inveigling my friend Ton That Dinh into joining the effort by playing on Diem's failure to award him a third star when putting him into that key command. To neutralize one potential source of resistance, the leaders killed the chief of the Navy, about whom they had doubts, the moment the coup began. The only defending force available to Diem thus turned out to be the Presidential Guard, who put up a valiant but hopeless defense of the surrounded Palace, holding off the attackers until they brought up tanks and artillery the following morning.

Lodge had only one other, and final, communication with Diem—on the telephone when the Palace was under full assault. Diem reported that some of his units were in rebellion and wanted to know the American position. Lodge avoided a direct answer, saying that he was not well enough informed and that Washington in the early morning could not have an opinion. Diem responded, "You must have some general ideas. After all, I am a Chief of State. I have tried to do my duty. I want to do now what duty and good sense require, I believe in duty above all." Again Lodge dodged the challenge for a clear statement of the American position: "You have certainly done your duty. . . . I admire your courage and your great contributions to your country," then added that the rebels had offered Diem and Nhu safe conduct out of the country. Diem got the message that there was no help coming from Lodge, said that Lodge had his telephone number, and that "I am trying to reestablish order."

After a futile attempt to rally forces outside Saigon to help them, Diem and Nhu secretly left the Palace during the night and sought refuge with a Chinese friend in the Cholon section of the city. When it was clear that there was no hope that the brothers could raise a force to support them, Diem contacted the generals at the Joint General Staff Headquarters and offered to surrender. They agreed to meet at a nearby Catholic church where they attended mass. Diem refused to leave Nhu, as he feared that Nhu would be killed if they were separated.

The generals sent an armored column to take them into custody, an aide of General "Big" Minh joining the unit at the last minute. When the Ngo brothers were picked up at the appointed place, they were placed in an armored personnel carrier for the ride to General Staff Headquarters near the airport. The route crossed a rail line, and a passing train forced the column to stop. Minh's aide entered the carrier, shot both brothers with a submachine gun, and stabbed them repeatedly. The column then proceeded to the Headquarters. The bloody bodies of the brothers were brought before the assembled generals, many of whom were horrified at this violation of the understanding they had insisted upon as they joined the coup—that Diem (though not Nhu) not be harmed.

Clearly the decision to murder the two was made by the coup's titular leader, General "Big" Minh, and by him alone. It was one of his few decisive actions and the most disastrous. The motive was simple: fear that if Diem had survived, he would probably have returned to wreak vengeance on Minh as the leader of the coup. Minh's action was typical of him—shortsighted, self-interested, and wrong.

Minh was not alone, however, in another direct murder during the coup—that of Colonel Le Quang Tung, commander of the Vietnamese Special Forces. An unbelievably mild-mannered, bespectacled, slight man, he was quite the opposite of what one would have expected in such a post. Deeply Catholic, he was dedicated to Diem, who had selected him for the post and, with Nhu, supervised his work with the Americans on the various projects conducted with the CIA Station. He also had directed counterintelligence operations for the brothers, searching out plotters and oppositionist figures, and earning himself the suspicion and fear of the generals. Tung's greatest sin in their eyes, however, lay in the fact that he and the Special Forces were not under the command authority of the General Staff; the attack on the Buddhist pagodas in August had been conducted by them without the General Staff's knowledge, but the blame initially was cast on the Army because of the uniforms the Special Forces were wearing. There was therefore general acquiescence among the generals assembled that Tung should be killed. After a final telephone conversation with Diem, in which Tung told him of his capture (confirming the lack of any hope of relief from the siege), he was taken outside the General Staff Headquarters and shot.

In Washington, the coup dominated the attention of the American Government. On November 1, 1:00 P.M. in Saigon was 1:00 A.M. in Washington. The first cables reporting the launching of the generals' coup came in shortly afterward, based on Conein's telephoned reports to the Embassy from the Joint General Staff Headquarters. A special meeting of the National Security Council had been called for that morning to bring the President and his advisers up to date on the situation in Saigon. There, as of our information at the hour of the meeting (by then mid-evening in Saigon), President Diem and his brother were holed up in the Palace protected by the Presidential Guard. The question was how a battle between the plotters and the Diem forces would go.

When the President, who was presiding, the Attorney General, and all the other principals were assembled in the Cabinet Room, John McCone asked me to give the briefing on the situation in Saigon, particularly the lineup of forces. I outlined the units in the area that might be expected to take part, stressing that an armored unit in the suburbs would be especially critical; if it went with the coup the forces against Diem would be preponderant, but if it stayed loyal a considerable battle would ensue. I did not know then, of course, the extent of the generals' careful preparations, which had covered this eventuality. They had carefully kept this to themselves, along with other negotiations to entice the Saigon area commander (appointed Minister of the Interior by Diem to keep him under control) to go with the coup. At this point, with the die cast in Saigon and Lodge clearly in charge of American policy at the scene, Washington had little to contribute other than to cling to the fiction that the coup was a purely Vietnamese affair, launched by the generals. In Kennedy's usual style, there were twenty-odd people in the room and the discussion was free flowing, even informal. The President, and others, did express concern over what might happen to Diem (though not to Nhu), and McCone cabled instructions to Conein to find out from the generals where Diem was.

But over the next night, most of which I spent at the communications center at CIA Headquarters, the news turned grim as the first reports that the two brothers were dead came through. The first stories—that they had committed suicide—were patently ridiculous in view of Diem's strong Catholicism (and his basic character), and it soon developed that they had indeed been murdered—General "Big" Minh's orders to his aide to this effect only being revealed later. When the news of the murders reached President Kennedy, he blanched and walked out of the room to compose himself.

The National Security Council met again the next morning, November 2, All Souls' Day in the Catholic calendar. I had stopped in our local church on the way to my premeeting appointment with McCone and asked my wife to say a prayer for "the brothers," whose fate I had learned during the night. The atmosphere of the meeting was sober, even somber. The triumph Lodge was expressing in his cables— that the coup had been "a remarkably able performance in all respects"—found little echo in that room. Only Dean Rusk of the State Department had sent a cable to Lodge stating his "highest esteem for your superb handling of a very complex and difficult series of events."

But there were no recriminations either, as it was clear that we had more important things to do. When the meeting began with the President's entrance, we bypassed the reports from Saigon of euphoric crowds celebrating in the streets to focus on the much more important problems of where we would go from here. Suddenly "the generals," on whom American policy had rested its hopes, had to be identified and their real capabilities assessed. The days when they were viewed simply as a happy alternative to the frustrations of dealing with Diem were over. The Attorney General asked me what had happened to that armored unit I had mentioned the previous day, and I could say only that obviously it had gone with the coup. The meeting came to no substantial conclusion other than to continue support of Vietnam under its new direction (whatever that might turn out to be), and to stress that the coup had been a Vietnamese, not an American, action.

When the meeting adjourned McCone told me to accompany him, and we went to the secretary's desk outside the Oval Office. In his forceful manner McCone said he wished to see the President, and we were ushered in. President Kennedy was alone at his desk, appearing thoughtful and subdued. He had recovered from the emotional shock he reportedly experienced when told of the deaths of Diem and Nhu—and he was also reported to have replied to a friend who said they were tyrants, "No. They were in a difficult position. They did the best they could for their country." But he knew he faced a serious problem because of his Administration's support of the coup.

McCone led off: "Mr. President, you know Mr. Colby." Kennedy nodded in friendly recognition. McCone continued: "In view of the confusion in Saigon, I would like to send him immediately to Saigon to make contact with the generals there and assess the situation on the basis of his close connections with them and his knowledge of the country. I would also like to be able to say that he is going on your authority." Unspoken between McCone and the President was the fact that both knew Lodge was in charge in Saigon, that they were both uneasy on the basis of their dealings with and through him, and McCone at least certainly recalled Lodge's opposition to my last appearance there with McNamara and Taylor and his order that I have no contact with Diem or Nhu. McCone, in establishing that I was going with the President's approval, was overruling any negative reaction to my visit by Lodge.

"Certainly," said Kennedy. He gave me a friendly look,

but he was obviously still under strain over the deaths of the Ngo brothers. Nevertheless, I felt a word of caution was in order. "Mr. President," I said, "I am glad to go, but I am not sure how much I can accomplish. I do know the generals, but I also know that they are aware that I was quite close to President Diem and his brother, and they might be somewhat reserved in receiving me. But I will do my best, and hope that I can be of help." "Thank you," the President answered, "I will be looking for your comments, and good luck."

Since the next available plane left the following day, I hosted a long-standing dinner that evening with the Noltings and Richardsons to conduct probably the only American wake over the deaths of Diem and Nhu. We all joined in expressing concern over how Vietnam—and the United States—would face the problems ahead without Diem's strength and leadership, and in wondering how our Government could have been so blind as to have contributed so directly to his overthrow and death. In this, significantly, we were joined by the Vietnamese Communists. Some days later, one of their representatives in Paris commented to an American that they had been surprised and shocked at our action against the strongest and most effective opponent they faced. The leader of the National Liberation Front, Nguyen Huu Tho, later called it a "gift from Heaven for us."

Part Four

THE SEARCH
FOR A
STRATEGY

10

Chaos and Confusion

ON THE LONG TRIP OUT TO SAIGON, I thought about where we were in the war and how we could put together the pieces of our effort without Diem. In principle, there was an option open to me personally—to resign in protest against the policies that had led to the dire situation we now faced. I did not even consider it. Much as I deplored what I was convinced were a long sequence of errors, I could not pretend to any personal complaint. I certainly had been given the opportunity to put my ideas forward through John McCone to the National Security Council and directly to President Kennedy. What is more, though I disagreed with the result, I appreciated the rationale that had pressed the President to move in a direction opposite to that which I advocated (pressures on him that included the daily barrage of press criticism of Diem's authoritarianism). In the early 1960s, we had not yet reached that national state of mind that considered any difference from one's own views as based on immorality or arrant stupidity and justifying the most extreme denunciations and rejection of authority. The basic discipline of the career officer, civilian or military, moved me to accept as mistaken even what appeared to be wrong; my attention was directed to the problems ahead that needed to be solved rather than to recriminations about the past.

The first problem was to determine who was running South Vietnam and in what direction. My first call was on Ambassador Lodge, who greeted me with effusive praise for the work of the CIA Station during the coup and its scrupulous adherence, under my instructions, to his direction. He also indicated full awareness of President Kennedy's endorsement of my mission, thus eliminating any repetition of his veto of Vietnamese contacts by me, as during my last visit.

I then was taken by our CIA officers to meet the new junta of the generals, who were equally enthusiastic about the way their CIA friends had worked with them during the coup. I was somewhat surprised at the way they received me—as a good friend and supporter of several of their pet projects in the past, as the boss of their CIA officer friends during the coup, and as someone who could sympatheti-cally interpret their new needs to faraway Washington. General Tran Van Don joked about having been my land-lord during my earlier tour, Le Van Kim reminisced about our discussions of strategy, and Ton That Dinh recalled the Mountain Scout program we had developed together among the tribal people in the highlands, in recognition of which he had given me a stuffed tiger. Only "Big" Minh, the nominal chief, was a bit reserved at first, but he soon warmed during the series of briefings we organized to outline the programs the CIA was conducting and how they could help the new authorities. No one mentioned my known close relationship with the Ngo brothers, Diem and Nhu.

Publicly, I put forward the most positive face that I could. But privately I was concerned that the new regime offered little to work with. The junta seemed overwhelmed with the responsibility of running a country and picking up the war effort. They looked anxiously to the Americans to show them how to do one and the other and even to do both for them—in the best French colonial manner under which they had grown up. "Big" Minh showed no inclination to take charge and provide the necessary leadership, much preferring to consult with his fellow generals in a series of briefings and discussions that led to no decisions. In the midst of the junta's indecision, Ambassador Lodge con-tinued his curiously detached attitude, remote from the mere details of getting an American mission to pull to-gether a strategy and a structure to carry it out. I drew my impressions together in a cable to McCone at the end of my visit, saying that we had an enormous job ahead to get the Government simply to work and to adopt and carry out a real strategy, and that Lodge, with all his virtues, was hardly engaged in it. McGeorge Bundy later told me that McCone had shared the cable with him and that he understood the problem.

I continued my efforts to understand the new forces at work in Vietnam. Much was to change, of course, in the fateful month of November 1963. One of those changes was a development on the ground in Vietnam. Its impact, if not as great as that of the fall of Diem or that of the other great loss still to come, was still considerable.

It stemmed, curiously enough, from the failure of the CIA's Bay of Pigs operation against Castro's Cuba. After that 1961 humiliation, President Kennedy appointed a Commission headed by retired General Maxwell D. Taylor to draw its lessons for future policy. One of the Taylor Commission's observations was that the CIA was not sufficiently staffed or properly organized to conduct such a large-scale paramilitary operation, with its needs for logistical planning, coordination of air, sea, and land forces, and a well-defined chain of command. The conclusion was therefore drawn—and accepted—that if a paramilitary operation, even one started on a covert basis, reached a large scale, it should be turned over to the Pentagon, with the CIA reduced to a supporting role in those areas in which its particular expertise would be useful.

By mid-1963, the CIA's paramilitary programs in Vietnam had indeed reached a large scale. The program of arming villagers had provided some 30,000 weapons to communities around the country, and some 450 American Army Special Forces troopers had been detailed to the CIA to supplement the organizing work of our case officers with on-the-ground training and help in the hamlets and villages. The other CIA programs—those in Central Vietnam directed by Diem's brother Can, the Mountain Scouts in the highlands, and the program to infiltrate agents into North Vietnam—all attracted intense attention among Vietnamese officials as well as modest but significant CIA resources in training camps, special air supply capabilities, and related logistics.

While all but the Northern program seemed to be working well, the inherent secrecy of the CIA made the effectiveness of any of them largely unknown beyond a limited core

of Vietnamese and American senior officials. Other Vietnamese and Americans saw them as cutting across established lines of command and organizations and diverting
resources and attention from larger-scale, regular military
and civilian programs. Even within the CIA, there were
many who felt it was dangerous for the institution to be on
the exposed forward edge of such potentially controversial
activities. An illustration of the risks involved—and a lesson
quickly noted—was Diem's and Nhu's use of the Vietnamese
Special Forces, which had been trained and funded by the
CIA outside the military chain of command, for the August
1963 raid on the Buddhist pagodas.

Thus one of my bureaucratic chores in mid-1963 became
the negotiation with Pentagon officials of Operation
Switchback, a misnomer given to the mechanism by which
the CIA's paramilitary programs in Vietnam would be
turned over to Pentagon direction. Even during the negotiations, it became clear that the transfer could not be simple.
It was plain that the informal and direct channels that the
CIA used to move logistics, weapons, and money to the
point of use were not available to the military. The Pentagon's procedures were to turn these vital supplies over to the
Vietnamese Government in Saigon and then hope that they
would reappear at the working level—a hope that was all
too often disappointed. Accordingly, a special arrangement
was devised by which the CIA's channels would continue to
be used to pass the materials for these programs to the
military in the field, although the military would control
the actual operations and budget and account for them at
the Washington level.

The CIA also had some experience to pass on to the
military. The Agency's offer to make some of its officers
available to help the transition was politely accepted but in
fact not utilized, as it was not really relevant to the more
extensive programs the military had in mind. This applied
particularly to the operations against North Vietnam.
There I had come to the conclusion that while air and sea
landings of agents might have worked in occupied Europe
or Asia during World War II in nations where the local
population actively resisted the occupier (and in fact had
helped me in my drops into France and Norway), they did

not work in a Communist-controlled society that exercised
unchallenged control over its subjects. My deputy, Robert J.
Myers, with long experience in Asia, pointed out that these
operations had uniformly failed against North Korea and
Mainland China, and I recalled the same lack of success of
similar ones tried in Eastern Europe and the Soviet Union
during the early 1950s.

As a result, at a strategy conference in Honolulu to discuss what pressures could be brought to bear against North
Vietnam and how Switchback might lead to a whole new
dimension of such efforts, I stood up to tell Secretary
McNamara and the assembled commanders, "They just
won't work, Mr. Secretary." I suggested that the most useful
unconventional operations against North Vietnam would
be psychological ones, with radios, leaflets, and other ways
of infiltrating ideas, rather than agents and explosives, into
North Vietnam. The advice was not particularly welcome
in the intense atmosphere of finding something "we could
do to them in North Vietnam to match what they are doing
to us in the South," and McNamara let my comment drop
without reply. The psychological effort was added to the list
of actions and left to the CIA to implement, but the main
thrust was to step up operations to drop agents and conduct
sabotage against the North.

But the major impact of Operation Switchback was not
seen until later. The fundamental strategy of the CIA's
paramilitary programs in South Vietnam was to build
strength in the rural communities from the bottom up,
arming the local inhabitants so they could participate in
their own defense, and gradually to extend the area of
security like Lyautey's *tache d'huile*. The local citizens in
such programs did have weapons, and full-time fighters to
come to their relief when under attack, but the purpose and
procedures were defensive, not offensive; political, not military. The objective was to involve the people of the community in a common effort to protect themselves, not to kill
the enemy.

The Army Special Forces understood this perfectly when
they worked under CIA direction and implemented the
concept with imagination and sensitivity. But within a few
months of the November 1 effective date of Switchback, the

strategy was changed. In the title "Citizens' Irregular Defense Groups," "Citizens'" became "Civilian" for reasons that escaped me then and still do but that apparently reflected the military belief that, not really being military, they must be civilian. More significantly, the mission for the forces was set as the conduct of "offensive guerrilla operations." The program of arming the safer communities in "oil spot" fashion was abandoned, and the weapons we had distributed there were picked up from groups we had trained to defend themselves. The full-time "strike force" units we had organized to bring reinforcement to embattled communities were bodily moved to isolated fortress bases along the Cambodian and Laotian borders, from which they were directed to conduct aggressive patrols, ambushes, and attacks in the jungles and mountains against infiltrators from North Vietnam. This was certainly a military mission, but it left the Communist strategy of the people's war in the villages essentially unopposed. We decided to fight our kind of war rather than the kind the enemy was fighting.

The new junta faced another problem in this context. During the summer and fall of 1963, the Communists had concentrated their efforts on destroying as well as discrediting Nhu's strategic hamlets program. They had identified it as a major strategic threat to their efforts to subvert South Vietnam. They had also correctly identified its weaknesses in execution, from its hasty proliferation pressed by Nhu to the facades erected by many local officials to satisfy the Palace's demands for instant results, instead of the slower but steadier buildup that sound procedure dictated. Diem and Nhu were aware of many of these shortcomings, as we learned from an inspector's report obtained independently at about the time of the coup, and Nhu certainly railed against them in conversations with me and with Richardson. In time they would have been corrected, but Nhu believed it more important to maintain the strategic momentum of the program than to perfect its every detail.

When the Buddhist crisis erupted, with its accompanying contest with the Americans, Diem's and Nhu's attention was perforce turned from the strategic hamlets program. The consequent lack of high-level supervision and emphasis, the weaknesses of the program and its officials, and concentrated attack by the Communists brought it to a halt over the summer and fall of 1963.

The Communists were not, however, prepared to exploit the opportunity provided by the overthrow of Diem. A number of them stated they found it hard to believe that the United States would so jettison their major adversary in the fashion it did, providing National Liberation Front leader Nguyen Huu Tho's so descriptive "gifts from Heaven for us." Their lack of preparation for so unexpected an opportunity, mixed with astonishment and disbelief, led the Communists to miss their chance for a devastating blow immediately after the coup.

But what the Communists did not do the new Government did. The strategic hamlets program was so prime an element of the Diem regime—and of Nhu's role in particular—that condemnation of it was inevitably a ritual demonstration of revolutionary bona fides. In my discussions with the new junta, I tried to explain the CIA's community programs in a fashion that would attract the new leaders' support for the concept. Obviously, I avoided pointing out similarities to the ideas underlying the strategic hamlets. The generals paid little attention to the community programs but a great deal to the frailties and falsities of the strategic hamlets program, further justifying its abandonment. With their agreement to dissolve the strategic hamlets machinery, the program vanished in the countryside.

The effect of this decision, together with that of Operation Switchback, was to leave the countryside open to the Communists' political offensive and its military accompaniments. After the Communists fully absorbed the fall of Diem and saw the drift and paralysis that followed, they gathered their energies to exploit the situation. From statistics of enemy attacks on Government personnel and installations, from the growth of Communist units thanks to increased local recruitment and infiltration from the North, and from the closing of substantial rural areas to outside access, it soon became clear that the Communists were moving to press the advantage afforded them by the confusion that had engulfed Saigon and the consequent new situation there.

As one of my efforts to comprehend that new situation, I invited one of the leading Buddhist bonzes to tea one afternoon. Resplendent in his yellow robe, he arrived in a polished limousine equipped with immaculate white cotton seat coverings, precisely as one of Diem's ministers would have. We had a long and pleasant conversation in which I sought some articulation of his goals for the Vietnam he had helped bring about and to learn how he saw his interaction with the military in the seats of power. I struggled manfully to bridge the gap between his Eastern mysticism and my Western pragmatism, drawing on all I had studied over the years of Buddhist doctrine and its variations—all to no avail.

We parted with expressions of amity and respect. But I realized that I could not write a memorandum of the conversation; not only could I not understand what he was trying to say, I was inwardly convinced that he did not know what he wanted to say. In a bewildering sequence of non sequiturs, he had restricted himself to short, pat phrases on the importance of Buddhism and good will. One thing was clear to me: he could generate crowds on the street, and, plainly aware of his political power, he wanted nothing done by the Government without his participation. But it was also clear that a Government dependent on his support would have a difficult time satisfying him.

I was not long back in Washington from this first inquiry into the aftermath of the Saigon coup when the next of that November's blows fell upon us. I heard the news of the senseless assassination of President Kennedy on a small transistor radio in CIA headquarters in Langley (followed in due course by the widowed Madame Nhu's bitter statement that this constituted a retribution for the deaths of her husband and brother-in-law, an observation that surely did the cause of Vietnam in America no good).

On hearing the news, I commented to Bob Myers that the results to flow from the loss of Kennedy's inspiring presence, which had so captured the imagination of the whole world, would be enormous. The hopes he raised of youthful and vigorous efforts to bring about a better and freer world were no more; the obstacles he had challenged us all to overcome seemed larger and more forbidding. And despite his responsibility for vacillation in our Vietnam policies between the two schools among his advisers, so opposed in their attitudes toward Diem, I am convinced that his sensitivity to the political aspects of the war waged by the Communists would have led him to insist on a strategy on our side to match them. I also believe that he certainly would not have let our effort in Vietnam change into the massive military affair it turned out to be.

The conjunction of the losses of Diem and Kennedy, then, set the course for the following years. If Diem had not been overthrown, he would have resumed his emphasis on the strategic hamlets strategy and firmly sat upon any effort by the Buddhists to disrupt his direction of Vietnam. In my view, there was a 50 percent chance that he would have repaired the deficiencies of the program sufficiently to once again seize the initiative from the Communists. This would have enabled him to wind down the war at the guerrilla level over the next several years with assistance from, but not massive participation by, the American military. If Kennedy had not been assassinated, his limitation of the American role to assistance and support without massive participation might have been enough to prevail, or it might have failed (Kennedy had privately indicated to several of his close associates his intention to limit further American involvement in Vietnam and even to withdraw from involvement there). But in the latter case, the failure would have been Vietnamese, not American. And the fall of Saigon in the mid-1960s, occurring ten years earlier than it actually did, would have saved at least a million Vietnamese lives and those of 50,000 Americans—and avoided the poisoning effects of the subsequent years of battle on the American political process.

In Saigon, a junta and confusion had succeeded Diem. In Washington Lyndon B. Johnson, in accordance with Constitutional procedures, succeeded Kennedy. Johnson is properly treated by many historians as a tragic rather than a malevolent figure. His personal convictions produced the Great Society and its commitment to the welfare of the disadvantaged of American society, the Civil Rights Act of 1964, as a major step toward repairing the unconscionable discrimination imposed on our black fellow citizens, and the Vietnam War as we know it.

In earlier policy discussions in the White House, Lyndon

Johnson had made no secret of his belief that we should have supported Diem and not tried to remake him into our own image of what a modern liberal democratic leader should be. This was the conclusion he reached during his 1961 visit to Saigon, when, with characteristic hyperbole, he dubbed Diem the Winston Churchill of Southeast Asia standing against the Communist threat. On that occasion, turning to his instincts and sense of priority and politics, he decided that Diem was in office, was doing reasonably well, and needed our support, not our criticism. During the National Security Council debates over the summer of 1963, he remained quiet as a Vice President must, while Kennedy presided over the differences among his advisers, but his occasional sharp comments and his demeanor gave full evidence that he believed the process misguided and mistaken.

Now that Diem was gone, suddenly the problem was his, but without the option he had supported all along. In this situation, those other elements of his character came to the fore—the tenacity and resolution legendary among Texans and the manipulative skills that had served him so well as Majority Leader of the assemblage of sovereigns that is the United States Senate. In an attempt to rally an injured nation, Johnson tried to project continuity with the fallen leader by retaining his Cabinet and advisers—McNamara, Rusk, Bundy, McCone, and their assistants. One he did eliminate was Roger Hilsman, whom he blamed for the anti-Diem campaign, but it was now too late for that to make a difference. The error in retaining his predecessor's chief deputies and counselors was not due to any personal defects or lack of competence on their parts. But in keeping this team he diluted the impact of his own leadership and encouraged the bureaucracy to continue to approach the problems of Vietnam in ways tried and found wanting—as events had already shown and were soon to show again. It is impossible to tell whom he might have substituted advantageously or the consequences of such changes, but it is easy to say that his own choices probably would have reflected more of his political approach and Texan simplicity than the intellectual outlook of the Kennedy team.

By the end of January 1964, it was plain to all that the

junta had failed. Increased attacks in the countryside were rapidly spreading Communist control. Not only had the junta no strategy with which to meet these attacks and their consequences; it seemed unable to make any decisions at all. After deliberating for hours, the generals would adjourn with no directions for their subordinates. In this situation, my earlier prediction that the former Chief of the General Staff under Diem during the attempted 1960 coup, General Nguyen Khanh, would assume the leadership came true. Without notice, Khanh suddenly arrested the junta members, sent them under house arrest to the hill station of Dalat, and took over the Government himself.

In my meetings with Khanh after the coup that had overthrown Diem, I had noticed that he had begun to grow a wispy beard—really a goatee. He was reticent about its significance, but the coincidence of the death of Diem and the appearance of Khanh's goatee convinced me that the two were related. He never clarified the matter for me, but related events led me to guess at the significance of this hirsute gesture. When Khanh seized power, General "Big" Minh's aide, who had actually killed Diem and Nhu, was promptly shot. Khanh kept his beard even after that, which convinced me that its significance was longer term than revenge for Diem's death and was possibly related to a commitment to ensure that Diem's work for South Vietnam's independence would be continued. Ellen Hammer, in her book *A Death in November*, reports that one of Diem's last remarks was "Tell Nguyen Khanh that I have great affection for him, and he should avenge me."

But Khanh proved unable to harness, or even contain, the diverse forces loosed in Vietnam by the destruction of the Diem regime. The nation descended into almost three years of political turmoil and internecine struggle. The success of Khanh's coup rested essentially on the belief among the military leadership that the first junta members just could not run the country and that Khanh might be able to. But Khanh's own closeness to Diem, and that of his principal supporter, General Tran Thien Khiem, who had also played a role in supporting Diem during the 1960 paratrooper attack on the Palace, raised the suspicions of the Buddhists that the Diem regime was returning without

Diem. They thus began, and continued, a series of disrupt-
ing demonstrations, their supporters and students attacking
whichever Government managed to assume what passed for
authority but offering no positive policies to help the nation
out of its dilemma.

Khanh initially put his emphasis on the need to combat
French-sponsored neutralism as a potentially popular attack on the French, and to rally the Army to carry on the
war against the Communists. He did not stand up to the
Buddhist challenges to his authority, but he tried to soften
them with concessions to their demands. This did not work,
but Khanh apparently believed this course preferable to
Diem's suppression of the Buddhists. Diem's policy, after all,
had aroused the antagonism of the Americans, whose response, viewed from the Vietnamese perspective, had been
to overthrow Diem.

But Khanh was dealing with different Americans. Lyndon Johnson had named a new Ambassador to Vietnam,
none other than General Maxwell D. Taylor. The President
and the Ambassador had little sympathy with the Buddhists, who by now had made themselves incomprehensible
and unwelcome to almost all Americans. Johnson's and
Taylor's main concern was with the anarchy engulfing
Saigon, which they thought a proper Government (and
perhaps Diem) might have overcome. Taylor's attitude toward Khanh was almost contemptuous, as he held him
responsible for the chaos of Saigon and the failure to bring
some semblance of order to both the society and the war
effort.

The Embassy used its influence to try to establish some
legitimacy in the new Government in Saigon. As a result, a
dreary series of antique civilian politicians were named
Prime Minister in a revolving-door sequence of so-called
"Governments" resting on little more than the American
insistence that they be there. When the Vietnamese military, in whom rested whatever actual power and authority
remained in the country, began to rumble about supplant-
ing them, the Americans gathered them for a dressing
down. Desist, they were told: any move risked eliminating
the little patience and hopes of support in Washington
essential to their continued existence. In one such session,

Taylor was so forceful that the Vietnamese generals complained he had treated them like a group of corporals—
which may have been how he viewed them.

Khanh also faced two coup attempts by Catholics. One
was led by Colonel Pham Ngoc Thao, the hapless former
chief of Kien Hoa province in the Delta, who in 1963 had
been plotting with former chief of intelligence and security
Tran Kim Tuyen against Diem. Thao launched a coup
attempt in February 1965, which failed, and he went into
hiding, only to be killed when his hiding place was discovered. After his death, his reputation was involved in a swirl
of intrigue and mystery as to whether in fact he had been
acting as a spoiler on behalf of Communist spymasters. A
leading Viet Cong figure, Truong Nhu Tang, who later fled
from Communist Vietnam, has alleged that Thao was
working with the Communists (his brother was North
Vietnamese Ambassador to East Germany) at the same time
he appeared to be serving Nhu and Diem as a loyal officer.
The evidence really suggests that Catholic Thao had his
own agenda for a nationalist Vietnam and was acting
against both the Diem regime and its military successors
rather than on behalf of the Communists. But the confusing admixture of motivations of this experienced Viet Minh
adherent and deeply nationalistic exponent of an effective
people's war was all too typical of the anarchic period of
Khanh's rule.

A principal source of confusion during this period was
the revival of a number of political parties and the emergence—or, in certain cases, reemergence—of civilian political figures. Some had worked with the French colonial
regime; others had opposed it as elements of the Commu-
nist-dominated, but not exclusively Communist, Viet Minh.
Several had been participants in the 1960 "Caravelle" protest against the Diem regime. Their credentials rested on
their anti-Diem records, but instead of finding unity in the
new regime, they divided and subdivided into a tangle of
contesting ambitions and claims to power and participation. All had great enthusiasm for intrigue and for endless
discussions of the ways they would bring new integrity to
the political scene. A few claimed a degree of mass support,
but there were no institutions through which their strength

and appeal to the public could be objectively measured. The American Embassy and the CIA Station wrestled each day with the dilemma of how to reconcile their claims to political participation with the absence of any substantiation of their political bases or support. What was abundantly clear was that the one thing they lacked was power.

11

The Military Answer

IN THE ANARCHY PRODUCED BY THE VACUUM in South Vietnamese leadership, power began to devolve into new hands. The original junta members were discredited and had little to offer from their exile, as I saw during a courtesy visit I made to them in Dalat during yet another of my visits to Vietnam. Khanh, in his attempts to survive by trying to please all sides, succeeded in pleasing none. A second tier of the military thus began to coalesce in order to provide a new base of power upon which the war could be fought. The Americans called them the "Young Turks." These Vietnamese officers represented a new generation of generals, such as the new head of the Air Force, Nguyen Cao Ky, who had flown the first CIA-supported parachute mission into North Vietnam, and Nguyen Van Thieu, who had supported Diem in 1960 but participated in the coup against him in 1963.

I knew Ky from our training flights together, but I did not know Thieu. The group included friends of CIA officers such as the leaders of the Navy and Marines and the paratroop commander of the 1960 coup attempt who had returned after Diem's overthrow, as well as other members of the Vietnamese military who did not have strong historical ties to the French. Their approach was national and professional, not political; their formation arose from shared revulsion at the machinations of the politicians and the political generals and the consequent chaos.

Watching the confusion in South Vietnam were two outsiders—the Communists and the Americans. The former had gradually exploited the opening the fall of Diem gave them. They stepped up their people's war to take over South Vietnam, concentrating on the major tactic of the political

175

struggle. In the countryside, this meant reinforcing the political cadres and apparatus to strengthen and spread the authority of the National Liberation Front. In the urban areas, now more open to Communist penetration, it meant the stimulation of calls for peace through negotiations between the national leadership of the Front and the battered Saigon Government, or what was left of it.

Beyond these political steps, in the fall of 1964 intelligence began to report the beginnings of preparations for action if the urban areas and the Vietnamese military forces based in them did not consent to negotiate power sharing with the Front. For the first time we began to receive reports of the movements of North Vietnamese military units down the Ho Chi Minh Trail through the mountains of Laos and the jungles of the Vietnam border area—intelligence since confirmed in historical accounts published by the victorious Communists after the war. These movements were a clear signal that the earlier tactic of sending Southern organizers and activists to build political strength in rural South Vietnam would be supplemented by military units to combat the South Vietnamese military and penetrate the final redoubts of authority in the urban areas.

Our knowledge of the difficulties of the Ho Chi Minh Trail and of the requirements for careful buildup of the necessary logistic support and assault forces made it clear that the threat was not immediate. But our equivalent knowledge of Vietnamese Communist determination meant that it was inexorable. As we looked at the dismaying scene in Saigon, we thought that end-1965 was a fair estimate of when the South Vietnamese collapse and the Communist takeover would occur.

But another outsider was looking at the scene from Washington. Lyndon Johnson, a tenacious Texan, did not take kindly to the idea of defeat, either of himself or of clients he had undertaken to support. Too much of his political life had been affected by the question "Who lost China?" and the frustrations of dealing with the intransigent Fidel Castro and his Moscow backers. He harkened to Soviet leader Khrushchev's aggressive 1961 call for Soviet support of "wars of national liberation" throughout the globe and saw it for what it was: a challenge to American predominance in the post-World War II world. In 1965, Chinese leader Lin Biao had expressed an equally aggressive determination in his call for the "rural" regions of the less developed world to rise against and isolate the "urban" developed world. Although Johnson correctly perceived the hostility of this call, he missed the subtlety of its address to a people's rather than a military strategy to achieve its goals.

No less determined were Johnson's principal aides. McNamara was convinced that the key to successful war-making lay with a rich nation such as the United States allocating resources such that no mere North Vietnam would dare contest it. He remained impervious to the question of "spirit" that Des FitzGerald had tried to draw to his attention. Secretary of State Dean Rusk believed the United States had both an interest and a duty to resist the expansion of hostile Communism in East Asia, where he had served, as it should have resisted the rise of Nazism to prevent the horrors of World War II.

The prevailing belief among these advisers was that the Vietnamese Communists should be convinced of the obvious fact that they could not win against the overpowering strength of the United States and that they would be punished if they persisted in trying. This gave rise to the many discussions of the "signals" to be sent to Hanoi by gradually escalating actions against Northern forces, communications, and bases—the participants in those discussions failing to perceive that Hanoi had in effect turned off its receivers of any such signals. There was no thought of seeking victory in North Vietnam itself. The 1950 advance to the Yalu River in North Korea and China's consequent intervention against the American forces there (leading, among the many fatalities, to the death—and posthumous Medal of Honor—of my boyhood friend Don Faith in the retreat from the Chinese human-wave attacks) set a firm precedent against any similar move against North Vietnam. From these beliefs, principles, personalities, and precedents flowed the thought processes that gave us the basic strategy the United States pursued: gradual escalation of military force aimed at the enemy's military forces in South Vietnam and at their logistics base and command links in North Vietnam.

It was an adaptation of the containment theory that had been basic American doctrine throughout the post–World War II years. On the ground in South Vietnam, the new American military commander, General William Westmoreland, limited to South Vietnam itself in what he could do to carry the war to the enemy, adopted a basic strategy of attrition of the enemy forces. But in warfare of this kind, there are no "front lines" moving encouragingly north or worrisomely south. How to demonstrate victory? The most gruesome answer to this dilemma was the "body count" of enemy—or at least those claimed to be enemy—troops. One of my more vivid memories of this device is of seeing one of Westmoreland's generals expounding on the need for higher body counts, stressing his point with an elongated arm and index finger strikingly evocative of the legendary skeleton Death.

Similarly, the air offensive against North Vietnam gradually escalated, in accordance with the many refined discussions of the "signal" that would be given Hanoi by moving the bombing line from the 18th to the 19th Parallel. The North Vietnamese authorities reacted by tightening their hold over the population of the area under attack and denouncing to them and to the rest of the world the brutal tactics of the American technological monsters against their "simple peasant society." Plainly, the "signal" was insufficient to divert the masters of the regime from the goal they had sought—and won—against the French and were still pursuing against the Americans. And the actions against the Ho Chi Minh Trail could not—and, of course, did not—stop successful delivery of the relatively small amount of logistics needed by the Communists in the South, whose tactics were to assert their secret political control in the rural areas and, except for short ambushes, to avoid conflict.

But all these were tactical considerations. The main problem Washington faced was strategic—its effort to fight its kind of war, a soldiers' war, instead of the people's war the enemy was fighting. In this situation, the Communist thrust simply went under the American military effort in South Vietnam. The American forces, trained to "find, fix, fight, and finish" the enemy, could not even find him, so

their enormous power expended itself against the jungles—
or the people in the rural areas who were the real objective
of the enemy. The finger of Death pointed too often at the
very people who should have been our allies, not our enemies.

At one point, as the American military role in South
Vietnam grew and increasingly preoccupied the American
policymakers, I spoke privately to McGeorge Bundy after
one of the White House meetings. I asked that instead of
fine-tuning the next increment of bombing North Vietnam,
we should organize some major attention to the real problem we faced: how to meet the Communist challenge at the
village level. He answered, "You may be right, Bill, but the
structure of the American Government probably won't
permit it." What he meant was that the Pentagon had to
fight the only war it knew how to fight and that there was
no organization in the American structure that could fight
any other.

In retrospect, even with Bundy's insight (no doubt correct
at the time), the gradual escalation of American power and
presence in Vietnam is difficult to comprehend, notwithstanding the considerable public support in the United
States at the time to assist our South Vietnamese ally against
the attacks from the North. The first air strikes against
North Vietnam followed the Tonkin Gulf incident in July
1964. For the next six months a variety of plans for further
attacks were considered, especially in retaliation for Communist attacks in South Vietnam aimed at Americans.
There was also a strong debate over whether American
military forces should be sent to Vietnam. President Johnson resisted both these steps. He felt the political chaos in
Saigon was the critical problem and that an American
military involvement would be both irrelevant to that problem and indecisive against the Communist threat. But increased Communist strength and, with it, greater audacity
led first to American retaliation and then to an exquisitely
intellectualized campaign of air attacks against the North.

Beginning in the border areas and then inching slowly
northward, their rationale was to convince the rulers of the
North that they should stop their war effort before the cost
to them became greater. So began Rolling Thunder. The

air campaign then brought the first U.S. troop units, Marines, on a mission ostensibly designed only to protect the airfield at Danang from which the air attacks were launched (one is reminded of Maxwell Taylor's suggestion in 1961 that American forces be brought to the Delta for a program of "flood relief"). Inexorably this defensive mission was expanded to patrolling, and the numbers increased, the military turning to its fundamental belief that the way to fight a proper war is to kill the enemy.

As this process continued, Johnson sought to offer Hanoi a carrot in the form of a promise of participation in a massive Mekong River development program funded by American aid if North Vietnam would stop the war. The Vietnamese Communists were no more influenced by this carrot than they were by the sticks of bombs. As they—and the Americans—continued to build their strength, our intelligence estimates anticipating South Vietnam's collapse by the end of 1965 included a qualifier: unless American troops held the country together. On the political side, American impatience with coups and revolving-door South Vietnamese governments grew. In a significant photograph, Secretary McNamara was shown lifting Nguyen Khanh's fist to show that he was "our" fighter.

In his determination not to lose, Johnson gradually increased the numbers of American military in the country—and their destructive effect. Over the months, he approved the Pentagon's recommendations that more increments of American military units be sent to Vietnam, each justified as necessary to stave off imminent defeat, but none offering the hope of real victory. During a visit to Washington, John Paul Vann was asked by Walt Rostow, Special Assistant to President Johnson, whether he thought the war would continue past 1965. In his iconoclastic manner, Vann replied that he thought the United States and the then Vietnamese Government could hold out much longer than that—hardly what Rostow wanted to hear.

Each increment of additional American military presence was wrung out of Johnson with great agony, and he tried to meet the need at a minimum cost to the American people—no call-up of the National Guard or Reserves. Nor were the budget requirements of his primary program, the

Great Society, touched. (The one program that did suffer from Johnson's preoccupation with Vietnam was Kennedy's Alliance for Progress with Latin America, which could have moved American Hemispheric relationships into new dimensions of cooperation and harmony.) But the attempt to conduct the war "on the cheap" lost any possible shock effect on the enemy and failed to arouse the dedication of the American people. Meanwhile the actual tactics used to wage the war were proving useless against an enemy who simply evaded whatever was done.

In the Washington policy discussions, I gradually dropped to a minor role as the focus of intelligence support shifted from whether to support the Vietnamese Government to how to employ our military forces, and especially which North Vietnamese targets to choose for air attacks— both being work more for the CIA's analysts than for its operators. This did not mean that there was not plenty to occupy me in the Far East Division of the CIA. Trying to learn what we could of developments in Communist China was time consuming, as were our efforts to follow and sometimes to influence events elsewhere in Southeast Asia. Vietnam was, however, the priority problem and engaged most of my attention, involving at least two trips there each year.

One result of the Switchback shift of covert operations against North Vietnam from the CIA to the Pentagon was that the CIA was freed of any responsibility for the events of August 1964 in the Tonkin Gulf, when the North Vietnamese attacked an American Navy destroyer in what was clearly a retaliation for a covert raid the previous night by maritime forces the CIA had initiated and turned over to the Department of Defense. A second attack two nights later also could not be attributed to the CIA's actions. My prediction to Secretary McNamara about these operations turned out to be right: they proved to be almost totally ineffective against the North. On one occasion, McNamara excitedly reported to the White House that a raiding team had been successfully landed on the North Vietnamese coast and had actually shot up a couple of trucks on the highway leading south. Having been on a similar mission in Norway in World War II, I knew full well that the trucks would be replaced the next day (as was my blown-up Norwegian bridge by the Germans) and that the only real significance of such operations is whether they reflect the resistance of the population in the area against their overlords. In North Vietnam they clearly did not.

The CIA Station in Vietnam continued to have the responsibility for covering the political machinations going on in Saigon among the contesting political groups and aspirants to power. Its reports were filled with references by the CIA's local contacts to the "necessity" for coalitions of national forces to contest the flawed credentials and performance of whoever was in office, as well as the coup plans of a variety of forces that sought American support for a new approach to the tangles of Saigon politics.

The influence of the CIA in this difficult period was probably affected to some degree by the changing personalities at the top of the American Government. Precisely the skills that had helped McCone with the Kennedy Administration caused him trouble with Lyndon Johnson. McCone's pressures for direct access to LBJ aroused the President's protective instincts against being pushed, and he was not impressed with McCone's efforts to dazzle him. On one occasion, McCone told me to take a rather large aerial photo and show the President some particular point on it that McCone was emphasizing. I could sense that LBJ felt he was being crowded, but I did as I was told. At one moment a corner of the photo came near the President's coffee cup, and he growled at me that I had better not spill it on him. I quickly agreed, and soon gave up the attempt to explain the obscurities of the photo to him, a process that would have delighted Kennedy. As LBJ gradually reduced the large groups that attended meetings with him to a few key advisers with whom he felt comfortable, it became clear that McCone's role was over. He resigned in April 1965. LBJ's first appointment to succeed McCone was an Admiral, William Raborn, who had presided over the construction program for the Polaris submarines. Admiral Raborn's enthusiasm for the PERT system of project control—Program Evaluation Review Technique—one of the early advanced "production management" techniques (which I actually found most interesting), and his innocence with respect to the subtleties of foreign cultures and their political dynamics led to a general belief that he was not the man for the job. In 1966 the President turned to the old Agency pro, Richard Helms.

Helms came, of course, from the operational side of the CIA, not the analytical. But his operational specialty was the professional collection of intelligence—the espionage trade—and its operations were what really attracted and engaged him. While as Deputy Director for Plans he had presided over and supported the Agency's political and paramilitary operations, the area in which I had spent most of my efforts, he was particularly sensitive to the dangers to which they could expose the Agency when they went wrong, as they had in the Bay of Pigs. His protective instincts for the Agency and its primary intelligence mission did not, however, in any way limit his support of the various projects I kept coming up with to help fight the Vietnamese War in the villages. He gave me almost full authority to run these operations as long as I kept him informed so that he could ensure the necessary policy approval within the National Security Council on behalf of the President.

When he became Director, Helms was equally protective of the analytical side of the Agency. In fact, the high quality and critical tone of many of the Agency's estimates about the Vietnamese War are in great part to Helms's credit. He encouraged the analysts to call the shots as they saw them, independent of whatever policy might be in favor at the time in the White House, and he protected the analysts from political pressures to "cook the estimates" in the direction of this or that advocacy. Helms was also a consummate pathfinder through the thickets of the interagency and Congressional relationships that are the key to success, and even survival, in Washington.

As the American military presence in Vietnam grew, so did the American military intelligence establishment. Much of this was very good, as it brought substantial resources to the painstaking job of filtering through masses of tiny items of information from interrogations of captives and defectors, intercepts, and tactical reports to build a comprehensive picture of the military forces facing the

South Vietnamese and American troops in the field. But the focus on the enemy's military strength again took the spotlight from his even more important political plans and activities. Moreover, the very weight of the American presence in Vietnam made it difficult for the CIA to use some of its traditional techniques for contacting and recruiting individual agents inside the enemy community, except through the South Vietnamese with whom the Station worked. This meant building the South Vietnamese capabilities to seek and maintain these delicate relationships, no small chore in itself. Involved was not just generalized training but careful one-on-one counsel through the complexities of different languages and cultures, as the American case officer carefully reviewed the identification of a possible agent in the enemy camp and discussed how he might be motivated, communicated with, and cross-checked so that his reports and comments could be turned into reliable intelligence.

As a result, there were few truly secret reports available from the inside of the enemy machinery. In fact, this was not a strategic lacuna, as the basic facts of the enemy's strategy were vociferously promulgated through its political apparatus and its radios to the Vietnamese citizenry, and the locations and ambush plans of its decentralized guerrilla forces could not have been reported in a timely fashion by secret agents. But it was another element adding to the basic American misconception of the war as an affair for soldiers on both sides, rather than a political attack by the Communists, supported by military forces.

In recent years, a false issue has been raised alleging that Westmoreland deliberately falsified the numerical count of the enemy to give a rosy picture of how the war was going in those troubled times. In fact, Westmoreland's position merely reflected the prevailing attitude that the enemy the Americans faced was a military one. An estimate of the strength of the military forces had been made by the careful processes of the order of battle specialists on the military staff. A CIA officer challenged the figures as unrepresentative of the entire enemy the Americans faced, as they omitted the various subversives who supported the enemy effort. The CIA supported its officer's position initially, but balked when he wanted to extrapolate from a small sample of how many such personnel were in the few communities on which the CIA had some figures, in order to create an estimate of what the total would be for the whole nation.

In the end, the estimate that went to the President said that the *military* forces our forces faced in South Vietnam were the total that had been determined, but that a real perception of the enemy would have to include an undetermined additional number of irregular supporters, providing food, shelter, information, and all the other contributions that would be expected from the people in a people's war. The military's estimate was not an attempt to falsify the situation they faced. Its more serious flaw was its failure to perceive that the situation they faced was a people's war.

The policy papers issued from the Pentagon under McNamara usually stressed that the mobilization of the population in support of the war effort against the enemy was the first necessity for a successful strategy. But to the military this meant establishing a government that could command the loyalty of the population through its policies—certainly not a military mission and, consequently, not their responsibility beyond recognition that someone—anyone—should take care of it. Alternatively, it meant establishing a barrier to protect the population against the nefarious influence of the enemy cadres, a strategy drawn from the Malayan experience dealing with Chinese dissidents dependent on Chinese communities. From this line of thought came some of the least effective and most counterproductive efforts of the war: a series of elephantine projects to resettle bewildered and hostile rural communities in new locations where it was believed they could be better sealed off from contact with the enemy (a few examples of which I had the misfortune to observe).

The concept was simple. The military forces would "sweep" through the selected area to drive away enemy military units, inflicting such casualties on them as they could. This action would be followed by a "screening" of the local population by Vietnamese military and civilian police to identify Communist activists or sympathizers, a process uniformly fruitless because of the lack of knowledge of the local scene on the part of the interrogators brought in from the outside. A group of prisoners would nonetheless be collected to demonstrate that the process was effective, and they would be carted off to prison.

In a particularly bizarre bit of theater, a part of the process would be designated a "county fair," meaning that the frightened inhabitants would be treated during the exercise with such niceties as music, the distribution of food, gifts for the children, and entertainment, in the hope that these palliatives would lure them into ignoring the exertion of military authority upon them. The cowed peasants would bow before these examples of authority and patiently await the end of the affair. They would then pick up the pieces of their lives in whatever new circumstances were presented to them and hope that their bending before the wind of superior power would allow it to pass while they, like the bamboo that surrounded their lives, could preserve the strength at the core of their family and village communities.

Despite the elaborate planning that went into these affairs, the results were unsatisfactory even to their military perpetrators. The numbers of enemy killed or captured were invariably small, since their units obviously faded away before the gargantuan force was deployed. The dispersed units would wait patiently for the soldiers to depart in search of new targets. The soldiery gone, they would resurface among the peasants, reassert their authority over them, benefit from the resentment at the intrusion of the hostile military, and, among themselves, chortle at their opponents' ineptness.

The resilience their strategy afforded the Communists, and their continued power in the face of the military's tactics, were decisively demonstrated on March 30, 1965, in Saigon. On that day a massive car bomb exploded in front of the American Embassy, killing two Americans and nineteen Vietnamese. Hundreds were injured, including our Chief of Station and several Agency employees, one of whom was permanently blinded. I met the evacuation plane bringing them to Washington for the care they needed to repair the devastation that flying glass had done to their faces. Greeting the family of one of those killed, and assuring them that their sacrifice was not in vain, was one of the most difficult meetings I have ever had.

There was one positive effect that came out of the frustrations of the military and their American political superiors: a renewed interest in pacification and a consequent resumption of the CIA's activities in this area. "Pacification" (I shall explain later the difficulties we had with the terminology of this activity) meant countering the Communist offensive in the countryside, in the thousands of South Vietnamese hamlets and villages where the Communists' people's war was being waged and their strategic plan was being fulfilled. In interagency meetings in Washington I had continued to press the subject, even to the extent of passing out copies of books by participants in French actions in Vietnam (which failed, but the failures were analyzed in clear terms); in Algeria (which came close to succeeding until displaced by revulsion at the atrocities the French Army committed there); and in the British experience in Malaya.

I particularly stressed the last, pointing out that the British and local forces deployed with them in successfully overcoming the Malayan "emergency" consisted of some 80,000 military, 80,000 police, and 400,000 home guards— compared to corresponding forces in Vietnam of about 300,000 Vietnamese and 200,000 American military, almost no police outside the cities, and no home guards. On most occasions my exhortations were received with great support, but when the discussion turned to which agency of the United States Government should take the lead in implementing them, there was silence. Mac Bundy's earlier comment to me was right. The structure of the American Government did not permit taking that approach.

But the ideas did spread, and the CIA Station in Saigon became alert to indications of local initiatives that offered promise. It gradually began to assist some, after securing the necessary approvals from the Vietnamese authorities and the Embassy. Thus, in Kien Hoa province (which I had visited in 1961 to meet the ill-starred Colonel Pham Ngoc Thao), the new Province Chief, Colonel Tran Ngoc Chau (later arrested for not reporting contacts with *his* North Vietnamese brother), had developed a program of sending small teams into the villages to conduct a census, in the course of which they would try to elicit the grievances of the villagers so that he could take steps to remedy them. The

Station began to support these "census-grievance" teams and to initiate the same activity in neighboring provinces. In other areas, the Information Ministry organized "armed propaganda teams"—armed for their protection while they circulated in the rural areas with the Government's word. In Central Vietnam the Station found an imaginative Vietnamese officer, Major Nguyen Be, who was putting together teams of about fifty youths to move into a village and reactivate its local government and services, moving on to another after a several-weeks stay. They also were armed, but for their protection only, as their mission was political, not military.

When I visited one such team with Be in a fishing village across the bay from Qui Nhon city in Central Vietnam, I carefully avoided any reference to their similarity to the teams launched earlier by Diem's brother Can, which we had supported, and gratefully accepted Ambassador Lodge's enthusiastic but somewhat farfetched definition of them as "precinct workers." (Lodge had returned as Ambassador in July 1965, ending General Taylor's brief and frustrating tenure. In his second tour as Ambassador in a completely alien polity and culture, Lodge still made a point of expressing himself in terms of American political life.) The Vietnamese named Major Nguyen Be's creations "People's Action Teams."

The CIA's flexibility allowed us to follow up on such experiments and local initiatives and thus to build from the bottom rather than impose a set structure from the top. The political sophistication of CIA officers enabled them to weave their way among all the civil and military authorities whose support, or at least acquiescence, was necessary to the activity. The low-key role played by CIA officers minimized the American aspect of the program and built up the importance of the Vietnamese leadership. This contrasted with some American military programs, such as the Army Special Forces' work in the highlands. There the Americans' tendency to identify with the doughty mountain people against the Vietnamese authorities eventually sparked a full-scale revolt in 1965 by the "Montagnards" seeking political autonomy. Once again the Americans were presented with a tangled dilemma: how to reconcile their basic support of the Vietnamese Government with the loyalties the Special Forces felt for their Montganard fighters.

During this period of groping for an approach that could get at the critical element of the war at the local community level, the U.S. Marines developed a program of Combined Action Platoons, which paired a Marine squad with a Vietnamese village force platoon to provide all-night defense for a village in place of the occasional visits of the regular military. The program was a success for as long as the Marines remained, but in due course it became clear that effective leadership was taken by the Americans and the Vietnamese merely followed. When the Americans departed, practically nothing remained of the security the local inhabitants so avidly desired.

At about this time, McNamara asked the CIA to create a technique for measuring trends in the countryside, where he recognized the real people's war was being fought. While this was, to some degree, an effort at quantification, it was also a recognition of the difference between Vietnam and the two previous wars fought by the United States. The Korean War had been simple to follow. If the Allied lines and troops moved north, we were winning—in the same way we had been able to follow General Patton's progress across France (or, for that matter, Grant's advance on Richmond). In Vietnam, where there was no such movement of armies until the very end, the military sought to define their progress in the atrocious "body counts" of the casualties they thought they had inflicted on the enemy—ignoring the fact that in a people's war a guerrilla and "the people" cannot be distinguished when they are dead.

The CIA's analysts in Washington took this on and went to the real purpose of the military actions to seek a means of judging whether the population was in fact being protected by the military. We turned to the advisory personnel who, living in each of the districts of Vietnam, were familiar with the villages and hamlets. Many a visitor to the Vietnamese countryside had witnessed the district Chief's sweep of his hand to say that *that* area was really quite stable, but—the arm sweeping again—*there* the enemy is present in force. We needed to make that distinction more specific.

In response to this need, the CIA produced a "Hamlet Evaluation System" (HES) to measure the security, political, and economic situation in each of the hamlets of South Vietnam as a better way to determine the status of the real war at that level than the military's reports of military actions and "body counts." The HES focused on simple indicators of the real situation in the rural communities, such as whether the village Chief slept in his community or sought safer haven in the nearby protected district center. It sought answers on a scale from good to bad for such factors as the prevalence of enemy attacks or presence in the area. It noted whether there was a functioning school, and other indications of whether life was nearly "normal" or dominated by the Viet Cong. The American district adviser, whether civilian or military, was required to file monthly reports on a computer form, characterizing the situation in each of the twenty to fifty hamlets in his district.

The various indicators making up the report were summed up in an aggregate grade for the hamlet or village as a rule-of-thumb indicator of how the people's war was progressing—or regressing—there. A community under full Communist control was assigned the letter V, and none of the detailed questions were answered—or perhaps they could not be. Correspondingly, a community with no Communist activity whatever, an elected leadership living calmly in the village which was equipped with a school, a local defense unit, a bustling market, and confidence, would be graded A. (There were not many of these, but there were some, especially in the province of the Delta peopled and controlled by the Hoa Hao religious sect, whose leader and saint had been killed by the Communists.) The scale originally ran from A to E, plus V. Much of the country lay between A and V, of course, from the B—not so well off as the A—to the E—heavily influenced by the enemy but in which some brave citizens were trying to maintain their independence of Communist rule. Many fell into category C, where the main battle for their loyalties and their participation on one side or the other was under way.

No one pretended that these categorizations were accurate in themselves. They could be influenced by the adviser's not getting to the hamlet that month, by his district Chief pushing him to give him a better grade, or by his own inexperience early in his one-year tour. But the results, in the aggregate, gave an overall estimate of how the war was going as the numbers of Bs or Ds rose or fell over the months and the contrasts among different districts and areas became clear. We all knew the weaknesses inherent in the system and, from the Ambassador on down in the years to come, stressed that the figures were merely indicators of trends, not absolute reports of the facts—complex as they were—on the ground. The media regularly held the HES up to ridicule, but it was useful to us who were managing the overall programs and determining which areas needed more effort, and it was equally useful to the Vietnamese authorities as an assessment independent of the self-interest of their local authorities, with their tendency to file rosy reports. And the system certainly related better to a people's war than did body counts.

When Lodge returned in 1965 for his second tour as Ambassador, he became fascinated with the subject of pacification and buttressed his interest by bringing back to Vietnam General Edward Lansdale as his personal adviser and counselor. With all his enthusiasm and advocacy of the importance of pacification, however, Lodge was no manager for an enterprise as large and complex as the American involvement in Vietnam had become. Each of the many U.S. Government agencies present tended to do its own thing and to run its own projects with minimal coordination, while Lodge exhorted Washington to put more stress on pacification. His advocacy paid dividends, however, in energizing the American bureaucracy to conduct a series of studies and conferences on the problems. In them I enthusiastically promoted the merits of securing the active participation of the local population in the improvement of their lives and security instead of sending alien forces to provide those improvements.

As we tried to develop a pacification strategy, it became clear that better coordination and interaction among the agencies involved were essential. The various studies and conferences, combined with additional emphasis on the subject by high Washington officials, produced a number of plans for greater efforts at pacification—and for greater coordination among the American agencies conducting the programs. But each contained substantial flaws in that they contemplated only coordination, not single command direction of the program.

The AID programs of assistance to education, health, and public works might be better related to the CIA-supported teams trying to improve the villagers' ability to obtain teachers, medical service, or better rural roads, for example, and the USIA might have more specific case studies of the effectiveness of these programs to broadcast to the population. But each one of these programs had to be carried out by the particular Vietnamese Ministry and its local representatives with whom the American agency would be dealing. No one was in charge in the province to concentrate all the programs on particular communities at the same time and in support of one another. All these plans for better American coordination also perpetuated the greatest flaw of all: they covered only civilian aspects of the program, leaving the military independent to conduct their war on their own.

Most important, these small steps toward integration of the pacification programs of the different agencies took place in the shadow of Washington's interminable debate over the bombing campaign against North Vietnam. Any possible light emerging from these lesser initiatives was completely eclipsed in the attention of the policymakers by the exquisite refinements of targeting and elaboration of the gradual escalation of pressure that was supposed to convince the North to abandon the war. The fascination of the higher levels of the Government with this subject, and their failure to perceive the nature of a people's war, was perhaps best expressed by Walt Rostow, Special Assistant to the President, when he said that bombing of North Vietnam would be our form of guerrilla war to match the attacks by the Communists against the Government in the South. At one point in these exercises, I exploded in total frustration to one of my colleagues, "For God's sake, let them go bomb something, anything, so they can get it out of their systems! Then maybe we can get them to turn their attention to fighting the war where it has to be fought." That place, as was finally but tardily realized, was the war in the villages.

12

Different Countries, Different Answers

THE AMBITIONS OF THE Indochinese Communist Party in Hanoi were not limited to South Vietnam. Two considerations turned the attention of the North Vietnamese leaders to neighboring Laos. One was geography. With the mountains of Laos being uncomfortably close to the Red River Valley and Hanoi, the North Vietnamese wanted to be sure that no threat could emanate from them. The other was history. Because Laos had shared Vietnam's subjection to French rule and the influence of France on its culture and governing institutions, the Party leaders considered it as much an element of the Indochina they hoped to rule as Vietnam itself.

The Kingdom of Laos was sharply divided between the Lao people, who lived in the west along the Mekong River at the foot of the mountains, and various tribal peoples in the mountains to the east, who shared an ethnic and cultural background with the numerous tribes occupying the mountainous areas of Southwestern China, Burma, Vietnam, and Thailand. To advance their aims in Laos, the North Vietnamese had formed a political vehicle called the Pathet Lao, and Lao supporters were recruited to be the token leaders of the effort, which depended for its direction and support on Hanoi.

In Laos there were two major political currents. One was frankly anti-Communist, chiefly military and colonial bureaucratic in composition, and welcoming Thai and American help in this microcosm of the worldwide Cold War. The other took its inspiration from the neutralism and nonalignment popular in other areas of South and Southeast Asia such as India and Indonesia, seeking to avoid involvement in great power contests and to be left alone.

During the late fifties and early sixties, the Eisenhower Administration had responded to the problems in Laos by increasing assistance to the Lao military and supporting nationalist military leaders in an effort to establish some form of stable government. At one point, there was a discussion of whether I should be detached from my assignment in Saigon to become the principal liaison officer to General Phoumi Nosovan, one of the leaders of the royal forces against the Communists and neutralists.

Early in the Kennedy Administration, Laos became front-page news. On nationwide television, the new President stood before a map of that faraway nation and asserted that the increase of Communist forces there, and the spread of their control, was putting Laos in danger of collapse. To demonstrate his resolve on the matter, Kennedy ordered preparations to send U.S. military and air units to Northern Thailand for use in Laos if necessary (though he acceded to the Joint Chiefs of Staff's objections to inserting U.S. forces into a region that presented so many operational and logistical difficulties). The President's problems were ostensibly solved by Nikita Khrushchev's acceptance of Kennedy's offer to negotiate the neutralization of Laos, Khrushchev believing that the country would drop into his hands like a "ripe tomato."

It was then that Kennedy assigned Averell Harriman to the negotiations, the objective being the neutralization of Laos, with the international control machinery needed to ensure that it remained neutral. Kennedy and Khrushchev made their deal over Laos at their 1961 meeting in Vienna, where the President first personally experienced the harshness of the Soviets' aims and maneuvers on the question of Berlin. Harriman's negotiations culminated in the 1962 Geneva Accords on Laos, in which all fourteen nations participating, including North Vietnam, agreed to recognize and respect a "neutral and independent Laos."

One of the provisions of the Geneva Accords was that all the nations would withdraw their "military and paramilitary" forces from Laos. The Soviet Union complied, and its Air Force planes that were resupplying the North Vietnamese and the Pathet Lao disappeared from Laotian skies. The United States did the same, and the American Special

Forces personnel and the CIA's paramilitary advisers left the country. The North Vietnamese, however, who had about 7,000 troops in the country—mostly in North Laos, where they were not exposed to outside inspection—left them in place. To the International Control Commission, charged with supervising the withdrawal, the North Vietnamese announced that they had removed forty soldiers— all they had in the country, they said.

It was Averell Harriman's role as chief American negotiator of the Geneva Accords on Laos and the President's chief action officer to make the Accords work, which, of course, made him so insistent about American compliance with them in my early discussions with him in 1962 when I took over the CIA's Far East Division. Harriman had no illusions that compliance on the other side would be easy to secure, but he wanted the fault for a breakdown, if one occurred, to be clearly theirs, not ours. At his insistence, our paramilitary advisers were withdrawn from the country, and our "private" Air America planes ceased their drops of arms and supplies to the Hmong and other tribal groups with whom we had established relations during the previous years. Harriman's approval, given somewhat grudgingly, to leave two CIA officers up in the mountain highlands to monitor the situation and report to us what was happening there was conditioned on a strict prohibition against sending them any weapons or military supplies, and each flight had to be personally approved in advance by Harriman.

The reports from the two CIA observers became more and more ominous. The North Vietnamese were not content simply to remain in Laos in violation of the Accords. They began to move aggressively to expand the area controlled by their puppet Pathet Lao, using regular North Vietnamese troops to do so. As this became clear, Harriman authorized me to approve resupply flights of ammunition and similar supplies but insisted that these be limited to use for "purely defensive purposes." This was easy, as the actions were occurring in areas where the North Vietnamese were pushing the Hmong communities out of their traditional areas; the flood of refugees moving to the west made clear the nature of the conflict. The clandestine flights lifting off from our base in Northern Thailand consequently became more frequent, and we were able to increase the numbers of CIA personnel on the ground to monitor what was being done with our supplies.

The CIA's capabilities for "covert" action became the key to our position with respect to Laos. Since its activities were officially secret, they could be conducted without official exposure or admission to the world—particularly the Soviet Union. As a result, the Soviets could officially ignore them. They in fact did so for ten years, keeping their Embassy open in Ventiane, the capital of Laos, and dealing there with the American Embassy, knowing full well that the Americans were operating and supplying in Laos. Since the Soviet position was that they had complied with the Accords by withdrawing their participation and that they had no responsibility for (nor in truth, much influence over) the North Vietnamese, they could stick to the Kennedy-Khrushchev deal that the United States and the Soviet Union not have a confrontation in Laos. Moreover, the fact that the CIA was the responsible agency on the American side meant that the U.S. military, with its traditional large staffs and support structure, was not engaged. The CIA Station took its instructions directly from the American Ambassador (and Harriman made sure that these were strong people of the stuff of William Sullivan and MacMurtrie Godley—not afraid to insist on full Ambassadorial control but also not afraid to approve and take responsibility for risky and dangerous missions).

From the Agency we sent our best officers, insisting that their responsibilities were not merely paramilitary but also political. The CIA had run across a natural leader among the Hmong named Vang Pao, who had been a Sergeant in the French Army but had risen to Major (about as far as one of tribal origin could go) in the Royal Lao Army after independence. Working closely with Vang Pao in the mountains, we had come to appreciate his courage, his understanding of his people, and his ability to fight the kind of guerrilla war against the North Vietnamese that was called for in the mountains of North Laos. We, and he, made it clear that he would give the orders and run the war and that CIA officers were there to help him with supplies, communications, air transport, and training, but not to supplant him.

One of the delicate political issues we faced was how to handle the relationship between the Hmong forces, directly supported by the CIA, and the Lao Government to which they were theoretically subordinate. Harriman was quite suspicious in the early period that the CIA might go off on its own in support of a nationalist, hard-line military leader, in conflict with his policy of convincing the neutralist Head of Government, Prince Souvanna Phouma, that the United States truly supported the idea of a "neutral and independent" Laos. As we gradually convinced Harriman that the CIA was following his directions, the North Vietnamese were simultaneously convincing the Prince that they had no intention of respecting his independence and neutrality. In the unfolding of this process, the Prince saw that the American assistance to his forces and his regime was being handled in a quiet and unobtrusive manner (by the CIA), without compromising his assertions of neutrality. Far from resisting the American intervention, he came to welcome it.

But there was the other side of this coin. How would the Hmong react to direct American aid? Would they take it as a warrant for assertion of their separation or autonomy from the lowland Lao, for whom they had little liking and whom they viewed as having exploited them for generations? The Agency's response to this problem was to stress the integration of the Hmong effort into the Lao nation. Vang Pao, after the exercise of some discreet influence, became a General in the Royal Lao Army; the King made a highly publicized visit to the main Hmong center in the mountains to receive the appropriate homage; and the main radio program developed by the CIA to communicate with the dispersed tribal peoples of Laos was named the "Union of the Lao Races" to make clear the national rather than ethnic basis for the struggle. The contrast with the tribal uprising that developed among the highlanders of Vietnam when the Agency's role there was eliminated under "Switchback" was dramatic.

Apart from their geopolitical importance, the significance of the Agency's operations in Laos was to prove the conclusions of the review commission after the Bay of Pigs to have been wrong. The CIA conducted a major paramilitary operation in Laos for ten years. The forces directly supported by the CIA numbered something over 30,000 full-time troops in the tribal areas, with their own officers and command structures. The total number of CIA personnel who supported this effort was between 300 and 400. Because of the strict orders they received not to participate in combat operations, the number of American CIA personnel killed was fewer than ten, those mostly in helicopter crashes.

The Agency's operations were supported by its "private" fleet of transport aircraft and helicopters, Air America, which delivered everything from rice bags for refugees to observation teams high in the mountains over the Ho Chi Minh Trail. (Occasionally I was part of the cargo, deposited with a crash landing on a tiny dirt strip on the top of a mountain from which, at takeoff, altitude was instantaneously 2,000 feet as one quit the runway's edge and the mountain dropped away behind and below; or we rocked from side to side during a ten-foot altitude approach along the Mekong under a morning fog bank, twisting and turning to avoid the islands in the river.) We even trained several Hmong to be pilots, flying spotter aircraft over their tribal homeland areas for U.S. Air Force attack bombers against the mutual enemy.

Most significantly, the enemy was fought to a standstill. After ten years the battle lines in Laos were approximately where they were at the start, although the North Vietnamese forces had increased from 7,000 to 70,000 (troops thereby not available to help fight the Americans in South Vietnam). The contrast with the engagements in Vietnam was striking. The nature of the Laotian people's war was guerrilla operations, ambushing North Vietnamese units dependent on the few roads and disappearing into the mountainous jungle when the enemy attacked—a mirror image of the positions of the two sides in South Vietnam.

Eventually, the North Vietnamese regulars built up the pressures against the lightly armed Hmong. Even though the Hmong developed regular battalions and artillery support from helpful Thai, escalation of the conflict worked to their disadvantage when direct American air support was reduced. The Royal Lao Army never really entered the conflict directly, remaining in the Mekong Valley (where some of *their* generals—not Vang Pao or his officers, and certainly not the CIA or Air America—profited from the opium trade instead of joining battle). But the success of the CIA's operation can be judged by the fact that the North Vietnamese finally accepted a second agreement, in 1973, which called for a "neutral and independent" Laos and the withdrawal of all foreign military and paramilitary forces from the Kingdom. Again, as in 1962, the United States (and the CIA) complied, and again the North Vietnamese did not, withdrawing only one of the three divisions they had in the country. Soon they resumed their pressures, but there was no American, or CIA, reaction, and Laos today is a Communist country under Hanoi's domination, with the CIA's friends in exile, dead, or living under oppression.

Neighboring Thailand also looked inviting to the Communists. In Northeast Thailand, there was a large colony of ethnic North Vietnamese who had moved there from Laos and North Vietnam during the First Indochina War against the French. They had been infiltrated by the North Vietnamese authorities and were considered a substantial threat by the Thai Government and security services. In addition, Communist China made threatening noises toward the Thai Kingdom. A substantial percentage of the citizens of Thailand are ethnically Chinese, from the great emigration into Southeast Asia at the turn of the twentieth century. A vigorous radio program, the "Voice of the Thai People," emanated from Yunnan Province in southwest China, calling for solidarity with the revolutionary forces of Asia led by China. An active underground existed in Thailand, supported from China with cadres, training, and revolutionary appeals. On Thailand's southern border with Malaysia, the remnants of the Communist revolt that had convulsed Malaysia during the 1950s continued to train and occasionally attack installations in the region, although they had effectively been defeated by the British and Malaysians in that "Emergency."

As the Thai saw insurgency increase in Laos and South Vietnam in the early 1960s, they considered how they should react. The Thai nation is unified in support of its royal family and in adherence to Buddhism, and its leaders properly assessed that it was not subject to the divisive problems of its neighbors without such a tradition of unity and loyalty. In addition, the Thai had a long tradition of independence, and indeed were the only nation in the region that never knew colonial status. They had cooperated over the centuries with a number of nations predominant in the area for a time, but had never subjected themselves to foreign domination or rule. The Thai armed forces played a major role in the life of the nation, but the police had been developed (more or less on the British model in their colonies) as the principal organ for rural security in support of the civil administration.

Out of these considerations, the Thai developed their own approach to the strengthening of their kingdom against the revolutionary forces around them. We in the CIA were deeply involved in helping them do so, to the extent that many years later I received an appreciative note from one of the leading figures of the Thai effort at that time to the effect that I had "introduced" the concept that the military, the police, and the civil administration work as a team during my various visits to Thailand during the 1960s. In truth, the Thai themselves came up with their own solution, and we in the CIA merely encouraged and supported them—a much more effective use of our influence. The Thai Police, and particularly the Border Police and its Police Aerial Resupply Unit (PARU), worked closely with the Thai military and the civil administration to produce a Volunteer Defense Corps to operate at the village level in the threatened areas. The Corps program was carefully coordinated at the national and regional levels with full representation of all three elements concerned. And the principal objective was *defense*, not the attack of the enemy, although that was included in the program.

One contribution to the Thai program was American, in the person of Ambassador Graham Martin. At an early stage, he made it clear that he, not the military, would be in charge of U.S. policy and operations in Thailand. He also insisted that the Thai would determine the strategy and the tactics of the program, and that the Americans would not impose their ideas. When he arrived in Thailand I was somewhat concerned as the CIA, in the person of a great, red-headed, friendly, and uncomplicated American who was our Chief of Station, had established warm and close relations with every important Thai leader. The apocryphal story was that he would be sitting behind the King when the Ambassador presented his credentials. My concern was that Martin would consider himself hopelessly outclassed in relationships with the Thai and decide that he had to change personnel. I therefore told my Chief in no uncertain terms that his first job was to gain the Ambassador's confidence that he was working for him, not independently of him. To the credit of both men, it worked out perfectly. My Chief fully accepted the fact that he was to do what he could to help the Ambassador in his mission, and Martin quickly determined that he could use the Chief of Station to say things and do things that no Ambassador could.

The unlikely two became a team, and an effective one, however many times my Chief (and, on my visits, I) had to listen to the Ambassador's recitation that he was the *President's* representative in Thailand, senior to any other American there. One thing they agreed upon, as did I, was that the American military should not take a dominant role in counseling the Thai on how to handle their insurgency. This aroused a substantial amount of opposition to Martin among some American military officials, who wanted to establish a proper Southeast Asian Command to provide formal military coordination for the different insurgency and military problems and operations in Vietnam, Laos, and Thailand. The Ambassador, like his fellows in Laos and Cambodia, thought the problems of the nations concerned sufficiently different that they needed separate, not uniform, treatment, and they were right.

The proof of the pudding was in the eating. The Thai approach to their insurgency problem worked, and the threat gradually diminished as the village and hill tribe programs brought economic and social benefits to the local communities—in the people's minds, the source of those benefits became linked to the representatives of the Thai Government who worked among them. By the late 1960s, the insurgency threat had essentially gone away, a tribute to the work of the Thai officials who saw the importance of a team effort among the civil authorities, the police, and the

military in building strength among the threatened communities rather than seeking to kill the enemy attacking
them.

Across the South China Sea from Vietnam, the Philippines in the 1960s were experiencing a revival of the insurgency that had been largely put down a decade before.
Responding to the (competing) calls by Khrushchev and
Lin Biao for revolutionary effort throughout the world, and
seeing the rise of the Communist insurgency in South
Vietnam, the Philippine Hukbalahap movement reappeared. While it did not encounter the inspiring leadership
of President Magsaysay, who, with Ed Lansdale's help,
stopped it in the 1950s, it did face a Philippine Government
with a number of the organizational tools and programs
needed to respond effectively in the local communities. The
Philippine programs of rural development, local government, and the work of the Constabulary (a rural police force
separate from the Army) had only to be combined to encourage the people of the barrios to work together in resisting the insurgents and in creating a better future with
Government support. I visited one of the training centers
for this effort in Tarlac province, north of Manila, where
the Hukbalahap had been strong in the early 1950s and
were now trying to restore their position. But the CIA role
here was minimal; the Philippine services knew exactly
how to go about their program, although our exchange of
experience and enthusiasm helped. The Communist revival
during that period never rose to a major threat. Under the
corrupt Marcos dictatorship years later, of course, it again
grew into a major problem.

Cambodia was another story. There the charisma and
leadership of Prince Sihanouk unified the nation and left
little room for any opposition. American policy overcame
its moralistic rejection of his neutralism, and accepted it for
the benefits he offered by ensuring that Cambodia would
not become the cause for another major crisis between
Hanoi and the United States. Thus we respected Cambodia's neutrality, despite the fact that its soil was used as a
base for supplying and sustaining the Communists attacking South Vietnam. The CIA Station there was quiescent,
merely trying to keep abreast of what was happening in the

country and the extent to which it was being used by the North Vietnamese.

Which was substantial, as we learned later. The CIA's analysts carefully measured what they thought was the required logistical support of Viet Cong operations in South Vietnam and determined (correctly) that it was so small that it could easily be carried over the Ho Chi Minh Trail along the Annamite mountains from North Vietnam. They therefore concluded that since there was no hard evidence of Communist use of the ports of Cambodia for supply purposes, there was none. Only after the overthrow of Sihanouk by his generals, concerned that he had sacrificed the sovereignty of the nation by allowing full exploitation of its territory by the North Vietnamese, did the evidence of the massive shipments to the South through Cambodian ports come to light, replete with bills of lading and detailed records of the trucking companies that serviced the Vietnamese border areas with the weapons, rockets, and ammunition used against the South Vietnamese and American forces there.

The Communists' use of Cambodian border areas as sanctuaries for their supplies, headquarters, logistics, and replacement processing centers was well known. What was less well known was the fact that these activities went on in parts of Cambodia that were almost empty of people, rather like the frontier regions of the Canadian and Alaskan Yukon. When the Americans decided that these Vietnamese Communist concentrations had to be attacked and concealed the "violation of Cambodian sovereignty" over the areas in question to do so, the uproar in the United States at this "illegality" was enormous. But Sihanouk's reaction at the time, and later, was not to protest this action by the Americans against their enemies in an area in which the North Vietnamese had already preempted Cambodian sovereignty and in which few, if any, Cambodians resided. On the contrary, Sihanouk in fact even welcomed it as a way to eject the North Vietnamese from Cambodian territory.

The key fact about Cambodia was that the Americans and their South Vietnamese allies essentially accepted Cambodian neutrality in the struggle between North and South Vietnam, while the North Vietnamese gave "fraternal assistance" to Pol Pot and his ultimately atrocious Khmer Rouge. The later takeover of Cambodia by the North Vietnamese was presented as a reaction to the genocide of a million or more Cambodians executed or starved by Pol Pot's Communists in their campaign to extirpate those who had in any way benefited as a result of French colonial rule. But that invasion came too late to save the Cambodian people. It is difficult to separate that invasion entirely from the North Vietnamese ambition to control *all* of Indochina—or from the hostilities with China that were largely coincident with it.

But the question pertinent to this inquiry that arises is whether an extension of the CIA approach to local security and development might have strengthened Cambodia against the obscene fate that awaited it—as the Agency's programs manifestly helped in Thailand and were effective in Laos for ten years.

13

Turning Point

THE YEAR 1967 MARKED A TURNING POINT in the war in Vietnam. It saw the emergence there of four men who would finally find a strategy to fight the war and invent the organization to carry it out. They built upon the preliminary work done by others before them, but they took an entirely new approach. Behind them all loomed the figure of Lyndon Johnson, as he shook the American and Vietnamese Governments (and many of our allies) in tormented lunges to find a formula that would overcome the exasperating confusion and lack of success he had inherited in South Vietnam.

Johnson's first move in this act of the Vietnamese drama took place in March 1966. It was his response to various appeals for more attention to the civilian side of the war on the ground in Vietnam, instead of only in policy papers in Washington, and to his own empathy for and sense of the political value of social progress. He demanded that what he called "the other war" be energized and given a priority equivalent with the military one. To make it clear to the bureaucracy that he personally would be keeping close score on how it responded to his orders, he appointed a Special Assistant in the White House to exercise "supervision" of the effort. He chose exactly the right man to do so.

Robert W. Komer was then on the National Security Council staff in the White House, covering the Middle East. He had begun his intelligence career in Italy at the end of World War II, studied at Harvard, advocated the "opening to the left" in Italy as a fervent Democratic supporter of President Kennedy, and then had turned his attention to the Middle East as a CIA analyst, from where he had been brought into the NSC. "Analyst" is too mild a term to describe Komer. No shrinking violet, he had utilized each of his positions in the most activist fashion possible, to the extent that a major crisis between Nasser's Egypt and North Yemen came to be called "Komer's war" by those in the American bureaucracy subjected to his pressures. Johnson had noticed his drive in his White House post and thought him the right man to get the bureaucracy moving on "the other war."

Komer came on to the Vietnam assignment with full force. He made it very plain that in his vocabulary "supervision" meant something more than the familiar bureaucratic rain dance of "coordination." He challenged foot-dragging in any department or agency by immediate reference to Johnson to apply the appropriate tongue-lashing to the Presidential appointee at its head. As chief of the CIA's operations in the Far East, I came directly under Komer's gun—and loved it. Finally I had found someone who understood the need for a pacification strategy and who had the clout to push the Washington agencies into producing it on the ground in Vietnam. He understood what the CIA Station was trying to do in its various experimental programs in the countryside. Insisting only that more be done, he provided the policy approval we needed to do it.

It soon became clear that Washington "supervision," however forceful, was not enough. The same kind of single authority was needed in the field in Vietnam. The halting steps that had been taken there were not proving effective. The military had set up a special section in the Command Headquarters to provide "Revolutionary Development Support" (RDS) in order to force some attention to pacification onto subordinate units, and to emphasize the subject in the military advisory teams that by now had proliferated beyond the regular Vietnamese Army units to the "sectors" or provincial units concerned with territorial security. The section was only one of the myriad elements of the Command Headquarters, however, and had little impact on the main line of thinking there.

The civilian agencies had been brought together in an "Office of Civil Operations" (OCO) under a Deputy Ambassador in the Embassy. It became a sort of traditional "Country Team," providing relatively passive "coordination" of the actions of the various agencies but no central strategic thrust. Certainly Lodge was not the man to impose and manage such a strategy. The Washington offices of the various agencies found the situation thoroughly satisfactory, as their lines of authority to their personnel and programs in Vietnam were undisturbed.

The civilian agencies had a serious reservation about altering this arrangement. They were fearful that a single authority in Vietnam would probably be a military one. Their experience thus far with the military convinced them that this would result in the civilian programs becoming only an adjunct to the military operations—cleaning up the battlefield behind the troops, so to speak, and lost in the staff structure with which the military ran the war. The military had their own concern—the sacrosanct necessity of unity of command during a war so that all aspects of it could be directed according to a single strategy. The military were willing to assume authority over the pacification program, but they were not willing to change their organizational structure to do so.

To resolve this impasse, Komer came up with an ingenious compromise. The pacification-related programs of all the agencies, military and civilian, would be placed under a single manager, not a coordinator, who would be named a Deputy to the American military Commander, General William Westmoreland. It was understood that this Deputy would be a civilian, in order to reassure the civilian agencies. The fact that the military personnel and programs related to pacification, especially assistance and advisory support of the local security forces in the rural areas, would come under his authority meant that all aspects of pacification, not just the civilian ones, could be conducted under a single strategy. The civilian programs would not be subordinated to the military's concentration on seeking out the enemy. On the other hand, the military insistence on unity of command was respected so that conflicts between the military and civilian programs could be resolved in Vietnam rather than in Washington.

Having come up with this solution to the problem, Lyndon Johnson sent Komer out to Vietnam to carry it out, to no one's particular surprise, including Komer's. Again he

came on to the scene with full force, insisting to startled
American generals that his position as Westmoreland's
Deputy (and the rank of Ambassador that Johnson gave
him) put him at four-star rank with the three other Deputies, his limousine equaling theirs in size with four stars on
its front. He was meticulous in his subordination to Westmoreland, who gave him full support and scope to bring
the various programs affecting pacification together, both
out of conviction that this needed to be done and with some
relief that he could let Komer do it while he continued to
conduct the military war that he saw as his primary responsibility.

Perhaps Komer's most important contribution was a serious effort to build up the territorial security forces in
numbers, weapons (at this late date in the war, they finally
received modern M-16 rifles, which the Army had had for
years), equipment, training, and advisory support, thereby
reversing years of American emphasis on the regulars of the
Vietnamese Army and neglect of the troops who bore the
brunt of the Communists' attacks at the village level. He
also compelled the disparate American civilian agencies
and the military to bring their rural programs under a
single American advisory team at the province level. He
placed major stress on getting good people to staff those
teams, taking good officers from each of the agencies and
putting them into fully integrated teams under a single
Province Senior Adviser. About half of these top posts were
filled by Colonels and Lieutenant-Colonels and the other
half by equally senior officers from AID, the Foreign Service, the CIA, and the USIA. The State Department made a
particular contribution when it peeled off about fifty of its
bright, young Foreign Service Officers and sent them to
language school to learn Vietnamese, making them particularly attractive candidates for these combined teams—in
effect ambassadors in charge of a full American mission to
a province or district. It was invaluable experience for the
real ambassadorial posts they would later be called upon to
assume.

But Komer could not have been as effective as he was
without the second key figure who emerged in 1967, Ellsworth Bunker. A true patrician, graduate of Yale (and

classmate of Averell Harriman), he was now in his early
seventies but held his trim body ramrod straight. He had
turned to Government service after a full career as a banker
and investor. A succession of Presidents had already used
him in posts of great challenge, as Ambassador to Brazil,
Italy, and India, as well as on such diplomatic tangles as the
Nasser/Yemen conflict (where he first met Komer), the
Dominican Republic crisis in 1965, and the West Irian
negotiations between Sukarno's Indonesia and the Dutch in
their struggle to hold onto the last piece of their East Indies
empire. It was in connection with the West Irian problem
that I first experienced Bunker's calm command of a complex controversy, his insistence that he be given the facts
without bureaucratic gamesmanship, and his clear focus on
the essentials of a problem. With his air of distinction and
formality, he was invariably mild and soft in manner, but
he exuded the authority of his office and made it clear that
he would brook no lack of discipline.

President Johnson sent Bunker to replace Cabot Lodge as
Ambassador to Vietnam in May 1967. Lodge had proven no
more able to manage the American mission on his second
try than on his first, but he had turned from antagonism to
the Vietnamese Government to sympathy, and, in a bizarre
gesture that only a few of us who had been around for some
time noticed, he dressed for his departure ceremony in the
Mandarin costume he had found so reeking of a medieval
court when he first saw it on President Diem. As one of his
first actions, Bunker presided over the announcement of
Komer's new authority and position and quietly made it
clear to the American civilian agencies that they would
comply fully with the new structural arrangement.
Bunker's aura of authority was equally impressive to the
military and to the Vietnamese and further solidified Komer's new role.

The third key figure who emerged during 1967 was
Vietnamese, General Nguyen Van Thieu. He had risen in
the ranks of the Vietnamese Army through his talent, his
background as a product of the Central Vietnamese province of Phan Rang, and a high degree of caution in working his way through the partisan disputes that characterized Vietnam in the 1960s. As a division commander located

to the south of Saigon, he had joined the forces relieving President Diem from the paratrooper coup of November 1960, but he had restrained his troops from any action other than quietly demonstrating their superiority over the frustrated paratroopers, thus allowing the insurgents to disband without a direct conflict. He had joined the coup plan against Diem in 1963 as a loyal member of the Army, and because he believed Diem could rule no longer, but had insisted as a condition that the coup be conducted without violence to Diem. He had remained aloof from the series of feckless juntas that had succeeded Diem but had become one of the group of Vietnamese officers the Americans named the "Young Turks," who began to insist on some coherent government for the country in order to conduct the war. His low-key style had left him in a secondary position to the flamboyant air commander Nguyen Cao Ky in this group, but his cautious tactics enabled him to remain as one of the leaders of the military who held the country together during the chaotic political turbulence of the mid-1960s.

By 1967, the string had run out on the old-fashioned civilian political leaders who had demonstrated their incompetence, and the Young Turks moved to assume power to provide some order and structure for the nation. American pressure translated this into the need for a formal Constitution, the first since Diem's. This was laboriously constructed by a Constituent Assembly in early 1967 calling for presidential elections to establish a political base for a Vietnamese Government. It was generally believed that Air Marshal Ky would be the Armed Forces and Young Turk candidate for the Presidency and easily elected by the few voters who could be corralled to the polls. At this point, however, Thieu made his move and insisted that the Armed Forces Council support him for the nomination. He prevailed, pushing Ky down to the position of Vice President despite (and perhaps partially because of) the American expectation that he would be the nominee.

The major American pressure was addressed to preserving the unity of the Vietnamese Armed Forces, whomever they selected as their nominee. In the event, the nomination of Thieu ensured his election as the new President, and it was clear that a new style of leadership was in store for

Vietnam. A wee bit dull, careful to maintain contact and confidence among the Americans, especially with Ellsworth Bunker, and relying fundamentally upon the Vietnamese military commanders who controlled the regions and divisions where real power rested, Thieu gradually assembled a power base of military subordinates and civilian experts (we would now call them "technocrats,") through whom he could run the Government from day to day, keep the enemy at bay, and adjust to the varying enthusiasms of the Americans upon whose assistance he realized any hope for Vietnam rested in the long term.

Thieu initially saw Komer's appointment as yet another variant of the many new American organizational devices that had proliferated in Vietnam. He patiently heard Komer out as the latter explained how he would be integrating the American machinery to support pacification. At first, Thieu saw little in the process which required that he be more than receptive to Komer's ideas, while maintaining his principal relationship with Bunker as the chief American representative and Westmoreland as the military commander. His interest increased, however, as Komer began to share with him the product of the reports of the provincial and district advisers who reported to Komer. He began to appreciate how this independent reporting service could help him keep track of the performance of his appointed province and district chiefs. He also had to pay attention when Komer used his reports of ineffectiveness or just plain corruption or malingering to demand that Thieu fire certain of these local officials, compelling Thieu to work out a solution to a Vietnamese-American difference of opinion without dissatisfying either side too much.

He certainly welcomed the attention Komer brought to strengthening and increasing the orphans of the Vietnamese defense forces—the local and provincial territorial units now named the Popular Forces and the Regional Forces. For the first time there was an American with responsibility for and interest in these essential units, so long neglected in the American military's enthusiasm for building up the regular Army, Navy, and Air Force—on those occasions, that is, when American attention turned from the disposition and operations of the American forces themselves.

Thieu had a sense of the importance of rural pacification from his own rural origins, his participation as a member of the "Revolutionary Youth" in 1945, and his involvement in Nhu's strategic hamlets program, which he believed did represent a correct strategy with which to combat the Communist people's war. He certainly did not have Diem's messianic attitude or his prickly insistence on Vietnamese independence and sovereignty in order to manifest his nationalism. He believed his role was to run the nation through the instruments available to him, particularly the Vietnamese military establishment, while making such symbolic gestures as were necessary to satisfy American expectations for the development of democratic institutions. The Americans had changed from the Diem days, of course. Under Bunker's careful handling, they found their main functions to be support of the steps Thieu made to build Government institutions and the programs that would strengthen the social and political structures—without calling for immediate "reforms" to bring the benefits of American democracy and separation of powers instantaneously to the Vietnamese peasantry.

The fourth figure to make a difference who appeared during 1967 was American General Creighton W. Abrams. A graduate of West Point just before World War II, Abrams in the expanding Army became a tank force commander under General George S. Patton in their dash across France in 1944. He later became a senior unit commander and commanded the troops sent by President Kennedy to the University of Mississippi during its integration crisis— certainly a challenge to his diplomatic skills. Abrams spent considerable time in Germany, where he developed his appreciation for the classical music with which he relaxed after busy days. His clenched cigar (of good quality), determined scowl, and occasional outbursts of profane rage over some misfeasance gave the image of a tough, fighting tanker—which he liked to project. Beneath this surface, however, was a man highly sensitive to subtleties, particularly able to relate to and respect allies of different backgrounds, and always willing to take a secondary position (especially to Bunker) if it in some way could advance the cause his country was supporting. In short, he was more the Eisenhower than the MacArthur or the Patton.

Abrams's first assignment was as Westmoreland's Deputy, with particular responsibility for the advisory relationship with the Vietnamese forces. This exposed him directly to the Vietnamese commanders and caused him to concentrate on the war from their point of view rather than from only the Americans'. This assignment was later interrupted by his dispatch to establish a unified advance headquarters for the American forces in the northern part of South Vietnam, but his interest in building the Vietnamese forces continued. Only later did he assume overall command of the American forces—when Westmoreland departed for Washington in mid-1968—but his approach was formed during 1967.

The impetus given by Komer at last to combating the political offensive in the countryside produced a number of initiatives in this period, both American and Vietnamese in origin. This was the point where we had to confront the semantic problems of defining what we were trying to do there. The Russians have long focused on the importance of names in strife: what we call "the Second World War," or "World War II," is "The Great Patriotic War" in Soviet life and literature—even with Stalin's role denigrated. When the Cominform tried to overthrow Tito, it launched a newspaper awkwardly entitled *For a Lasting Peace and a People's Democracy*, for two reasons: first, the slogan, no matter how false, said what they wanted others to hear; second, knowing the journal would be quoted in the West, each quote would require repetition of the Russians' slogan in their adversaries' heartlands. Khrushchev announced Soviet support for "wars of national liberation," and a nauseating series of grim totalitarian satellites adopted the title of "People's Democratic Republic." In Vietnam, the appellation *My-Diem* ("American-Diemists"), created and used by the Vietnamese Communists to isolate Diem from his compatriots because of his foreign support (successfully ignoring their own support from nearer, and far from disinterested, foreigners), was an example of what can be done with a name.

Thus one of the most difficult aspects of the struggle against Ho Chi Minh's aptly titled "people's war" was what to call the other side of the fight. A variety of names surfaced over the years, none of which proved satisfactory. Part of the reason was that during most of the time there was no real consensus as to the fundamental nature of the effort, so it was hard to define a name for something that did not really exist. The early Diem program of *action civique* took on a different meaning when put into the English "civic action," which refers to health services, entertainment, and small development projects conducted by the military to benefit the local population near an airfield or other U.S. installation to create goodwill toward the military unit there. My own concoction of "Citizens Irregular Defense Groups" tried to state the essence of their function. The military's replacement of "Citizens" by "Civilian" when they assumed authority over the program under Operation Switchback, presumably to differentiate it from the real "military," was an example of destructive nomenclature— destructive because it confused the purpose of the program.

Diem had also started a "Rural Development" program (*Xay Dung Nong Thon*), but it had no security component and disappeared into the strategic hamlets. Nhu's "strategic hamlets" name was certainly apt but of course died with him, to be replaced by "New Life Hamlets," which never caught on as the program went nowhere in the confusion of the mid-1960s. The most imaginative was "Revolutionary Development," which was constructed out of whole cloth by Air Force Chief Nguyen Cao Ky to please President Johnson, in theory asserting the "revolutionary" purpose of the Young Turks. Its only problem was that it existed only in English, the Vietnamese version sticking to the term "rural." The word "pacification" had come out of the French experience and became a generic word without clear program implications. It had the drawback of suggesting that peace would be imposed on the population—reflecting the military or colonial view of what was required—and it certainly contradicted the essential element of engaging the population in a common effort to defend and develop their communities.

In some frustration, I nevertheless decided that we should accept "pacification" despite its drawbacks and count on the component programs to clarify its nature. But when Komer constructed the unifying civil-military program for pacifi-

cation under the military command, uniting the military's
"Revolutionary Development Support" (RDS) staff section
and the Embassy's "Office of Civilian Operations" (OCO),
the acronym CORDS was chosen (the *CO* from *OCO* and
the *RDS* from the military). Later I quietly changed the *R*
from the artificial "Revolutionary" to the more apt "Rural."

These problems of names reflected the confusion that
existed concerning the nature of the war. In contrast to Ho
Chi Minh and his associates' careful articulation of the
fundamental political strategy of the people's war, neither
the Americans nor the Vietnamese (except perhaps Nhu)
approached the conflict as a political struggle. The absurd
phrase "winning hearts and minds," which was broadly
used (but never by me), implied pleasing the population as
an almost inert audience rather than engaging its participation in a common effort. The fundamental aim of a political strategy instead should have been to stimulate the local
population to work together under local leaders, in support
of and supported by, the Government, as an alternative to
Communist rule. It would not work if they merely ap-
plauded the military combatants or simply obeyed the
Government directives imposed upon them. Activating and
supporting local efforts of this nature was the best way to
counter the competing efforts by the Communists to establish their governance over the rural communities.

To the question of whether the peasants would in the end
cooperate with the Government, the only answer was to try
out the approach, in confidence that they did not want to
live under Communist direction if they had an alternative.
It took many years for this basic lesson to be accepted and
the necessary supporting programs to be developed. In the
meantime, huge efforts were expended in other directions
that were essentially irrelevant to this fundamental task.

Among the programs that grew to maturity during 1967
were People's Action Teams of Colonel Nguyen Be. They
were seen as an important initiative, and the CIA was
encouraged to expand them and to establish them on a
national basis for use throughout the country. We thus
established a national school for the "cadres" who com-
prised the teams ("cadres" being a deliberate adaptation of

the Communist word *can bo* to clarify that their mission
was fundamentally political and their weapons merely for
self-defense in the exposed communities in which they
worked). As the concept grew, and it became obvious that
the teams needed the support of various Government services for their efforts, the Vietnamese Government established a special Ministry to back them up, and to integrate
their efforts with the other pacification-related programs.

The school had one crisis when its first commander, an
officer the CIA had identified in the provinces and found
especially understanding of the political dimension to be
taught, was ousted by the Ministry when it discovered that
he was supplementing the curriculum by recruiting the
student "cadres" to join his favorite political party, in a bid
to give it a nationwide base of organizers and activities.
This opened the post to Nguyen Be, who demonstrated his
commitment to a new basis for Vietnamese society, arising
from the rural communities rather than from a partisan
attempt to impose authority from the top down. Be created a
bit of a problem when he told Vice President Hubert Humphrey, on a brief visit, that the training was intended to
displace the corrupt political and social class that ran
Vietnam—a phrase highlighted in the American press accounts of his visit. Thanks to the CIA's continued support,
and to the fact that his Vietnamese superiors had heard him
say the same thing many times before—in fact agreed with
his approach as the best way to counter the Communist
appeal to the rural audience—Be survived, despite the
American press's delight at his apparent attack on the
Vietnamese establishment.

Another project developed out of local initiatives and
local need was the Provincial Reconnaissance Unit (PRU).
CIA officers in a number of provinces noticed that the
Province Chiefs had no effective forces who could seek out
the enemy guerrilla forces and their leaders. The formal
military units in their area were either not under their
command or were ill armed and poorly trained for aggressive operations, since they still were the stepchildren of the
American military aid program that focused on the regular
Army. And in the mid-1960s, the atmosphere in many
provinces was one of the frontier—the enemy coming in the

A World War II Office of Strategic Services Mission to Vietnam—Americans assisting Ho Chi Minh, Vo Nguyen Giap, and other Vietnamese Communists fighting the Japanese and the Vichy French.

On the Vietnam-Laos border on Route 9, 1960.

Ngo Dinh Nhu, counselor and brother of President Ngo Dinh Diem, in his study at Independence Palace, Saigon, September 1963. (Associated Press)

Madame Ngo Dinh Nhu, sister-in-law and hostess for President Ngo Dinh Diem, Independence Palace, Saigon. (Associated Press)

Ngo Dinh Nhu visits a strategic hamlet with a Nigerian journalist, myself, and local officials in 1961.

A visit to a Delta village with National Assemblywoman Pauline Nguyen Van Tho in 1960.

President John F. Kennedy, outgoing CIA Director Allen W. Dulles, and incoming CIA Director John A. McCone, September 27, 1961. (Courtesy of JFK Library)

A visit to the mountainous A Shau Valley on the Lao border, 1962: Generals Nguyen Duc Thang (later Minister of Rural Development), left; Nguyen Khanh, center; Tran Van Don, right; and myself.

A Citizens' Irregular Defense Group, the Mekong Delta, 1962.

A chat with president Ngo Dinh Diem at Independence Palace, 1962.

The defense built around a strategic hamlet by the local population (1962) with the sharpened bamboo sticks pointed out against Communist would-be invaders.

The Colby front yard after the November 10, 1960, paratrooper coup attempt against our neighbor, President Diem.

Talking with the Rural Development Cadre Team before it goes out to its night positions—in Delta province, 1968.

Inspecting the Mountain Scout Training Center in the highlands, 1962, with General Ton That Dinh and my replacement, John Richardson.

General Duong Van Minh, Secretary of Defense Robert McNamara, and Ambassador Henry Cabot Lodge, March 11, 1964, Saigon. (Associated Press)

In the Oval Office, 1963: Secretary of Defense Robert McNamara briefs President Lyndon B. Johnson and his advisers Averell Harriman, John McCone, Roger Hilsman, and McGeorge Bundy, with myself as McCone's backup.

Ambassador Robert W. Komer visits—and sings with—a Vietnamese youth group outside Saigon, 1967.

Off on the open-door helicopter for a night in the country, 1969.

The "one war" command in 1969, General Creighton Abrams at the center, with his deputies around him: Andrew Goodpaster (later NATO Commander) to his left; myself as Deputy for CORDS to his right; George Brown as Deputy for Air (later Chief of Staff of the U.S. Air Force and then Chairman of the Joint Chiefs of Staff), next left; Elmo Zumwalt as Deputy for Navy (later Chief of Naval Operations), two seats to the right.

Ambassador Ellsworth Bunker and President Nguyen Van Thieu during a visit to the countryside, 1973. (Associated Press)

General Creighton Adams lights Secretary of Defense Melvin Laird's cigar during an inspection trip to the field to review the Vietnamization program, February 13, 1970. (Associated Press)

John Paul Vann, a valued friend and coworker, in the photo he rather liked.

Pressing the pacification message at John Vann's regional conference, 1969.

President Nguyen Van Thieu visits National Training Center for village and hamlet officials at Vung Tau and is received by Colonel Nguyen Be, originator and leader of the center, wearing the traditional peasant black pajama uniform, October 1970.

A visit to a Montagnard center and a traditional drink of the rice wine—
Pleiku, 1969—with Colonel Ya Ba, the Province Chief of Montagnard origin,
to the left.

The Delta, 1970: a friendly chat with the District Chief on the canal.

A night motorcycle tour of a pacified district of Quang Tin province in Central Vietnam in 1970. The Prime Minister accompanied me on the back of another motorcycle.

Testing the new motor rice plow to help rice production, outside Hue, 1971.

A visit to a community near Hue—with the Prime Minister, myself, and Colonel Than (the Province Chief).

President Ford and his National Security Council, 1974, from right: Secretary of Defense James Schlesinger; Deputy National Security Advisor Brent Scowcroft; President Ford; Chief of Staff Donald Rumsfeld; Secretary of State Henry Kissinger; Deputy Secretary of State Robert Ingersoll, and myself.

A chat with the President, 1975.

A North Vietnamese tank, no barefoot guerrilla, crashes through the gate of Independence Palace, Saigon, April 30, 1975, (NBC)

The National Security Council meets on April 29, 1975, to decide on the evacuation of Saigon. Around the table, left to right: myself; Deputy Secretary of State Robert Ingersoll; Henry Kissinger, Secretary of State and National Security Adviser; President Ford; Secretary of Defense James Schlesinger; Deputy Secretary of Defense William Clements; Vice President Nelson Rockefeller; and George Brown, Chairman of the Joint Chiefs of Staff. (Courtesy of Gerald R. Ford Library)

windows and attacking at will. Several of the Province Chiefs turned to their CIA officers for help in meeting the challenge, having taken note of the Agency's flexibility in bringing help to where it was needed. In this way, a number of provinces developed small units of tough fighters, armed and paid by the CIA, who were prepared to locally develop and exploit intelligence directly and immediately. The example paid off in effectiveness, with the result that neighboring Province Chiefs asked for the same help. The Agency agreed on two conditions: one, that the Province Chief in each province assume direct charge of the units and the operations they were to undertake; and two, that the personnel be given serious training for their operations.

Because of the inherent secrecy of the Agency's procedures and the dispersed nature of this program, the PRUs became the subject of much controversy. Their operations were characterized in lurid terms; it was charged that they were made up of draft dodgers and deserters from the regular military, and the wealth of their armaments compared to that of other programs produced envy and complaints of "lack of coordination" with other American programs. The one group who did not complain were the Province Chiefs. They were enthusiastic. Several years later, as the entire situation in Vietnam improved, we integrated the PRUs into the National Police.

We in the Agency were sensitive to the charges of atrocities frequently leveled at the PRUs. We did what we could to get them to adhere to the normal rules of war, with a helpful influence but not with complete success. At a period when the enemy was mining and rocketing the civilian population and assassinating Government officials, their families, and innocent people at will, it was hard to get men chosen for their toughness and aggressiveness to adhere to every one of the rules of fair play. But we kept trying, and the complaints increasingly turned to hearsay and generalities—the "war stories" always heard in combat situations. I do not excuse any bloody misdeeds, but I do insist that they be considered in the context of the situation prevailing in the mid-1960s and in light of the effective influence the Agency *did* exert to improve PRU performance.

Better intelligence was, of course, a constant demand. In

the early 1960s, at the start of the war, the CIA had responded by working with the Vietnamese to train their
officers, both police and military. Under Diem we had
helped build a Central Intelligence Organization (CIO)—a
deliberate play on the initials—to provide a national-level
analytical center to review all information and produce the
kind of considered studies we expected from our analytical
staffs in Washington. There were an ample number of
intelligence collection agencies in the Vietnamese machinery. The gamut ran from the regular G-2 of the military
and the Military Security Service comparable to the Counter Intelligence Corps of the American Army, through the
National Police Special Branch in the British and French
traditions, to the private activities of various political leaders, such as Colonel Le Quang Tung's Special Forces working for Ngo Dinh Nhu or the hidden network of Nhu's Can
Lao party. Each acted as a separate fiefdom, however, so
that information known to one was zealously guarded and
used for its own purposes and only rarely shared with
others.

In some situations there was good reason for this reticence, as the information might be used against its originator in the chaotic period of the mid-1960s, but the result was
that frequently the CIA was the only agency that had the
confidence of a number of the different Vietnamese groups
and could put the bits and pieces together in a fashion that
gave the overall picture. When one added to the proliferation of Vietnamese agencies the existence and separate
interests of the many American equivalents, each serving its
separate commander, the result was a tangle of reports, a
limitation of perspective, and a confusion of conclusions.

The predominance of the American military during the
mid-1960s produced the problem that intelligence concentrated on the military aspects of the enemy. Obviously—
and legitimately—American military commanders and,
consequently, their intelligence officers were concerned
primarily with intelligence about enemy military units that
might attack them or that they saw as their targets. Their
focus, therefore, was the Communist military enemy rather
than the "civilian" activists who inhabited the rural communities or visited them to conduct the basic elements of the

people's war strategy—proselytizing, taxing, conscripting. Military interrogators of prisoners thus would ask every detail of the activities of a main or local force unit in the neighborhood, or even of a guerrilla squad, but ignore the identity or activities of a local tax collector or *agitprop* activist.

The CIA's interest in precisely this aspect of the war led it to try to improve intelligence concerning it. The CIA had no possibility—or even desire—to match the manpower commitment of the American military to their combat intelligence interests. The CIA's approach was, therefore, to help the Vietnamese build the kind of structure that could inform us both of the political enemy we faced in the clandestine apparatus the Communists maintained in Vietnam. The concept was simple: create intelligence centers in which all intelligence agencies participated and to which each could contribute intelligence that might be of value to the others, but with each agency allowed to retain under its own control the critical sources and techniques that it felt it could not share without risk of exposure to the enemy (or to a political rival).

The addition of a central staff to focus on the enemy's political apparatus permitted an analysis of all the information given and the development of reasonably accurate lists of local Communist cadres, their organizational structure and strengths, and even a projection of their tactics and strategies for the people's war in the area. By the end of 1967, the earlier experiments with the process produced the idea of a national program to carry it out. President Thieu incorporated the concept in a directive in December of that year establishing a national *Phuong Hoang* (roughly translated as "Phoenix") program. A late development, perhaps, but it represented an attempt to provide the intelligence base upon which to conduct the necessary counter to the Communist people's war in the rural communities. It was a Vietnamese program, in line with the CIA's basic concept that the Agency's role was to help the Vietnamese develop the tools and techniques to fight the war, not to do it for them.

These CIA-sponsored programs that began to focus on the local aspects of the war were matched by other agencies.

Thus the United States Information Service developed a national television network to bring information to the isolated rural communities. After initially destroying the Government-supplied receivers and generators, the Communists learned that the village communities insisted on continuing to receive the programs. The Agency for International Development concentrated its efforts on the macroeconomic problems of how to keep the Vietnamese economy in some degree of viability despite the impact of the American troop presence with its inflationary—and corruptive—effects. AID also accomplished prodigious results in health care, in support for education, and in the introduction of the first stages of the "green revolution," the enormous advance in rice productivity that grew out of the Rockefeller Rice Research Institute (and other similar institutions) in the Philippines by carefully integrating fertilizers, pesticides, and new strains of rice. At the beginning, the canny Vietnamese farmers regarded the last suspiciously, but in short order they seized upon it as the bonanza it was to their productivity.

By late 1967, therefore, the situation in Vietnam seemed promising to the Americans on the ground. A stable and constitutional Government was in place, ending the revolving-door experiences since Diem's fall. The American forces were nearing 500,000 men and women, clearly sufficient to prevent the regular North Vietnamese Army troops from achieving victory. The South Vietnamese forces had been increased and were undergoing new programs to improve their training, equipment, and effectiveness. The Americans had built an organizational structure by which to prosecute the pacification program, which was now recognized as the key to developing sufficient strength in South Vietnam to permit the gradual drawdown of American troops over the next several years. There was still some debate as to the exact way such a program would be carried out (e.g., whether the Vietnamese Army should be assigned to the pacification mission while the Americans handled the "big war" against the Communist regular forces). There was no doubt that the Communists remained determined to carry on the war, not yielding to the pressures of the air war against North Vietnam and the supply routes of the Ho Chi Minh Trail. But there did seem to be "light at the end of the tunnel," in the phrase used at the time to indicate that a favorable outcome was ahead—even at the cost of considerable darkness en route.

This was the message presented by Ellsworth Bunker and General Westmoreland during a visit to the United States in late 1967. While the public statements were carefully hedged to exclude an early success, the usual media dialectic translated them into expressions of great confidence that a happy ending was in store, seeming to naysay the pessimists who contended that the cause was hopeless. Indeed, I myself felt the same careful optimism. So when CIA Director Richard Helms offered me a chance to shift from my long service on Vietnam and the Far East to become chief of the CIA's clandestine attempts to penetrate the Soviet Union, I welcomed it. I felt that I had made what contribution I could to Vietnam and that the programs of both Vietnamese and Americans there seemed reasonably well conceived and promised success in the end if we pursued them for the time required.

The Soviet target was (and is) a high priority for our intelligence services. I was aware that our operations there were difficult and had had some problems in themselves, especially in internal disputes within the Agency over the approaches taken to the target. While knowing little of them because of the necessary compartmentalization of intelligence activities for security reasons, I welcomed the opportunity to try my hand at them and to concentrate on professional intelligence activities after my long focus on political and paramilitary operations. In response to my enthusiasm, my daughter Catherine bought me a Soviet-style fur hat for Christmas to equip me properly for my new role.

But it was not to be. Dick Helms interrupted one of my briefings on Soviet operations with a call to come to his office. He was obviously annoyed and quickly explained why. In a meeting of the "Tuesday lunch" (Lyndon Johnson's strategy session with his senior advisers on Vietnam—which could take place at a Friday breakfast), the President had turned abruptly to Helms and said that Komer had been in town and wanted a fellow named Colby to be sent to

Vietnam to be his Deputy. The President had turned away equally abruptly to imply that it had been accomplished. Helms apologized to me for the way it had happened and asked me to think about it overnight to see what we should do about it.

It did not take me long to recognize that Komer and the President were right despite my own interest in the Soviet assignment. I could hardly claim great expertise on that subject, and I had spent the past six years as one of the resident Washington experts on Vietnam. Moreover, the ideas I had long been promoting were now finally coming to center stage there. Besides, it is impossible to say no to a President who calls you to a task—especially as I had sent dozens of CIA officers from their specialties all over the world to Vietnam to contribute their talents to our effort there. So I returned to Helms to say, as he expected, that I would go and that I hoped I might get a crack at the Soviet target some other time.

As I prepared to return to Vietnam, one of the principal American figures of the Vietnam War was leaving the scene. On November 27, the White House had announced that Secretary of Defense McNamara would resign and be appointed to head the World Bank. This action reflected McNamara's increasing disillusionment with the war and his part in setting our governing strategy. Architect of the "numbers" approach, he had finally recognized that it would not work. He has since stated that his first doubts about the war had arisen in late 1965, but his continued direction of it along the same lines has still to be explained. By the fall of 1967, however, his disaffection was such that President Johnson had lost confidence in him at exactly the time when Johnson was seeing what he thought were the pieces coming together (a constitutional Government in place in Vietnam, an increase in the numbers and effectiveness of the Vietnamese forces—including the territorials—and the American mission properly organized to direct the American effort) to permit the war to be wound down, at least, if not won. McNamara stayed in office for some additional time while his successor, longtime Washington insider Clark Clifford, awaited Senate confirmation. That finally came on the inauspicious date of January 30, 1968.

Coincidentally, Helms and I had set that date for me to leave my job as Chief of the CIA's Far East Division and transfer to the Agency for International Development, which would be paying my salary during my forthcoming tour as Komer's Deputy. The date's true significance became clear as the first cables came in from the CIA Communications Center in the Embassy in Saigon that the Embassy was under direct attack.

Part Five
STRATEGY FOUND

14

Tet 1968

THE FIRST FLASH CABLE FROM SAIGON ALERTING us to a Communist attack came into Washington during the afternoon of January 29, 1968; it was then early morning on January 30 in Saigon. That cable reported that a violent attack against the American Embassy was in progress, with the attackers possibly within the Embassy itself. I flashed back that the Communications Center should button up its steel doors, a bit of gratuitous advice that was the subject of some amusement in the calmer times that developed later. The news services and other reports from the Embassy and the military soon brought us more detail. It was clear that similar attacks were in progress in many cities and provincial towns throughout the country. These fitted in with reports we had received the day before of Communist attacks in some cities in Central Vietnam and with various indications the military had picked up of Communist intentions to launch some kind of action around the Tet period, the several days of the lunar New Year—in East Asia the most sacred holidays of the year, on which each family is expected to gather to reassert its primacy as the fundamental social unit.

These reports were fuzzy and imprecise and by no means solid reflections of operations orders given to the Communist units that would launch the attack. Again this was a reflection of the nature of the war. It did not involve major Communist military units assembling their logistics and moving their heavy weapons to the line from which they would strike. Instead, an order was passed from the secret Communist networks to the guerrilla units hidden in the forests to surreptitiously position themselves on the outskirts of the urban and Government centers, and be pre-

227

pared to attack the sites of Government power when directed. Our intelligence efforts had not penetrated this secret network to the point of obtaining such orders when sent; the Communists were well aware of the danger that they might and had implemented sophisticated security procedures to protect themselves against just that possibility. Only in retrospect is it clear that the attacks in several cities in Central Vietnam, where action began a day earlier, reflected confusion among the Communists as to exactly when to launch the assault.

But in response to the initial vague indications that the Communists appeared to intend some kind of attack, General Frederick Weyand, commander of the several U.S. divisions and supporting units in the region around Saigon, moved the U.S. 25th "Tropic Lightning" Division nearer to the capital from its operations in the wild country farther north. President Thieu had limited military leaves to no more than 50 percent of the Vietnamese forces. The latter action seems minimal, of course, but it must be measured against the facts that those forces had been fighting for many years and would be doing so until victory, defeat, or death—not the one-year tour of most Americans. Also, for most of them the family gathering would not be far from their normal duty stations. But Vietnamese history could have given better warning. One of Vietnam's historical heroes, Nguyen Hue, had gained a legendary victory over an invading Chinese army by attacking during Tet 1789, rather on the order of George Washington's crossing of the Delaware to attack the British and Hessians at Trenton on Christmas Eve of 1776.

The reports gradually made it clear that the attacks had taken place nationwide. In most cases, they were carried out by small sabotage and assault groups targeted on important urban centers (such as the American Embassy), followed by guerrilla units to assert authority and main force units to hold off the reactions of the Vietnamese or American forces. Plainly the Communists were counting on the exercise generating their doctrinal *khoi nghia*, or general uprising, by the local citizenry, thereby quickly multiplying their entering forces. While the initial, secret infiltrations generally went reasonably well, producing tactical surprise, the remainder of the plan proved a disaster for the Communists.

The Vietnamese and American forces quickly rallied and counterattacked, and the population simply fled from the Communist forces. Most of them were left to fight holding actions or to attempt to retreat, while exposed to superior firepower and taking enormous losses. In most of the cities attacked, the invaders were defeated within the first day or two, although they holed up in the ancient castle of Hue to resist for three weeks. The resulting death and destruction were enormous as American and Vietnamese artillery and heavy weapons pounded the cornered Communists, destroying large sections of the towns and cities in which they had gone to ground.

The fighting generated over a million refugees. The Communists sought refuge and concealment in the homes of the population, who fled both them and the devastation of the ensuing battles. In much of the countryside the Communist attacks were effective, and they assumed authority over those villages and hamlets in which they had killed the Government defenders. The main Government forces were so engaged in expelling the attackers from the cities and towns that they had no forces to spare to recapture the outlying settlements. But from a strategic point of view, it became evident within a couple of days that the Government and American forces had effectively stopped the attack, that the Communists could not win the engagement they had begun, and that the battle henceforth would consist of mopping up the attackers.

In the areas where the Communists exercised authority for any length of time, they failed to try to organize the population—which is surprising considering the rationale of their strategy and, in the case of this particular operation, their ultimate dependence upon a show of popular support. They limited themselves essentially to killing representatives of the Government, or others they deemed hostile, as they did in a mass execution of some three thousand persons in Hue, whose collective grave was discovered some months later. In the smaller communities, while they had power, they cut down the local representatives of the Government and those who had openly sympathized with it. But in no case were they able to develop any political momentum or mass support of the type their own doctrine called for.

If the widespread nature and simultaneous timing of the attacks were not anticipated by the Vietnamese, or by the Americans, the Communist intelligence system's appreciation of the strength of the Vietnamese-American forces and of the political attitude of the Vietnamese population was more disastrously faulty. The losses to the Communists, especially to their Southern leaders and cadres, were enormous and had long-term effects on their ability to conduct the people's war there. In effect, they were forced to turn more toward a military war conducted primarily by Northerners.

But the war involved another theater, as did the First Indochinese War against the French. Certainly the Communist leadership hoped the Tet attacks would be victorious and produce the same effect on faraway American public opinion that the victory at Dien Bien Phu in 1954 had on French opinion. Initially, the failure of the offensive must have disappointed them and called into question the value of the losses suffered. But in fact the attack became the turning point of the war—in their favor.

This was the result not of some deep-seated conspiracy of the press and liberal opinion but of a combination of factors endemic to the American democratic system and to the impact of technological developments upon it. The conviction of responsible American officialdom that at long last the tools for a successful outcome of the war were at hand, stressed by Lyndon Johnson and in the visits to the United States of Bunker and Westmoreland in late 1967, sounded to the public as though all would be downhill from then on. The fact that the Communists were able to mount a nationwide offensive at Tet—entering the grounds of the American Embassy itself—seemed to directly contradict this.

The real source of the impact of the Tet 1968 Communist offensive on the American public was the sudden eruption on nightly television of the enormous toll of the attack in blood, violence, and destruction. Much of the Vietnam war can be marked by a few dramatic photographs, such as that of the Buddhist bonze burning in protest against Diem. Tet provided a whole portfolio of such images, especially the execution by Police Commander Nguyen Ngoc Loan of a Communist captive, caught in excruciating detail by Associated Press photographer Eddie Adams (who later said he wished he had not taken it). The drama of the photo drowned out Loan's fury over the murder of his men—and, in one case, of a whole family—by the Communists. The bloody and torn bodies, the explosions, the fires, repeated night after night as the camera crews moved on from towns where the attack had been defeated to ones where it continued, such as Hue, gave the impression that the whole country remained convulsed.

The American body politic suffered a shock similar to being awakened from a warm sleep by a dousing with a pail of cold water. Dispassionate analysis of the actual outcome of the attacks could hardly be heard against the resounding impact of such imagery—and was not. Thoughtful journalists have expressed concern at this process. Some have raised the question of whether their profession needs to develop some disciplines to try to present the whole picture in such dramatic circumstances rather than only those startling events that dominate the TV screen. These questions can be left for others to solve; the important thing to note here is that the effect of the media—most importantly TV—coverage in America of Tet 1968 was to turn public opinion critically to the belief that the American effort in Vietnam was hopeless and should be ended.

On February 27 Walter Cronkite, everyone's national TV uncle, summed up a visit he made to Vietnam after Tet with the conclusion that "the bloody experience of Vietnam is to end in a stalemate." Clark Clifford, the new Secretary of Defense Johnson had chosen to replace McNamara (who had become too dovish for Johnson), conducted a review of the military recommendations for increasing the U.S. force commitment to Vietnam and recommended that no increase in strength be sent.

Following a dinner and briefing by the State Department, the Pentagon, and the CIA on March 25, a group of Washington "wise men" who had previously been consulted by and supported the President, urged disengagement from the war. Since they included some of the grand Establishment figures of the nation—no doves they—such as Dean Acheson, McGeorge Bundy, Douglas Dillon (former Secretary of the Treasury), Robert Murphy (a leader in American diplomacy from North Africa in 1942 to Japan in the postwar era), John McCloy (High Commissioner in postwar Germany), and Henry Cabot Lodge (reappearing in the Vietnam scenario), their views placed additional pressure on Johnson.

Their views were reinforced by the Democratic primary returns in New Hampshire, which saw antiwar advocate Eugene McCarthy almost upset the incumbent President of the United States, and by Robert Kennedy's announcement that he would be a candidate for the coming Presidential elections and would run on the issue of the war. Johnson took these blows like the brave Texas politician he was and determined that he would not be a candidate for reelection, so he could try to end the agony decently without the pressure of a campaign.

But I didn't agree, nor did many of the Americans on the ground in Vietnam. We were looking at the reality of the situation, not just its appearance on American television. We saw that the Tet attack had been a defeat of the enemy and that the Vietnamese and Americans in Vietnam were finally positioned and organized to take advantage of it. The enemy had been devastated by the losses they had suffered, especially of their South Vietnamese cadres, which were the essential base for their strategy of a people's war. The South Vietnamese had been buoyed up by their successful defeat of the greatest offensive the Communists had launched against them, in which their forces, and not just the Americans, had acquitted themselves with courage and success. The time was ripe to step up the war against the enemy, but now at the level at which he had posed the challenge—in the villages of Vietnam.

As I went through the bureaucratic processes during February to take leave without pay from the CIA and join AID, I thought about what needed to be done in Vietnam. My children had all lived there. My elder daughter, Catherine, though burdened with epilepsy and poor vision, was particularly fond of the Vietnamese and knowledgeable and respectful of their culture. Taken aback in 1964 by an

especially crass interpretation in *The Washington Post* of a
Vietnamese incident, she wrote to the editor, "Having lived
in Vietnam for more than three years, I read with great
interest any articles on that country. So as I began to read
[the] article in your Oct. 25 issue, I was hoping to get the
facts accurately and with a sympathetic perspective. But as I
read on, I realized that [the author] was sometimes mistaken
in facts and narrow in judgment. . . ." From there she went
on, "accurately and with a sympathetic perspective," to
detail the mistakes in "facts and . . . judgment." It was thus
my habit to speak with my children of the (nonoperational)
issues surrounding my work, as I did on this occasion. We
went skating on the C&O Canal outside Washington, during which I managed to break my ankle. I shed the cast in
time to leave on schedule, though on a cane. But in our
talks I explained to my children—indeed, promised them—
that the most important thing I wanted to accomplish in
returning to Vietnam now was to form self-defense groups
in the villages—so many of which they themselves had seen.

Again a long plane ride across the Pacific afforded me a
chance to think about what I should do when I got to
Vietnam. Obviously I had to adjust to Komer's hard-driving
style, managing the CORDS program under him as his
Deputy. He would have the broad role, maintaining the top-
level relationships with the military, the Embassy, and the
Vietnamese leadership. My job would be to shape the specific programs for him so that they constituted a strategy for
pacification and to supervise their execution. In so doing, I
would have a chance to put forward my ideas of a political
approach and of the importance of local community self-
defense, and to integrate the various CIA programs that had
evolved over the last few years into a national approach. I
knew Komer would support me in this, as he had supported
the CIA programs before CORDS was established. But I
also realized that we had to produce results soon in view of
the adverse effect of the Tet attack on support at home for
the war. Our results had to be so effective that they would
revive support at home for our efforts. If not, they had to so
put the enemy in trouble and so strengthen the Government
that it could survive with a major reduction in American
assistance. It promised to be a close race, but I looked

forward to the chance to compensate for the wasted years produced by the overthrow of Diem.

As the Pan Am plane dove steeply into Tan Son Nhut Airport (to avoid possible ground fire) on March 2, I noticed a Vietnamese plane on a bombing mission off our right wing, probably against one of the guerrilla groups still fighting in the outer suburbs. I realized there was still a lot to do to translate our programs into effect on the ground. Throwing back Communist military and guerrilla units was one thing—and it had been accomplished in the urban centers—but providing an atmosphere of security and confidence against terrorist bombs and ambushes in the countryside was another. There was also an enormous amount to do simply to repair the physical damage to homes and whole sections of towns, to reopen roads and bridges, and to care for and resettle the million refugees uprooted throughout the nation by the Tet attack.

Komer greeted me warmly and told me to concentrate on getting into my new job, actually as his Deputy, officially as an Assistant Chief of Staff (among many others) in the American military command structure for Vietnam. This involved getting to know my fellow Assistant Chiefs of Staff for such matters as operations, intelligence, personnel, logistics, planning, and all the other specialties that a military headquarters controlling 500,000 troops can produce—and being instantly available to the Chief of Staff, who was the stage manager of this large orchestra in support of the conductor, Westmoreland, and his Deputies. I found that my background as an "Army brat"—child of a regular Army officer—established a link to the predominantly professional military with whom I was dealing, though for a time I had a major psychological block in talking to anyone with stars on his shoulders without referring to him respectfully as "General." (There were few generals in the Army when I was a boy, and then one approached them with awe.)

But my main job, and interest, lay outside the Command Headquarters in the field. Early on, I decided that the best way to stay out of the troubles of Saigon life and do the field job I saw as the real purpose of my being in Vietnam was to spend as many nights as possible in the provinces. With the ultimate luxury of being able to call for a helicopter or fixed-wing aircraft to take me where I wanted to go, I could put in a full working Saturday at Headquarters, leave in the late afternoon, have dinner and the evening with some province or district Advisory Team, examine local activities in the morning, and be brought back to Saigon by late afternoon for a swim and dinner, ready for work at Headquarters on Monday morning—having happily missed the Saigon Saturday night festivities.

These nights were an education in what the war was like in the provinces. My helicopter making a tight circle to land inside the provincial capital of Vinh Long in the Delta showed—convincingly—that the enemy were just outside the narrow outskirts and were ready to shoot us down if they could. A night in Ban Me Thuot, not far from the village of Buon Enao, where we had started the protective belt of armed mountain villages in 1960, was enlivened by listening to the exploding mortar rounds marching methodically up the street toward our quarters. Fully armed, we manned the second-floor balcony in case a ground assault followed. (It didn't.) If these provincial capitals were this closely threatened, it was obvious that the enemy had free rein in the rural villages from which it had driven all representatives of the Government. The American and Vietnamese military could, of course—and did—sally forth at daybreak in search of the major Communist units they hoped to find and destroy. Generally, the searches were fruitless.

There were also shorter daytime visits to the areas near Saigon or in the Delta, more carefully arranged field visits by various Washington officials, regional conferences of the provincial Advisers attended by the Saigon staff, and attendance at assemblies of the military officials of an area to represent the pacification program in their deliberations. Obviously Komer took the lead in the more formal meetings, but I would, to the degree possible, strike off alone to get my own impressions.

One of my first visits was with John Paul Vann, then and now a legendary figure of the Vietnam war. As a young nineteen-year-old, he had trained to join a bomber crew during World War II to fly missions against the Japanese.

When the war ended before he saw combat, he opted for a military career and worked up through the ranks (including a stint in the war in Korea) to become a Lieutenant Colonel of Infantry, assigned in 1962 as adviser to a Vietnamese division in the Mekong Delta. Almost totally irrepressible even by the Army's discipline, Vann first came to public prominence after the January 1963 Battle of Ap Bac. The division he advised had bottled up a Communist unit there but, with a combination of laxity and disinclination to close, had allowed the enemy to escape through a gap conveniently left in the lines around them. The Vietnamese force had lost eighty dead and over a hundred wounded and the Americans five helicopters, with three from their crews dead and eight wounded.

With his usual forcefulness, Vann had exploded to the press that highlighted the affair as a further indication that the Diem regime and its Army were unworthy of American support. Vann became so incensed at the official American reaction to the affair, in his mind condoning the ineffectiveness of the Vietnamese unit and its commander and trying to muzzle his protests, that he resigned from the Army. A short exposure to life in the United States convinced him that his heart lay with the effort in Vietnam. In a very few months, he reappeared there in the role of a provincial representative of the Agency for International Development, serving, typically, in one of the more dangerous and challenging provinces surrounding Saigon. He had worked himself up to the post of regional AID chief for the area around Saigon and was naturally chosen by Komer as regional head of the new, combined advisory organization for pacification there.

Neil Sheehan has written a lengthy and intense book about Vann, focusing on him as a prototype through whom to present the war in Vietnam. Sheehan's research is exhaustive, his writing brilliant, and his conclusions, in my view, wrong. His conclusions are essentially three: that the young reporters, such as Sheehan, who were in Vietnam during the early period of the war and played such a role in attacking Diem were correct; that the Vietnamese generally (not just Diem) were hopeless; and that the Americans who were heavily engaged in the war were flawed.

My view of the Diem regime, fully stated previously—in sum not perfect, certainly, but better than what followed it—casts doubt on the wisdom, if not the specifics, of the reporters' themes, even though much of their criticism came from Vann himself. I shall describe what I believe were effective performances by other Vietnamese, high and low, after Tet 1968, in sharp contrast to the view that they were uniformly hopeless. As for unattractive aspects of Vann's private life unearthed by Sheehan, I can say only that they never, in my experience, impeded his qualities of leadership or his outstanding execution of his responsibilities. To be truthful, I never heard of them until Sheehan saw fit to detail them.

I had met Vann only once, on one of his trips to Washington, when he visited CIA headquarters to tell me that the cadre teams the CIA was building up were not as good as we thought they were and spent too much of their time simply protecting themselves instead of doing the political job they were supposed to accomplish. I had not contested his comments, but I said we knew the teams were far from perfect and needed more time, work, and supervision, but they were certainly a step in the right direction. When I arrived in Vietnam as his boss's Deputy, Vann expressed some concern that I would be resentful of his negative comments about the CIA's pet project. He confronted another problem when I showed up with a cane for my broken ankle, which he had to explain to his staff and Vietnamese friends was not because I was handicapped, but had simply been foolish on the C&O Canal ice (a hard concept in itself to get across in Vietnam).

Vann had done his homework on me carefully, however, and the first night I spent with him he took me to a village to visit a vigorous village chief who had armed the young men of the community with rude swords made by sharpening discarded automobile springs. When I laboriously limped to see their outposts, the young men were fiercely brandishing these homemade weapons. The main point of the visit came, of course, when the village chief, pressing for real weapons for his men so they could provide a proper defense for their community against Communists well armed with AK-47s, gave me one of these swords. Carefully, to avoid raising false hopes, I said I would certainly try to obtain real weapons for them (and later did). The important result of the evening, however, was a clear understanding between Vann and myself that the real way we should be fighting the war was by building communities such as the one we visited, and gradually pressing the Communists away from the population.

But at that time we were in fact not really pursuing a pacification strategy. The Tet attack had produced such a legacy of destruction, some by the Communists and some by the Vietnamese and American forces reacting to them, that there was an enormous job to do to reconstruct the economy and the communities. The total number of refugees who had fled for protection from the violence—the Communist attack and the Vietnamese and American response—numbered over a million. They looked to the Vietnamese Government for shelter, sustenance, and care. Many were fearful of returning to the areas where they had been attacked and huddled in the camps established for them, expectant that the authorities would care for them. The Vietnamese Government accepted the obligation, as it had for the 900,000 refugees from North Vietnam who had arrived in 1954 and 1955.

Large numbers of homes and public buildings, such as marketplaces and schools, had been destroyed and had to be rebuilt, for which cement, tin roofing, and labor had to be supplied. The wounded had to be healed and basic Government services gingerly reestablished in areas the Communists had occupied even temporarily during the Tet attack. And to exacerbate the situation, the Communists were to make another surge of attacks during the coming months to try to pick up the momentum the initial Tet attack had lost.

The pacification program was seen as the natural organization to take on these reconstruction tasks while the military concentrated on the threats the Communists still posed, counterattacking them whenever they could be located. Komer threw himself, and the program, into the task with gusto to show that the new pacification organization could perform under pressure. But one effect of the effort was to focus all our attention on the physical requirements of rebuilding, postponing to a better day the more political and intangible elements of a real pacification program.

These early days of getting into the job were interrupted by another visitor from Washington. Clark Clifford, the new Secretary of Defense, was in Vietnam for his first look at his greatest responsibility. Loyal Democrat to the core, he had served and counseled a series of Presidents and other leaders of the American body politic. Johnson had named Clifford to succeed McNamara notwithstanding—and perhaps even because of—the fact that Clifford, arguing to the President in 1965 against committing U.S. combat forces to Vietnam, had added the almost uncanny prediction "If we lose 50,000 plus [men] . . . it will ruin us. Five years, billions of dollars, 50,000 men, it is not for us." Part of the new Secretary's effectiveness came from his courtly manner, confident air, and deep voice, inspiring confidence and even awe in whatever he might say. But his most impressive trait was his clear judgment of the political realities a President must deal with, and Vietnam was the most important one with which President Johnson was wrestling.

Clifford was accompanied by Paul Warnke, his Assistant Secretary of Defense for International Affairs, whom I had known from his days in the Washington law firm of Covington and Burling, where I had several friends from my law school days. I knew that Warnke was a firm liberal Democrat, though I did not know then that he was in the forefront of those circles with rising doubts about the war who were looking to an American disengagement.

Neither Clifford nor Warnke, burdened as they were by the American domestic perception that the commitment in Vietnam was not working, as displayed by the dramatic events of Tet, were much impressed by the upbeat briefings the military command put on. Komer and I had little opportunity to put forward the promise of pacification, itself then overwhelmed by the devastation of Tet. Rather than a strategy, it appeared only as a program for physical reconstruction of the damage a successful enemy had wrought upon the Vietnamese scene, without promise for the future. The two visitors departed with no successful contradiction of their attitude on arrival—to wit, the United States was deep in a quagmire, and the sooner it withdrew, the better.

In April 1968, a new move occurred on the enemy side that made it clear to me that the political effort had nonetheless to be revived. The radios announced the organization of the "Alliance of National, Democratic and Peace Forces," an obvious new effort by the Communists to establish a front organization to incorporate non-Communist, nationalist forces in a coalition against the South Vietnamese regime. The tactic was familiar to me from my experiences in New York political circles and in Europe in the 1940s and 1950s, and from my studies of the way the Communists had led anti-Fascist fronts during the 1930s. The Vietnamese Communists also announced the formation of self-styled local Liberation Committees as vehicles to establish local government in the areas under their control. They were obviously meant to provide a base for the assertion of their authority in the event they were able to negotiate some compromise on the ground between their forces and those of the Vietnamese Government.

Having failed in their bid for conquest in the Tet attacks, the Communists were now laying the groundwork for a claim to political power, or at least participation, and for an effort to negotiate a compromise political solution with the Americans over the heads of the Vietnamese Government. Clearly the response of the Vietnamese Government and its American ally had to be political: to establish legitimate local authority to counter the claims of the Communists and their fronts. But much organizational and political homework on our side was necessary before this could be accomplished. To do so, the pacification program had to be turned from its concentration on tin roofs and cement.

15

Rebound

FOLLOWING MY PROMISE TO MY CHILDREN on my departure from Washington—and my more cautious assurances to the village chief I had met with John Vann—the first thing I set out to do was produce local self-defense units in the villages. Komer's program of a year before to improve the local security forces of the country, the Regional and Popular Forces, was a fortuitous precedent. Thanks to his having taken the responsibility for American support for those forces under CORDS, for the first time there was a locus within the American structure that focused on them for their own value, not just as recipients of hand-me-downs after the regular Vietnamese forces were taken care of.

Unbelievably, Komer had found these local forces still armed with a collection of second- and thirdhand weapons of uncertain vintage from French days and from whatever odd equipment American modernization of the regular forces had made available. Komer stressed that these security forces were bearing the brunt of the fighting against the Communists and surely deserved better weapons. As a result of his pressure, the decision had finally been taken to arm them with the modern American M-16 rifle, allowing them to trade in their collection of antiques from World War II and before. The opportunity this offered was too good to miss. The weapons they turned in could be used to arm local self-defense groups in the village communities.

Easier said than done. The idea of distributing weapons in the countryside met with resistance. Some contended that it would merely be a way to arm the Communist guerrillas, to which I responded that they showed no need for such supplies, being amply armed with the Communist AK-47, a more modern and better constructed guerrilla weapon than any we had available. Some said the idea was of little value, as the untrained villagers who would use them would not be effective soldiers and would probably fade away rapidly in the face of the enemy. Here my answer was political— that the object of the exercise was not to produce trained soldiers but to recruit to the Government's side the very individuals who would otherwise find excitement in joining the local Communist guerrilla groups.

Experience had shown that a disarmed village community could be entered and dominated by a five-man enemy squad. If they met no opposition, they could assemble and harangue the population with their message, collect taxes and supplies, and conscript or recruit some of the local youths into the Communist forces. Even a modest local defense element, however, could block this intrusion and allow the villagers to resist if they so wished. The key point was that giving the villagers arms was a Government show of confidence in them that would have a major favorable impact. It would be the best possible way to enlist the villagers' participation in the struggle against the Communists—essential to a people's war strategy. Even if some of the weapons went astray, the net benefit in enlisting most of the people would be well worth it. My own estimate was that we would probably lose about 20 percent of the weapons but would gain 80 percent of the population—in my view a very good trade.

Perhaps the most difficult argument against the idea was made by Prime Minister Tran Van Huong, an elderly and respected former teacher in the French school system who had participated in the resistance against the French (and Diem) but stood firmly for non-Communist nationalism. From his memory of the sect wars that had convulsed Vietnam in the mid-1950s, he said that the weapons would become fuel for similar internecine struggles after, or even during, the fight against the Communists. To meet his arguments, I laboriously constructed a letter to him in French, which he had once taught and was thus easier for him than English, essentially making the point that the immediate problem was the Communist threat, and that the dangers to which he pointed could be taken care of after the major threat was eliminated or at least substantially reduced. When we met at a ceremony shortly thereafter, he graded my French as *execrable* (atrocious) but said that he had accepted my arguments.

Komer carried the same arguments to President Thieu, whose reaction was much simpler: the Government, he said, had to rest upon the support of the people, and it had little validity if it did not dare to arm them. As a result, a national program to create a "People's Self-Defense Force" was established, the title again being carefully chosen so that each word indicated its mission. Over the next three years, some 500,000 weapons were made available to the villages for their use.

The concept was simple. Able-bodied men (and later women) in the villages, too young or too old for service in the armed forces or the territorials, were required to contribute a certain amount of time to guard duty for the community, such as one night a week. A small stock of weapons was made available to the village chief to be issued each night to those on duty. Those who could not be armed were to help as lookouts. The weapons were turned in to the village center in the morning for issuance to the next contingent the following night. No pay was given to the participants for this service to their community, but an effort was made to give them armbands or identifying insignia to incite their pride (and that of the local young women in them).

The program was first carefully applied in areas basically safe, both to gain confidence in it and to avoid exposing the self-defenders to more than they could handle. This procedure, and the daily exchange of the weapons under the careful control of the village chief, brought the surprising result that weapons losses were no more than 2 or 3 percent of those issued—far below the 20 percent I had anticipated. Some firefights with the enemy took place, and predictably the self-defenders proved not very fearsome warriors, but the primary political purpose of the program began to be achieved as the number of participants mounted from the hundreds to the hundreds of thousands. Because of the informality of the procedures involved, I never really believed the million-or-more figure that was reported as the number of participants, but I certainly saw evidence of the spread of the activity in my nights in the field.

There was one feature of the program for which I cannot claim credit, since it was generated by the Vietnamese. The idea that the self-defense groups would be unpaid volunteers (albeit pressed by the community to perform the service) was understood by us both, but the Vietnamese authorities conceived the procedure of collecting the weapons each morning and issuing them to a new group of young people the next evening. The fact that the weapons did not stay with individuals permanently meant that their service would be only occasional. The result was that we did not build up vigilante squads who would threaten fellow villagers as much as the enemy, as has happened in some other nations where the program was tried. I could only give the idea my full support and steadfastly reject proposals that the members of the units be paid for their service, which would indeed have made them semiprofessionals.

The other program I thought it necessary to revive was Phoenix, which had been initiated in a decree by President Thieu in December 1967. It had been almost totally set aside by the Tet 1968 offensive: first by the need of all the intelligence agencies to focus on the military and guerrilla threat of the attack and its aftermath; and second by the pacification program's concentration on the requirements of reconstruction and relief after the massive damages Tet produced. The outlines of the program were still there, however, and the need to concentrate on an understanding of the political enemy was even greater in the face of the Communist development of the more sophisticated tools of the Alliance and the Liberation Committees to prosecute a political offensive.

The Alliance was simply another front, comparable to the National Liberation Front set up in 1960 to give the impression that non-Communist elements were involved in the struggle against the Government. But the Liberation Committees were much more significant as preparations for the claim that they represented local government in their communities and had to have a role in any settlement of the war. If our side of the dispute approached the problem as

simply a military one, we could have found ourselves out-
maneuvered by these political tactics and forces of the
enemy. The first job was to understand them.

The Phoenix program may have been moribund at that
juncture, but it provided the base for a new effort. In a series
of meetings, planning papers, and discussions with Vietnamese and American intelligence agencies, we put together a whole new start to the effort and gave it a new
priority. The result was a new decree by President Thieu in
July that established it as a national priority program, the
key to which would be the establishment of a center in each
of the nation's 244 administrative districts at which all of
the intelligence and security agencies present in the area
would be represented. Each was directed to contribute its
knowledge of the Communist "infrastructure," the term
chosen to describe the Communist political apparatus that
acted as the area's political command and control machinery against the Government. The objective was described as
seeking to identify and understand the Communist "political order of battle" in the same way military intelligence
traditionally tried to comprehend the military order of
battle it faced.

A special arrangement was made on the American side to
provide a corps of advisers to these district centers, who
would work with the local Vietnamese officials, military,
police, and civilians. The American military, in their
customary rapid response to a requirement for a new contribution to the war effort, immediately identified a number of
officers to serve at the district centers and set up training
and orientation courses for them. With the typical flexibility of American military officers, they saw the point of the
exercise as soon as it was explained to them and developed
as much enthusiasm for identifying the members of the
local tax-collecting committee as the location of the local
guerrilla unit—all covered, in the abbreviated American
parlance, by the initials VCI, meaning "Viet Cong Infrastructure."

One decision about the program was made at the outset:
that it would not be a secret police activity. Accordingly, the
launching of the program took place in full public view,
with new Prime Minister Tran Thien Khiem leading a

parade through the streets of Saigon, making it clear that the Government wanted and needed the help of the citizenry to identify the leaders of the secret Communist apparatus who were responsible for the bombs in the marketplaces, the assassinations of village authorities, and the taxation and conscription of villagers for the Communist enemy. In effect, it constituted not only a declaration of war on the secret Communist enemy but also a call to the people of South Vietnam to join the war effort and not merely cheer on the soldiers.

It recognized that the enemy was not a faraway, structured force but a presence the villagers had become accustomed to living with. The skeleton of the small motorcycle bus that hit a mine on its way to morning market, the random mortaring of the refugee camp to drive its inhabitants back to the countryside, where they could act as couriers and food suppliers to the local guerrilla forces, the murdered schoolteacher or village official—these were the aspects of the war familiar to the rural population. They were a regular part of village life, more constant than the sporadic uproar of the American or Vietnamese Army units, which were certainly frightening and devastating but mercifully soon gone.

Some idea of the scope of this assault on the ordinary people of South Vietnam can be seen from the fact that in 1969 alone, more than 6,000 officials and citizens lost their lives in this terror and some 15,000 were wounded. Among those killed were 23 village chiefs, 126 hamlet chiefs, 229 refugees, and 4,350 private citizens. Of the total, also, over 1,200 were the victims of selective assassinations rather than of merely the random mine, rocket, or mortar round. These 1969 figures were rather lower than those of 1968, and the decline continued, but their sheer numbers show the extent of real danger facing the rural citizens of Vietnam and the ever-present threat of nonmilitary Communist attacks with which they lived.

The Prime Minister thus struck a responsive chord when he named the shadowy figures of the "infrastructure" as the source of the permanent fear and terror felt by the rural villagers, whose only real desire was to till their land and raise their families with as little interference as possible. He called upon all to help the fight against them by reporting what entire communities well knew about them—their identities, their habits, their threats. And the parade and ceremony were purely Vietnamese. The ubiquitous Americans took no part, most being baffled by the banners and slogans, all in Vietnamese. In this sense too, the affair was a new declaration of war by the South Vietnamese against their enemies, not a part of the American soldiers' war.

To clarify the program for the American personnel, military and civilian, who would be supporting and working with it, I developed a Command directive to govern their actions. I wanted to make it clear that they would not be involved in a campaign to attack, by fair means or foul, the secret forces of the enemy. The directive explained the role of the infrastructure as the central line of command of the enemy subversive apparatus in Vietnam. I then said very plainly that the program was not a program of assassination but an intelligence program, and that any actions against the apparatus and its personnel it identified would be conducted according to the laws of war. The language of the instruction is worth repeating:

> The PHOENIX program is one of advice, support and assistance to the GVN Phuong Hoang program, aimed at reducing the influence and effectiveness of the Viet Cong Infrastructure in South Viet-Nam. The Viet Cong Infrastructure is an inherent part of the war effort being waged against the GVN by the Viet Cong and their North Vietnamese Allies. The unlawful status of members of the Viet Cong Infrastructure (as defined in the Green Book and in GVN official decrees) is well established in GVN law and is in full accord with the laws of land warfare followed by the United States Army.
>
> Operations against the Viet Cong Infrastructure include the collection of intelligence identifying these members, inducing them to abandon their allegiance to the Viet Cong and rally to the government, capturing or arresting them in order to bring them before Province Security Committees for lawful sentencing, and, as a final resort, the use of

military or police force against them if no other way
of preventing them from carrying on their unlawful
activities is possible. Our training emphasizes the
desirability of obtaining these target individuals
alive and of using intelligent and lawful methods of
interrogation to obtain the truth of what they know
about other aspects of the Viet Cong Infrastructure.
U.S. personnel are under the same legal and moral
constraints with respect to operations of a Phoenix
character as they are with respect to regular military operations against enemy units in the field.
Thus, they are specifically not authorized to engage
in assassinations or other violations of the rules of
land warfare, but they are entitled to use such reasonable military force as is necessary to obtain the
goals of rallying, capturing, or eliminating the Viet
Cong Infrastructure in the Republic of Viet-Nam.

If U.S. personnel come in contact with activities
conducted by Vietnamese which do not meet the
standards of the rules of land warfare, they are
certainly not to participate further in the activity.
They are also expected to make their objections to
this kind of behavior known to the Vietnamese
conducting them and they are expected to report the
circumstances to next higher U.S. authority for decision as to action to be taken with the GVN.

There are individuals who find normal police or
even military operations repugnant to them personally, despite the overall legality and morality of
these activities. Arrangements exist whereby individuals having this feeling about military affairs
can, according to law, receive specialized assignments or even exemptions from military service.
There is no similar legislation with respect to police
type activities of the U.S. military, but if an individual finds the police type activities of the PHOENIX
program repugnant to him, on his application, he
can be reassigned from the program without preju-
dice.

I have been asked why I issued this directive and particu-

larly why it mentioned assassination. The answer is simple.
I knew that the French Army, after their defeat at Dien Bien
Phu in Vietnam, had given much thought to their tactics
there and had developed a doctrine of how to combat the
new *guerre revolutionnaire* by concentrating on building
security in local communities rather than thinking of the
war as a military one, as the French had largely done in
Vietnam. Faced with the challenge of the *Front National de
Libération* in Algeria, the tactic had been carefully applied
in several experiments and grew to larger scale. It had
proven quite effective, bringing about a distinct decline in
FLN strength.

But it contained a flaw that had proved fatal. Through
euphemism and subterfuge, the French services adopted a
conscious program of torturing prisoners to obtain information. It even tried to justify torture morally as protecting
the greater number of innocent bystanders from the terrorism deliberately conducted by the FLN to demonstrate that
the French authorities could not protect the population. An
enterprising French journalist penetrated the scheme and
published his denunciation of it under the title *"J'Accuse,"*
with devastating results for the Army's effort in Algeria.
Metropolitan France, which was none too happy with the
struggle in Algeria in any case, was roused to indignation
at what was being done in its name, and much of the
sentiment for withdrawal stemmed from this incident.

I was by no means naive enough to believe that atrocities
had not taken place on both sides in Vietnam, or that they
would not occur again, but I was resolved that the issue of
lawfulness be brought into the open and clearly decided for
the Phoenix program. The directive therefore specifically
described the operations that would be conducted as induc-
ing VCI members to rally to the Government, capturing or
arresting them, and, "as a final resort the use of military or
police force against them." It stressed that we wanted to
obtain them alive in order to use "intelligent and lawful
methods of interrogation" on them. The specific prohibition of assassination, or other violations of the rules of land
warfare beyond the use of reasonable military force, was
designed to make our position clear, as were the instructions specifying what Americans were to do if they encoun-

tered Vietnamese violating these standards. The purpose
was to put our policies clearly on record so that the personnel involved would have them as direct instructions and as
part of their training. There was to be no misunderstanding that headquarters was giving them a free hand and
winking at whatever they might do. We were also providing
the basis to enforce the directive in the years ahead to ensure
that Americans conformed and that cases of Vietnamese
violations that came to our attention would be reported so
that we at the command level could take them up with the
Vietnamese leadership. In later years, in appearances before
Congressional Committees, I was glad I had written the
directive.

Despite these instructions, Phoenix has, of course, become a synonym for brutality in Vietnam by the Government and the United States—not by the enemy. Part of this
has arisen because of confusion between the primary *intelligence* function of the program—gathering and analyzing
information to determine the identities and organization of
the Viet Cong Infrastructure—and the *operations* conducted against them. Those *operations* were undertaken by
all the forces engaged in the battle there—the regular armies, the territorials, the police, the Provincial Reconnaissance Units (PRUs), and even the self-defense forces. They
all operated under their own command systems and used
Phoenix information, but they were not part of Phoenix.
Some units, especially some of the American military, used
the term "Phoenix" to refer to any operation against the
VCI or other irregulars, even when the operation had no
connection with the Phoenix program at all. Indeed, some
of the more lurid accusations heard in public have turned
out, on examination, to be in exactly this category.

But because the key to Phoenix operations was the careful targeting of individual VCI leaders, the work would
clearly be more akin to police work than normal military
operations against enemy units. This was the reason I
included in the directive the offer to allow regular military
officers to drop out of the program if they did not want to be
involved in "police-type" activities, in the same way that
conscientious objectors are authorized by law to be excused
from military operations. I was trying to make it clear that

the program was well within the laws of war and also that it was an essential element in the kind of war the enemy was fighting.

Meanwhile, the program Komer had launched in 1967 of strengthening the territorials, the Popular Forces at the village level and the Regional Forces at the provincial level, began to bear fruit in the increase of units and personnel, the better weapons of the M-16, training camps and activities for existing as well as new units, and more American advisers to work at these levels. It was apparent that the tools were being developed for a real effort on pacification. The enemy's actions to prepare the ground politically for negotiation and participation in government made it clear that the need was urgent.

Ho Chi Minh had correctly read the American public reaction to the Tet attack, dramatized by President Lyndon Johnson's decision not to be a candidate for reelection, as indicating that the American will to continue the war, like that of the French after their defeat at Dien Bien Phu, was failing. In April the Communists signaled their readiness to negotiate to end the war, and the delegations met—and stalemated—in Paris on May 10. Ho anticipated that some face-saving formulas might be necessary in order to actually secure the withdrawal of the Americans, so he was preparing the political structure that could allow the Communist Party to manipulate the political scene in such negotiations and lead to its assumption of power thereafter.

Komer and I were concerned that this scenario might not be sufficiently appreciated in the military command. We thus decided to present a briefing at the monthly command review of the situation and strategy, conducted by the new commander, General Creighton Abrams, who had taken over from Westmoreland in mid-1968. The session was also attended by Ambassador Bunker and the senior American military commanders in the four regions of the country. It was an Americans-only meeting to encourage the frankest possible discussion of problems and alternatives. The horseshoe table included the American high command in Vietnam and much of the military leadership of the United States for a number of years to come. Aside from Bunker and Abrams, there were General Andrew Goodpaster, formerly aide to President Eisenhower and later NATO Commander, General George Brown, Commander of the Seventh Air Force covering Southeast Asia and later Chief of Staff of the USAF and Chairman of the Joint Chiefs of Staff, and Admiral Elmo Zumwalt, later to become Chief of Naval Operations. In Vietnam Zumwalt had broadened U.S. Navy participation from coastal patrols to include small attack craft sailing up the winding and dangerous Delta of the Mekong and other rivers as deep into the country as the Cambodian border.

They were surrounded by their staffs and assistants, including many who would play important roles in the future, such as George Keegan as Chief of Intelligence for the Air Force, Daniel Graham, later head of the Defense Intelligence Agency, and John Singlaub, one of my parachutist companions in France in 1944, who in 1968 was running the covert operations against the North that the CIA had turned over to the military in 1963. The horseshoe table faced a translucent screen, behind which a supporting cast changed the dozens of colored slides and statistics charts to show on cue everything from the number of air operations run that week to the latest reports of traffic on the Ho Chi Minh Trail. Komer asked me to give the briefing on the political side of the war to these worthies, which I was glad to do, although, of course, I checked it out in detail with him in advance.

The briefing proved a critical step in our effort in Vietnam. I reviewed the political structure of the enemy and the various stages it had passed through. The original Indochinese Communist Party had been renamed the Vietnamese Workers Party (Lao Dong) and never again identified itself as "Communist." In 1960, the National Liberation Front had been established to repeat the successful front technique employed by the Viet Minh League against the French. In 1962, a separate party (in name), the People's Revolutionary Party, had been established to present the picture of a separate (Communist) party for South Vietnam, "independent" of the Lao Dong Party in power in North Vietnam. The spring and summer of 1968 saw the next logical step in this progression, the formation of the Alliance of National, Democratic, and Peace Forces, in order to associate ostensibly (and, to the extent possible, actual) non-Communist elements with the program of replacing the Thieu Government, either by such pressure that it would collapse or as part of a negotiated solution in which power sharing would permit the withdrawal of the American forces.

To supplement the political picture the Alliance presented (in conjunction with the People's Revolutionary Party as the controlling element and the National Liberation Front as the overall cover for the fight against Thieu and the Americans), I outlined on the map of the country the locations of reports of the formation of Liberation Committees and described their purpose as the assertion of local government authority, not mere political representation. The maps made clear their clustering in areas of heavy Communist presence (as reported by our Hamlet Evaluation System) and also their tendency to expand toward areas more favorable to the Government. The enemy strategy thus described, it became easy to point out the need for an appropriate counterstrategy for the Vietnamese Government and the Americans, i.e., a vigorous extension of security and political presence by the Government, with American support, in order to preempt the areas not yet penetrated by the Communists and to spread the Government presence into the contested areas.

I pointed out that this was a job for the local security forces of the Vietnamese, now properly armed and being trained for the job, and for the civil institutions of the Government. The military role, Vietnamese and American, was to screen these areas from incursions by regular Communist forces, attacking them in "spoiling" operations to keep them off balance and away from the settled areas, since the Vietnamese local security forces, if left to themselves, could be overwhelmed. But I made no call for either the Vietnamese or American military to participate in the pacification exercise itself.

I added that this campaign needed a political element as well, one that, by establishing democratic legitimacy in the villages through local officials, would provide a non-Communist structure to counter the claims of the Liberation Committees. As a final flourish to the briefing, I said we should set ourselves the target of seizing the initiative in this key aspect of the battle and turn around the course of the war by the anniversary of the Tet attack at the end of the coming January.

I had, of course, addressed my remarks most directly to General Abrams, and I was not disappointed. He listened intently, following each point with obvious understanding of the essentially political analysis I was giving. At the end he tapped his cigar thoughtfully, thanked me warmly for the briefing, and gave Komer his full approval and support to go ahead and work out such a campaign with President Thieu.

Komer reacted with the same drive and force he had shown when President Johnson first told him to "supervise the other war" in Washington and when he arrived in Vietnam to assert the coequal status of the pacification program in the American military command. He called upon our staff for details of the situation in the provinces, what assets existed, what were already programmed to be available, and what additional ones could be brought in. Working against the end-January target, and allowing time to do the necessary planning and briefings of the local authorities, we decided on a three-month blitz starting November 1, which Komer christened the Accelerated Pacification Campaign, or APC, as it came to be known even to the Vietnamese.

Komer insisted that the Campaign not be merely a rhetorical exhortation but a plan of specific accomplishments to be achieved. Of our Hamlet Evaluation System's six rankings, reflecting the hamlets' degree of security and development, the first three (A, B, and C) described levels of a "secure" state. The next two (D and E) applied to locales that were "contested." V, of course, denoted that the hamlet was under Communist control. We thus incorporated in the APC an objective of bringing 1,000 hamlets from a "contested" to a relatively "secure" state—C on the scale—during the three months, and this thousand was broken down into specific province and district goals. Similarly, 200,000 weapons were to be distributed to self-defense groups in the rural areas, also broken down into individual requirements for each province and district. If some province advisers protested that their allocated objectives were not realistic, Komer listened and was even ready to reduce goals in response to a good argument, but he was forceful with anyone who he sensed merely wanted to do business as usual.

Over the years, the Americans had come up with a series of great ideas and programs to turn the war around, all of which had foundered on a Vietnamese inability or unwillingness, sometimes for good cause, to execute the programs according to the American formula. Komer and I were acutely conscious of this sad history and realized that the key to making the APC work lay with President Thieu and the Vietnamese chain of command down to the provinces and districts. If they could be convinced that the program was in their interest and the interest of a non-Communist Vietnam, they would support and work for it. Whatever the American role in conceiving and supporting the program, it was essential that it be executed by local Vietnamese, and felt by them to be theirs rather than an imposition of the American successors to the French.

Komer approached the subject in this way in his first description of the idea of the Campaign to Thieu. Thieu liked Komer and his clear commitment to the best interests of both the Vietnamese and the Americans. He appreciated the careful staff work Komer had done and his development of specific goals for the Campaign, together with his access to the independent monitoring service of the American advisory network to check on how the subordinate Vietnamese officials would implement the programs involved. Most of all, Thieu appreciated the strategy the Campaign reflected, meeting the Communist challenge at the local political level where they fought the war. He had contested with the Communists over the years, understood the attraction of their nationalist approach, and knew it could be met only by a more effective political approach on his side. Thieu was not philosophical by nature but pragmatic, and he had seen the futility of the French military and colonialist approach. He knew and was a part of the Vietnamese military that had provided the only structure for the state in the face of the Communist assault.

Thieu also had learned something of the Americans—

that to handle their enthusiasm it was not appropriate to challenge them directly, as Diem and Nhu were wont to do, but it was sensible to accept their ideas rather than reject them and then try to adjust them to make them more practical. In this manner he retained the Americans' goodwill, and channeled their support to what could practically be accomplished in the real world of Vietnam, which the Americans frequently did not fully understand. So he eagerly accepted and endorsed Komer's proposal for the Accelerated Pacification Campaign and put his full weight behind it. This had an immediate effect on the subordinate Vietnamese officers at the regional and provincial levels, where the detailed plans were drawn up for exactly which hamlets would be upgraded, where the self-defense weapons would be distributed, and where the cadre teams would work to reestablish village government.

As the plans were drawn up, I made one major suggestion for the strategy of the Campaign: that its first priority be placed on the Mekong Delta provinces south of Saigon. The Tet attack had devastated many of the communities of that area, but it was clearly the key to a successful national pacification campaign, since it contained a disproportionate percentage of the people of the nation, especially the rural population—some six million in all—and was the rice basket for the whole country. Komer agreed to the logic, even though we both knew we were taking on a large job, as the density of Vietnamese Army units there was thin compared to some of the more northern areas, and there was only one American division stationed in that area. But this was the point of the exercise. Pacification was not a military chore but one of local security and development, so that it was in the Delta that the need for it was obviously the greatest.

We thus gave the Delta provinces priority on the allocation of self-defense weapons, the newly authorized increases in Regional Force battalions and Popular Force platoons, and cadre teams. To make our point crystal clear, Komer accepted my idea that John Vann be transferred from his leadership of the pacification program in the provinces around Saigon and take over as head of the program in the Delta. After first objecting to the move as taking him away

from what he thought he could finally accomplish in the
Saigon area after so many years of frustration, Vann agreed
to accept the challenge, as we knew he would when he saw
that we considered the Delta the area in which pacification
could at last make a major contribution to the war.

In a whirlwind of briefings of regional and local officials, drafts of plans, and preparations of supporting personnel and logistics, the Campaign was launched on schedule on November 1. So many ideal plans had been put
together over the years in Vietnam that it received little
attention outside the pacification community and the local
officials who had to carry it out. They, however, were
acutely conscious of the fact that President Thieu was
demanding real performance, and that the American advisory chain had been fully mobilized not only to help but to
judge their performance as measured by results and report
them directly to the President. Only a few did what they
could to convince their local American advisers to fudge the
reports and found them unwilling. Others who thought the
Americans could hardly measure their real success or failure found that the Americans insisted on visiting the communities planned for inclusion in the Campaign and
looked for the facts to see whether the plans were being
carried out. This is not to imply that the American reports
were totally accurate, either in their myriad statistics or in
the detail called for by the report forms. In fact, however,
with all their inaccuracies, they did give a better picture of
what was happening at the local level than we had ever had
before.

Just as the Campaign began, however, a change took
place on the American side. President Johnson was facing
his last days in office and wanted to do what he could to
thank some of his aides who had worked long and hard for
him. Prominent on the list was Bob Komer, and the President knew that his first interest had been the Middle East.
He thus appointed Komer to become Ambassador to Turkey, where he hoped the drive he had shown for Johnson
could be repeated in that important area for his successor.
Thus, on November 6, I accompanied Komer to the small
Air Force jet that would take him to Hong Kong for the
connection to Washington and thanked him for all he had

done to get pacification finally launched as a major strategy of the war. I thanked him also for arranging for me to succeed him in the job of making it work. I did not then know that I also should have thanked him for arguing that I should also succeed to his personal rank of Ambassador, which he insisted would be necessary for me to have the status and clout to make the program work.

As Komer flew away to his new challenge, highlighted by a welcoming riot in Ankara that overturned and burned his car (to his undisguised delight), I turned to the job of making pacification work and making certain that its political purpose remain its priority, however much it had to be surrounded by the practical elements of guns, tin roofing, cement, and roads. And in this I knew I had a strong supporter. In one of my first discussions with General Abrams as his new Deputy for Pacification, Abrams said he looked forward to a fine relationship with me. He highlighted his approach by saying in one of his command conferences that he wanted to hear no more of "the other war" of pacification—henceforth the entire effort was to be "one war."

16

Pacification on the Offensive

THE ACCELERATED PACIFICATION CAMPAIGN WAS a great success. Perhaps its most important result was to energize the Government and local officials to take the offensive in the war and to do so at the level of the people's war. In the vital matter of rural security, after some cross-checking at the outset of the Campaign, we had made some alterations in the original targeting of hamlets to eliminate localities that had already reached the midpoint for security (and in some cases had been proposed by local officials for just that reason, thereby assigning themselves tasks that were in effect already accomplished). The basic objective of increasing the population living in security from the enemy was indeed achieved: over a million people inhabited the hamlets which were upgraded and where the Government's authority had been established locally.

The reports indicated that the Campaign's statistical goals were generally achieved. Some of the statistics, though, we thought were fairly soft, to put it mildly. A case in point was the claim that more than 7,000 members of the Communist apparatus had been taken out of action by being captured, by accepting amnesty, or by being killed in military or police actions. Our complaint was over the tendency to credit to the Phoenix program almost any local guerrilla who surrendered, or was captured or killed, as being a part of the hard-core leadership apparatus the Phoenix program was seeking to identify. We took with a grain of salt the figure of 1.1 million recruited into the People's Self-Defense Force, with 400,000 trained. But there was no doubt that, as reported, 170,000 weapons had been distributed to the villages, and it was notable that this figure did *not* meet the 200,000 goal. The 8,600 amnesties

much exceeded the 5,000 goal, but they were disproportion-
ately in the Delta area and included, in our view, many who
had had only a minimal connection with the Communists
and were now free to assert their preference for the Government's side in the war.

Our overall assessment was that the Communists had not
resisted the Campaign—and perhaps had viewed it as nothing more than another of the Government's campaigns
more visible on paper than on the ground. But this was
irrelevant to our strategy; it was precisely our intention to
extend the Government's writ first into the areas of least
enemy presence as a base for later expansion, and not to
confront the enemy in his strong points. The main purposes—seizing the initiative in a fundamentally political
struggle, gradually engaging the population in the war on
the Government's side, and depriving the enemy of his
earlier access to the population—had been achieved.

The Campaign brought to the Vietnamese something
beyond initiative: it brought organization. President Thieu
quickly understood that a major strategy of pacification
required the kind of unified management structure the
Americans had finally produced in the CORDS machinery.
In response, he set up a Central Pacification and Development Council to direct the Campaign and the work of all
the Ministries and agencies of the Government involved in
it. He placed the Council in the Office of the Prime Minister with its own integrated staff, led by an effective Major
General, Cao Hao Hon, who could speak with the direct
authority of the Prime Minister. All of the Government
Ministries, including Defense plus the Joint General Staff,
were represented on the Council, so that its directives were
specific and binding on all the local organs involved in the
pacification Campaign. None could ignore them by asserting that it had not received instructions from its parent
Ministry.

What developed was a pyramid on the Vietnamese side,
starting with the President on top, the National Council
under him, followed by the four Regional Councils under
the Regional Commander, and then the forty-four Provincial Councils under each Province chief. The latter gathered all the representatives of the different Ministries in his

Province into one body to put together and implement a coherent plan for the pacification of that Province. Each Government service made its contribution to the effort. The day of each Ministry, agency, or service doing its own thing, in whatever direction it might think best, was over. As now organized, the plan went up this integrated pyramid for review—sometimes modified if it was too cautious or did not fit well with the plans of neighboring Provinces—and final Vietnamese approval.

The Americans had an overlay of the Vietnamese structure. We repeated their pyramid: the national CORDS staff working with the Central Council and the different Ministries and national programs, then the Regional CORDS staffs, and then the vital level of the Province Advisory Teams, each under a single Province Senior Adviser who controlled the American advisers to all the different programs, civilian and military, working in his area.

Reporting chains and systems, from the Hamlet Evaluation System to a number of special ones for such programs as amnesty, Phoenix, and Territorial Forces, went up both Vietnamese and American channels. They were fully shared at all levels. The computerized analyses produced by the American side became the working tools both the Vietnamese and Americans used to measure progress.

During visits to the regions and provinces, the President and the Prime Minister conducted reviews of how well the provinces were implementing the plan. These visits included not only a formal briefing but tours of some of the villages to see whether what was reported in the statistics was being matched by actual performance. In this process, the CORDS advisory network played a major role. I could bring their independent reports of weaknesses and shortfalls to the attention of the President or the Central Council staff, who in turn would prod the local officials. In these reports, the Americans were not shy about criticizing Vietnamese officials—or recommending their replacement—all of which I would quietly pass on to the Prime Minister.

There were, of course, differences and difficulties in these relationships from time to time. Vietnamese officials would take issue with the local American assessment of the situation in a particular community, saying the American's lack

of Vietnamese language and too occasional visits had pre-
vented him from understanding the true situation. Since
most such protests were that the situation was better than
the American had judged it, the Americans were quite
willing to check the matter out by a joint visit. The size of
the escort proposed for the visit would generally indicate
the degree to which the Vietnamese officer really believed
his more favorable assessment. At the same time, the Americans had to be wary of becoming the target of political or
bureaucratic frictions among the Vietnamese.

There was also a delay before the Ministries, under continued persuasion from the Central Council, abandoned
the finely crafted directives they were accustomed to issue
from their air-conditioned offices in Saigon. But finally,
accepting the transfer of direction and control of their
programs to the province chiefs, they turned to their true
function of supporting them. After the Vietnamese began to
realize that their President was serious about the goals of
the program and would hold them to account to achieve
them, the principal arguments were usually over what
goals it was feasible to include in the next plan. Here the
American local adviser might support his Vietnamese
counterpart, and pressure from above might be needed to
convince both that the Campaign was a serious exercise to
change the pace of the war, not to continue business as
usual. In some situations, of course, the American had to be
restrained from reinventing a wheel that he conceived as he
started his tour but that his Vietnamese counterpart had
seen tried and found wanting or impossible too many times
before.

The question of whether the Campaign was American or
Vietnamese had to be faced constantly, with the answer that
it had to be both. The drive and initiatives that came from
the American side as a result of the long overdue integration
of the American effort in CORDS, plus the independent
advisory chain from Saigon to the farthest province and
district, were certainly essential to the program; many of its
basic elements came out of the ferment among the Americans seeking new ways to apply the basic strategy. But the
Americans also knew full well that the strategy would fail
if it became only an American program. It depended upon

Vietnamese motivation and organization to make it work at the local levels. We therefore put the word out through the advisory chain that the American function was to advise, not command; to suggest, not direct; and to support, not displace, local Vietnamese leadership. Attending the briefings and conferences, the Americans would be seated at the side, clearly leaving management of the meetings to the Vietnamese.

This technique was also followed at the senior levels, where ideas might be discussed in general terms but the directives were written by Vietnamese, followed by further consultation as to how they might be made better. The Vietnamese chain of command was understood as the primary one. Translations of summaries of the Vietnamese directives were sent through the American chain so the advisers could see what their Vietnamese counterparts were directed to accomplish and could make their assessments of how it was working on the ground. From time to time this required that the Americans accept something less than they would have preferred, simply to stress the support rather than the command role.

For example, midway in the APC, the directive came through Vietnamese channels that the Vietnamese would not use the terms we had established for the Hamlet Evaluation System, i.e., A, B, and C on the scale as "Government controlled" (in different degrees), D and E as "contested," and V as Viet Cong controlled. Instead, we were told, President Thieu had directed that the A-B-C-D-E categories be carried as "areas controlled by the Government" and V as "not yet fully controlled by the Government." We initially suspected that the change might be a deliberate effort to slack off on the essentials of the Campaign. We found out, however, that President Thieu believed he had to protect himself in the negotiations in Paris from any "admission" by his own Government that it conceded control of some of its communities to the enemy. The matter was solved without great difficulty by the Government using its nomenclature but showing within the first category the usual degrees of A-B-C-D-E. We continued to assess the hamlets according to the original reporting system, which continued to be used as the measure of the Campaign.

The APC was only a start, of course, and its main accomplishment lay not in its actions on the ground but in its concentration of the Government's and Americans' attention on the need for a long-term pacification strategy. In order to make that a reality we were already devoting considerable time, even during the three-month APC, to the next steps—the specific pacification plans for the coming year, 1969 (Tet 1969 to Tet 1970). A general set of guidelines and principles was developed by the Central Council. This was sent to the provinces to be applied in preparing their plans (for ultimate approval at the regional and national levels).

The principles called for the same kinds of specific goals for expansion of the pacification campaign that characterized the APC, but also for several new features designed to emphasize the longer-term political nature of the strategy. Certain areas were delineated as "national areas of precedence." Others were listed for priority treatment within certain provinces. Large areas of the country were left unspecified, meaning that we would worry about them later. These priorities closely followed our knowledge of population density, so that the geographic precedence we established was directly adapted from Marshal Lyautey's "ink spot" pacification strategy developed decades before in Morocco: starting with the population centers we were gradually spreading outward, so that the base was first consolidated, then expanded. We were using tactical defense in a strategic offensive.

The political component of the year's plans focused on the revival of locally elected government. Village elections had been scheduled for 1967, but few had actually taken place because of insecurity. The 1969 plan called for such elections to be held in all villages where security permitted, as determined by looking at their ratings under the Hamlet Evaluation System. In order to create incentive, the funds provided (by CORDS) for local development projects, one million *dong* per village, were made contingent on such elections actually having been held. Villages that held no election were allocated a smaller amount.

In addition, the procedures decreed that no project would be eligible for village development funds unless it had been selected by the elected village council after public discussion in the community as to which alternative the council should select—a new footbridge, irrigation ditch, schoolhouse, or whatever. Further, projects costing less than a moderate amount could be implemented directly by the village chief and council, without submission for approval by the district or province authorities.

To ensure that the new political message of reliance on local communities and their own authorities went out to the nation, the rural development cadre training center under the indefatigable Colonel Nguyen Be was turned into a national training center for newly elected village chiefs, councilmen (and women), and hamlet chiefs. The principal lessons taught at the center were that these elected officials were truly the leaders of their communities and that they were to administer the various Government programs in their areas with the participation and support of the people. The approach stressed that their authority and direction came upward from the people of their community and were not to be imposed upon them. One village chief heard with near disbelief that he would be given authority to decide on anything as important as the expenditure of money without superior approval, even in the relatively minor amount set in the plan. The idea brought tears to his eyes.

The courses were for six weeks, with over 2,000 local officials in attendance, and each ended with a dramatic ceremony attended by the President, the Government Ministers, and a goodly selection of the members of the National Assembly. One can sense the impact of such a center if one would imagine the value to an American Presidential candidate of meeting directly with the Selectmen and Mayors of every town and village of the United States at the conclusion of a program describing their responsibilities and stressing their authority in their local communities.

Another step in the 1969 plan emphasizing its political thrust involved the rural development cadre teams. Clothed, like the peasants whom they were enlisting in the community effort, in the black pajamas that made a Vietnamese rural scene viewed from a distance seem to be populated by so many ants, the teams had been operating in fifty-nine-man groups that provided their own defense and security in the villages where they worked. We now divided them into thirty-man teams. For their defense and security, they were to rely on the increased local security forces and self-defense groups in the communities to which they were assigned. They were directed to concentrate on their primary mission to stimulate a community spirit aimed at improving the villagers' lives, in place of being simultaneously preoccupied with their own basic security.

All the other elements of an integrated pacification campaign were also included in the year's plan, building up from the districts and provinces to the national level. Each aspect set specific goals: the Self-Defense Force was to be increased from one to two million members, 400,000 of whom were to be armed, rather than the 170,000 achieved in the APC; a goal of 20,000 amnesty claimants was set, with special incentives to be offered to family members and others who induced them to leave the enemy and rejoin the national community; provisions were included to reintroduce them into local life or, in some cases, to resettle them to protect them from Communist retaliation for their defection. The goal for refugees was to reduce the total below one million, primarily by assisting 300,000 to resettle in the communities newly secured against enemy military action by the expansion of the pacified areas.

The Phoenix program was to reduce the Communist apparatus by some 33,000 cadres by increasing the Phoenix identification activities and passing the information to the military, police, and other elements, who were to induce defections, capture them, or attack them in their strongholds. Rice production was to be increased from five million to six million tons over the year by pressing the use of the new "miracle rice" just recently been developed in the Philippines. The plan covered a jumble of different programs, but they were to be integrated in the provincial plans so that the spread of miracle rice, for example, would occur in the communities where new local territorial forces were assigned and self-defense groups organized. We were avoiding having each program operating on its own without mutual support or strategy.

Important as the development of such integrated plans

may be, the proof of the pudding is, again, in the eating. And here we met a problem. The APC had indeed had a major impact, engaging the attention of the Government machinery and many of the local communities affected. Its three-month duration, however, set a limited attention span for it, and its termination at Tet brought a feeling of accomplishment and relaxation. The fact that the 1969 plan was for an entire year removed the sense of short-term urgency the APC had produced. As a result, the Vietnamese machinery essentially coasted for a considerable period.

When the American advisory network began to point this out in its reports, and we expressed concern that the strategy could well become another paper exercise in Vietnam's long list of such, President Thieu reacted quickly and began to press the 1969 plan with the same urgency he had accorded the APC. He insisted on a series of visits to the four regions, to begin with a briefing at the regional command with all province chiefs and their American counterparts in attendance. There the reports of actions taken to comply with the new plan were reported and reviewed against the independent reports of the American advisers as to what changes were actually occurring on the ground. This would be followed by a visit to one of the provinces for a closer look at the situation in a particular district or even village, the selection having been checked against the American reports to ensure that not only a Potemkin-like facade would be presented.

Again the Presidential interest and insistence on the importance of the program brought results. The local province chiefs turned to their American counterparts to discuss just how they should work together to accomplish the results called for by the plans—and to ensure that they were properly included in the reports. The Americans' monthly written reports, apart from the statistics fed to the computer-run measuring system, would resound with their concern at slow progress in certain areas or programs, and with their calls for corrective action to overcome problems in support or direction of individual programs, from the availability of fertilizer to the tendency in the Phoenix program to meet its goals by actions affecting low-level Communists rather than the leading cadres at which the

program was aimed. The problems cited would generate
intense discussions between the Vietnamese and the American staff officers at the regional and national levels seeking
to refine the programs or to remedy their deficiencies.

The Americans also held separate sets of regional meetings. We reviewed the details of the various programs and
worked out how best the American influence could be used,
and at what level, to build up the needed pressure for
concrete results. We did not hesitate to modify the plans to
achieve the real goals of strengthening the local communities, engaging their members in the struggle to keep free of
Communist pressures, and producing a better life for their
children. But a late-night helicopter ride home from the
Delta (at 3,000 feet to avoid possible shots at our running
lights) after one of our meetings showed me vividly that
there was more to be done. Below we saw the flashes as the
artillery fired rounds into enemy-held areas, and occasionally flares appeared over some local outpost under attack.
Some areas, however, were peacefully dark, so some progress was being made.

Did the Americans come on too strong, taking initiative
and self-reliance from the Vietnamese? We certainly came
on strong to the officialdom with whom we worked, but the
thrust of our pressures was always to engage the rural
population in a common effort to establish more secure and
better lives. Our pressures were aimed at the officials, not
the population itself. Moreover, they accurately reflected the
policies of the Vietnamese leadership seeking a better way to
defeat the Communist effort. The planning and statistical
reporting systems were technically advanced, and they were
certainly complex, but they were designed to impose a
discipline on the effort, and they did so.

We Americans had no apologies for putting major pressure on the officials, in view of our nation's huge commitment to defending Vietnam and our own conviction that we
had at last developed a winning strategy that could defeat
the common enemy of both nations. Also, we were working
with the full endorsement and assistance of President Thieu
and the Prime Minister's Central Council, all of whom
eagerly sought our ideas and welcomed the reports of the
Americans in the field. Thus we operated the whole system
of plans, execution, and evaluation as a piece of compli-

cated and sensitive machinery, to induce and support the individual decisions and actions of millions of simple Vietnamese citizens and families. The answers were to be found in the villages and the cities, not in the computer printouts, but the latter did help us identify weak spots and direct attention and resources to them.

Throughout all the planning, the revising, the countless meetings, I continued my program of twice-weekly evening visits to the provinces. There I frequently could learn more of the real situation over an evening gin and tonic or beer with the Province Chief or the American Advisory Team than in the formal briefings and escorted visits of the daytime. As I rode the helicopter or plane to such a visit, I would review the accumulated statistics, plus recent monthly reports, for what they said of the province and note the comments the Saigon staff had suggested for my attention. During the discussions, and in my room during the night, my notebook would fill up with problems of support or misunderstanding of the various programs at the provincial or district level, which I would pass on the next day to the Saigon staffs to work out solutions or clarification with their Vietnamese counterparts.

In effect, the Central Council on the Vietnamese side, its regional and provincial counterparts, and the CORDS structure on the American side worked as a joint team to push the pacification program under President Thieu's overall direction. I grew accustomed to being the lone American (with my wonderfully fluent friend and helper, Major Jean Sauvageot, muttering translations into my ear from his seat behind me) attending a Central Council meeting—in effect, a Vietnamese Cabinet meeting—or going with President Thieu as one of his staff, the sole American on his aircraft, on a visit to the countryside, eating strange and exotic foods in a fishing or farming community. At one point, a senior Vietnamese official with whom I was working said, "The pacification program is the best organized and conceived operation we have had in Vietnam since Ngo Dinh Nhu's strategic hamlets program." We could share the perspective since we too had experienced both programs, but his remark was a chilling indictment of the lost years of the middle sixties.

By 1969, the CORDS team counted some 1,000 American

civilians and 5,000 American military, from the Saigon headquarters staff to the five-man Mobile Advisory Teams working with the territorial units at village levels through-out the country, helping establish the nightly ambushes to protect against enemy incursions, training the local self-defense forces how to use their weapons, and teaching them how to call during the night for support from the fearsome "Spooky" gunships if under attack. On the Vietnamese side, the balance of forces began to reflect the requirements for a people's war, as the village-level Popular Forces rose to 215,000, the province-level Regional Forces to 260,000, and the People's Self-Defense Forces to some 400,000 armed—finally exceeding in numbers the Vietnamese Army of some 400,000. The National Police also had grown from some 75,000 toward their goal of 120,000, with the 1969 plan calling for half of them to be assigned to villages rather than almost exclusively to the urban areas.

Nowhere in the plan was there a requirement that these local forces produce a "body count," as their purpose was protective, not offensive. The one exception—the Phoenix program aimed at the Communist political infrastruc-ture—had goals of reducing the enemy presence, but its directives made clear that capture or amnesty were the most productive ways of doing so, since they provided informa-tion no "body" could.

Among the Americans, the urgency of the program grew with changes in the United States. The aftermath of the 1968 Tet attack had led to the opening of American (and, reluctantly, South Vietnamese) negotiations with the North Vietnamese and the "Provisional Government" that the Communists had established to receive the surrender or assume authority after a hoped-for American overthrow of President Thieu's Government. But newly elected American President Richard Nixon had no intention of surrendering to the North. At the same time, he realized that the Ameri-can public demanded something more promising than a continuation of the war and American casualties for what appeared a lost cause. His solution was the Nixon Doctrine, stating that the United States would furnish support to nations fighting Communism but would not do the job for them with its own troops. United States forces would be withdrawn from Vietnam, and Vietnam would have to defend itself, but with American economic and logistic support.

Nixon announced this policy during a press conference held on Guam in July 1969. Following that announcement, he made a quick—five-and-a-half-hour—visit to Vietnam. He met with President Thieu at the Presidential Palace to discuss the withdrawal of American ground troops. That action having already been agreed upon and announced, the meeting, which I attended alongside my old friend Marshall Green, then Assistant Secretary of State for East Asia, was purely a formality. Nixon naturally had to spend a good part of his short time visiting U.S. troops for the photographers. But in the Saigon meeting Nixon made clear his high regard for Thieu's leadership of his country, and the U.S. commitment to continue to support him and Vietnam. The point of the visit was, in fact, to reinforce the basic strategy of building up the Vietnamese military to carry the burden of the soldiers' war on the ground and to press the pacification program to win the people's war in the countryside—a welcome Presidential endorsement of my efforts.

From the Nixon Doctrine quickly emerged its corollary, the policy of "Vietnamization," or turning the war over to the Vietnamese and sending the American forces home. The implications of the policy can be seen from the numbers involved. In mid-1968, the American forces numbered some 550,000 troops, with a heavy proportion of support elements. The elimination of the substantial American element of the combined American and Vietnamese forces fighting the enemy would have to be made up in some fashion, or the result could only be victory for the Communists. The answer lay in strengthening the Vietnamese forces to take care of the military threat—and in pacification. If the countryside were cleared of the enemy sufficiently that the Vietnamese regular forces could be withdrawn and assigned to the task of fighting the enemy's regular forces—the major task of the Americans—the balance could be maintained.

The challenge, therefore, was to accelerate pacification to match the withdrawal of the Americans, which began in

July 1969. The first troops, happily, were taken from the Delta, to remove all American units from its heavily populated terrain, so inappropriate for the American "body count" mentality. The geographic objectives of pacification did not greatly change, but, as I said to John Vann, our real objective now was to free the regular Vietnamese Army units from the Delta to replace the departing American units facing the regular North Vietnamese Army units in the northern and mountain provinces on the nation's frontier. My job was to see that this went forward at full speed so that General Abrams could extract the Americans and build up the capabilities of the Vietnamese forces, while Ambassador Bunker tried to calm the fear aroused in the Vietnamese by Henry Kissinger's attempts to negotiate a settlement of the war with the obdurate North Vietnamese, whose basic proposal was the overthrow of Thieu so that they could inherit the land.

On my night visits to the provinces, I frequently invited a guest observer—an American or foreign journalist, a visitor from Washington, or one of the foreign Ambassadors resident in, or accredited to, Vietnam. I stressed that they should accompany me to the briefings and other meetings and ask any question they wished, as the program contained few, if any, secrets. I did ask that the journalists, in whatever copy they filed afterwards, omit the names of the local Vietnamese and American officials with whom they had spoken, thus protecting those lower-level officials from the displeasure of their superiors that was bound to fall upon them if they were named as the source of complaints we heard—and invited—about problems and difficulties in the various programs (of many such trips, only one journalist violated this request).

I was hoping to generate some understanding of the program not only among my traveling companions but among their audiences. With the officials, it generally worked. With the journalists, the record was spottier. Stewart Alsop, a World War II fellow parachutist to the French Resistance who had become a *Newsweek* columnist, spent a long day with me and John Vann driving over washed-out roads from the farthest south province of An Xuyen to the regional capital, at one point passing an artillery battery shooting off into the mangrove swamp from a base next to the road. The title of the article he wrote after our day of discussion in the lurching vehicle and at various stops at district and village centers was "They Just Might Make It"—one of the more positive remarks to appear in the American press at that time.

Another journalist, however, best put the dilemma of our mutual situation on the helicopter ride back to Saigon in the morning by saying that the night had not produced much of a dramatic story he could write about. I agreed that we had not been rocketed or mortared—had not, in fact, been involved in any "dramatic" military action at all. I added, however, that he might have found something quite dramatic had he asked an elderly woman in the village center to compare her present situation with that of the year before. A year ago, I said, she had probably been huddled in a refugee camp wondering where her sons were. Now she was back in her own village, in a house rebuilt by one of the sons who had taken the amnesty program, and was beginning to produce rice on her old property, protected by the other son in the local self-defense unit against the third, who might still be in the Communist guerrilla force in the area—a "dramatic" contrast and story indeed. My visitor accepted the point, but neither of us had any very good idea of how to solve the problem of getting media attention for an essentially undramatic program.

One journalist, a woman, had aggressively challenged me to take her with me as I had her male colleagues. When I did, she ignored the main discussions of the elements of the pacification program to extract from a nice old gentleman, who was a member of the provincial council, his complaints about the dominance of the military in the affairs and hierarchy of his province and the nation. He reminded me of some of his colleagues in the intellectual circles of Saigon who had offered only their disdain to the various Vietnamese leaders trying to organize some form of community strength against the Communists.

Many of my trips were with the President, the Prime Minister, the Minister of Rural Development, or other officials and their delegations to see the workings of the program and how their particular part of it fitted into the whole strategy. This led to some fascinating insights, such as listening to an irate Province Chief protest in a regional meeting that allowing village chiefs to decide on local development projects without the Province Chief's prior approval would lead to the waste or theft of the funds involved. The Prime Minister's reply could not have been more direct: "The President and I are creating a democratic society in which locally elected leaders will hold real authority and responsibility. If they steal the funds, the Province Chief should punish them. But if their decision merely turns out to be unwise, it is up to their community to choose someone better."

President Thieu's strong leadership came through on the trips to the regional headquarters and to the remote villages, as did his clear message that the regional and province chiefs were to give the program their full support and to work with the local American advisers in the same fully integrated way in which the CORDS Saigon staffs worked with the Central Council. Nor did he hesitate to point to his treatment of me as a member of his staff as an example of the integration he wanted.

During this period, I also made a few trips by road or canal just to prove that they were possible and that our reports that the enemy no longer dominated certain areas were true. I had a great day with John Vann on the Cho Gao, the principal rice-carrying canal from the Delta to Saigon; our two outboard motorboats sped along without incident, and I could report from personal observation to Ambassador Bunker at the next Embassy meeting that it was full of rice barges moving steadily, interrupted only by periodic maritime police checkpoints (at least in the daytime then).

One trip on the main North-South highway went northward from the province of Quang Ngai, where the U.S. American Division had its base, through the province of Quang Tin to the province of Quang Nam and the city of Danang and its U.S. Marine headquarters. The first province was the prototype of a war-ravaged region: ruined houses, refugee camps, bridges down. It had also been the scene of the atrocity of My Lai, where a unit of American troops had slaughtered a community of Vietnamese villagers, men, women and children, in furious frustration at their inability to distinguish friend from foe among the local population.

The second province to the North, Quang Tin, was a picture postcard of a green and fertile tropical farming area. I knew the rich land extended beyond the highway area because I had spent a night there in an isolated village along the coast listening to faraway rockets being shot at the American base camp to the south. At the border of the third province, Quang Nam, the war reappeared: temporary bridges, mud defense posts ringed with barbed wire, the pervasive sense of insecurity.

I knew the reason for the different appearance of the middle province: a thoughtful and intelligent Province Chief, Colonel Hoang Dinh Tho. He so clearly understood the human fundamentals of the war that he made it a point to invite any member of the enemy who chose the amnesty program to dinner with him at home for a long discussion of his background, his motivation, and his experiences, and then made sure that the guest would be well treated during his resettlement. The result was good intelligence on the enemy forces he faced, but, more important, additional amnesties induced by earlier ones. He also pressed a pacification program in the province that stressed local leadership and projects appealing to the rural communities that would otherwise turn to the enemy in hope of betterment.

One of Colonel Tho's district chiefs was equally effective and, after a visit to get to know him, I persuaded the Prime Minister to spend a night with me in his district. The most memorable moment of the evening was our late-night sortie on the back seats of a set of motorbikes through several of the rural communities of the district. We were protected not by American or Vietnamese regular forces but by the local security forces—and the community cohesion the district and province chiefs had created in their island of calm in the region. The contrast between the district and its war-torn neighbor to the north could not have been more dramatic.

Significantly, it was in the neighboring province that the U.S. Marines were searching for the enemy to fight. Both provinces had North Vietnamese regular forces in their western mountain areas, but the difference in the populated areas demonstrated the value of pacification over a solely military approach to the war. I remember the candlelit shrine I visited one night in a coastal village in pacified Quang Tin. The pictures of the village youths who had died in local fighting showed that the peaceful atmosphere had come only at a cost, but at least their younger siblings could farm the rice fields in peace rather than die in renewed combat.

17

"... Security to the People ..."

ONCE THE 1969 PROGRAM HAD PICKED UP SPEED, we began to think of the next installment, 1970. Confidence that
the individual programs really seemed to work was leading
to willingness to extend them into additional communities.
The graduates of the national training center found that
the lessons learned there were reflected in the authority they
could exercise in their home communities. Some of the
programs, of course, continued to show weaknesses in
concept or execution, with the result that confused local
officials were frustrated that their efforts did not pay off in
benefits for their communities. But we were dealing with a
multiyear strategy: the need to ensure a solid base before
pushing into the more contested areas meant that building
strength outward could be done only gradually.

The 1970 plan offered a chance to integrate more Government programs relating to the population into the strategy
so that they could benefit from the strong direction that
came out of the Central Council and its CORDS support
structure. Several major new directions were inserted into
the plans for the 1970 program. The stress of the APC and
the 1969 programs had been to extend security to cover
more of the population, to engage the population in the
process by giving them a role through local elections and
allowing local officials to wield real authority, and to enlist
large numbers of the population in the exercise through
self-defense groups and other forms of community activity.
By late 1969, basic security for most of the population had
been achieved, as measured by the high percentage of the
national population who lived in communities ranked C or
above on the Hamlet Evaluation System, and confirmed by
the assessments of our local CORDS advisers (and the on-

site reviews of many of our senior officers, such as myself).

The challenge for the next phase was to move above this basic level of security to one more solid, where the community would function without concern for the incursions of the Communists, merely sporadic at this stage. Status of this kind we delineated as in the A or B categories of the measuring system. Of the well over 90 percent of the total national population which by the end of 1969 had reached C or above, only about half was in the A or B categories. The goal of the new plan was to bring 90 percent into the top two categories.

This goal could be met only if there were continued improvements in the security situation *and* if there was also progress in the political and economic aspects of the HES measurements—meaning, of course, the villagers' lives. Our aims were to produce a forward momentum in all aspects of Vietnamese rural life and to continue to assert the initiative in the Government's contest with the Communists for the support of the population. President Thieu summarized the change of emphasis by insisting that the Vietnamese title for the plan be changed from Pacification and Construction (really, reconstruction) to Pacification and Development. The name change was significant to the Vietnamese but was hardly noticed by the Americans; in our English version, we were already calling it by what was now the new Vietnamese title.

The second major theme of the new phase was the application to the pacification program of the policy of Vietnamization. The American military was already well launched on the process of withdrawing American troops and turning the responsibilities for military action over to the Vietnamese forces. The pacification program's execution had, of course, been Vietnamese from the outset; Americans could not, to take but one example, induce community cohesion in a Vietnamese village by themselves participating in the local elections. But now the word went out to the American advisers at the national and local levels that the plan should be written and worked out by the Vietnamese, the Americans to be as helpful as they could but not to dominate the planning process—as they certainly had in the APC and the 1969 phase. The ideal was not always achieved, of

course. As the American advisory chain identified problems
that needed attention but were not receiving enough of it,
they would insist—sometimes not overly subtly—that certain actions be taken or would respond to recalcitrance by
urging that Americans higher up the line stimulate Vietnamese at that level to exert pressure on their subordinates.

We made a host of major and minor changes in the
content of the plan and in the procedures for its implementation. Foremost among them was a new land reform program under the title "Land to the Tillers." Remembering
the failure of Diem's land reform because of its requirement
that farmers pay mortgage fees on land they had actually
occupied when the landowning system broke down as a
result of the Communist rebellion, the new scheme required
no payment by the occupier and new owner. The titular
landowner was paid in Government bonds; their value was
perhaps dubious, but they were better than nothing. Land
reform was incorporated into the CORDS program with
specific emphasis on the fertile Mekong Delta. It was a
remarkable step ahead in the concept of land reform; in
Asia, there had been programs in postwar Japan and Taiwan that successfully distributed land against mortgage
obligations, but they had not had a Communist insurgency
to contend with.

A variety of steps to strengthen the authority of locally
elected officials were included in the plan. The village chief
was given authority over the National Police unit in the
village and the local Popular Force platoon, whose orders
formerly came only through the military chain of command. Arrests of local citizens under the Phoenix program
had to be reported to the village chief so that his knowledge
of the families and individuals involved could correct obvious mistakes. The level of village development funds that
could be dispensed without prior approval was doubled.
And a beginning was made on applying the concept of
locally elected authority to the provincial level. It was not
feasible to think of elected province chiefs in the French-
originated administrative structure in the middle of a war.
But the plan did require the election of Provincial Councils
and gave them their first taste of financial authority and
responsibility by providing for a provincial development

fund that could be disbursed only by vote of the Council.

The Phoenix program required particular attention. Most American monthly reports for the provinces complained that it was working poorly, if at all. Some said it was only a revolving-door process, those arrested being released to resume their activities after only a few days or weeks. Some decried the merely ostensible fulfillment of the goals for reductions in the Communist infrastructure by the practice of crediting every low-level guerrilla caught up in military operations to Phoenix. Others denounced the corruption whereby arrestees could bribe their way out of incarceration. Still others complained of an atmosphere of live and let live which seemed to keep local officials from disturbing particular Communist base areas.

The least of Phoenix's problems was the one American critics concentrated upon—brutality. Certainly there was some of that, but the instructions to the American advisers were direct: They were certainly not to participate in such activity; beyond abstention they were to remonstrate against it to the degree they could; and they were to report any incidents of brutality up the line for correction. One such case illustrated the complexities and pressures of war. A Province Senior Adviser reported to me that following the capture of a woman Communist leader the local district chief had come across the district, jumped out of his jeep, and shot her. I complained about the incident to the Prime Minister, who promptly fired the district chief. At this my Province Adviser protested to me that he was the best district chief in the province and that the reason he had shot the woman, as the Adviser had since learned, was that she had been directly responsible for the deaths of several members of the chief's family.

We worked hard to remedy the problems of Phoenix. As we began to receive the young U.S. military intelligence officers who had been specially trained to serve as Phoenix advisers at the district and province level—some 500 in all, eventually—we tightened up the framework of the operation. We established categories of Communist infrastructure members: A meant a Party member or an important Front or local official; B meant an important cadre in one of the key committee posts, such as taxation, or a guerrilla unit leader; C meant an ordinary supporter of the Communist cause as a member of the local organization, a courier or logistics assistant, or a member of the local paramilitary unit. Instructions were issued to ignore the C category as not being the objective of Phoenix. Those in the B category were to be given a minimum of one year's detention and those in the A category the maximum allowable two years, renewable on review of the case.

New, detailed instructions required three separate reports of an individual's involvement in the Communist infrastructure. We developed training courses, teaching how to keep dossiers, and how gradually to build up a diagram of the local Communist apparatus in a community, with identifying information of those we did not know. We then began the laborious process of developing a computer program for Phoenix—the basic personality and functional information to be completed at the local level and then consolidated and correlated by the machines—in order to impose better discipline on the program.

An imaginative USIA officer came up with the idea of placing in the local marketplaces posters describing the local Communist apparatus, with names and photographs as available. The posters had purposes beyond their appeal to the people to help in capturing the subjects. They were intended to elicit local protest if our information was wrong. And, in a significant contrast to the old Western posters offering a reward for the subject "dead or alive," a statement at the bottom of the poster conveyed the word to those described on the poster that the amnesty program would receive them without punishment for whatever they had done. We saw none of these steps as panaceas, and the complaints from our field advisers continued. But I was determined to continue with improvements and adaptations for Phoenix, because it seemed to me to be the essential counterpart to the rest of the pacification program. The main line of that program was designed to build security and strength by enlisting the population in the process of protecting themselves and improving their communities. Phoenix was an essential weapon in fighting the attempts of the Communists to infiltrate and impose *their* authority on the communities we were helping to assert their own authority.

The changed focus of the 1970 plan was also reflected in

attention to the urban population. As a result of the pressures on the countryside, the economic effects of the American presence and demands for services, and the distinct growth of commerce and light industry, the cities and towns now held some 60 percent of the South Vietnamese population. In my travels around Asia as Chief of the Far East Division of the CIA, I had studied and visited Singapore and had become fascinated by the way the People's Action Party there had developed a network of community centers in the different sections of that city-state to provide a focus for community action. The centers had all the qualities of the Tammany Hall Assembly District association I had participated in during my young lawyer days in New York City, providing a place for social activity, help in dealing with government bureaucracy, and opportunity for political participation.

The need for such centers to serve as magnets to bring urban residents together and replace the attraction of the Communist agents and their secret networks was even greater for Saigon and the other Vietnamese cities than it had been for Singapore. The 1970 plan thus called for the establishment of such centers in the urban communities. It also established self-defense units in the urban communities. There they could provide patrols and protection, and generate neighborhood projects—clean up the garbage and improve the bamboo sidewalks over the mud and slime beneath—by an allocation of the "village" development fund to provide financing on the basis of a neighborhood vote. I thus came to include Saigon in my schedule of trips to the "countryside." I would accompany the Mayor to evening ward meetings at which local residents orated eloquently on the need for a better source of clean water while their children competed vigorously in ping-pong upstairs. It was obvious that the future hopes of a free Vietnam depended upon such community identity in the urban areas as well as in the rural, and that such centers were a way to avoid city disturbances that could be as dangerous as rural guerrillas.

The Montagnards—the mountain people—presented a special concern. Their cultures and economies were truly primitive, little changed from their origins before the Vietnamese moved down from the North and pushed them from the rice-growing coastal plain into the mountains, where— as did the other primitive tribal peoples of Southeast Asia— they followed the slash-and-burn agricultural practices of their ancestors. They were divided into a number of tribes, with little interaction among them. The French had treated them separately from the Vietnamese and had used a number of them in special paramilitary units. They proved to be uncommonly good fighters, in part because of their anti-Vietnamese sentiments.

In the early 1960s, the CIA had begun its paramilitary efforts among the members of the Rhade tribe in the vicinity of Ban Me Thuot, helping them establish local defense groups against infiltrating Communist Vietnamese who were utilizing them against the Vietnamese Government authorities in the region. As we saw, the CIA's efforts proved to be particularly effective, since they stressed only the simple concept of self-defense of the local communities in which these tribal people lived. But these early CIA programs had been taken over in 1963 by the Army Special Forces, whose new orders had been to concentrate the tribal people on "offensive guerrilla operations" in the high mountain jungles.

The prevailing Vietnamese attitude toward the mountain people had about the same degree of compassion we Americans had displayed for our Native American population in the West. In 1965, the situation in the area exploded into a rebellion of the tribal groups against Vietnamese authority, seeking autonomy and believing their cause to have the support of the U.S. Army Special Forces. This caused a crisis with the Vietnamese military and political authorities until a solution could be worked out clarifying that the Americans would work only in support of and through the Vietnamese authorities—something the CIA had understood from the outset.

The new pacification program offered a vehicle with which to work again on the difficulties inherent in the relationships. In the mid-1960s the CIA had developed political action teams to work among the mountain people, somewhat like the ones it had developed for Vietnamese communities along the coast and that had spread to the rest of the nation under the name of Rural Development Cadre. Their function was to help organize the mountain communities and to assist them in obtaining the services the Government had available for them. Now these teams and their training center in the highlands (which I visited one day to imbibe the ceremonial rice wine of dubious vintage) were integrated into the overall pacification program in the mountain provinces; they were put under the local authorities, with support from the local CORDS advisory teams. Similarly, the territorial security forces and self-defense force programs supported by CORDS were directed to give special attention to providing better security to the mountain communities.

A considerable amount of effort went into the care and resettlement of the mountain refugees from the fighting between the regular military forces in their home areas. And here arose the issue of forced resettlement. Some of the local Vietnamese commanders were moving mountain communities from isolated and exposed positions to central areas where they could be protected from enemy pressures. As a first step, this usually meant a refugee camp. Sympathizers with the mountain people condemned this uprooting of the Montagnards from their homes, while the practical area commanders contended that this was the only solution in view of the impossibility of protecting each distant collection of two or three long houses (the most passionate on both sides of the argument being their American friends and advisers). I finally devised what I thought was a reasonable compromise by inserting into the directives to the pacification officials a prohibition against forcible resettlement unless the specific move had been approved by the Central Council at Saigon. President Thieu set the tone with the statement, repeated several times, "The object of the program is to bring security to the people, not the people to security." He even appointed one of the leaders of the 1965 revolt to be his Minister for the Ethnic Minorities and named a highlander officer in the Army to be the Province Chief of Pleiku, one of the most important mountain provinces.

In another indication that Vietnam was coming together behind the Government's program, Dr. Phan Quang Dan, the Harvard-educated nemesis of President Diem, accepted an appointment as a Minister in Thieu's Government to resettle refugees and others uprooted by the war in new settlements. He went at it with intense enthusiasm and with the full support of CORDS. Perhaps only I noticed the irony that his efforts bore a strong resemblance to what Diem had tried to accomplish in many of the same areas.

The pacification program certainly did not end all forcible resettlement, but it did limit the earlier simplistic approach. And it was obvious that the enemy was hurt by the whole exercise. I understood this when, during a visit to a refugee camp in the highlands, my foot happened to kick the rusting tail fins of a Chinese 82-millimeter mortar round that had recently been fired into the camp to try to drive the mountain people back into the hills where the enemy could use them.

The changeover to the 1970 plan was accomplished without the pause that had occurred between the APC and the 1969 plan, since by now everyone understood that pacification was making a real change in the war and that the priority accorded it by the President was correct. Thieu continued his monthly visits to each of the four regions to review how it was going and to keep pressure on the provincial leaders. I grew accustomed to sitting in the hot sun listening to his exhortation in Vietnamese (which I could follow in substance if not in detail) or seeing him ceremonially hand out land titles to grateful Delta farmers. On the edge of his delegation, I could also pick up useful sidelights about some of the programs. On a trip to the northernmost province of Quang Tri, for example, I noticed an empty schoolhouse whose tin roof had been blown off in a typhoon several months before. I asked what had been done with the roofing and was told that the local farmers had taken the pieces to use on their own houses. When I expressed surprise that they were unconcerned that their children had no schoolhouse, the local citizen I was speaking to said the schoolhouse belonged to the Government, so they considered it the Government's job to repair it.

Returning to Saigon from this trip, we took up the question of how we could improve the tax revenues of the villages so they could assume a greater role and therefore a greater sense of responsibility for such local expenses as their own, not the "Government's." This opened up a whole discussion with the Central Council staff as to how to develop local revenues for local purposes in place of the traditional "from-the-top-down" colonial system managed by the Saigon bureaucrats in their comfortable offices.

The scope of our programs and the intensity of the efforts in support of them attracted Washington's attention. Defense Secretary Melvin Laird was especially interested and supportive, seeing pacification as the essence of his policy of Vietnamization, strengthening the Vietnamese Government and forces to replace the Americans now being withdrawn in accelerating increments. Laird was the unsung hero of the whole war effort. A clever midwestern politician, he saw the need to adjust American strategy to maintain the support of the American people in political terms—"the art of the possible." Coming into office in the aftermath of the Tet 1968 attack and the defeat of Lyndon Johnson (and the exhaustion of the Democrats), Laird, while perceiving the need to adjust the war effort to what could be sustained, fully agreed with his President that we should not lose the war or dishonor our effort by surrender. His formula for reconciling these potentially conflicting principles was Vietnamization of the military effort and pacification of the countryside of South Vietnam. In the latter, he fully supported us with resources and personnel and was invariably helpful to me whenever I needed his support. His policy was to be fully vindicated in the Easter Offensive of 1972.

The American press still gave pacification only occasional coverage because of its "nondramatic" nature and because of a high degree of skepticism with respect to its statistics. But the Foreign Relations Committee of the Senate under Chairman J. William Fulbright decided they should have a look at the program. Hearings were scheduled for January 1970 in Washington. Given the rising antiwar sentiment in the nation and the Congress, we expected them to be hostile.

I nevertheless decided that we should take a different approach and use the interest in our work as a great opportunity to put clearly before the American people the nature of the pacification program and the bases of our confidence

that it was working. We assembled a group representing the
CORDS effort at all levels: myself, my Chief of Planning,
the Chief of the refugee staff, John Vann for the Delta
region, a Foreign Service Officer who was the Senior Adviser in a mountain province, a military officer at the
district level, a military Adviser to the Territorial Forces in a
province, an Army captain who led a mobile advisory team
in a village in the Delta, and a Marine sergeant who led one
of the Marine squads integrated with a Vietnamese Popular
Force platoon in a village in Central Vietnam. We tried to
cover the different geographic regions, as well as a variety of
situations, from areas that had already seen substantial
improvement to those where fighting was still going on.

We prepared a series of background papers describing the
program in detail. I asked each witness to prepare an
opening statement of what he wanted to say about his
activities, stressing that I wanted it to be both accurate and
complete, and to draw as fully balanced a picture as possible. I did not review their statements in advance, but as an
erstwhile practicing attorney, I did give some hints as to
how to handle questions with an honest response but without feeling obliged to volunteer material that could be taken
out of context and sensationalized.

The Committee had arranged that one of the four days of
the hearings was to be behind closed doors to discuss
Phoenix, as it involved classified information. I initially
protested this, saying that I could give a full account of
Phoenix in open session and that I thought this was the
best way to demystify and desensationalize it. The Committee insisted, however, so I made certain to cover Phoenix in
the unclassified background papers. In addition, the Senators quickly went to the subject, so our answers got the
exposure we wanted. The closed session went largely over
the same ground, the testimony being later declassified
except for some sensitive CIA names and similar material.

I was particularly heartened by a sensible *Washington
Post* article about Phoenix that appeared on the opening
day of the hearings, a normal journalistic technique to
capture attention. Its basic theme was that the program was
not working well, and it recounted some of its weaknesses
that appeared in our monthly province reports. But the

author added that his efforts to find evidence that it was a
program of assassination had been unsuccessful. The corresponding *New York Times* article concluded that the
program appeared "more notorious for inefficiency, corruption, and bungling than for terror." Since the sensation-
alism was removed, the press quickly lost interest; by the
third day, the TV cameras had gone and the press table was
nearly empty.

Even the Senatorial attention span ran out as Chairman
Fulbright manfully tried to keep up his own interest in the
complicated details of the many programs being covered.
One memorable moment came, however, when the Marine
sergeant made a casual reference to a "hunter-killer" team
in his area. The Chairman awakened to the possibility of
pay dirt in the investigation, only to be deflated by the
sergeant's explanation, in answer to his next, probing
question, that this was the name given to some of the night
patrols of the American Marine division in the area.

During the year the statistical reports indicated constant
progress. More importantly, my trips to the countryside
brought the same message. By year's end I was staying
overnight in areas that had been "Indian country" the year
before, driving on local roads or going up canals where
prudence had dictated no penetration earlier. I especially
enjoyed an uneventful trip with two jeeps through a central
Vietnam province. My last trip over that road had generated
an armored cavalry escort organized by the local American
unit to be certain that nothing happened to the Ambassador and General Abrams's deputy.

Perhaps most impressive was an overnight visit John
Vann arranged for me and a visiting journalist to a small
village in the province of Kien Hoa, which was known
locally as the birthplace of the Communist resistance in the
Delta region. One of its principal features was a well-built
house that local reports said had been the home of Madame
Nguyen Thi Binh, who, as Foreign Minister of the Communist Provisional Government, was prominently displayed at the Paris negotiations and in encounters with
various American antiwar activists. The community also
contained a cemetery, where the headstones of the buried
Communist fighters still bore the red stars that had been put

on to honor them. But the remarkable aspect of our visit was that John and I and three or four other Americans spent the night in the village protected only by the regular Territorial and self-defense units normally in the area. Plainly, the situation in the area had changed.

Since the statistical reports were bringing so much good news, they also became less useful, their indicators beginning to cluster at the tops of the scales. We made some changes to make them more useful, stressing political and developmental factors in the areas where security had improved so much. We also began announcing only the A and B total as pacified, and considered C as unsatisfactory against the goals we had set.

We also initiated a wholly new reporting system to try to measure the population's attitudes through polling. To measure the political changes that were the true objectives of the program, we thought we needed a better indicator than the objective statistics on enemy incidents, the presence of an armed self-defense group in the community, local elections, and nightly locations of village and hamlet officials. We were fully aware of the danger of generating the answers canny peasants would think we wanted to hear, so the questioners were specially trained to conduct relaxed conversations about subjects of local interest, to encourage complaints as well as direct answers to rote questions, and then to summarize the answers according to a scale on the selected topics.

The questioners were, of course, Vietnamese—teams who had assisted some of our evaluation staff over the past several years, and new members recruited and trained for the task. We were conscious that some local officials might be resistant to such displays of curiosity in their communities, so the process by which questioners were deployed required some diplomacy as well. President Thieu and the Central Council saw the value of such polling of attitudes as a possible means of measuring the reality of the results we sought in the pacification program, so with their support the surveys were gingerly launched, local officials being assured that the results would be made available to them in summary form (but without the identities of the sources). As with the other reporting systems, we had little confidence in the accuracy of the absolute results of the system but looked instead for trends, differences in areas, and confirmation or negation of what other reporting indicated.

After the usual birth pangs, the system began to produce valuable indicators of the people's major concerns and of their estimates of the various programs. Somewhat to our surprise, we found a generally high degree of confidence in the protection provided by the American forces where they were present and almost as much in the regular Vietnamese military. At the bottom of the list—no surprise—were the Vietnamese Police. We found the expected concern over the Phoenix program and its operation but were surprised by the support that existed for its objectives of strengthening defenses against the secret Communist infrastructure. The universal interest in economic and social improvement, and the increasing confidence in local government, were a welcome ratification of the basic pacification strategy.

The improved atmosphere permitted some change in the intensity of our schedules, too. As my helicopter took off from the Marine headquarters pad in Danang one day, I noticed below me the surprising sight of two day sailboats of clearly Western origin. A bit of inquiry revealed that they were part of the Navy's special service activity for some of its sailors who wanted to keep up their Annapolis-hewn skills. A bit more inquiry resulted in my being able to borrow one of the boats for a sail on sparkling Danang Bay. A few weeks later, during a pause in a serious inspection visit in the area for Ambassador Bunker and his bride, visiting from her duties as Ambassador to Nepal, I was able to treat them to a day of sailing. When the Navy discovered Bunker's interest and skills in sailing, it arranged more outings for us, the crew sometimes consisting of Navy officers with Olympic experience. Though only a brief break in our normal seven-day week, these few hours away from the intensity of the war were refreshing. Most of all, they were encouraging indications of how far we had come in only two years.

Part Six
VICTORY WON

18

Tet 1971:
A Ride in the Countryside

AS WE BEGAN TO LAY OUR PLANS FOR 1971, it was clear to us all—Vietnamese and Americans working in the pacification program—that the situation facing us had changed, and substantially, opening wide the possibility of major improvements in the lives of the Vietnamese rural—and urban—people.

The increases in the numbers, equipment, and training of the Vietnamese forces, especially the Territorials and the self-defense units, were providing twenty-four-hour security in many sectors that had previously buttoned up each night in anticipation of Viet Cong attacks. The regular Army was being freed to step into the shoes of the departing Americans, whose remaining troop levels were dropping visibly in each weekly report. The Vietnamese Army would never be as lavishly supplied with helicopters, armor, and heavy artillery as the Americans, but General Abrams's and Secretary Laird's Vietnamization program was giving it capabilities representing a massive improvement over conditions two or three years earlier. Thanks to the mobility and firepower they now possessed, they could use the American tactics of a forward defense, seeking out the North Vietnamese regular units in the mountain areas rather than passively awaiting their attacks.

In the countryside, large areas had been brought to the point where the population could focus on building their communities and improving their economic circumstances, and not have to worry anymore about the danger of military action. Except in the more isolated areas, the morning trip to market was free of fear that a mine planted the night before would destroy the small bus with its cargo of vegetables, fruits, and chicken or fish with an overload of villagers

perched on top. The random rocket attacks on the cities and
bases had stopped, and the main route from Saigon south to
the Delta was open all night to handle the volume of traffic
in fruits and pigs going North and consumer goods going
South.

The obvious improvements in local security and the
economic advances of the villages, the citizens riding Hondas instead of walking, the village councils deciding on
which local community projects to spend the central government's grants, the villagers working their rice plots in
the conviction that the harvest would be theirs and watching their children benefit from a reopened school or malaria inoculations—all this provided the basis for a feeling
among the population that welled up through the Army
and the Government that momentum was on South Vietnam's side.

Throughout the execution of the 1970 Plan, President
Thieu continued his vigorous promotion of the pacification program through trips to the regions and the provinces, invariably inviting me to go along, not as a curious
foreigner to be impressed (although he occasionally asked
them too) but in effect as one of his staff. And in one casual
remark to me while returning from one of our day inspec-
tions in the country, Thieu commented that he thought
Diem had run the country quite well. This may have reflected his awareness that he was running it along somewhat similar lines, but he was doing so with American
acquiescence, as distinct from Diem's difficulties with the
Americans—as our cooperation in the pacification program, among much other evidence, showed. The Vietnamese Central Pacification and Development Council staff and
the American CORDS advisory network, for example,
jointly served as the general staff of the program.

As 1971 approached, President Thieu and the Central
Council, eager to maintain the momentum, began to prepare the Plan for the new year. Over the years the Plans,
and the statistical and informational techniques that went
into their preparation, have been criticized as forcing complex Western techniques on an Asian society and economy
for which they were at least unsuitable, if not actually
irrelevant. I can attest that in the struggle for control of the

villages we did apply a lot of advanced management techniques in Vietnam. And I can also attest that they worked. Compelling the Vietnamese military and civilian structures to work from a common plan, at both the national and provincial levels, permitted President Thieu to impose a fundamentally political strategy on the South Vietnamese effort. He could focus that effort on enlisting the participation of the people in the struggle to keep the Communists from taking over *and* to build a better society and economy that would provide the people with better rewards than the enemy could ever offer.

Breaking the plan down into specific goals for each community and for each year allowed gradual execution of the strategy, and furnished a gauge of whether or not subordinate officials were carrying out that strategy on the ground. The separate and independent reporting system provided by the American advisory network was an important element in evaluating subordinate response and activity and local needs, particularly in reporting the way the programs were affecting the population, instead of merely counting the physical actions taken, as had occurred too often with Nhu's strategic hamlets.

The fact that the national plan had to be matched by a provincial plan ensured that local reality—and not just the paper dreams of Saigon bureaucrats—would be reflected in the final product and action. The incessant inspection visits by the President and Prime Minister convinced the Vietnamese power structure that the program was serious, and holding the province chiefs directly and personally responsible for executing the plans they helped prepare fixed responsibility at a level that could actually implement the "ink spot strategy." The fact that the stated goals were reasonable and real produced confidence that at last a winning strategy to end the war's agony had been found. Visible progress toward those goals, in the form of safer travel, better crops and markets, and less military combat in populated areas, reinforced that confidence. The intensity of the effort reflected the universal hope that the war would be ended, and ended well, by carrying out a strategy that seemed to be working.

The 1971 Plan exemplified and reinforced the new atmosphere that prevailed. To underline the change from the aggressive recapture of control over the countryside ("pacification") to longer-term aims of helping communities defend themselves and improve their welfare, President Thieu directed that the title of the program be changed from Pacification and Development to Community Defense and Local Development. "Program" is a misnomer. The effort as a whole was a conglomeration of different programs and activities, all aimed at reinforcing the basic strategy. Searching for a way to express the common aims of the strategy, and the multitude of activities included in it, our planning chief, Clayton McManaway (later our Ambassador to Haiti), and I hit upon a theme that seemed to express it all—"self-defense, self-government, and self-development." When we presented our suggestion to President Thieu, he not only accepted it but improved on it by adding "local," to stress the key role of the communities. Thus the 1971 program was organized around the three watchwords—Local Self-Defense, Local Self-Government, and Local Self-Development. The following components of each theme in the 1971 Plan, with their functions, show the Plan's breadth:

LOCAL SELF-DEFENSE
Territorial Security:
• Regional Forces (province-level companies and battalions): training, equipping, operations
• Popular Forces (village-level platoons): training, equipping, operations
• People's Self-Defense Forces (unpaid part-time village militia): organizing, training, equipping
• National Police Force: increase in strength, deployment to rural villages, training, equipping, operations
• Phoenix: identifying and fighting the secret Viet Cong Infrastructure
• *Chieu Hoi* (amnesty program): inviting and resettling defectors from the Viet Cong

LOCAL SELF-GOVERNMENT
• People's Administration: village and provincial council elections and training local officials at the National Training Center

- People's Information: the Government Information Service—distribution to the villages
- People's Organizations: encouraging private organizations—agricultural, labor, social, etc.
- Youth Program: sports, civic projects, etc.

LOCAL SELF-DEVELOPMENT

- Land Reform: "Land to the Tillers" program
- Agriculture and Fisheries: Government assistance programs
- Local Economic Development: local taxes for local projects
- War Veterans: programs for support of military veterans, especially disabled
- War Victims: refugee assistance and resettlement, "return to village" program, rehabilitation of wounded, etc.
- Public Health: extension of medical services beyond central hospitals to village aid stations
- Education: local schools, teacher training and support
- Manpower Development: labor training programs
- Public Works: roads, bridges, irrigation, etc.
- Post and Communications: village post offices
- Rural Credit: rural development banks
- Province/Municipal Development Program: grants for local use decided by elected provincial or municipal councils
- Village Self-Development Program: grants for village projects chosen by village councils

SPECIAL PROGRAMS

- Urban Programs: community centers and local development projects
- Ethnic Minorities: programs for highlanders and Cambodians

The three major themes of the Plan were neither word games nor publicity gimmicks. The three slogans, by providing reference points, aided in the organization of the 1971 program and in explaining the program to the communities, rural and urban, that would carry it out and benefit from it. They clarified the thrust and purpose of the activities to the military and civilian staffs responsible for them: it was essential that the staffs engaged in their disparate and widespread activities understand that their work was part of an overall strategy and that each part was essential to the whole effort to keep the initiative in Government hands in the contest with the Communist enemy. As for "public relations," practiced by many a government agency, they were not part of our effort. We were not out to seduce. Beyond my overnight visits to the countryside with a few journalists, we did little or nothing to impress the press, although the Embassy press officer once commented that my invitations to the journalists were among the best public relations efforts of the mission.

The 1971 Plan included a special effort to improve the legal procedures for sentencing under the Phoenix program and to obtain better accounting of prisoners and their terms of detention. I initially worked out these improvements in Phoenix with Gage McAfee, a brilliant young lawyer who had joined AID and been sent to Vietnam, where I thought his special talents better applied to the problem of Phoenix legal standards than to those of some remote district. We quickly discovered that the legal basis for Phoenix lay in a system of preventive detention of suspects considered threatening to the state in time of national emergency. The system was common to a number of nations that had faced this kind of problem, and was at the time still being applied in India, Northern Ireland, and some former British colonies. We even found that the United States Congress, in the Internal Security Act of 1950, had authorized preventive detention if the President declared an internal state of emergency.

In Vietnam, a special problem was whether an accused would have the right of counsel to help in his defense. A fundamental of American Constitutional rights, its application in Vietnam was problematical simply because in the entire country there were only two hundred lawyers—and most of them were in the few urban centers, whereas Phoenix activity was primarily in the rural districts.

Seeking to introduce procedures to guard against abuse, we discussed the problem with the Central Council, seeking a way to improve the situation without calling for unrealistic standards that could not be met. The result was a revision of the rules of sentencing to preventive detention whereby the province chief was to be assisted in his decision by the elected chairman of the provincial council and by the local prosecutor, making the process less arbitrary and including a legally trained officer and an elected official to represent the local population. Here again we stumbled, this time on the discovery that, outside of a few urban centers, there were no prosecutors in most of the provinces. This led us to the Minister of Justice.

The Minister's reaction to our suggestion of the need to dispatch some of his young lawyers to the provinces revealed aspects of the social system the overall program was trying to alter. His first objection was against sending talented young law graduates to some of the primitive communities that passed for provincial capitals. As we worked our way over and around that one, he then said it was essential for his young lawyers' dignity, and that of their office, that they be housed in quarters appropriate to their station.

Not without difficulty, I held my temper in check. I told the Minister of the young Vietnamese lieutenant I had met in a province up the coast the previous weekend who was living in a tent because the Regional Force company he commanded provided security for a village whose original population, after years in a provincial refugee camp, was now returning. I added that I thought the Minister's young men might be expected to endure some hardships for the reestablishment of law in the provinces. This was useful but not decisive. My ultimate threat was to report to President Thieu that the Minister was not fully committed to the pacification program that the President had set as the nation's first priority. The Minister now came around to a more positive approach—in principle.

But, as was so often the case with our programs, a decision in principle did not mean the problem had been solved. Some days later, the Minister brought to our attention the fact that the quarters previously occupied by the prosecutor in one of the Delta provincial capitals had been requisitioned for several years past to house the American advisory team there. Would I, the Minister asked, kindly arrange for the house to be vacated for the use of the prosecutor and his family whom he was sending there? After a series of discussions, the Minister finally consented to his nominee occupying the somewhat less ostentatious, one-family quarters that the provincial team had located for a prosecutor. Over the next few months, at last, we saw prosecutors assigned to most if not all of the provinces to play their role in the sentencing procedures.

The major thrust of the earlier plans, upgrading and extending the security of local communities, was continued in the 1971 Plan. Literally hundreds of thousands of refugees were resettled in their native villages, now accompanied by the needed Territorial Forces rather than seeing them assigned elsewhere for "military" reasons. In the local communities, the self-defense forces not only stood guard but became more and more the central vehicles for organizing self-help projects, identifying Communist infiltration, and disseminating the political messages of self-government and self-development. To extend the enthusiasm that the "combat" self-defense forces had aroused to the many other chores basic to improving the surroundings and lives of the villagers under their own management, the "combat" self-defenders elements were supplemented by "support" self-defense groups. The "combat" self-defenders stood guard and handled the village's weapons, while the "support" groups of children, elders, and others dug the trenches, reported sightings of Viet Cong, and otherwise participated in the community development efforts.

The importance attached to the village level of government pervaded the new Plan. Decisions on the land reform program, such as measurements of property lines and eligibility of claimants as "tillers" of plots over past years, instead of being made in the time-honored fashion by a visiting Saigon bureaucrat, were delegated to a village "screening committee." The Ministry of Post and Communications was given the goal of extending postal and telephone services to every village instead of merely the urban communities. The provision of rural credit, in order to finance the land reform and agricultural production, was managed through village credit committees, which could best gauge local credit risks, and which had an obvious incentive to protect the available funds from waste at the expense of worthy local applicants.

Several years before, on a visit to Malaysia, I had observed a practice that we now inaugurated in the Vietnamese villages. It was a basic "development book," recording in one place the security situation, the elements of local government such as elections and committees, and the economic and social resources such as rice production, schools, health centers, and public works in the village. These accounts of the current situation were used as the basis for plans for improvement during the next year. This gave the local citizens and visiting officials a quick overview of the village's realities and its plans for the future, not in ritualistic generalities but in solid geographic and statistical form, against which actual progress could be measured. On another trip, through rural South Korea, I had seen an adaptation of the same technique when the village budget and development objectives were painted on the wall of the village headquarters so that all villagers could see them and measure whether the local authorities were accomplishing them. On several occasions I observed President Thieu, on his trips to villages, look at the book and then go out to see the progress on the new bridge over the local canal it called for, exactly as Prime Minister Razak did regularly in Malaysia.

We moved in another new direction. We continued to strengthen the interchange between province authorities and the villages, but we also noted the increasing need for village autonomy. As authority had been increasingly devolved upon the villages, it became clear that their full *self-management* would come to fruition only as they assumed the responsibility for funding village projects out of local resources, taxing themselves to do so. This is a difficult transition everywhere, not only in Vietnam, and an even more difficult threshold from centrally subsidized to locally supported activities. Aware that this process had to be traversed in stages, we and the Vietnamese set 1971 targets of some 200 villages to take full responsibility, and 300 half-responsibility, for their local development projects and their financing, just short of a quarter of the total of 2,150 villages (embracing 10,494 hamlets) nationwide—in a nation torn and tortured by war.

The Plan we worked out also called for new directions for the national programs. Hitherto, military and civilian

hospitals in Vietnam had functioned as two separate enti-
ties—with the military obviously better off, since they
benefited from American assistance from the Pentagon's
budget, while the civilians received only what could be
squeezed from the foreign assistance program. We inaugurated steps toward joint operation of the two to serve the
citizenry as well as the military, especially for war-related
civilian wounds. A new Ministry was established to provide
special care for the 200,000 war veterans, 40,000 disabled
veterans, and the 70,000 widows and almost 300,000 orphans of the men who had already paid the cost of the war
in full.

There were other special provisions: fisheries and freez-
ing plants (one of our young Navy officers introduced and
spread the technique of constructing fishing boats of cement stretched over wire netting to avoid the rot which in
that climate so quickly affected ordinary wooden boats);
plastic identity cards, distributed by the National Police,
with photos and internal indicators of tampering or coun-
terfeiting; youth programs augmented by a variety of projects for sports, cultural activities, and congresses—all assigned to village leadership. Beginnings were made toward
democratic pluralism. The villages were encouraged to
organize private community organizations in each of three
categories: cultural or educational (including sports and
youth); social or charitable (including health); and economic (including trade unions and farmers' organizations)—none to be supported by Government funds. The
objective for the year was to enlist each citizen in at least
one such community activity.

With the experience of the previous years to guide us, the
planning for 1971, and then the transition to the new year,
went smoothly. The President continued his regular reviews in each of the four regions. In most cases, they were
held in one or more village centers to hear the reports and,
on occasion, complaints of regional, provincial, and local
officials and representatives. Particular emphasis was put
on including in these sessions the locally elected officials
and provincial council chairmen.

On one occasion Thieu convened a gathering of all forty-
four provincial chiefs, the chairmen of their provincial

councils, and the Government Ministers for a full day's briefing and discussion on the Plan and how it appeared to be working at the local level. After opening the proceedings and outlining the major elements of the program, the President, in a display of Oriental tact, left so that his presence would not inhibit the discussion. The Prime Minister then presided, referring questions or complaints about particular parts of the program to the responsible Ministers. At the beginning the provincial chiefs, all military officers, carried the bulk of the exchanges. But as the hours passed and the atmosphere eased, the provincial chairmen became increasingly vocal and sometimes critical. One could sense their assumption of a genuine political role as representatives of their own communities. They were not yet the equivalent of New England selectmen in their powers and participation, but they were beginning to perform the same functions.

As the first weeks of 1971 passed and Tet approached, we could sense the breadth and solidity of the forward movement created in the villages. I decided on an experiment. It was now getting on to three years since I had transferred John Vann from the Saigon area to the Delta and all the challenges it then posed to pacification. In the interval, I had to intervene three times to save John from high-level wrath at his outspokenness and criticism to the American press. The most recent occasion had involved an irate Ambassador Bunker, who told me flatly to fire him. Vann had been amply warned, the Ambassador said, and had gone ahead with his insubordination. I pleaded with him that Vann was too valuable for us to lose and gave him my assurances that it would not happen again, after which I took John to the proverbial woodshed. Vann was contrite and assured me he would obey (which I hoped for but would never bank on), and he stayed on in the Delta.

But now I approached John in a different vein. Knowing his enthusiasm for motorcycling over the back roads of the Delta, often at great risk, I asked if I could join him for a ride. I suggested we take a trip together to celebrate the Tet holiday. He was more than game. We planned a motorbike ride across the entire Delta, from the regional capital of Can Tho, not far from the South China Sea, to a provincial capital within sight of the Cambodian border. We were going alone. Although we were both sure we would make it, John arranged for a couple of helicopters to be on alert to respond to our radios if trouble did arise.

John and I had become quite close, but still professional, friends. We were often on the telephone discussing what we ought to be doing about the pacification program in the Delta and just how far we could go in giving that region the priority on Regional Force and Popular Force allocations of new forces and M-16 weapons against the competing demands of the other regions of the country. We both agreed that it had to have the very first priority: if we could defeat the Communist challenge in the most populous region of the nation, and its economically most productive, the people's war could indeed be won. No, he did not confide in me the sexual and private aspects of his life—which Neil Sheehan in his 1988 account of John's life and work made so much of—nor did I inquire about them, considering them his own business and extraneous to whether he was doing the job confided to him. (It was no more relevant, certainly, than the private life of John F. Kennedy.)

My evaluation was that John Paul Vann was performing those duties in a spectacular manner, swooping into the various districts and villages of the area without notice to check whether the situation was what the local advisers' reports said it was. He was a familiar figure to the local Vietnamese officials in the region as well, and they knew that his reports went up the line to the President and the Prime Minister, so they gave him their full attention. He spent many a night in distant outposts and had more than his share of combat time when they came under attack, his radio crackling with his demands for support from helicopter gunships and for reinforcements.

I certainly agreed with John when he extolled the fighting qualities of General Ngo Quang Truong after they had shared a tiny, isolated fort that came under attack during the night. But when Truong was transferred by President Thieu to take over the Northern Region directly facing North Vietnam, certainly the best place for his talents, I expressed some doubt over John's enthusiasm for his successor, General Ngo Dzu. With all John's fine qualities and

time in the country, he had never learned to speak Vietnamese, and I thought his enthusiasm for Dzu rested heavily
on Dzu's excellent command of English and his willingness
to do what John said.

Here Neil Sheehan's observations about John are correct;
he really wanted to be in command, perhaps operating
through a Vietnamese shield, but still in command. His
impatience with failure, lack of proficiency, or just plain
ineffectiveness made the long process of building Vietnamese self-reliance and independence, which I thought necessary if Vietnamization and pacification were to be achieved,
very difficult for John. My own view was that despite the
heavy hand John (and many of the rest of us) might wield,
Vietnamese self-reliance—and proficiency—was growing,
and would continue to grow, and that meanwhile we could
profit from the benefits of American effectiveness without
losing the long-term objective of Vietnamese self-reliance.
Obviously, if the American troops were to be withdrawn
fully, and soon, as Vietnamization (and American antiwar
sentiment) required, the short-term strengthening of South
Vietnam was the first priority, with the longer-term self-
reliance growing as it could. And if John Vann was impatient with the latter, he was devoted to the former.

Tet being a holiday, the road was full of other Tet cele-
brants off to visit their families, and we weaved among and
around them over the pockmarked road. When the brake on
my motorcycle malfunctioned, John insisted that I exchange it for his out of concern that "the Ambassador"
might hurt himself, thus losing the whole point of our trip.
He insisted that he could manipulate a faulty vehicle better
than I, and, as he probably could, I agreed. Continuing on,
at one point we came upon an American engineer unit
working to repair, and in some places rebuild, the road. The
road had to be fixed, and Tet was not an American holiday,
so a lone American GI had been posted to control traffic to
permit the heavy equipment to work. When we arrived he
had called a halt to the swarm of Hondas, bicycles, and
farm carts. As the machinery swung back and forth and the
delay in the hot sun lengthened, the ever-growing crowd
became impatient. Those in the rear began to push those
ahead to move. We watched, without identifying ourselves,

as the poor GI gradually lost control of the crowd and, with it, his temper. He shouted in English at the uncomprehending Vietnamese and pushed one older man roughly back in line. No use. The flood finally broke through and flowed past him.

When the GI finally gave up and let the crowd (and us) go by, I wondered aloud to John whether the benefits of the better road were worth the frictions involved in its repair. (On returning to Saigon I recounted the incident, pointing out that the GI had been placed in an impossible situation and that the local advisory team should have been consulted to provide a Vietnamese National Policeman to share crowd management with him—only to be told that had been done as a matter of regular procedure, but the officer had not shown up on the Tet holiday. Reality in the countryside is not as simple or clear as it sometimes seems viewed from high command levels.)

As it turned out, this was the sole unusual event of the trip. It is difficult to conceive of anything being "fun" in wartime Vietnam, but if anything could be, that trip was. At the end of the day John and I completed our journey in good order, and shared an evening drink looking over the Cambodian border where the Communists had taken refuge. The contrast between this peaceful traverse and the ambushes, roadblocks, and enemy battalions we would have met had we tried the same trip three years before was striking. Tet 1971 in Vietnam was a different world from that of Tet 1968.

If proof were needed, John Vann provided it. That evening he told me he had come to believe so much in the way the pacification program was working that he had decided to keep his mouth shut to the press about his criticisms of the excessively military American approach to the war and the weaknesses and failures of various Vietnamese and American officials. I wasn't certain his conversion would last, but I accepted it with pleasure.

19

The Delta and Hue:
Rural Peace

AS VIETNAMIZATION PROCEEDED DURING 1970 and 1971 with the drawdown of the American forces, it began to affect the pacification program as well. We maintained that pacification had always been Vietnamized, since the channels of command were Vietnamese and the work was done by the Vietnamese, but we still had a large advisory network playing a major role in suggesting and counseling, and in monitoring the program at all levels from the Central Council to the farthest village. We now began to close out the small teams in quieter districts where security had been brought under control, even if the enemy had not been entirely eliminated.

We also began to transfer the reporting systems. First we arranged that reports such as the Hamlet Evaluation System be prepared jointly by Vietnamese and Americans. Then we sent copies through both Vietnamese and American channels. Finally, we sent them through Vietnamese channels only, with the local American advisers merely commenting upon the results and giving their views of the reports' accuracy. At the Central Council, the staff under quiet and efficient General Cao Hao Hon took full control of the planning and monitoring process, speaking directly in the name of the President and the Prime Minister to each of the Ministries about what they should be doing to help the program and criticizing them for shortcomings. We could sense the initiative and responsibility for the program passing from the Americans to the Vietnamese.

But this was a program the real measure of which was out in the myriad communities dotting Vietnam and not in the Central Councils or Ministries. A look at the Mekong Delta, the rich, crowded, and once dangerous region south-

307

west of Saigon, can perhaps illustrate the changes the program produced in the countryside.

The province of Vinh Long is in the center of the Delta. I had stopped in Vinh Long in 1959, during my car trip to the southernmost part of the country. I had visited it again several times during that first tour of duty in Vietnam, in 1959, to see one of Diem's "agrovilles," assembling sufficient population to support the amenities of quasi-urban life and later to observe its skeleton after it had been overrun by the Communists. On another occasion I stopped there to visit the school Ngo Dinh Nhu had set up to indoctrinate Vietnamese civil servants in his doctrine of personalism. As Nhu turned his attention to the broader approach of producing new leadership for Vietnam from the rural population through the strategic hamlets program, he lost interest in personalism, and his wife turned the school into a center for the rehabilitation of former Saigon prostitutes.

Vinh Long had also been the site of one of the first serious sociological studies of rural Vietnam by an American. I had studied Gerald Hickey's *Village in Vietnam* early on in an effort to understand the attitudes and customs of the villagers I saw as the key to hopes for a free Vietnam. I visited the village Hickey had dissected to see firsthand the area he had delved into so effectively, driving up the side road off the main highway to the village and then walking freely about its homes and canals to see its *dinh* or village shrine, its market, and its rich paddy fields. But by the mid-1960s the province was under very strong Communist influence, and no longer the place for Americans conducting sociological studies in the countryside.

My insistence on spending a night in a village during one of my trips from Washington in the mid-1960s was humored by the local authorities selecting one just outside the provincial capital of Vinh Long and assigning to it that night a substantial defense force. In 1968, just after the Tet offensive, my helicopter made a tight circle to avoid ground fire from the periphery of the provincial capital and landed in the middle of the town. That evening the Province Chief (who had commanded the tank unit in which President Diem and his brother were killed) and I inspected the barbed-wire defenses at the edge of town and checked the readiness of the armored personnel carriers (APCs) in their regular night positions. We went no further into the darkness outside, where the Communist cadres controlled the countryside. There the guerrillas attacked the few outposts of the Government's wretchedly equipped local forces, and laid mines on the roads to strike early patrols "opening" the main routes and to block the morning traffic. The strategic hamlets had been smashed and replaced by the authority of Communist cadres taxing, exhorting, conscripting, and dominating the population, and executing any who might have had residual ties to the Government.

As the pacification program began to work in 1969, the main roads started filling up with the multicolored, ramshackle buses and Honda-powered small carriers overloaded with enterprising Saigonese descending on the countryside to pick up fruits and vegetables for the markets. By 1970 the principal road to the Delta, Route 4, was opened at night to accommodate the traffic. My overnight village had by then been included in the "ink spot" of security spreading out from the capital, and the western part of the province had been freed of threat, except for occasional forays by main force enemy units from the neighboring swamps of the Plain of Reeds and Cambodia, which provided work for the regular Vietnamese Army units in the area. The eastern edge of the province, however, was adjacent to a more difficult area with a strong Communist presence; the ink spot did not yet extend that far.

On one of my visits to Vinh Long, I met a young AID officer and spent too far into the evening discussing his ideas for the revival of the villages in his district—which included the one where I had overnighted several years before under heavy security precautions. He urged that that village government be rebuilt as the foundation of a new Vietnam, developing individuals in the countryside who could rise in the system and provide better leaders at all levels of the society—and in the meantime could contest effectively with the disciplined Communist cadres for the loyalty of the people. Stephen Young was the son of Kenneth Young, Vietnam Desk Officer in the State Department in the early years of the Diem regime and later Ambassador to Thailand, where I had met him. While on holiday with

his family in Thailand from his studies at Harvard, Steve
became curious about a peculiar shard he had, quite literally, stumbled upon. Pursuing the origins of his relic, he
had unearthed a previously unknown prehistoric site. It is
now accepted as fundamentally changing the established
wisdom that bronze and its associated developments emanated from the Middle East. Steve's find was dated as before or
contemporaneous with the Middle Eastern Bronze Age sites.

Steve's flair, imagination, and pertinacity, plus his fluent
Vietnamese and intense interest in the village communities,
so attracted me that I arranged—over his violent objections—his transfer to our Saigon headquarters. It seemed to
me that his ideas and drive could be translated into programs that would benefit the country at large rather than
his district alone.

By late 1970 the war in the Delta essentially had been
won. Security was so improved that there remained only a
"residual level of violence," such as the pop-pop-pop of an
AK-47 firing at our helicopter as we flew over the mangrove
swamp along the sea in a distant southern district. As I told
a reporter friend who was with me on one such occasion,
that sort of thing would probably continue, but it would not
threaten the security of the state or substantially interrupt
the development program. Long An, one of the provinces
just south of Saigon, had been the location of a series of
military attempts at pacification during the middle 1960s,
to little or no avail. By the end of 1970, I could drive over the
back roads of that province in a jeep with no escort. The
Phoenix program reported that the Communist provincial
committee was now located at one of the sanctuaries over
the Cambodian border and had lost all direct contact or
influence with the provincial population.

The most convincing reason for this change came to me
from a twelve-year-old girl who, as I visited a community in
the course of rebuilding, quietly expressed her happiness
that she was attending school again after a five-year lapse. I
thought her account more reliable than our statistics.

John Vann and I luxuriated in the new security in the
Delta. We organized a day trip along the Mang Tiet Canal,
which in linking the two principal arms of the Mekong
Delta, passes through the previously dangerous eastern area

of Vinh Long province. It proved to be uneventful, aside from the vision of the rich rice fields and the heavy barge traffic carrying their product to the Chinese rice wholesalers of Saigon. On another occasion we went into one of the southernmost provinces, deep into the marshes, to spend the night in an isolated community of resettled refugees. In the gathering dusk we saw, a few hundred yards ahead, a nondescript assembly of armed men on the canal bank. As we drew near, not without misgivings, they greeted us with waves and smiles. With us was a journalist friend from *Newsweek*, who was sufficiently impressed to refer in his survey of Vietnamization to the "extraordinarily successful" pacification program. Praise we heard little of in those times.

At this point, John Vann felt—and rightly—that he had accomplished what I had sent him to do three years before. He therefore asked me to transfer him out of the Delta to the north. There the contest was still going on, as I had experienced in a lonely drive along the spectacularly beautiful coast on a road with no traffic and the sound of machine gun and rifle fire somewhere in the brooding hills above. In a war zone, stillness is a signal of danger, as the normal sounds of the countryside are quieted by the presence of armed men aiming their weapons at what they hope will soon be targets, and the stillness of that ride was threatening indeed. On some of my overnight visits to the region, the morning jeep transit to the local airstrip to meet the aircraft to take me back to headquarters in Saigon still produced what we called the "pucker factor," a tightening of the nether sides in anticipation of what might erupt from a mine placed in the road by a Communist sapper squad during the night, despite the sandbags carefully placed in the jeep floor against just that possibility.

We had deliberately given the Delta the priority for pacification and for the resources in new territorial force units, training slots at the national school for village chiefs, and the land reform program, so its faster progress was only to have been expected. In addition, of course, most of the provinces further North abutted on Cambodia or Laos, with regular North Vietnamese troops raiding over their borders. Pacification, we frequently said, was designed to

counter—and even to recruit—enemy guerrillas, but we had
no pretensions that it could fend off enemy battalions.

John had a special request. He asked that he become the
senior American authority in his area, with control over the
remaining American military units there as well as the
advisory contingents. This was a large demand for a former
Lieutenant Colonel who had resigned his commission in
protest against the United States Army's actions in the early
1960s, and who had since been the source of numerous
critical comments to the press about the military. But when
I took the idea to General Abrams, he agreed—after I
stressed that John had obviously mended his ways. The
General's decision was perhaps influenced by the fact that
most American forces would soon be gone from the central
highlands and coast the new region covered and that John
had not asked for the northernmost region, where the military threat still dominated and the last American divisions
still operated.

I had rather hoped Vann might take over that northern
area, the most difficult in which to apply the principles of
the pacification strategy. The intrigues of the various political parties there were particularly inhospitable to a common strategy against the Communists, who were as abhor-
rent to the party leaders as their non-Communist rivals—no
more, no less. The narrow, flat plain on which most of the
population lived was dominated by mountainous jungle.
The Government's hopes of establishing communities in
the foothills that would survive were repeatedly dashed by
the sallies from the mountains of North Vietnamese units.
The Laotian border was only a few kilometers away, providing the North Vietnamese with a secure sanctuary in
which they could organize their supply depots and lines of
support from North Vietnam. The necessarily dominant
role of the military, Vietnamese and American, in this
region near North Vietnam made it especially difficult to
promulgate the doctrine that authority and allegiance
should be built from the local community upwards, not
imposed by the military in fear of the nearby invader. In
forward battle areas, it is difficult to assert the supremacy of
the political arts over the harsh demands of the military.

There had been, nonetheless, some successes in the northern region. They were usually thanks to a perceptive and

wise province chief who saw beyond the need to win in combat with the enemy to the possibility of winning the enemy over. I recounted earlier the success of the brilliant Colonel Hoang Dinh Tho in his tranquil island between two war-ravaged Provinces. The Province Chief of the Hue area, Colonel Le Van Than, was equally effective.

Despite the presence in his province of the 1st Vietnamese Division and the 101st American Airborne, Colonel Than had devoted himself to the pacification program in the populated coastal plain from which the military launched their daily search-and-destroy operations into the mountainous areas of the A Shau Valley and along Route 9 leading west to Laos, where I had visited with my son Jonathan so many years before. His results reflected his dedication. Once when I was in his area, the Colonel had used me to promote the farmers' requests for small mechanical plows, leading me out into a muddy rice field to slog barefoot in the mud behind a chugging Japanese motorized plow to demonstrate its value for increasing rice yields.

But my most impressive visit to Hue came in the spring of 1971, with the British Ambassador as my traveling companion. After dinner Colonel Than asked whether we would like to go for a ride in the countryside. Confident in our host, I immediately accepted. We set off in two jeeps, Colonel Than driving one with the Ambassador and myself as passengers, the Provincial Senior Adviser and two other officers following in the other. We quickly left the city behind and were soon turning and twisting on country back roads. At one point the headlights shone on a group of young men without uniforms, carrying weapons. The chief drove confidently up to them. I confess I experienced some qualms as to what I might have exposed Her Majesty's Ambassador. But as we exchanged greetings, they proved to be one of the local village defense units on their nightly patrol. The Ambassador had accepted my confidence in Colonel Than, but both of us were well aware that the territory over which we were traveling that night had been the location of major battles between North Vietnamese and American divisions less than three years before. The episode convinced us both that, whatever the statistical reports said, the situation in the Hue area had demonstrably changed for the better.

20

The Test Passed: Spring 1972

NOT EVERYTHING HAD GONE WELL IN VIETNAM during these years, of course, and we had never expected it would. In early 1971, I stepped out of my usually reticent attitude toward military matters in a private talk with General Abrams to say that the pacification program might be going well but the key to the war seemed to me to be whether the infiltration of North Vietnamese forces along the Ho Chi Minh Trail through Laos could be cut off. I had deliberately tried to avoid injecting myself into the military part of the war, as I had enough to do with pacification and thought to avoid resentment among the military officers at a mere civilian asserting a role in military decisions. Abrams had included me in every major command briefing and clearly welcomed my comments, even when I pointed out on one occasion that the Royal Lao Air Force seemed to be making an exceptional record of missions flown and bombs delivered in comparison with the other air units at work in the area. I was not included in the private meeting Abrams held daily to decide on the B-52 strikes for the next day, and I did not question this as it clearly had little to do with the pacification campaign. Abrams obviously appreciated my deference on these matters to his command position, and we were the best of friends and colleagues in a common effort, it being clearly understood between us that I was not about to tell him how to run his business, the military, while he gave me full support in mine—our common goal of pacification.

In response to my gingerly intervention into the military dimension in suggesting that something needed to be done about the open flow of North Vietnamese forces through Laos, Abrams replied that he was in full agreement. We both knew that the extensive air bombardment of the area reported in our weekly strategy briefings had not stopped the supply of essentials to the North Vietnamese forces. General Abrams gently told me to wait a bit and that I would see something done about the problem. I did not inquire further into what was clearly a purely military aspect of the war, but I felt better about his recognition of the problem.

In a few days, I saw the operational reports of the first Vietnamized military operation over the border of Laos to try to cut the Ho Chi Minh Trail. It took place in the region of the Demilitarized Zone. Beyond some helicopter units, no American combat forces were involved. The Vietnamese went into an area that North Vietnamese regulars had completely controlled for years and in which their reserve forces were readily available. The South Vietnamese were understandably cautious, and when they met a massive counterattack they withdrew.

The American media focused on pictures of South Vietnamese hanging onto helicopter skids and pronounced the operation a defeat. Victory it was not, but it did demonstrate that the Vietnamese had developed the beginnings of a capability to mount a forward defense outside their own borders. The first exercise had ended in disaster, no less, but it set the objective for the South Vietnamese for the future— better to organize such operations in areas where the enemy was not so strong as to be overpowering. The first halting steps had been taken to apply the Nixon Doctrine that the United States would support the South Vietnamese in defending themselves but American combat troops would not do the fighting for them.

There were political problems as well. President Thieu's term was to end in 1971. It was obvious that he would run again and that he would be reelected. But it was essential to the Government's future credibility and to its claim to legitimacy, as against the Communists and their front organizations, that the election be seen at home and abroad as free and honest. So long as the peace negotiations in Paris were without result, there was no way in which the Communists could be included in the election process. At Paris they were calling on the United States to overthrow

Thieu for them—at one point suggesting, as Kissinger reported in his memoirs, that he simply be assassinated (as, of course, had happened to Diem). I had once suggested to the Embassy that a start might be made toward bringing the Communists into the political process by allowing them to participate in village elections. The idea was to bring them out of their armed opposition and begin to incorporate them into the political process, but at a safe level initially. But the suggestion aroused no enthusiasm from the Embassy, which was after all in charge of such political matters.

Thieu did begin preparations for the election by organizing a Democracy (Dan Chu) Party on whose ticket he could run, but this ran into the same troubles that had afflicted Diem's National Revolutionary Movement. The officials of the Government apparatus, civil and military, took it over and ran it as an element of the Government administration. While regrettable, this was probably inevitable. The Government apparatus had been in effect the only real political body in the country since 1954. Aside from the Communists and their fronts, the so-called political parties were simply small conspiratorial groups engaged chiefly in plotting and complaining. It was really the Government that, through the pacification program, was fulfilling the function of political formation and representation of the people's interests.

But some opposition was needed to present a valid picture of an election, and there was a name available. General Duong Van ("Big Minh") Minh had returned from exile in Bangkok, where he cultivated orchids, to do the same in Saigon. As he had grumbled about Diem's Government, so did he continue to complain about Thieu's. He had some justification for this continuity; as I noted earlier, Thieu had once mused to me after a day in the country that he thought Diem had run the country fairly well. But now few Americans were criticizing Thieu's authoritarian ways, since the results in the countryside seemed so positive—and the sequel to Diem's removal had been such a disaster. Moreover, Minh had wide name recognition in the country and, as he made no secret of his opposition to Thieu, he was a natural candidate to oppose Thieu in the election.

In his usual indecisive way, Minh put out hints of his readiness to undertake the challenge. Then he backed away. Then his interest was revived. Both Thieu and the Americans hoped Minh would run; both were sure Thieu would win, but the contest would provide the necessary legitimacy. Finally, at the last moment, Minh backed away for the last time. The election provided an overwhelming endorsement of Thieu, but it was flawed by the absence of an opponent. Grumble as he might, Minh's decision plainly reflected his, and everyone's, judgment that Thieu would soundly defeat him—a loss of face and a favor to Thieu that Minh simply did not want to offer up.

Our judgment in this episode relied on more than guesswork. Some months before the election, we in CORDS had inserted a few significant questions in our public opinion surveys. We first asked for some recognition of the identities of the self-proclaimed political parties. The results were minuscule. This did not surprise us, as the polls covered primarily rural areas, but it was satisfying to see our judgments confirmed. We then sought some indication of popular recognition of or response to possible candidates for the election. We indulged in some rather arch phrasing here, suggested by some of our people who had had experience with polling: to avoid asking how people would vote, we asked merely who they thought would run for President. Again the results brought no surprises. Some 80 percent named Thieu first, and another 10 percent put him as their second choice. Minh received a respectable but losing recognition by about 15 percent as first named and another 3 or 4 percent as second. As a fair prediction of the likely outcome of a contest between the two, this seemed about right—even welcome. Minh's withdrawal was apparently based on the same conclusion.

We were later criticized in some of the media for conducting so political a poll. I defended it as giving us information about popular attitudes and preferences of obviously vital interest to the United States. Some said we were partisan in giving the results to the Thieu Government and not to his opponents—as though we could have even conducted the poll without the Government's knowledge and assent and without giving them the results. I did not feel we had an

obligation to search out "Big Minh" and give him the
results, or to solicit his questions. In fact, I had rather hoped
that he would not learn of the polls, as they would suggest
to him that he do what he did, i.e., withdraw, which was
hardly an action welcome to American policy.

The Presidential election of 1971 was a disappointment.
But the real test of the American effort in Vietnam lay
elsewhere: whether the Communists could win the war.
That vital test was still to come. By the time it was posed, I
had returned to Washington. Our daughter Catherine was
suffering some severe psychiatric and physical problems as
a result of the epilepsy she had endured since childhood,
magnified with the onset of adulthood and the social pressures it brought. I had made several emergency visits to the
United States in early 1971 to try to help, but her situation
had not improved, and my place was clearly at home. As in
my first departure from Vietnam in 1962, I thought I should
stay to continue the momentum we had built up, but I had
to respond to other obligations. And I left in 1971 with the
feeling I had in 1962: that the prognosis was certainly good
on the basis of what was going on in the countryside.

Coming back on my schedule rather than the Government's obviously raised the question of what to do with me.
The State Department, for which I technically worked
because of my Ambassadorial rank, most generously offered
me the position of managing its concerns with Vietnam, a
logical assignment for one who had spent so much time
there. But Dick Helms, remembering my giving up the
Soviet assignment he had planned for me in 1968, offered
me instead the post of Executive Director of the CIA, a
senior position concerned with management, preparation
of the budget submission to the Congress, and coordination
of the Agency's operational, analytical, technological, and
administrative activities. Needless to say, I accepted with
great appreciation his offer to return to the Agency where I
had spent most of my professional life.

In Vietnam, the vital test that had been looming when I
left came in the spring of 1972. It was won by the South
Vietnamese and the Americans.

The contrast between the Communist attack at Tet 1968
and their Easter Offensive in 1972 was both marked and
momentous.

By the time the North Vietnamese attacked in 1972, approximately 500,000 American troops, with their enormous firepower and support mechanism, had been withdrawn from Vietnam. In place of 1968's nationwide assault by hundreds of small guerrilla units against the urban centers of South Vietnam, the 1972 attack consisted of a regular military assault by many North Vietnamese divisions, with their supporting artillery and armored units moving across the borders of South Vietnam from their bases in North Vietnam, Laos, and Cambodia. They struck across the Demilitarized Zone in the north, from Laos into the highland regions in the center, and from the Cambodian sanctuaries against the Saigon area.

Almost nothing in the way of guerrilla assaults occurred in the interior of the country, in the populated areas of the Delta, or in the coastal regions. The southern and central attacks over the frontiers were quickly contained by the South Vietnamese Army. The direct attack from North Vietnam, through the Demilitarized Zone, had some initial successes. A newly formed South Vietnamese division cracked when its commander panicked and fled. The North Vietnamese overran the northern province and its capital. The pacification successes there could not withstand the onslaught of regular forces and their supporting arms. Refugees and defeated troops streamed southward into the Hue area, which seemed as though it too would fall.

In Washington, I reviewed the intelligence and operational reports. My conclusion was that Hue might indeed fall but that the attack would be contained before it reached Danang. It turned out differently. The Vietnamese Army, buttressed by President Thieu's assignment of one of its best generals, Ngo Quang Truong, who had shared the remote outpost in the Delta with John Vann, picked itself up from the initial onslaught, reformed its defenses, and fought the enemy to a standstill before Hue. During the ensuing weeks, it forced the North Vietnamese forces back North, freeing the northernmost province, although by then its cities consisted of little more than rubble.

The attack in the central highlands was more easily and effectively contained by the substantial force the South Vietnamese had maintained there against the possibility of precisely this attack. The probe just north of Saigon proved

the most serious threat of all. The North Vietnamese had
assembled a force of several divisions, hoping to overwhelm
the South Vietnamese there and go on to the urban center of
the country. The South Vietnamese who took the first blows
responded well, but the power amassed against them soon
threatened their defeat.

It was then that all the work of John Vann and our
advisers in the Delta over four years was vindicated. President Thieu ordered the 21st Vietnamese Division to leave its
station in the South of the Delta and to move up to the area
north of Saigon to reinforce the division facing the brunt of
the enemy attack there—in theory exposing the southern
Delta to enemy action. But Thieu was confident that the
Communists were capable of little more than marginal
harassment in that area, which could be easily handled by
the Territorial Forces. And he was right. Pacification had
accomplished the mission Vann and I had discussed of
freeing the regular forces to defend the frontiers of the
nation. And Vietnamization had done its job of preparing
the Vietnamese Army to meet this massive military assault
and defeat it after some tense and heroic fighting.

While half a million American troops had been taken
out of the equation of force between North and South
Vietnam, and practically no American combat forces participated in the defense of South Vietnam in that spring of
1972, this did not mean that the Americans had no role in
the defeat of the North Vietnamese offensive. The Nixon
Doctrine enunciated in 1969 did not propose that the
United States wash its hands of the problems of its friends
and allies; only that we would not do their fighting for
them. American support did play a critical role in the 1972
contest.

Lavish American logistical *support* in the form of ammunition, fuel, and advanced weaponry such as helicopters
allowed the South Vietnamese troops to apply effectively the
tactics of overwhelming firepower and rapid maneuver
their American advisers had advocated. From its sophisticated electronic apparatus, American intelligence provided
the Vietnamese with reliable indicators of enemy action
against them flowing from our worldwide network of collection of data, its analysis in fantastic computer centers in

the United States, and its instantaneous delivery to field units. The enormous power of B-52s, Naval carrier strike forces, and Air Force tactical bombers was brought in from Guam, the South China Sea, and Thailand with great effect against concentrated targets of conventional North Vietnamese armor, artillery, and infantry units—in contrast to the thin logistical lines those same forces had tried so ineffectually to interdict over the previous years. But the Nixon Doctrine was obeyed. The South Vietnamese bore the main burden of the fight on the ground; few Americans were involved other than in logistics and air support.

This was the test. And the South Vietnamese met it. The North Vietnamese units did not take Hue; they were repulsed in the highlands. The major attack against the Saigon area stalled before the heroism and strength of the South Vietnamese Army. A free Vietnam had proven that it had the will and the capability to defend itself with the assistance, but not the participation, of its American ally against the enemy to the North assisted by Soviet and Chinese allies. On the ground in South Vietnam, the war had been won.

But victory, as well as defeat, has its high costs. In the heat of the action in the central highlands, John Vann had taken his helicopter across the fighting in the night and had crashed when it struck a tree in the darkness, killing him. The North Vietnamese claimed to have shot it down, but their claim was no more valid than any of their others. John himself would have said that he had accepted such risks countless times, and that being in the center of the attack, in full command of the Americans supporting the Vietnamese in the cause in which he believed, was fulfilling his greatest ambition. Komer found the words, in his eulogy of John at the funeral in Arlington National Cemetery: "We sent our best."

Part Seven
VICTORY LOST

21

"America Out of Vietnam!"

IN THE SPRING OF 1971, I BEGAN TO APPRECIATE a new factor in the war—the virulence of the antiwar movement in the United States. It had erupted earlier, of course, over our incursion into Cambodia in 1970, but that seemed only a faraway and misguided protest against what on the ground was a clearly justified effort to clean out the Communist base areas along the frontier with South Vietnam. The scale of the Khmer Rouge atrocities in Cambodia that were to follow on the Communist victories was a shock to the world when the news finally leaked out of that unhappy land, but this prospect was unperceived in the early 1970s by the antiwar activists, who saw only American and South Vietnamese faults in Indochina.

We in Vietnam were, of course, focused on the situation we saw before us. The Americans were leaving, the pacification program was doing very well, the Vietnamese Army was being strengthened to take over the military defense of South Vietnam, and it finally seemed that a positive outcome from the years (and blood) committed by our Vietnamese friends and by the Americans to the cause of a free South Vietnam was possible. Such incidents in the United States as the killing of four students at Kent State University in Ohio by a National Guard unit in May 1970 certainly demonstrated that there was a major protest at home about the war. We mourned those deaths, as we did so many during those years, and they pressed upon us the fact that the time available to complete our Vietnamization and pacification tasks was, as we knew, short.

Problems related to antiwar sentiment arose in Vietnam itself, giving us concern. One was the rising use of drugs by American troops. Another was the increasing number of

incidents of "fragging"—troops surreptitiously attacking
their own officers by rolling fragmentation grenades at
them. The erosion of national will at home was being
reflected in an erosion of discipline and morale among the
remaining American troops in Vietnam.

I had a curious personal encounter with the degree to
which antiwar sentiments had penetrated even our military
in Vietnam. I chatted at dusk one evening with an American soldier standing guard at the rampart around a rural
team site I was visiting on one of my nights in the country.
He mused that he really didn't understand why we, and he,
were in Vietnam. I replied from my World War II perspective that we were protecting our country and our allies
against the spread of a Communist threat, and doing it far
from home rather than finally at home. He responded that
he did not agree with that, and that we should fight only if
we were directly engaged. I then asked whether he thought
we should fight in Europe or Canada and in each case
evoked a "No." Somewhat startled, I asked whether he (from
New Jersey) would fight in Maine and got another "No." I
gave up at that point, wishing him well as he stood guard
over us in that faraway place. I was confident that he would
do his duty to protect us while we slept, but I could not help
but marvel at the far reach of his negatives.

But my own direct experience of the intensity of the
antiwar ferment at home began when I was asked to return
to Washington in April 1971 to testify about our assistance
to refugees before Senator Edward Kennedy's Subcommittee
on Refugees of the Senate Judiciary Committee. In Washington, jurisdiction over refugee programs rested with the
Administration for International Development in the Executive Branch and, in the Senate, with the Judiciary Committee, which would presumably control American immi-
gration policy. In Vietnam, the program had been
integrated into CORDS to ensure that it would work in
close coordination with the pacification program and the
military, with a separate Ministry of the Vietnamese Government managing the refugee centers and dispensing the
necessary benefits to the refugees. I was thus the appropriate spokesman to present the situation to the Senate Committee when it wanted to be brought up to date on what was

being done for the refugees in Vietnam with American support. In preparation, I had spent several days just before the trip home visiting each of the refugee centers that I knew the Committee's staff had focused on so that I could testify about them from personal knowledge.

As I testified, in the rear of the hearing room a group of antiwar veterans in beards and camouflage uniforms hooted denunciations of me as lying or supporting an American policy of genocide. This did not particularly bother me, especially as Kennedy made it clear that he insisted on order at his hearing.

What was unnerving was the surreal atmosphere of discussing American and South Vietnamese actions as though there were no enemy at all in Vietnam. Kennedy repeatedly tried to make the point that refugees were generated by U.S. military action. When I made it clear that most of the cases he referred to involved South Vietnamese military action in response to Communist attacks (many American forces having gone home by then), he turned to using the term "U.S.-supported actions," to which I replied "Vietnamese action primarily." He referred to one incident as "in the area of My Lai" (the site of the 1968 murder of Vietnamese civilians by an American unit), and I had to point out that the incident was some thirty or forty kilometers from My Lai, which made the reference irrelevant, however dramatic. I also had to point out the elemental fact that the greatest surge in refugees came at the time of the Tet attacks in 1968.

When I tried to stress that millions of refugees had been cared for at least to some degree by the Vietnamese Government's programs over the past several years and that the program had been expanded to cover "war victims" (people who had been hurt but were still in their own homes) rather than only refugees, Kennedy turned to the small scope of South Vietnam's civilian social welfare program, which we had been able to broaden in the preceding year but which could hardly match that of Massachusetts.

At one moment, I had to ride over his question to insist on the full story:

MR. COLBY: In June 1970, Senator, in Quang Tri
    Province, what that stemmed from was an effort

by about three companies of North Vietnamese to
sally down into the lowlands.

SENATOR KENNEDY: Doesn't it appear that those
are the ones . . .

MR. COLBY: When they got there the friendly forces,
including the local self-defense and local territorial forces, held them and fought with them and
the ARVN [South Vietnamese Army] came and
chased them out and destroyed them. In the
course of that kind of fight you do get that kind of
damage to the houses, because there was a lot of
shooting going on and a lot of shooting done by
our forces and the Vietnamese forces. I don't think
there were any American forces involved in that
one. But I think that is the origin of that particular incident in Quang Tri Province.

We then got into a theological discussion of whether
populations should ever be relocated so that their isolated
settlements would not be involved in our battles with North
Vietnamese forces. When I tried to stress President Thieu's
policy of moving security to the people rather than the
people to security wherever possible, and his requirement
that relocation be conducted only with high-level approval
and with proper preparation, a few cases of inadequate
handling (which our officers had reported and which we
were trying to correct) were adduced as evidence sufficient
to denounce the entire effort. My reference to the fact that
many nations had relocated populations in wartime situations (e.g., the Japanese-Americans from California in
1942) was set aside as not justifying the action in a more
enlightened today.

I had brought along a Chinese 82-millimeter mortar fin I
had picked up in one refugee camp in the highlands to
illustrate the Communist practice of attacking refugees in
order to drive them back into Communist areas to serve as
porters and food growers. But I decided that displaying it
would just be contentious, have no effect on the overall
atmosphere, and detract from, rather than strengthen, the
impression I was trying to project that the situation was by

no means perfect, but that the Vietnamese and the Americans on the spot were working on it and fully understood its moral dimensions. My approach seemed to pay off to a degree when Kennedy summed up saying that I had done "an excellent job in attempting to defend an indefensible policy." But the gulf between the reality of making progress in the myriad problems in Vietnam and the American insistence on immediate perfection still persisted; everything bad was blamed on American and South Vietnamese actions.

On June 13, 1971, more fuel was added to the fire directed against our efforts in Vietnam by the start of publication of the so-called Pentagon Papers, followed by the Supreme Court decision, over the Nixon Administration's objections, allowing their publication in full. I had no real problem with their accuracy, but I did with their scope, their coverage ending in May 1968, just when CORDS had begun its work. They thus focused on the Diem period and his overthrow, the revolving-door governments that followed him, the major American military buildup, and the dramatic Communist Tet 1968 offensive. Their description of the formation of CORDS ended on the hopeful note that "at least the Mission was better run and better organized than it ever had been before, and this fact may in time lead to a more efficient and successful effort" (Gravel edition II, 622). The years that followed certainly showed this to be an accurate statement. But the main effect of the publication of the Papers was once again to call attention to the confused and ineffective conduct of the war prior to the period of success that followed 1968, and to reinforce the feeling of futility about Vietnam, which by then had become fixed.

At the end of June 1971, I returned from Vietnam to Washington for the last time. My daughter Catherine, as I have recounted in the preceding chapter, was extremely sick. Some critics have alleged that her sickness and later death in 1973 was a protest against my work in Vietnam and particularly my direction of the Phoenix program. I know this to be false, as she was invariably supportive of my efforts on behalf of Vietnam, where she was perhaps happiest during her childhood. After my return she had a series of good and bad periods, but her epilepsy and her depression gradually slipped into anorexia, which finally took her life in 1973 despite the efforts of the medical experts in Washington and at Johns Hopkins in Baltimore.

When I left Vietnam, I turned CORDS over to my most helpful Deputy, George Jacobson, who had begun his service in Vietnam as a military officer, had left, returned in the early 1960s, and had been there since. George enjoyed some fame for leaning out of an upstairs window next door to the Embassy during the 1968 Tet attack to ask that a friend throw him a pistol, with which he then disposed of an attacker heading up the stairs toward him—the incident making great television drama. He was to lead CORDS until its dissolution at the time of the 1973 Peace Treaty, but he stayed thereafter until the last days in 1975.

My return in 1971 fully opened my eyes to the intensity of the antiwar movement. In July the Subcommittee on Foreign Operations and Government Information of the House of Representatives Committee on Government Operations decided to hold hearings on our assistance program in Vietnam, and I took the full impact of the new atmosphere. The Committee began on the somewhat mundane subject of accounting for the budgets devoted to the CORDS effort. A General Accounting Office team had recently visited Vietnam to examine the subject and had been startled at my statement that I did not know in dollar terms what my program cost. Being an intelligent team, they soon understood that I did know about the funds we actually managed in the field but that the full cost of our programs frequently included the costs of weapons or other equipment that were written off when shipped from the United States and delivered to the Vietnamese Government. Also, some assistance programs were handled by different agencies in the United States and in Saigon, but by CORDS at the rural level. The GAO examiners even accepted my statement that we had been putting our efforts into fighting the war rather than into accounting, extracting in return my concession that things were in fact now going well enough that it was appropriate for us to devote some attention to better accounting and financial controls.

The House Subcommittee huffed and puffed a bit about this problem and then repeated much of Senator Kennedy's concern over refugees and the civilian victims of the war. Two Congressmen bored in, however, on Phoenix. One, Paul McCloskey of California, had been to Vietnam, where he was escorted around by one of the best of the CORDS officers, Frank Scotton, on detail to CORDS from the USIA. Scotton spoke Vietnamese fluently and operated under my instruction to let the Congressman see anything he wanted to, to tell him the truth even if it hurt, but to try to give him some sense of proportion and of the wartime reality in which we carried on our work. McCloskey was having little of that, however, and focused on nuggets he could use to denounce the program.

The other Congressman, Ogden Reid of New York, concentrated on whether Phoenix met the standards of American Constitutional due process, with right to counsel, court procedures, etc. Since my Constitutional law studies were as good as his (we both graduated from Columbia University Law School), I frankly said that they did not, but that we were doing all we could to improve the procedures under which this necessary program of the war would be carried out. My defense that a war clearly involves an attempt to achieve the capture, the surrender, or the death of the enemy cut little ice with my critics, whose simplistic position was that a war should not be going on in Vietnam and would not be if the Americans were not there.

While I had opened my description of Phoenix with the fact that the Viet Cong terrorism that it was designed to combat had killed some 6,000 South Vietnamese local leaders and ordinary citizens during the past year, the statistics that caught the attention of the press in its accounts of my testimony were those of the effects of Phoenix on the enemy. I recounted that during the years since it began in 1968, the Phoenix program had brought about the capture of some 28,978 Communist leaders in the Viet Cong Infrastructure, that some 17,717 had taken advantage of the amnesty program, and that some 20,587 had been reported as killed. I made it quite clear that those killings occurred "mostly in combat situations" and supported that statement with the further details that some 87.6 percent of those killed were killed by regular or paramilitary forces, and only 12.4 percent by police or irregular forces. Mr. Reid then asked,

"Can you state categorically that Phoenix has never perpe-
trated the premeditated killing of a civilian in a noncombat
situation?"

"No," I replied, "I could not say that, but I do not think it
happens often. I certainly would not say never," adding,
"Phoenix, as a program, I say, has not done that. Individual
members of it, subordinate people in it, may have done it.
But as a program, it is not designed to do that." Reid then
tried to get me to make an admission in specific numbers of
people who may have been inaccurately identified as members of the VCI, which I successfully resisted. I did not know
the answer, and I understood that he was seeking a good
headline.

We then had a direct debate over Mr. Reid's contention
that the United States should cut off its assistance to the
program. I countered this by stating that if we did not
approve, we should go further—we should use our influence to have the program stopped. But I said that the
program was designed to eliminate the problems he was
concerned about and should be continued. Then I said:

> Mr. Congressman, I have said on several occasions
> that unfortunately the Vietnamese are not going to
> live happily ever after. They are going to face a
> security threat from North Vietnam and from the
> Viet Cong over a number of years. They are going to
> lose a few and they are going to win a few. But I
> believe that the probabilities are very clear that they
> will be able to sustain themselves in the future
> without the U.S. presence there that there has been
> in the past.

My testimony was followed a day or so later by an account
by a former American soldier who presented the most sensational and bloody picture of his "role as it was peripheral to
the Phoenix program" and "associated with both military
intelligence and the CIA." Mr. K. Barton Osborn never did
say precisely with which unit he had served, but he claimed
he had worked with the U.S. Marines and Army and that he
did not "work with the Vietnamese in any capacity"—a
clear indication that he could not in reality have worked
with Phoenix, which was by definition a Vietnamese pro-

gram with our U.S. military Phoenix advisers in a support
capacity. Mr. Osborn also indicated that he left Vietnam in
1968, when the Phoenix program had just begun to work as
part of the Accelerated Pacification Program, again indicating that whatever he may have done had nothing to do with
Phoenix. But his lurid testimony of throwing Communist
captives and suspects from helicopters and my report of the
numbers affected by this struggle cast in concrete one of the
most repulsive, and flatly wrong, images of the Vietnam
war, namely, that the Phoenix program under my control
had murdered some 20,000 Vietnamese.

This was despite my emphasis that the deaths involved
were mostly during military actions and had been identified
on the battlefield after the fight as known members of the
Communist apparatus. My problem was that I could not
and would not say that no wrongful death had ever occurred, so that the sensational item for the press was my
admission that some had happened. The Congressmen also
did not pick up the key facts about their witnesses, which
any attorney would have caught as affecting their credibility, but instead wallowed in the accounts of bloody misdeeds, with the media recording it all. A small solace was
that the next day's report in the *New York Times*, while
repeating my statistics, gave a straightforward account of
the hearing, headlining that I had defended the program
"despite killings of civilians" and stating that with "quiet
persistence" I had argued that "the program was designed
to protect the Vietnamese people from terrorism."

But the fact that Phoenix was reducing the arbitrary way
in which the war had been fought was lost in the impression of wrongful death. The fact that the figures were only
supplemental to those I had reported during my testimony
to Senator Fulbright in early 1970, and not different in
proportion, was more a mark of the different atmosphere
that had grown up around the question of Vietnam than of
the figures themselves. I was moved to consider the words of
the moralist that if one is not concerned with the death of
each person, one is not concerned with the death of any,
and thought my critics were concerned primarily with the
political capital that could be made of the statistics.

Over a year after this dramatic testimony, the Subcommittee submitted its report on the hearings, which was more significant for what it did not say than for what it did, so it received practically no media coverage. The sole recommendation dealing with the Phoenix testimony was that the Secretary of Defense investigate the allegations of crimes committed by U.S. military personnel against civilians. The Subcommittee also recorded its concern over the problems of the Phoenix program about which I had testified and that our advisory teams were working to overcome. But no recommendation issued from the Subcommittee that the program or its American support be halted.

The Subcommittee and its staff apparently concluded, on a conscientious review of the full record, that the sensational allegations of the witness did not really stand up as an indictment of the Phoenix program, although some of the incidents may have happened and should be prosecuted. But this is a rather subtle conclusion to be drawn from the report, and it drew no attention from the media or the antiwar movement, both of which continued to repeat the sweeping charges of the witness and to apply them to Phoenix as a whole. It was clear from the experience surrounding the testimony that many Americans, including my two Congressional interrogators, were totally opposed to what we were trying to accomplish in Vietnam. They wanted, in the slogan used by the antiwar movement, "America Out of Vietnam!"—without condition and without consideration of what the Vietnamese might want.

In this account of the Vietnam war, I have omitted any discussion of the various diplomatic efforts that were made to settle it. This was not from inadvertence, nor was it from the fact that the subject never really fell within my responsibilities either in Vietnam or in Washington. Rather, it reflects my belief, then and now, that the process was largely irrelevant to the struggle in the countryside. I was convinced that the North Vietnamese Communist leadership was determined to conquer South Vietnam and would accept nothing less than victory in any negotiations that might take place. They had certainly given full evidence of their determination to prosecute the war, whatever their casualties on the battlefield; I was certain they would not be turned from their objectives by diplomatic persuasion or bargaining.

At various stages, the political leadership of the United States—President Johnson, President Nixon, Henry Kissinger, their aides and diplomats—thought that approaches to the Soviet Union could produce pressures on the North Vietnamese to get them to accept some compromise solution. My own view was that this did not give sufficient weight to North Vietnamese determination and that it missed the most interesting of the balancing acts that occurred during the Vietnam conflict—the exquisite skill of the North Vietnamese in manipulating their Soviet and Chinese sources of supply to extract the maximum from each. Locked as the two Communist giants were in rivalry between Mao's Cultural Revolution and Moscow's revisionism for leadership of the Communist cause worldwide, the North Vietnamese involved them in a competition in which each sought to demonstrate superior credentials as fellow Communists—the gauge being support of Hanoi.

Some of the CIA's counterintelligence personnel considered this Sino-Soviet ideological dispute a charade to confuse the West and advance the cause of Communism, but I accepted it at face value as reflective of an internal theological dispute, and of the national antagonisms that had characterized Russian and Chinese relations for centuries. The North Vietnamese correctly saw in the dispute a chance to play each supporter off against the other and to derive a rich reward in military hardware therefrom. The one thing that seemed obvious to me was that in this situation the Soviets did not have enough influence over the North Vietnamese to halt their operations against South Vietnam. With the frustrations Americans suffered trying to make the South Vietnamese conform to American ideas of what was good for them, I saw little chance that the Soviets could control their far more tough-minded and determined cousins in the North.

I accordingly paid slight attention to the various secret probes and intermediaries or to the direct approaches to Moscow that diverted high-level concentration from the war in the South during the mid-1960s. Even when formal negotiations began in Paris in 1968, it was plain to me that no compromise solution was possible through diplomatic channels. The North Vietnamese had the French model to sustain them. Their steely determination had finally worn down French willingness to continue the war effort in 1954, leading to concessions from Paris far beyond what the Communists had actually won at Dien Bien Phu. And in that performance lay at least one of the factors that kept the North Vietnamese to a hard line in the 1960s and 1970s. It was that they had actually compromised in Geneva in 1954 under the pressure of the Soviets and China, only to see their hope for subsequent "inevitable" total victory frustrated by the unexpected ability of Ngo Dinh Diem, with American support, to revive South Vietnam.

The principal North Vietnamese negotiators in the 1968–1973 period often were quite frank in their references to the strength of the American antiwar movement as a principal factor that would force the United States to withdraw from the war in South Vietnam and cease its support of the Thieu Government. This was put directly to Kissinger by senior North Vietnamese negotiator Le Duc Tho. Despite Kissinger's sharp replies that Tho had no idea of how to deal with an opposition and that Kissinger would not discuss American public opinion with him, the many contacts of the North Vietnamese with Americans in Europe and visiting North Vietnam convinced them that they had only to be intransigent and the Americans would give in. The North Vietnamese attitude was perhaps best expressed by their suggestion at one point that the principal obstacle to a "solution" to the impasse that persisted between the parties could be removed by the simple act of assassinating President Thieu—perhaps in their view a fair comment on how the Americans had treated his predecessor, President Diem, when he failed to follow American direction.

We in Vietnam were well aware of this firm attitude by our enemies across the battle lines and were fearful that the North Vietnamese were correct, so the only hope was to build up the South sufficiently rapidly so that it could sustain itself against the North without American participation. But we knew it would need American logistics and air support, as we had provided in 1972.

The invisible participant at the negotiating table, on which the North Vietnamese depended to split the American delegation from its South Vietnamese negotiating partner, was the American antiwar movement. The North Vietnamese assiduously courted its members through contacts in Europe, visits to Hanoi, and appeals to liberal sympathy with anticolonialism. This was immensely assisted by the American media's full access to South Vietnam and their inability to penetrate North Vietnam's tight security screen, thus providing the American public with a rich diet of stories of the failures and imperfections of the South Vietnamese regime and little or nothing about North Vietnam beyond the image Hanoi wished others to see. What the American public saw, read, and heard was, on balance, another element in the pressures the North counted on the antiwar movement to put on the American Government to ultimately withdraw from Vietnam and, as the French Government did in 1954, leave South Vietnam to its fate.

The most difficult aspect of the antiwar sentiment for us in Vietnam to understand was the fact that when public interest in Vietnam declined with the withdrawal of American troops and the consequent reduction of American casualties, prevailing liberal and antiwar opinion shifted its emphasis from halting American military action to stopping the Vietnam war entirely—at the cost of North Vietnamese victory if need be. Indeed, many antiwar leaders actually believed that a North Vietnamese victory would be the best possible outcome.

These pressures weighed especially heavily on President Richard Nixon and his National Security Assistant, Henry Kissinger. Nixon faced the election campaign in 1972 opposed by George McGovern's flat call for an end to all American involvement in South Vietnam. Kissinger realized that the only possible answer to that challenge was to bring about a peace agreement, and he searched insistently for a formula that would satisfy the North Vietnamese, yet allow President Nixon to assert that the United States had achieved an honorable settlement.

The North Vietnamese had an additional card to play in the persons of the American military captives held in North Vietnam, mostly Air Force and Navy airmen shot down there. Their captors cynically exploited them at the same time they abused them, parading them before antiwar activists like Jane Fonda in order to add this public pressure

on President Nixon to yield to their demands. Their own
spectacular courage and discipline under pressure (one
blinking out the Morse Code letters T-O-R-T-U-R-E with
his eyelids before the television cameras recording such a
meeting; a group giving a rude hand signal to the still
photographers, which *LIFE* magazine had the bad taste to
publish, thus ensuring punishment for the captives) were
hardly recognized by a nation that had decided that what
they had done in the service of their country was flawed,
and that they should be repatriated out of charity, not pride.
The effect of this cynical manipulation of these prisoners
was summed up in a remark Kissinger later made to me (I
had no role in the negotiation from my administrative post
in the CIA) when I commented that I could never understand how anyone could have believed that the North Vietnamese would comply with the "Peace" Agreement they
finally signed: "You have no idea of the pressure we were
under to get the POWs out."

The fundamental issue in the negotiations came down to
whether Hanoi could maintain the presence in South Vietnam that they had lost to Thieu's pacification campaigns.
Thieu saw this as an impossible outcome, as he fully
realized that a peace agreement would mean only one
thing—that the United States would end its involvement
and support of South Vietnam while the North Vietnamese
would return to the attack as soon as the situation seemed
propitious. North Vietnam's assistance from its Soviet and
Chinese allies would certainly continue, but America's to
South Vietnam would as certainly dry up. Thieu thus
resolutely refused to accept continued North Vietnamese
presence in the South, which would give the North a clear
advantage for the succeeding, and inevitable, attack.

Kissinger's accomplishment in the negotiations of finally
obtaining North Vietnam's acceptance of the authority of
the Thieu Government as an equal to the Communist
"Provisional Government" in South Vietnam was of no
value to Thieu, who knew that the war would resume as
soon as the Americans were removed from the scene, and
that the balance of forces without the Americans would
certainly favor the Communists and their allies. Kissinger
was seeking the best possible compromise with the Com-

munists, trading agreement for their continued presence in South Vietnam, albeit with a promise that they would stop further infiltration, for acceptance of a continued role for the Thieu Government. He asserts in his *White House Years* that he assumed that the South Vietnamese Army, with American support, could handle minor violations of the agreement and that the United States would return to aid against major ones in the way it had done in the spring of 1972. He did not contemplate only a "decent interval" between an American departure and a South Vietnamese defeat.

Thieu was both suspicious and resentful during his dealings with Kissinger. In later interviews for Nguyen Tien Hung and Jerrold L. Schecter's *The Palace File*, a book based on the many assurances he received of American support if he would agree to the "peace" conditions Kissinger had arranged with the North Vietnamese, Thieu recounted the various and sometimes petty and denigrating ways in which Nixon and Kissinger handled him very much as a colonial dependent, meeting him in Midway rather than Honolulu and giving him a smaller chair than Nixon (which Thieu changed), keeping from him some of the critical negotiations with the North Vietnamese, and even presenting only an English text of an agreement they had negotiated when the crucial question was the meaning of some of its key phrases in Vietnamese. The pressures to which Thieu was subjected understandably raised in his mind the image of the two Ngo brothers as the victims of an American-encouraged coup, lying finally in their own blood in a Vietnamese Army vehicle.

Kissinger recounts his version of the final negotiations in great detail. He had to overcome Thieu's resistance to allowing the North Vietnamese to remain in the South (which Kissinger had already conceded to the Communists), and his first try was to assert to Thieu that later elections to be arranged by the two Vietnamese parties could gauge the balance between the rival authorities. Kissinger's problem was that the conditions he had obtained in his secret bargaining with the North Vietnamese were better from the viewpoint of the South than the ones Thieu had previously authorized him to offer, so that Kissinger knew that the political consequences in the United States, particularly from the antiwar movement, would be severe if he did not now secure Thieu's agreement to the settlement. Thieu's problem was that he had indeed given Kissinger such authorization but had done it when the prospects of a favorable outcome of the negotiations through Hanoi's acceptance of any future whatsoever for Thieu's Government seemed remote. Now that an agreement appeared logically imminent because of the concessions Kissinger had extracted from the North, it was clear to Thieu, as it was to the North, that any agreement that left the North in the South would only mean a resumption of the war without American support, with defeat almost a certainty. Thieu thus dug in his heels and used every stratagem possible to avoid agreement with Kissinger's program.

While President Nixon made it clear that Kissinger's negotiations should not be affected by the forthcoming American Presidential election, both of them were in fact pressed by the manifest evaporation of American public and Congressional support for Vietnam, and were anxious to extract a peace agreement to forestall a unilateral suspension of American assistance. The North Vietnamese were equally anxious for an agreement to fix an American withdrawal, which they correctly foresaw would bar any return, and made a series of concessions, such as agreeing to withdraw from Laos and Cambodia, to obtain it.

Thus the two actual negotiators had come to an agreement, but were unable to complete it because Thieu was resisting. Even the promise of a pretruce massive infusion of military supplies to South Vietnam, which could thereafter under the agreement be replaced on a one-for-one basis, did not overcome Thieu's resistance. He judged that the key question was continued American will and involvement, which he correctly thought would melt away, rather than the words on the paper of the agreement. Thus he reacted with a combination of hysterical tears, fears that the United States was planning a coup to overthrow him, rudeness to the American envoys, and intransigent rejection of the carefully constructed agreement, despite President Nixon's strongly worded expressions that American support would be forthcoming if the agreement were violated but that he would be unable to maintain American support if the agreement were not signed. The impasse with Thieu became obvious to the North Vietnamese, who then decided they would hold up the agreement to get better terms than those they had already agreed to.

The situation was opened up only by a forceful thrust against both Vietnamese parties. The North Vietnamese were subjected to a powerful bombing attack at Christmas 1972 at President Nixon's express order to make clear to them that this attack was different from the delicately applied, gradual bombing campaigns that had characterized the 1960s. Its force, despite the hysterical opposition aroused among the antiwar factions in the United States, was both precise and effective. The North Vietnamese massively publicized the destruction of a hospital in Hanoi but omitted reporting that it was across the street from the railway yards. They made a mistake in announcing the death toll as 1,300 to 1,600, which to anyone familiar with World War II bombing casualties in urban communities indicated clearly that the attack had been no "carpet bombing."

And it worked. The North Vietnamese quickly requested a resumption of the negotiations they had stalled, with a view to coming to a final peace agreement along the lines of the concession they had made. Nixon has since stated that he regretted not having hit the North Vietnamese as hard in 1969 as he did in 1972. He is right.

President Nixon's forcefulness was equally effective with President Thieu and the South Vietnamese. To convince him that the Christmas bombing did not reflect any change in the U.S. determination to make an agreement with the North Vietnamese along the lines that had been negotiated, Nixon advised Thieu that "you must decide now whether you desire to continue our alliance or whether you want me to seek a settlement with the enemy which serves U.S. interests alone." Thieu gave a response that withdrew some of his objections but said that he could not "accept" the continued presence of North Vietnamese troops in the South. He thought this formulation would not stop the Americans from the negotiations but would have kept his conscience clear that he had not acquiesced in a provision that he accurately foresaw could lead to the defeat of his country. Nixon then supplemented his forceful letter to Thieu with another that offered his "assurance of continued assistance in the post-settlement period and that we [the U.S.] will respond with full force should the settlement be violated by North Vietnam." And Kissinger returned to Paris to wrap up the arrangement with the North Vietnamese.

When the final Agreement had been settled in Paris and was taken to Saigon for Thieu's acceptance, it was accompanied by a Nixon letter saying that he would sign the Agreement "if necessary, alone. In that case I shall have to explain publicly that your Government obstructs peace. The result will be an inevitable and immediate termination of U.S. economic and military assistance." Despite a flurry of last-minute attempts to salvage something for his country, Thieu accepted the American decision. The die was cast for "peace" in Vietnam. The Peace Agreement was initialed in Paris on January 23, 1973, and finally signed on January 27. The day was marked by the announcement that the American draft was ended, perhaps a more important concession to antiwar movement adherents than the Peace Agreement itself. An emotional television bath followed the return of the POWs from Hanoi, giving them the honor they were due, but clearly putting the final stamp on the fact that America's war, and interest, in Vietnam was over.

It was plain that the Peace Agreement was not a formal treaty, which would have engaged the United States Senate in a ratification vote, with presumably some responsibility for ensuring compliance. To the North Vietnamese, the Agreement was no different from the others they had signed, as was their violation of it in a matter of days after the signing by shipping further military forces and supplies south. The American military had flooded South Vietnam with as much military equipment as it could before the ban of the Peace Agreement was effective so that it could be legally replaced one-for-one while the Agreement was in effect. The North Vietnamese were less concerned with such legalities, for their supplies were to continue in defiance of the Agreement.

22

Double Defeat

DURING THIS PERIOD, I HAD LITTLE CONNECTION with the negotiations. I did stop in once at Paris to brief the U.S. Delegation on our progress in pacification, with the thought of strengthening them in their negotiations, and to urge them not to "give away the store." But my job by then was that of Executive Director of the CIA, responsible under Director Richard Helms and Deputy Director General Vernon Walters for management problems in the Agency. Essentially, the position cut me out of the Agency's substantive work. I still had, however, the quite intimate connection with it of preparing the Agency's budget, and the more onerous one of defending that budget before the Office of Management and Budget in the Executive Branch and the leadership of the Appropriations and Armed Services Committees of the Congress. The Congressional leaders reviewed it in the polite and cursory fashion that was their tradition—soon to be upended. But my long involvement with Vietnam did not allow me to turn off from it entirely, and I followed the intelligence reports on what was happening there and in Paris with particular attention.

What I saw did not alter my basic belief that South Vietnam would have to fight for its continued existence and that United States support was a critical factor in whether it would be able to sustain itself. Certainly, South Vietnam had proven in 1972 that it could sustain itself with American logistics and air bombing support, but its vulnerability if the Americans abandoned it was clear.

It was also clear that the political contest had been won—the Communists offered no attraction whatsoever. The Thieu Government had designed a program of economic and political improvement that meant a better life for the

343

Vietnamese people. Foreign and American complaints persisted that authoritarianism and corruption still made the
South Vietnamese system far from ideal, but the disengagement of the Americans from the war produced a far less
intrusive and preachy interest in Vietnamese affairs than
had characterized earlier years.

The euphoria that greeted the return of the brave men
who had endured Hanoi's imprisonment seized the national
consciousness, and Vietnam sank into oblivion. In South
Vietnam the Northerners set up a Liaison Mission in Saigon pursuant to the Agreement, which the South Vietnamese effectively sealed off from the countryside. In contempt
of the Agreement, the North Vietnamese began the construction of a network of roads through the Annamite
mountain chain around the Demilitarized Zone between
North and South Vietnam down to the area just north of
Saigon, which had been one of the principal points of
attack during the 1972 Easter offensive. A four-power International Commission was established to monitor compliance with the Agreement. It soon fell into the same
paralysis that had marked its predecessor created after the
1954 Geneva settlement. The Communist members of the
Commission, Poland and Hungary, could never perceive
any violations by the North Vietnamese, and the Northerners simply ignored the requirements for reporting to the
Commission.

Both North and South made last-minute efforts to extend
their areas of control as the Peace Agreement went into
effect in January 1973. The South Vietnamese Army acquitted itself well in this exercise, essentially confining the
Northerners to the remote and isolated mountain and
border areas without substantial population, and regaining
control of the northernmost city and province of Quang
Tri, which had been taken by the North Vietnamese in the
1972 spring offensive.

The one aspect of the Peace Agreement fully complied
with was the American commitment. Within the prescribed
sixty days the last American military left Vietnam, leaving
only a Defense Attaché's office and a few Marine guards at
the American Embassy in Saigon. These were supplemented by some 8,500 American civilians, most of them

logistics and technical personnel assigned to maintain the technology left to the South Vietnamese military and civil organizations. The United States did continue bombing support of Cambodia against the continued assaults of Pol Pot's Khmer Rouge forces, which had not been included in the Peace Agreement and which the North Vietnamese had indicated they could not control. In the last days before the Agreement came into effect, there had been a surge of American military equipment to Vietnam, giving the South Vietnamese large stocks and the basis for future replacements item by item as authorized in the Agreement. But future replacements depended, of course, upon continued American will to provide them, initially in the form of Congressional appropriations.

It was this will that proved to be wanting. The Nixon Administration loyally tried to continue a healthy level of aid to South Vietnam within the limits allowed by the Agreement, only to face rising resistance to continued American involvement in Indochina. In June 1973, the Senate and the House of Representatives passed bills to bar any funds for U.S. military activities in Indochina and were persuaded to delay the cutoff date until August 15 only by Administration urgings that American support to Cambodia continue in order to provide pressure for a cease-fire negotiation there. In October 1973, the Congress passed the War Powers Act, limiting to sixty days the President's power to commit American forces abroad without specific Congressional approval, thereby limiting President Nixon's power to carry out his pledge to President Thieu to "respond with full force" to North Vietnamese violations of the Peace Agreement. In November, the Congress overrode President Nixon's veto.

The declining rate of South Vietnam's American support almost symbiotically matched the increase of North Vietnam's buildup in South Vietnam and in its adjacent Cambodian and Laotian border areas with weaponry provided by the Soviet Union. By October 1973, the North Vietnamese had increased their forces through infiltration by some 70,000 men and hundreds of tanks, artillery, and antiaircraft weaponry and built an all-weather road to the region near Saigon. They were also well on their way to producing an oil pipeline on the same route to provide fuel for the modernized military force they were assembling in and adjacent to South Vietnam. To those of us in the CIA's headquarters in Langley who followed these intelligence reports and the photographs from the sky, their intentions were crystal clear: they would resume the assault on South Vietnam whenever they deemed it auspicious, but this time by an overpowering military attack rather than the laborious people's war tactics that the South had decisively defeated.

In May 1973, President Nixon announced that he was nominating me to become the new Director of Central Intelligence to replace James Schlesinger, who was named Secretary of Defense. My confirmation hearings before the Senate provided another opportunity for the antiwar movement to wave aloft my albatross of Phoenix (to mix metaphors a bit), this time by affixing posters around Washington with an unflattering picture of me as I looked up, an ace of spades in the background, and the familiar charge that I had assassinated 20,000 people in Vietnam through the Phoenix program. But the Senate confirmed me, and I was sworn in on September 5, 1973.

As the new Director, it was my duty to brief the Congress and to keep the Executive Branch up to date on developments in Vietnam, despite the competing attention of other trouble spots in the world such as the Yom Kippur War in the Middle East. I felt the responsibility about Vietnam particularly keenly, however, as I had the feeling that President Nixon had in good part selected me for the Director's post because of what he and Alexander Haig had heard of my work in Vietnam in the pacification program. But my briefings to the Congress fell on very deaf ears. The Members and Senators were far more interested in reducing American involvement abroad.

The results were starkly evident in the decline of American assistance to Vietnam during 1973, 1974, and for 1975. The $2.8 billion in military aid to South Vietnam for 1973 (which included the last-minute surge of supplies before the Peace Agreement) was cut by Congress to $700 million for 1974. A mark of the national attitude in 1973 was that President Nixon in April 1973 could invite President Thieu, our ally in the long Vietnam War, to visit him only in San Clemente, because of the political hostility a normal state visit to Washington would have aroused. When Thieu did visit Washington, he could be received only by Vice President Agnew, who had a difficult time assembling even a token reception committee.

The South Vietnamese were fully aware of the erosion of American support for their continued struggle against the growing force from the North, and it had its inevitable effects on their morale and hopes for the future. Commanders were frank in their statements to old American friends and visitors that they had real doubts whether their troops could be relied upon to fight off another invasion after their obvious abandonment by the Americans. President Thieu arrested the gradual growth of democratic institutions when he suspended elections in the villages and appointed the village chiefs, which he justified by the continuing Communist threat. He also pushed his Democracy Party and effectively erased others, providing the forms but not the reality of political life. The Government bureaucracy filled the key positions of the new party, excluding new blood from the rural and lower classes, in a reprise of Ngo Dinh Diem's National Revolutionary Movement, to present a facade of political participation without its reality.

Faced with declining American support, the Army began husbanding its supplies, reducing its allocations of ammunition and fuel for forward defense operations against Communist units in the mountain and jungle areas, and limiting itself to static defensive tactics. The Territorial and self-defense forces saw their firepower reduced and the general sense of initiative on behalf of extending local security replaced by a wary limitation of risk. Various indicators such as the allocation of artillery daily rates of fire, or helicopter and air sorties, reflected the increasingly cautious approach. The South Vietnamese Army, trained in American weaponry and tactics, was adjusting to being deprived of the American logistics that were essential to the lessons it had been taught.

The political initiative that had characterized the period of Vietnamization and pacification with full American support and encouragement was replaced by a reversion to a military-dominated administration. Thieu believed the rise in Communist conventional military strength left him no choice but to rely increasingly on his military chain of command to meet the coming onslaught. The military, facing a last-ditch battle, increasingly convinced they had been abandoned by their American mentor and supporter to wage a hopeless fight, began to think of the survival of their families rather than the need to sacrifice. But despite the decline in effectiveness of the security forces in the countryside, there was no concomitant rise in Communist presence or strength there. The rural population showed little or no inclination to join the Communist-led "revolutionary" effort, and the Communists seemed to have put the people's-war strategy aside while they built up their conventional forces for frontal attack when the time was right.

An additional development was to have a major impact on the American response to North Vietnamese violations of the Peace Agreement. As the tawdry tale of Watergate unfolded, bits of the Vietnam story, including ex-CIA employee Howard Hunt's scheme to discredit President Kennedy by rewriting his role in the fall of Diem, emerged. Watergate's primary effect on the Vietnamese drama was to further weaken the ability of President Nixon, and even of his successor, Gerald Ford, to utilize American force or to mobilize other American support of South Vietnam. President Nixon's forced resignation in August 1974 was the high-water mark of Congressional power over the Executive, climaxing public distrust of Presidential leadership over the years of the Vietnam War. Nixon's departure revealed the fragility of his personal pledge to react "with full force" to any major violation of the Peace Agreement by Hanoi.

By December 1974, it was clear that North Vietnam had amassed an overpowering force on the borders of South Vietnam. The question was what the Northern leaders would do with it. They discussed this intensely in Hanoi. Intelligence analysts in Washington were engaged simultaneously with the same question. Both sets of discussions came to roughly the same conclusion: Hanoi would make its main attack on South Vietnam in 1976, to benefit from the pressures that would stem from the American Presidential elections. In the meantime, however, it would launch preliminary attacks during the spring of 1975 to maintain the pressure on South Vietnam and American public opinion. Of course, if a target of opportunity opened, Hanoi would exploit it and press as far as it could.

To meet the new and growing pressures, the Ford Administration in January 1975 requested a supplemental Congressional appropriation of $300 million in military assistance for South Vietnam. The request was received by the Congress with undisguised hostility. My briefings in support of it, pointing out the increases in North Vietnamese forces in and around South Vietnam, aroused little or no interest. I could not concentrate my effort on Vietnam, moreover, since from Christmas 1974 on I found myself heavily engaged in defending the CIA from a massive assault by the Congress. The issue involved various instances over the twenty-five-year history of the Agency in which it had overstepped its proper bounds, which were exaggerated and sensationalized to a degree sufficient to put the CIA's continued existence in jeopardy. The atmosphere bore strong similarities to the way Phoenix had been approached.

In January 1975, the North Vietnamese launched a strong attack on the province of Phuoc Long some seventy-five miles north of Saigon. "Province" is something of an exaggeration in describing the area, as in truth it consisted of essentially empty, jungled hills with a few isolated communities connected by thin dirt roads. President Diem had made it a province in order to force Government administrators to pay attention to it, and had resettled some North Vietnamese refugee communities there in order to build a defense against the expected North Vietnamese exploitation of this access route to the Saigon area. But the Northerners selected it for their first attacks in 1975 to determine what the South Vietnamese—and American—reaction would be to this harbinger of the reopening of formal hostilities despite the Peace Agreement. It was also conveniently adjacent to the supply depots and rest areas the Communists had built up at the end of their all-weather roads and pipeline from the North.

Their test was successful. President Thieu decided he

could not risk or devote the necessary helicopter lift to react forcefully to the Communist attack, and it was apparent that the Americans would take no action. President Ford's request in January for supplemental assistance for South Vietnam attracted no greater Congressional attention or support than his report that the North had 289,000 troops *in* South Vietnam, together with hundreds of tanks, heavy artillery, and antiaircraft weapons. The North could escalate its attack with confidence that the Americans would not intervene and that Thieu would thus be forced to fight with limited firepower rather than the way the Americans had trained the South Vietnamese Army.

The North Vietnamese leadership now had a new appreciation of the situation on which they could build: the South would not be supported by the American ally, would have major morale problems among its own troops, and would be outgunned and overpowered by the heavy forces the North would deploy against them. They therefore prepared a large-scale attack to take advantage of these new elements. But they did not consider the coming encounter as being without difficulties. They realized that the South Vietnamese forces were still substantial and that the Northerners were essentially outsiders seeking to overwhelm a possibly still resilient South Vietnam. Taking into account the fact that their efforts to penetrate South Vietnam with a subversive and guerrilla force had failed, their way to victory would have to be by conventional military assault. The hope of undermining the South through the people's war strategy was abandoned.

In the revised circumstances, the new strategy worked better than they could have dreamed. They launched their major attack at approximately the same points on the border areas where they had attacked in 1972. Tactical failures and mistakes caused local defeats for the South Vietnamese forces. The regional commander of the highlands gave orders to withdraw his forces from the exposed highlands pursuant to President Thieu's strategic instructions, and then left his staff and subordinates to complete the maneuver. The troops—and their families—were withdrawn over a totally inadequate road system, where they were completely bogged down and then chopped up by the enemy forces. In the North, President Thieu issued a confusing set of contradictory orders to his best airborne troops: first to resist the enemy onslaught, then to withdraw to meet the main attack in the South, and then to defend the ancient capital of Hue.

The result was a total collapse of the military resistance to the oncoming North Vietnamese forces in the northern and central parts of South Vietnam. The North Vietnamese followed their basic strategic plan to exploit the weaknesses that opened before them. The South Vietnamese forces melted before their attack into individuals seeking their own and their families' salvation. In Washington, we in the National Security Council could only watch helplessly as the intelligence assessments, which I presented, showed the steady advance of the North Vietnamese regular forces down the peninsula and indicated that the disintegration of the South Vietnamese defenses was imminent.

It reminded me forcefully of the collapse of France before the blitzkrieg of the Nazi panzer divisions in 1940, when the inadequacy of the defensive forces foreordained not only their defeat but their fragmentation into individuals seeking escape from the juggernaut and occupation. Nonetheless, to give them credit, there were individual South Vietnamese commanders and whole units that offered a desperate last-minute resistance to the superior enemy forces, such as the 18th Division at Xuan Loc just north of Saigon, whose identities in any long history of Vietnam should be accorded recognition for the heroism they displayed against hopeless odds.

The comparison with France in 1940 had another referent point: the neutrality of the United States as it watched the progress of the battle—and the final outcome of its long involvement in Vietnam. President Ford and his Administration were powerless to influence the result of the contest, despite its repudiation of the efforts and the investments the United States had made in supporting a free South Vietnam. The experience had been rejected by the Congress and the people of the nation.

These last days involved a number of frantic efforts to salvage something from the imminent wreckage of a nation. Our CIA Chief of Station, Thomas Polgar, who had been chosen for the job by reason of an exceptionally effective performance in several other nations (including an incident in which he had climbed aboard a hijacked plane and convinced the hijackers to surrender), came from a Hungarian family and had struck up an acquaintance with the head of the Hungarian Delegation on the International Commission, which was supposed to monitor compliance with the Peace Treaty. This generated a flood of cables to and from Washington about whether the Hungarians could intervene with the North Vietnamese to persuade them to accept a cease-fire or some nonviolent way of ending the conflict. My own view, expressed in the endless meetings that occupied Washington, was that there was little or no hope that these probes would be any more successful than the many efforts we had made to get the Soviet Union to reason the North Vietnamese into a settlement, especially as the balance of forces on the ground so clearly indicated that they would soon achieve the total victory they had sought for so long and for which they had sacrificed so many of their people.

I did intervene with a strong negative, however, to a suggestion from a Vietnamese in Saigon that a settlement might be obtained if the United States would support a coup against President Thieu to replace him with someone more amenable to the Communists. I sent an immediate reply that we would have nothing to do with any such move. If South Vietnam was to fall, so be it, but not with the ultimate indignity of a push from its American ally. We did not need to add another Vietnamese President overthrown with American complicity.

There has been an intense debate over the evacuation of Vietnam, amid charges that many individuals who should have been helped to depart were abandoned and that sensitive material was left behind to compromise those who had worked with the CIA and other American agencies. Certainly, many who should have been helped to depart were not, but many others were. Some departed a number of days in advance, thanks to the help of many Americans, by special flights and arrangements set up outside the formal procedures. My private channels to Tom Polgar allowed me to direct him to move a number of key people out, including the two blinded young Vietnamese women who had been working with the Station as interpreters. One such effort ended in tragedy, however, when a special U.S. Air Force mission to evacuate a load of handicapped orphans lost a door and crashed outside Saigon, presenting perhaps the ultimate atrocity of the whole experience.

A feature of the final helicopter evacuation was the fact that the crowd around the Embassy entrance many times allowed Americans to pass through to the gate, a last courtesy to the Americans who had been so important to the now frightened Vietnamese. But the collapse of a nation does not allow for the methodical removal of all who might have wanted to escape the new regime they had fought against for so long. The true test is how many escaped, either through their own efforts or assisted by their allies. The numbers are impressive: some 130,000 Vietnamese, and all the Americans, escaped Hanoi's rule.

As for documents, the Embassy and the CIA Station spent a great deal of their final energies burning documents to keep them from the enemy's hands, and we have not been treated to the show trials that would have shamed us for the plight of our secret friends. Great numbers of South Vietnamese were later sent to "reeducation" camps, but these were open members of the nationalist cause or sources betrayed by documents left behind in various Vietnamese offices, not in American or CIA files. The evacuation was supplemented by a number of private efforts by some officers and former officers who returned to Vietnam on their own, including several former CORDS officers such as Gage McAfee, to help as much as they could by rounding up former Vietnamese colleagues and ensuring that they were included in the airlift. One former CIA officer, Tucker Gougleman, was not so lucky; he came by sea to the south coast only to be captured and later die in prison.

Finally, however, the end was clear and near—the occupation of Saigon by the North Vietnamese forces. President Ford cut through any last-minute hopes to order the complete evacuation of the Embassy by 3:45 A.M. on April 30. Shortly before that hour, the CIA Station Chief, Tom Polgar, sent me a message that he would soon terminate all communication so that the codes and equipment could be destroyed. He then added:

It has been a long and hard fight and we have lost. This experience unique in the history of the United States does not signal necessarily the demise of the United States as a world power. The severity of the defeat and the circumstances of it, however, would seem to call for a reassessment of the policies of niggardly half-measures which have characterized much of our participation here despite the commitment of manpower and resources which are certainly generous. Those who fail to learn from history are forced to repeat. Let us hope that we will not have another Vietnam experience and that we have learned our lesson. Saigon signing off.

In Washington I was aware that communications with Saigon would soon end, and I thought it only appropriate to record recognition of the CIA's efforts there over the years. So I sent a message that crossed the incoming one:

As we approach end of communication with Saigon, I would like to record the Agency's pride and satisfaction with the job its representatives did there, and at no time during its twenty-odd-year history is this more true than during these past few weeks. The courage, integrity, dedication, and high competence the Agency displayed in a variety of situations over these years has been fully matched and even surpassed by your performance during this difficult final phase. Thousands of Vietnamese owe their lives and future hopes to your efforts, your Government has profited immensely from the accuracy and breadth of your reporting, and your country will one day learn with admiration of the way you represented its best instincts and ideals. Good luck and many thanks.

Soon afterward, the North Vietnamese entered Saigon. An NBC television crew caught one of the more significant pictures of the event. It filmed a huge North Vietnamese tank with its monstrous cannon as it broke open the main gate to the Presidential Palace. The people's war was over, not by the work of a barefoot guerrilla but by the most conventional of military forces. During the last days of the South Vietnamese collapse, as Colonel Harry G. Summers reports, one of the most trenchant comments was made by a naval fighter pilot flying cover for the helicopter evacuations. Returning to the *USS Coral Sea*, he said excitedly, "They're fighting our war!" The ultimate irony was that the people's war launched in 1959 had been defeated, but the soldiers' war, which the United States had insisted on fighting during the 1960s with massive military forces, was finally won by the enemy.

Part Eight
A BETTER WAY

THE FALL OF VIETNAM WAS FOLLOWED BY A SERIES of
revelations of the nature of the Vietnam War that con-
founded many who had been critical of the conflict while it
was being fought. The victorious North Vietnamese commander, General Van Tien Dung, contributed an account of
the final campaign to the April 1, 1976, issue of the Hanoi
journal *Nhan Dan*, which made clear that it was a massive
military assault, in which Southern guerrillas played
hardly any role. He exulted that the lack of American
support meant that Thieu had had to fight "a poor man's
war" against Dung's fourteen well-armed and armored
North Vietnamese divisions. Most interesting to the analysts
in the CIA, he recounted that the North Vietnamese strategy
was to launch an attack in early 1975 but to approach it as
the start of a two-year campaign, to culminate, of course,
during the 1976 American Presidential elections—unless a
target of opportunity developed earlier. This was exactly
the estimate that the CIA had made of the enemy's intentions in the winter of 1974–1975.

Over the next several years came a number of other
revelations confirming assertions by the American and
Vietnamese Governments during the War that had been
contemptuously dismissed at the time by the antiwar forces
in the United States. One such revelation confirmed that the
decision to launch the "people's war" against President Ngo
Dinh Diem had been taken in late 1958 and put into effect
the following year. The first two moves in 1959, it was
explained, were the dispatch of Southerners who had
moved to North Vietnam in 1954 back to the South to
rebuild the political and organizational base for revolt
there, and the establishment of a transportation command

to open what became the Ho Chi Minh Trail. Another confirmed that the first regular North Vietnamese military units moved South in late 1964 to exploit the chaos that followed the overthrow of Diem in hopes of bringing the War to an early end.

Still others were frank statements that the Phoenix program was the action undertaken by the Southern Government that had been most damaging to the Northern strategy, and that it had almost broken all contact between the Communist political structure and the South Vietnamese population. In my own view, this was an exaggeration of what Phoenix by itself had achieved. It stemmed from the erroneous impression (prevalent among many who were—and still are—not well informed about the CORDS effort) that Phoenix equated with the broader pacification program conducted by the Thieu Government. The latter, of course, included its stress on territorial security in the villages, the strengthening of local government, in addition to the direct attack by Phoenix against the Communist secret apparatus, the self-defense and Territorial forces, and the programs of local economic and social development. Taken together, these indeed had had results the North Vietnamese ascribed to Phoenix alone, but I believe they had more to do with the rejection by the South Vietnamese rural population of the authority the Communists tried to exert over them than the Phoenix program alone.

Of course, a number of other "objective facts," as Marxist-Leninists would call them, also belied the claim that the Communists led a popular revolution. The million or more refugees who fled Vietnam, many to die in the South China Sea over the next years, repeated the exodus from North Vietnam that followed the Communist victory in 1954. The fact that they included large numbers of simple farmers and fishermen showed that this was not a flight only of the privileged class under the French or the Diem or Thieu regimes, but that they represented a broad mass of South Vietnamese who refused to accept the gray future imposed by the Northern, doctrinaire Communist, regime. A rough but fair way of judging nations is whether refugees move toward or away from them, and by this test the verdict against the North Vietnamese was conclusive, both during and after the War.

The leadership of the Southern "revolution," the members of the National Liberation Front and the Provisional Revolutionary Government, essentially disappeared from political sight after the 1975 "victory," when they were replaced by North Vietnamese functionaries reinforced by a permanent garrison of North Vietnamese troops. This preparatory step was followed by the "unification" of the Socialist Republic of Vietnam in 1976, in which the rule of South Vietnam was permanently assumed by Hanoi. Interesting to us in the American intelligence community was the fact that practically no senior officials of the South Vietnamese regime or military surfaced after the victory as long-time agents and sympathizers of the North. The principal one touted by the North, Pham Ngoc Thao, former chief of Kien Hoa province in the Delta, who had plotted against Diem in 1963 and against Khanh in 1965, was by this time safely dead, so he could not gainsay the honor.

The situation in Vietnam after the Communist victory, in fact, bore an uncanny resemblance to the predictions made by Douglas Pike, one of the most astute students of Vietnamese Communism, in the conclusion of his study for the United States Information Service of the murders of South Vietnamese during the month in 1968 that the Communist forces occupied the ancient capital of Hue, slaughtering over 3,000 South Vietnamese:

> If the Communists win decisively in South Vietnam (and the key word is decisively), what is the prospect? First, all foreigners would be cleared out of the South, especially the hundreds of foreign newsmen who are in and out of Saigon. A curtain of ignorance would descend. Then would begin a night of long knives. There would be a new order to build. The war was long and so are memories of all scores to be settled. All political opposition, actual or potential, would be systematically eliminated. Stalin versus kulak, Mao versus landlord, Hanoi versus Southern Catholic, the pattern would be the same: eliminate not the individual, for who cares about the individual, but the latent danger to the dream, the representative of the blocs, the symbol of the force, that might someday, even inside the regime, dilute the system. Beyond this would come

Communist justice meted out to the "tyrants and lackeys." Personal revenge would be a small wheel turning within the larger wheel of Party retribution.

But little of this would be known abroad. The Communists in Vietnam would create a silence.

The world would call it peace.

This almost precise prediction of what actually transpired in Vietnam after 1975, with the exception of the mass exodus that occurred, was disputed by the antiwar movement at the time as alarmist and contentious, as well as unlikely. We have seen that it was directly on point.

In the aftermath of the collapse of South Vietnam, a number of explanations were offered by American and Vietnamese authorities and commentators. Some, of course, held the whole experience to have been a monstrous exercise in American arrogance and colonialism, interfering in a civil conflict between an *ancien* and authoritarian, colonialist regime and a truly nationalist and revolutionary force whose victory was inevitable. Frances FitzGerald's final comment in her *Fire in the Lake*, written before the collapse, typifies this attitude: "The moment has arrived for the narrow flame of revolution to cleanse the lake of Vietnamese society from the corruption and disorder of the American war." Some saw the cause of defeat in a failure of American public support caused by hypercritical and one-sided media reporting that deliberately misled the public. Others blamed America's political leadership for trying to conduct the War without revealing its intentions or the War's difficulties that a real public debate, such as a call-up of the reserves or a call for other major commitment by the American people, would have produced. Some military men have criticized the incrementalism of the Government's approach to the War, both in the gradual force buildup and the bombing campaigns, in lieu of striking the enemy with full force and, if necessary, following General Curtis LeMay's formula to "bomb North Vietnam back into the Stone Age." Others believe in hindsight that the U.S. forces should have been used to establish a blocking force across Indochina to Thailand at the 17th Parallel, thus barring North Vietnamese personnel and supplies from reaching the South, and leaving the fight against the Southern guerrillas to the South Vietnamese as more fitted for it than white and black Americans on one-year tours.

Robert Kennedy once said that enough errors were committed over Vietnam for everyone to have had responsibility for some. While there may be truth in his statement, it does not help in drawing lessons from the tragic experience to serve as guides for—and tests of—future challenges to American interests and allies. Certainly there are no pat rules that can be derived from the Vietnam War that would be automatically applicable to the different situations, conflicts, and cultures of other regions of the world. But it is equally certain that lessons, both positive and negative, exist from an experience as extensive and intense as those sixteen years from 1959 to 1975 of American involvement in Vietnam. To derive them we need to identify the turning points within the period and the decisions taken with respect to them, their rationale, and their effects.

The simplest lesson lies in the difference between the American and Vietnamese responses to the North Vietnamese attacks of 1972 and 1975. As noted earlier, the attacks were essentially similar—major military forces entering South Vietnam at approximately the same three points, with no substantial guerrilla action. The South Vietnamese response initially was also similar—resistance by the Army mixed with local tactical failures by a few individual units, with the catastrophic difference of later collapse in 1975. The real difference between the two was in the American dimension. In 1972, the Americans provided massive logistical support, the assistance of American advisory elements and intelligence units on the ground (but no combat forces, 500,000 having been withdrawn from Vietnam during the preceding three years), and the deployment of American air power directly against North Vietnamese military targets in massive and effective doses. In 1975, all three of these American elements were lacking. This difference was the major factor producing the collapse of morale and discipline that led to the end.

This refusal to provide the essential logistics and airpower must be considered the final of three major errors of the American performance in Vietnam. The absence of this relatively small increment of assistance made the downfall of South Vietnam certain and rendered futile the years of blood and sacrifice by Vietnamese and Americans leading up to it. This is not to say that the outcome certainly would have been different, but there is at least a substantial chance that it might have been, based on the 1972 experience. In any case, failure in 1975 would then clearly have been a Vietnamese failure, not the result of the refusal of Vietnam's American ally to respond in its hour of need, with all the implications that refusal presents to other American allies and adversaries around the globe.

The reason for the difference between the American role in 1972 and that in 1975 is not so easy to define. One obvious factor was the Watergate resignation of Richard Nixon, who had made the pledge of acting with "full force" against any North Vietnamese violation of the 1973 Agreement to End the War and Restore Peace in Vietnam. But in Nixon's place, Gerald Ford certainly tried to provide the assistance the South Vietnamese needed, so the change in Presidents is not the whole explanation. The cause is more clearly identifiable in the Congress's refusal of the monetary and material components of American assistance, reflected in its sharp reductions in appropriations for the military aid South Vietnam needed and in the adoption of the 1973 War Powers Act limiting the authority of the President to employ American military force abroad. In part, this Congressional attitude stemmed from the belief that "peace" had been achieved in Indochina by the 1973 Agreement (at least for Americans). But the refusal of further American involvement had even deeper roots.

The rise in the antiwar movement after Tet 1968, and its increasing support by the U.S. public, must be ascribed to a feeling of frustration among Americans that the use of American military force in Vietnam had been ineffective, brutalizing, and costly in the blood of Americans and Vietnamese beyond any worthy objective. The dramatic images of the Tet attack had turned off America; the low-key reports of the success of the Vietnamese Government in the countryside of Vietnam thereafter could not counter the established image of American failure. Here responsibility

must be assigned to the penultimate major error of the
Americans in Vietnam: insisting upon fighting an Ameri-
can-style military war against an enemy who, through the
early years of the war, was fighting his style of people's war
at the level of the population. American troops only rarely
could find the enemy; since it proved almost impossible to
fix him, fighting him generally consisted of fighting off his
attacks, not finishing him according to the best military
tradition. As a result, Americans troops frequently reacted
with frustration and fury and the American public with a
sense of futility and rejection.

The enemy made no secret of either his doctrine or his
strategy. The intelligence reports were replete with references to them, classified and unclassified. The explanation
for the American error must be found elsewhere than in
surprise by a wily enemy. It lies in two areas, institutional
and political. Robert Komer has produced perhaps the best
summary of the former in his phrase "Bureaucracy does its
thing." The American military expected to perform its role
in fighting a military enemy, despite its many historical
experiences of extending that role to the pacification of
such disparate hostile forces as American Indian tribes,
Aguinaldo's guerrillas in the Philippines, and Sandino in
Nicaragua.

The American dismissal of the French experience in
Indochina and Algeria, of the British in Malaya, and of the
plain warnings of Mao Tse-tung, Khrushchev, and Ho Chi
Minh and his lieutenants that Vietnam would be a different
kind of war than the Americans contemplated on the North
German Plain or experienced in Korea, is difficult to understand. Yet it certainly characterized the American approach until Komer produced the institutional and ad hoc
innovation of CORDS. But CORDS's gradual success after
Tet 1968 fatally lagged behind the American public's rapidly growing perception that the Vietnam enterprise was an
exercise in futility.

The political level was equally responsible with the institutional bureaucracies for the overmilitarization of the
American approach. John Kennedy had tried to press the
institution of the military in the direction of a greater role
for special forces and counterinsurgency, but his death

removed this stimulus. Lyndon Johnson's impatient insistence that American military forces stem the eroding position in 1965 was supplemented by Robert McNamara's faith in statistical power to overcome such a puny force as that fielded by Ho Chi Minh and his colleagues. The result was that the United States confidently increased the application of power by cautious steps designed to impress Ho with the futility of *his* enterprise against American military might, successively increasing it again when it was evident that Ho was not yet impressed. When the American force level reached a half million with no perceptible effect on the enemy's will and determination (or even, apparently, his power), it was the American people's turn to be unimpressed.

But the decision to deploy American forces in full power had an origin as well—the predictable collapse of the Vietnamese in 1965 and the absence of any other option for Lyndon Johnson to forestall it. While John Kennedy might have found another way out of the dilemma after a successful 1964 reelection campaign, and repudiated his 1961 inaugural pledge to "pay any price to assure the survival and success of liberty," it is clear that the overthrow of President Ngo Dinh Diem left a legacy of anarchy in South Vietnam to Johnson. Many contributing causes can be blamed for the overthrow—the ambitions of Vietnamese generals such as Duong Van Minh, Buddhist unrest—but the American Government's role clearly was crucial. And the basis for that role still seems almost incomprehensible: the beliefs that greater democratization and effectiveness could be brought to the Vietnamese by an unidentified general or generals than by Diem's continued rule, and that American interests would be better served by assuming the responsibilities of fine-tuning Vietnamese political leadership and policies than by supporting what existed.

The coup against Diem, then, must be assigned the stigma of America's primary (and perhaps worst) error in Vietnam. The two later ones—fighting the wrong war, refusing help to an ally at the critical moment—stemmed inexorably from it. As we have seen, there was at least a chance that Diem might have repeated his spectacular performance of 1954 and 1955, suppressing the Buddhist religious revolt as he had the Hoa Hao and Cao Dai, and then resuming his concentration on the strategic hamlets program as the proper strategy for contesting a people's war. And in the worst case, if Diem had remained in office but fallen to the people's war of Ho Chi Minh in 1965, Vietnam, the United States, and the world as a whole would have suffered less in all ways than by postponing the event to Thieu's fall in 1975.

The lesson is not that the United States should avoid involvement in revolutionary situations or that counterinsurgency is a hopeless, and dangerous, art for Americans. Rather, such programs may be the easiest and least violent way to protect real American interests and allies. But their foundation must be intelligence of the enemy and his strategy and tactics and of the ally and his culture, strengths and weaknesses. Only upon such a base can the United States design programs capable of meeting an enemy challenge that will at the same time be consonant with the interests and culture of the ally, and definable to the American public as worthy of their support.

To be willing to give their support, Americans must be confident that the results are commensurate with the involvement. They have a natural preference for involvements that are minor and for shorter terms. But they will sustain a major involvement over a short term, or a minor involvement over a longer term, if convinced that the results are demonstrably worth the effort. What pragmatic Americans cannot support is a major involvement over a long term whose results cannot be shown. Therefore, whatever the level or term of involvement, the appropriate organizational structure must be designed, ad hoc if need be, to bring unity of execution to a definable program instead of a cacophony of effort confusing to allies and ourselves, and pleasing only to an enemy.

That some of these lessons have been absorbed in the United States can be seen in El Salvador. There both the Carter and the Reagan Administrations conducted a strategy that profited from them and from some participants in the CORDS experience among the Americans involved. The American military presence has been strictly limited to the grand total of fifty-five soldiers (a sharp contrast to

Vietnam's 550,000) and rigorous rules of engagement—even to the absurd degree of a media scandal resulting from an American military officer being photographed actually carrying a rifle. The stress was to support the authority of the elected leader, then Jose Napoleon Duarte, and to help him establish himself against the right-wing death squads who would challenge him and the rule of law, as well as against the revolutionary left. Assistance to the security forces has been matched by programs to strengthen economic development and social growth for the population (although the scope of these programs has been inadequate, even minimal). And attempts have been made to open a dialogue with the hostile forces to seek the possibility of reincorporating at least their reasonable elements once again within the national political framework.

But there is much evidence that the lessons of Vietnam have been ignored or not learned. The Reagan Administration, in its determination to oust the Sandinista regime from Nicaragua, clearly put its faith in a military—even if paramilitary—approach through support of the contra forces and put this cart in front of the essential horse of a political cause and structure. Mining harbors, sending raiding forces supported by a covert airlift, and building border base camps preceded the development of the political ideas to attract support away from the Sandinistas. These "operations" took attention from essential preliminary steps such as developing a real political cause and organization and arranging for their propagation through radio broadcasts, wall markings within Nicaragua, and patient political agents gradually and secretly building resistance networks. Only when these are created does it become useful to stimulate and support internal sabotage actions and assemble committed guerrilla bands made up of local residents, in the best people's-war tradition. Such "people power" is the way to develop an alternative to an organized and determined political apparatus that uses a combination of revolutionary appeal and harsh discipline to maintain its authoritarian control. But impatience with this long and difficult process led the Administration to seek the seemingly quicker solution of direct military action. In so doing, it condemned its efforts to futility and to the loss of the American people's support.

The Communist success in Vietnam, the mid-1960s and the failures of the sabotage teams sent into North Vietnam should have given a better guide for the efforts in Nicaragua. The Kissinger (Jackson) Commission Report had the correct stress of building economic and political strength in the Central American nations outside of Nicaragua in order to develop a clear contrast between their success and the regimented and unproductive life within Nicaragua. But these prescriptions, among them the proposal for a Central American Development Organization, received only limited attention from the Congress, while the Administration focused on circumventing the Boland Amendment's prohibitions on the military and paramilitary approaches.

The United States does seem to have learned a lesson from Vietnam in the matter of challenges for change in leadership in nations dependent on American support. In contrast to the way it acted with respect to Diem during his travails with the Buddhists and other oppositionists, our Government now seems capable of a high degree of caution and restraint. The overthrow of Somoza by a national outburst against his corruption and abuse of power took place in Nicaragua, not in Washington. In fact, the slow American adjustment to Somoza's departure was influenced by the ghost of Diem. In the Philippines, the departure of Ferdinand Marcos, albeit by American aircraft, was the clear work of Filipino "people power," to which the United States acceded at just about the proper moment. American reticence with regard to the succession process in Pinochet's Chile is at least partially ascribable to the same attitude, although reinforced there by the necessity to overcome the myth that the United States brought down his predecessor, Salvador Allende. One of our greatest losses, the replacement of the Shah of Iran by the religious zealot Khomeini, demonstrated a commendable disinclination to turn against a leader who had been praised by every American President since Franklin Roosevelt—although, obviously, the succession in Iran was not within our power to decide.

Out of these experiences, we may perhaps be learning that we must not try to determine the leadership of small and faraway states whose cultures are different from ours, but that we should be true to our own values of democracy and human rights, expressing our influence to these ends but not asserting an authority over others' affairs that is not ours.

An indication of this learning process has been the establishment of the National Endowment for Democracy (NED) by the Reagan Administration. This institution, funded by open Congressional appropriations and operating without secrecy, has been commissioned to provide grants to applicants around the world who will use these funds to promote the development of democratic institutions and programs—from Poland's Solidarity to the campaign in Chile for "No" to further Pinochet rule. In effect, it provides overtly the assistance to political action that the CIA formerly provided secretly, since at that time there was no alternative to doing it covertly. Just as the CORDS ad hoc structure was established to carry out openly, and within the normal American Governmental structure, the village-level support activities that the regular military and AID bureaucracies were not able to conduct (and that the CIA's secret processes posed difficulties for that Agency to conduct on the national scale required), so is the NED able to focus on those political forces and institutions on whose success or failure rest the hopes for democratic rather than totalitarian solutions of the serious economic and social challenges so many nations face.

The NED does not solve the problems of integrating American military and paramilitary assistance with "civilian" economic and social assistance programs, but it is recognition that the political dimension must be addressed. It is also recognition that this dimension must be addressed from the posture of providing American assistance to groups struggling within national political processes to advance toward democratic objectives known to and supported by the American public, rather than attempting to manipulate foreign situations according to the preferences of the American Government operating through the secret machinery of the CIA. There will be situations in which overt American assistance may be impossible in the face of rigid rejection by hostile authoritarian governments, and in some of these cases it may be appropriate to turn to the clandestine capabilities of the Agency. But the existence of the NED means that these will be necessary only when all other means are barred, so that the use of the Agency for these purposes because of the freedom from Congressional or public challenge its secrecy offers will become a thing of the past.

The American superpower, meanwhile, has still not come to terms with the question of how to express, and use, its superpower. This is most clear in the area of nuclear forces. The continuing faith that these huge arsenals have utility is similar to the mid-1960s faith that America's regular military forces could easily overpower the poorly equipped, ragtag Vietnamese Communist guerrillas, and that, as the exquisitely calibrated bombing campaigns marched up the parallels toward Hanoi, Ho Chi Minh would see that he had no choice but to abandon his effort to seize South Vietnam. Any reasonable person can quickly perceive that our nuclear weapons are unusable for the simple reason that any use would be met by devastating retaliation from the equally huge arsenals of the Soviet Union. It is also plain that the arms race in these weapons has long since passed the limits of reason, as both the Soviets and the Americans possess more than enough not only to destroy each other but to threaten the very existence of human life on this unique blue sphere in the vastness of space. It is equally clear that any advance by one of the two parties in this kind of weaponry is quickly met by an equivalent advance by the other, with no change in their relative positions of power—or of vulnerability.

The debates over the Strategic Defense Initiative ("Star Wars"), the MX Missile ("Peacekeeper"), and similar technological marvels are direct descendants of the discussions of the "McNamara Line," the bombing campaigns, and the attrition strategy against the North Vietnamese and their Southern recruits. After Vietnam, one would believe the Americans to be more sensitive to the ancient biblical account of a combat between an overarmored, overarmed, and muscle-bound Goliath and a young stripling named David with the right weapon precisely aimed at the enemy's vulnerable spot, or to the usual result of pitting a powerful but muscle-bound bull against a supple matador. In the face of the bankruptcy of our "strategic" weapons, one would expect a revision of the strategy that led to the present stalemate, wastage, and danger they represent, and a search for other ways to reduce the threat they pose to both sides. One is there—negotiations—but the fearful way in which these are approached until recently gave little hope that they would be eliminated or even reduced substantially by either of the great superpowers.

It is plain that super weapons and forces are sometimes not applicable to the problems the United States faces. Their application in situations for which they are not appropriate, or in which their very superpower cannot be addressed to the target, leads to a discrediting of the United States' will, wit, or wisdom—witness the Marines in Lebanon, Desert One in Iran, the almost fatal missteps during the invasion of Grenada, and the USS *Vincennes* tragedy in the Persian Gulf.

Congress has forced a reluctant Pentagon to give greater attention to our special operations forces, but there is still a paucity of analysis, organization, and doctrine as to how to integrate the political factors so important in modern struggles into a comprehensive strategy. The Pentagon's efforts to deal with "low-intensity warfare" still seem to approach the problem with a military bias, seeking to frustrate or eliminate an enemy. The political objective of incorporating the enemy or his individual members into a consensus, either through negotiation or through programs designed by their substance (not merely their appearance) to secure the defection of his supporters and the adhesion of the uncommitted, is left out of the equation.

The American weakness in this regard is particularly apparent in the omission of a role for police operations, which provide a careful use of force appropriate to the purpose under strict legal control. Integrating such activities into a Pentagon strategy is difficult enough; the Wyatt Earp U.S. tradition of police action is far from the doctrine of nations like the British, the Japanese, and others which have used police effectively. But one truly despairs at the prospect of trying to surmount the simplistic reaction of Congress of barring any U.S. involvement in Latin American police programs because human rights abuses have occurred, instead of using them for training and advisory efforts to produce better practices.

We thus are still in the situation we faced in Vietnam from 1959 to 1967, trying to articulate and implement what should be a single strategic effort through the independent baronies of the established American Governmental structure. In 1967, we established an ad hoc solution to that problem in the CORDS structure; this worked, but the experience has hardly been noticed in the accounts of the Vietnam War. A new situation could thus well require the same laborious and costly process of experimentation that preceded CORDS. It was a better way then, but it came too late for the American people, whatever its successes on the ground. We cannot afford to stumble again before some new challenge.

Perhaps the saddest example of our inattention to the need to develop a better way of integrating our military and civilian efforts abroad is the Vietnam Memorial adjacent to the Lincoln Memorial in Washington. This moving but ambiguous sunken wall names some 58,000 of America's fallen in that conflict to give *them* honor, if not the cause for which they died. But it holds only the names of military personnel. The civilians who died serving with the military in CORDS, and otherwise, are not recognized as having made the same sacrifice. When one cannot find the name of John Paul Vann on the wall, despite his death in full action in the 1972 Easter offensive, when he commanded all U.S. military and civilian personnel in the highland region, one can only conclude that the American view that Vietnam was a soldiers' rather than a people's war still prevails.

If that were to be the conclusion drawn from the sixteen years leading up to the finale of April 1975, I would feel it a double defeat. It would mean the defeat not only of America and its allies' defense in Vietnam against the Communist threat to us both but also of the entire learning process we went through there. After years of trial and much error, we had finally learned how to meld our military, political, and economic efforts in support of a single strategy and of a unified mechanism for its execution. But then the hopeful years of 1962, 1967, and 1972, through which I had lived, had been followed in each case, in the kind of inconstancy one would hope a great power would not display, by the ghastly years of 1963, 1968, and 1975—through which I also had to live.

I do not assert that America should take on the task of defending—and directing—other nations, but there is, in my mind, a clear obligation on our part to support our allies in common efforts to defend us both against the enemies whose hostility to us both is manifest. With the withdrawal of almost all American forces from Vietnam by 1972 and South Vietnam's successful repulse of the North Vietnamese Easter offensive that year with our air and logistics aid, I had hoped that our policies had settled into a long-term posture that could protect us and our ally in South Vietnam against the threat trumpeted by our adversaries. That posture had worked in Korea; it seemed it could be equally productive in Vietnam. I had looked ahead to the same favorable prospects for Vietnam that were already beginning to appear in Korea, as the energies of its people could turn to the challenges of economic growth and social development and away from the agonies of war.

Instead, the following months saw a steady erosion of American support and interest in Vietnam, while the North Vietnamese carefully prepared the next effort against South Vietnam. American aid to South Vietnam was reduced by large proportions, and the Thieu Government was faced with the need to husband its military resources for the day when, assuredly, the North Vietnamese would resume the assault. In the United States, by now preoccupied with the internal crisis of Watergate, there was no stomach for further involvement in—or even assistance to—South Vietnam. This retreat by the United States from its status as an ally of South Vietnam forecast a disastrous end to a long enterprise.

Daily informed of the consequences to which our course was leading, I did my best to convey the ominous facts to the Committees of the Congress in support of Presidents Nixon's and Ford's concerns over the unmistakable North Vietnamese intent to resume the assault. But among the members of the Congress there was little response to, or indeed interest in, the fate of our ally. The great lesson of the 1972 North Vietnamese attack—that the South Vietnamese could defend themselves without American ground troops if they

continued to receive full American support in other areas—
was ignored.

It was very painful, of course, to see policy go so awry.
But the human dimension of the collapse hit me hard as
well. The most tragic facts to face were the million or more
Vietnamese and 58,000 American lives sacrificed for such a
defeat, and the hundreds of thousands of exiles the event
was sure to generate (although I had not foreseen the
trauma and tragedy of the boat people). Friends and co-
workers from many years were scattered about the globe as
refugees, trying to reestablish their lives. Over the years
since 1975, I have seen many of them to express my sympathies with their difficult situations and done what I could to
help, while they have labored to restore some of the human
dignity that was theirs as they struggled and fought in
Vietnam. America's welcome to so many of them has reduced their physical suffering, but it cannot rebuild the
future they looked for in their vision of a free Vietnam.

The relief of the American people generally that the War
was over at last avoided a repetition of the 1950s dispute over
"Who lost China?" Politically, the subject of Vietnam
quickly dropped into oblivion. I grieved over the lost people
and opportunities but did not see that I personally could
have done anything much better to bring about a different
outcome. But this did not dissolve the frustration aroused
by the knowledge that the South Vietnamese would be
subjected to a draconian regime augmented by the type of
"reeducation" and punishment the Communist regime in
China had imposed after its 1949 victory. I was certain that
the prospects for South Vietnam would indeed prove so
grim under its new masters as to clearly and justly repudiate
those Americans who had gone so far as to urge the victory
of Ho Chi Minh and his heirs.

Today there are some indications that the Communist
authorities who "won" are aware of the hollowness of their
own "lost victory" and of the continued suffering of the
Vietnamese people under their misrule. A new generation
of leaders of Vietnam gives some slight promise of realizing
that their predecessors may have been able to win a war but
were unable to win against the challenges of "peace."
Vietnam has not become an open and democratic society,

but its new leaders are taking some tentative steps toward withdrawal from their adventure into Cambodia. They seem to be trying to normalize their relations with the rest of Asia—and the world. They have far to go, but they may have begun the long journey. One of the many tragic aspects of that journey, with its origins in the War itself, is the heavy—and self-created—baggage they carry.

When I came to reflect on the experiences and lessons of Vietnam, during subsequent years, I gradually realized that the responsible positions I had held throughout most of sixteen years gave me an almost unique vantage point for analyzing the American experience in Vietnam—what had occurred and how, and how it might have been different. If I could at least help to find a better way for future American action in other areas, some benefit might flow from the misery inflicted on so many during those years and afterward. To try to do so is not to engage in casting blame or in justifying self. If some of my ideas of how to fight a people's war may have been right, I was not sufficiently forceful to cause them to be adopted at the time or on the scale needed. Again, as Robert Kennedy said, there is enough blame for Vietnam to go around. We all have a share.

The challenge for Americans is to approach the problems of our relations with friends and foes from the point of view of the real lessons of Vietnam. In human affairs nothing is truly inevitable, and men and women of goodwill have learned from the past to improve the future on many occasions. With the perspective of over twenty years from Tet 1968, it is not too much to ask that the lessons of the Vietnam experience, bad and good, be drawn upon to prevent similar failures in the future. This will not redeem the dead or sweep away the many agonies leading up to the final one of defeat. But it should prevent a repetition elsewhere of that final outcome.

There was, after all, another conceivable outcome of the Vietnamese War. With other human decisions, it might have been that South Vietnam, under a Thieu or other non-Communist Government, would gradually have improved its economic, social, and political systems to become a modern, even democratic nation. To many, and especially those in the antiwar movement, this seemed totally unlikely, but the experience of Vietnam's fellow nations on the rim of Asia now suggests that it was a highly likely possibility. Those countries also were charged with having governments that were military, authoritarian, and corrupt, unworthy of support by the United States. But the dramatic economic successes of South Korea, Taiwan, Singapore, and Thailand have been followed by the distribution of the benefits of progress to their peoples and the inexorable growth of democratic aspirations, which are now well on their way to fulfillment in most of these countries.

Steady American support of these nations in their resistance to Communist threats against them over the years, especially in South Korea and Taiwan, have played a major role in these success stories. At the same time, the Communist powers—China, North Korea, and Vietnam—have alternated between mistaken panaceas for change and isolated stagnation of every aspect of their national lives.

The entrepreneurial instincts of the Vietnamese people are no less strong than those of their neighbors, and it is plain that they would now be a fifth "Tiger" of Asia if the 1975 attack had been defeated and North Vietnam became convinced—as North Korea has been—that an attack to its south would be unsuccessful and too costly. This conviction need rest only—as was shown in the 1972 attack and has been shown in North Korea—on the assurance that aggression would be met with the "full force" of American logistics and air power in support of South Vietnamese armed forces kept to the strength necessary to deal with such aggression with, as a consequence, little need for American ground troops.

In a political sense as well, it is clear that the beginnings of democratic government in South Vietnam would have grown at least as effectively as they did among those neighbors, as nationalist leaders gradually would have relaxed— or been compelled to relax—the military rule they imposed in the face of military threat. As in those other nations, the choice would not have been only between a suffocating totalitarian Communist rule and the corrupt vestiges of a colonial regime, for a new generation of leaders would have risen from within the nation itself. An America that saw such a development could have had the same pride and satisfaction from its long, costly, and bloody contribution to such a new nation as it did when it saw a successful and democratic South Korea host the World Olympics. Certainly a better ending for the Vietnamese—and for America as well.

Even as I have been writing this book, striking changes have taken place in our world. Some hold promise of a decline in international tensions and the huge arms budgets. Others bear witness to a surge of enthusiasm for democratic institutions and processes throughout the world, despite temporary, authoritarian setbacks in some lands. Still others indicate a growing sense of responsibility in international affairs, a recognition of the pressing need for cooperation in worldwide problems. But none of these developments guarantee the future security or welfare of the United States of America. For that, as always, we must rely on ourselves—and, in a world where power is now more dispersed, on the allies joined to us. In doing so, we would be sadly remiss in not taking to heart what we learned in Vietnam about the primacy of "people power" at home and abroad.

Afterword

I cannot close this effort without several words of thanks. First, of course, to my patient and helpful coauthor, Jim McCargar, who turned the long and abstract sentences I had drafted into clear prose and pressed me to bring life to the people and events I presented. And Bernard Shir-Cliff of Contemporary Books had faith that this book would come even when it appeared that it might not. It is a better book also for his good editing suggestions.

But I also owe thanks to the many men and women, Vietnamese and Americans, with whom I shared the experience of the years 1959 to 1975. We agreed and we disagreed over many programs and issues, but I respected the integrity of their positions throughout and appreciate all those who helped me go through the many difficult times involved.

I also thank the Publications Review Board of the Central Intelligence Agency and its (anonymous) contact who patiently went through my several drafts from the first tangled typed version, pursuant to the contract I signed with the CIA many years ago, to assist me in ensuring that the book would not reveal classified information. That review, however, neither constitutes CIA authentication of my material nor implies CIA endorsement of my views.

Finally, I dedicate this book to my deceased daughter, Catherine Ann Colby, 1949–1973, because during her too short and difficult life, she was happiest when she lived in Vietnam.

Appendix A:

Key Dates

1945–1946   Communist leader Ho Chi Minh receives support from U.S. Office of Strategic Services for operations against Japanese; makes bid for Vietnam's independence from France; requests for U.S. assistance ignored; French power reestablished

1946   Initial attack on French by Viet Minh under Ho Chi Minh's leadership begins lengthy hostilities

1951   United States establishes aid channels direct to South Vietnamese instead of passing through French

1954   French defeated at battle of Dien Bien Phu; Geneva Accords separate North and South Vietnam; Ngo Dinh Diem assumes leadership of South with U.S. aid; Communists assume power in North; 900,000 refugees move from North to South; 90,000 Communist cadres move from South to North

1955–1956   Ngo Dinh Diem suppresses religious sect armies, secures leadership of South; establishes Republic of South Vietnam; "Land Reform" repression in North Vietnam

1956–1959   Diem pushes economic development in South with U.S. aid; maintains full political power in own hands

1959   Decision taken in North Vietnam to launch war against South; cadres dispatched to begin organizing

1960–1961   Communist activity increases in South Viet-
             namese countryside; U.S. discusses increased
             military aid and democratic reforms of Diem
             government; CIA initiates experimental pro-
             grams in local community self-defense and
             develops actions to penetrate North Vietnam

1961–1962   Ngo Dinh Nhu takes leadership of strategic
             hamlets program; American military advisers
             and assistance to Vietnamese Army increased

1963   Buddhists oppose Diem government; strategic
             hamlets program slows; U.S. Government
             abandons Diem and encourages Vietnamese
             military plotters; Vietnamese military over-
             throw and kill President Diem and brother
             Nhu

1964   Vietnamese Government and strategic hamlets
             program in effect collapse in absence of leader-
             ship; North Vietnamese regular military units
             begin infiltration into South Vietnam; Naval
             incident occurs in Tonkin Gulf involving at-
             tack on U.S. ship; Congress passes Tonkin
             Gulf Resolution authorizing U.S. forces to act
             in Vietnam

1965   U.S. combat forces enter Vietnam, bomb North
             Vietnam; security in South Vietnamese coun-
             tryside deteriorates

1966   Communist and U.S. strength in South Viet-
             nam increases; South Vietnam formulates new
             Constitution; "Young Turks" led by Air Force
             leader Nguyen Cao Ky and Army General
             Nguyen Van Thieu assume control of Army
             and Government

1967   U.S. organizes CORDS to unify military and
             civilian support for pacification; Nguyen Van
             Thieu elected President; Antiwar movement
             grows and demonstrates in U.S.; U.S. forces in
             Vietnam rise to 500,000

1968   Widespread Communist attacks on Tet (lunar

New Year-end January) are defeated on ground but dominate media, implying that war not being won as U.S. officials report; President Johnson announces he will not stand for reelection; Accelerated Pacification Campaign launched November 1

1969–1971   Twin strategic campaigns of pacification and Vietnamization succeed in weakening Communist presence in countryside, strengthening Vietnamese regular and territorial forces while U.S. forces are withdrawn from Vietnam

1972   "Easter offensive" by North Vietnamese military forces is defeated by South Vietnamese military with massive U.S. logistics aid and air bombardment but without U.S. ground forces

1973   "Peace Agreement" supposedly ends war; U.S. forces leave Vietnam; U.S. POWs freed by Hanoi

1974   North Vietnam builds military force and logistics bases in violation of Peace Agreement; U.S. assistance to South Vietnam sharply reduced; President Nixon resigns

1975   North Vietnam launches full-scale military assault on South Vietnam; U.S. does not react; South Vietnam collapses; over a million South Vietnamese flee Communist rule

Appendix B:
Pacification Programs in Vietnam

Dates	Name	Description	Fate
1950–1954	GAMO (Groupe Administrative Mobile Organization)	French program directing Vietnamese cadres to organize local communities; assisted by U.S. aid	Ended with defeat of French
1956–1957	Civic Action	Early Diem program to send teams to work with peasants to improve local communities—1,800 cadres	Collapsed with death in 1957 of Kieu Cong Cung, spark plug of the program; cadres folded into Ngo Dinh Nhu's secret Can Lao Party and Diem's "mass" National Revolutionary Movement
1960–1963	CIA-supported experiments: Buon Enao, Force Populaire, priest-led communities, Mountain Scouts, CIDG (Citizens Irregular Defense Groups)	Ad hoc programs in different areas mobilizing local population for self-defense and development; supported by Ngo Dinh Nhu and CIA, assisted by U.S. Army Special Forces	Phased into Ngo Dinh Nhu's strategic hamlets program; CIA support passed to USAID Rural Development Program, U.S. Army Special Forces, and MACV Rural Development Support Program
1961–1963	Strategic Hamlets	Ngo Dinh Nhu's national program to organize local hamlets for self-defense and to provide	Successfully seized initiative in 1962 from Communists; drew increasing attacks from Commu-

		new social and political base to Vietnam; assisted by USAID and U.S. MACV	nists; overextension and false reporting created more facade than reality in many hamlets; collapsed with overthrow of Diem
1964–1966	Various military-directed pacification operations: Sunrise, Long An, Hop Tac, etc.	U.S. and Vietnamese Army military programs to "clear and hold"	Heavy on military aspects, minimal on political; marginal effects initially, even those lost when military went to other operations
1965–1968	Peoples Action Teams, later to become Rural Development Cadre; Census-Grievance teams; Armed Propaganda Teams; Provincial Reconnaissance Units; Combined Action Platoons; National Police Field Force	Programs generally at local level to seek rural security and influence; supported by CIA, USIA, USMC, USAID Public Safety Program	Varying effectiveness; later merged into overall pacification program
1967–1968	CORDS	Combination of MACV Rural Development Support Division and U.S. civilian agencies' Office of Civil Operations; initiation of an integrated civil-military approach to pacification	Initial steps disrupted by Tet 1968 attack, causing focus on refugees and reconstruction
1968	Accelerated Pacification Campaign (APC)	Three-month program to take initiative on pacification in the rural areas through fully coordinated GVN civil-military actions	Convinced President Thieu and U.S. officials that pacification should become top-priority GVN effort with full U.S. support

Dates	Name	Description	Fate
1969–1972	Central Pacification and Development Council (CPDC)	Chaired by President Thieu and Prime Minister Khiem to produce and execute annual national and provincial pacification and development plans and programs—close coordination with CORDS Sub-programs: Territorial Security—support and increase of Regional and Popular Forces for permanent rural security; strength grew from approximately 150,000 to 400,000 People's Self-Defense Force—unpaid part-time defense groups in local communities; 500,000 weapons issued Phuong Hoang (Phoenix)—intelligence coordination to identify and combat the secret Viet Cong infrastructure Village Elections—revival of local elected governments and training local officials People's Information—information centers and programs	Cleared rural areas of Communist guerrillas and infrastructure; programs integrated into regular government structure; swept away by North Vietnamese military attack in 1975.

Amnesty Program—attraction and care of defectors from Viet Cong

Refugee Program—care and return to home communities when secure

National Police—training, support, and increase of National Police and deployment to rural areas

Rural Development Cadre—teams to revive village government

Village Self-Development—funds for local improvement programs voted by elected village councils

Provincial and Municipal Development—funds for improvements voted by elected councils

Land Reform—distribution of land titles to tillers

Ethnic Minority Development—for highland tribal groups

Urban Programs—community centers

Youth Programs—development of youth, sports, etc.

Appendix C
Glossary

Vietnamese place names (provinces, cities, towns, villages) are given as they were in the Republic of South Vietnam.

A Shau Valley   Strategic valley in the Annamite Mountains in Thua Thien province, bordering on and exposed to attack from Laos.

Abrams, Creighton W.   U.S. General, Commander MACV 1968–1972, in succession to General Westmoreland.

Acheson, Dean   Lawyer. Assistant Secretary of the Treasury. Assistant Secretary of State. Under Secretary of State. U.S. Secretary of State, 1949–1953. Subsequently adviser to Democratic Presidents.

agitprop   Term derived from Soviet Communist Party organization, indicating Party section with responsibility for "agitation" (rousing the "masses" to desired responses) and "propaganda" (spreading the Party line). Has come to mean the content of the work as well as those who do it.

Agnew, Spiro   Vice President of the U.S., 1969–1973. Re-elected 1972, resigned October 1973, and pleaded no contest to tax evasion on payments made to him while Governor of Maryland.

agrovilles   Program initiated by Ngo Dinh Diem in mid-1959 to build "agricultural cities" in the Mekong Delta in order to concentrate sufficient population to support medical centers, schools, and viable markets. Their wide expanse made them vulnerable to Communist attacks, and the program collapsed during 1960.

389

Aguinaldo, Emilio   1869–1964. Commander of Filipino forces in rebellion against Spain, 1896–1898. Led insurrection against American authorities, 1899–1901. After his capture in March 1901, he took oath of allegiance to U.S. and retired from public life.

AID   United States Agency for International Development.

Allende, Salvador   Became President of Chile in 1970, with plurality of one-third. A Marxist, his economic programs failed in part because of U.S. pressures against him. In September 1973, a military junta seized power. They claimed that Allende, who held out in the National Palace, committed suicide, which was denied by Allende's family and supporters.

Alsop, Stewart   American journalist (*Newsweek*) and commentator. He served in the O.S.S. during World War II.

American-Diemists   Literal translation of the epithet *My-Diem*, by which the Vietnamese Communists referred to Ngo Dinh Diem, his Government, and supporters.

Annam   Central part of Vietnam and largest of the three historic regions of the country. Originally a kingdom that included Tonkin (northernmost region of Vietnam) and some southern Chinese provinces, then an Empire, at times embracing Tonkin, Annam, and Cochin China (the southernmost region). Name employed by the Emperors in dealing with Europeans. Superseded by Vietnam only in the nineteenth century.

Annamite Mountains   Mountain chain running along both sides of the Laos-Vietnam border from about the 19th to about the 14th Parallel. Some summits rise to over 8,000 feet.

An Xuyen   Southernmost province of Vietnam.

Ap Bac   South Vietnamese hamlet near the Cambodian border, site of battle in January 1963 in which South Vietnamese forces lost eighty dead and over a hundred wounded, the Americans five helicopters, with three crewmen dead and eight wounded, and the Communist unit escaped back to Cambodia. This fiasco led to Lt. Col. John Paul Vann's resignation from the U.S. Army, though he returned shortly thereafter to Vietnam as a civilian.

APC   (1) A U.S. Army armored personnel carrier. (2) Acronym for Accelerated Pacification Campaign, inaugurated by Robert Komer in November 1968 to run to Tet 1969.

ARVN   American acronym for the South Vietnamese Army (Army of the Republic of Vietnam).

Ataturk   1881–1938. "Father of the Turks." Name taken by Mustafa Kemal, later Kemal Pasha, when he embarked on creating the new, secular Turkey after World War I. President of Turkey 1923–1938.

B-52   U.S. heavy bomber, mainstay of American heavy bombardment support of ground troops in Vietnam and of bombing of North Vietnam.

Bac Lieu   Province with capital of the same name, bordering southernmost province of Vietnam.

Ban Me Thuot   South Vietnamese provincial capital in highlands about 180 miles northwest of Saigon. Site of decisive 1975 battle.

Bao Dai   Last Emperor of Vietnam. Last of Nguyen dynasty. (*See* Gia Long.) Forced by Ho Chi Minh to abdicate in 1945, he was recalled to the throne by the French in 1948. He was finally deposed by Ngo Dinh Diem in October 1955.

Ben Hai   River marking the border between North and South Vietnam at the 17th Parallel established by the Geneva Conference in 1954. (*See* DMZ.)

Binh Xuyen   Bandit gang and vice overlords of Saigon. Eliminated by Ngo Dinh Diem in the mid-1950s. Owners of the vice center, *Grand Monde*.

Boland Amendment   Legislation adopted by Congress in 1985 prohibiting military and paramilitary actions by the CIA in Central America.

bonze Buddhist priest or monk.

Braestrup, Peter Author of study of the Tet 1968 Communist offensive. Former Editor, *The Wilson Quarterly*.

Brown, George U.S. General, Commander, Seventh Air Force (Southeast Asia). Later Chief of Staff of the Air Force, and Chairman of the Joint Chiefs of Staff.

Bundy, McGeorge National Security Adviser to Presidents Kennedy and Johnson.

Bunker, Ellsworth American Ambassador to Vietnam, 1967–1973.

Buon Enao Village six miles outside Ban Me Thuot (*supra*), site of early successful CIA experimental pacification project.

Burchett, Wilfred G. Australian pro-Communist journalist in Far East.

Ca Mau Cape at the southernmost tip of Vietnam. Also name of capital of the southernmost province.

can bo Vietnamese Communist term meaning "cadres."

Can Lao Party Ngo Dinh Nhu's secret organization, largely of civil servants, intended to act as "vanguard" and movers of the modernization of Vietnam.

Caniff, Milton American artist whose comic strip "Terry and the Pirates," later "Steve Canyon," centered in the Far East, was very popular from the 1940s to the 1960s, and featured an exotic female character called "The Dragon Lady," with whom Americans tended to identify Madame Ngo Dinh Nhu.

Cao Dai Religious sect, mixture of Buddhism, animism, and Catholic hierarchy, founded in Saigon in 1926. Maintained a powerful army until defeated and disarmed by Ngo Dinh Diem in 1956–1957.

Cao Hao Hon South Vietnamese General. Chief of the Pacification Central Council Staff.

Caravelle Hotel Modern (in 1960) Saigon hostelry, which was site of meeting and subsequent manifesto against

Ngo Dinh Diem launched by Saigon politicians and intellectuals prior to the 1961 elections.

Chams People of Indonesian origin, living in Vietnam and Cambodia, descendants of the founders of the Kingdom of Champa, established in A.D. 192, with its capital at Hue. The Chams came under Hindu influence in the fourth century, adopting Buddhism. Later they experienced Chinese penetration and sometimes domination. It is the Chams' stamp on the country that later gave it the name of Indochina—the place of mixed Indian and Chinese civilizations. The "March to the South" of the Vietnamese state forced the Chams continually to the south and west, and their kingdom disappeared in the seventeenth century.

Chi Hoa Prison in Saigon.

Chiang Kai-shek 1886–1975. Member Chinese Revolutionary Party of Sun Yat-sen 1911. Graduate Tokyo Military Staff College. Creator of Kuomintang army. President of Chinese Nationalist Goverment, 1928–1931. Chairman, Executive Yuan of Nationalist Government, 1935–1938, 1939–1945. Supreme Allied Commander, Allied Air and Land Forces, China Theater, 1942–1945. President, Nationalist Government, 1943–1975 (from end of 1949 on Taiwan).

Chieu Hoi South Vietnamese amnesty program for Communist defectors.

Cho Gao Principal rice-carrying canal from the Mekong Delta to Saigon.

Cholon Chinese quarter of Saigon.

Clements, William U.S. Deputy Secretary of Defense in Nixon-Ford Administrations. Later Governor of Texas.

Clifford, Clark Adviser to Democratic Presidents. U.S. Secretary of Defense, 1968–1969.

Cochin China Southernmost of the three historical regions of Vietnam (Tonkin in the north, centered around the Red River, Annam in the center, Cochin China in south, centered about the Mekong Delta).

Cominform   Communist Information Bureau, established by Stalin in Bucharest in 1948 after rupture between Soviet Union and Yugoslavia. In effect, successor to the Third Communist International (Comintern), abolished in 1942 as a gesture by Stalin to the Western Allies. Published a newspaper, *For a Lasting Peace, and a People's Democracy.*

Cong Ly   "Justice." Name of street in Saigon on which Independence Palace was located.

Conein, Lucien   Member of CIA staff, Saigon. Liaison between the U.S. Embassy and the military plotters against Ngo Dinh Diem. O.S.S. in World War II.

CORDS   Acronym for U.S. pacification program in Vietnam, 1967–1968, which combined military's Rural Development Support Division, and U.S. civilian agencies' Office of Civil Operations. Established by Robert Komer, it was first integrated civil-military approach to pacification.

Dai Viet   The "Great Viets." Underground non-Communist party dating from French times. Also, historic name for unified three regions of Vietnam.

Dalat   Capital of Tuyen Duc Province. Vietnamese equivalent of a "hill station" in British India, i.e., a place of repose, thanks to its elevation, from the heat of the cities and lowlands.

Dan Chu   Democracy Party, formed by President Thieu for the 1971 elections.

Danang   (Also Da Nang). Port, capital of Quang Nam Province. Site of U.S. Marine Headquarters. In French period was called Tourane, France having received sovereignty over the city as early as 1787.

Dien Bien Phu   Site of 1954 defeat of French by Vo Nguyen Giap, which ended French dominion over Vietnam and led two months later to the division of the country by the Geneva Conference into North and South Vietnam by a line drawn at the 17th Parallel, with a Demilitarized Zone (DMZ) on both sides of the line.

DMZ   *See* preceding.

Dulles, Allen W.   Lawyer. O.S.S. Representative in Bern, Switzerland during World War II. Deputy Director, Central Intelligence Agency, 1950–1953. Director of Central Intelligence, 1953–1961.

Dulles, John Foster   1888–1959. Brother of preceding. Grandson and nephew of U.S. Secretaries of State. Lawyer. Counsel, U.S. Delegation to the Versailles Conference. Member of post–World War I Reparations Commission. Adviser to Senator Vandenburg at founding of U.N. Conference, 1945. Negotiated Japanese Peace Treaty. U.S. Secretary of State, 1953–1959.

Duong Van Minh   South Vietnamese General. Known as "Big Minh" to distinguish him from another South Vietnamese General Minh. Headed 1963 plot against Ngo Dinh Diem and ordered murder of Diem and his brother Nhu. For a time was Chief of State but was deposed with other members of the military junta by General Nguyen Khanh when he seized power in 1965. Resided in Thailand for several years. Returned, he finally decided not to run against Nguyen Van Thieu for the Presidency in 1971. With military defeat of 1975, Minh assumed Presidency in order to surrender, but the conquering North Vietnamese disdained to deal with him.

Durbrow, Elbridge   U.S. Ambassador to South Vietnam, 1958–1961.

EXCOM   President Kennedy's Executive Committee for international crises.

Fishel, Wesley   Michigan State University professor with whom Diem maintained private contact.

FitzGerald, Desmond   Chief of Far East Division, CIA. Head of special Cuban Task Force, 1963. Deputy Director for Plans, CIA, 1966. Died of heart attack, 1967. Father of Frances FitzGerald, author of *Fire in the Lake*.

Forrestal, Michael   New York lawyer (son of first U.S. Secretary of Defense). Officer in charge of Vietnam affairs on National Security Council staff under President Kennedy and McGeorge Bundy.

Fulbright, J. William   U.S. Senator from Arkansas, 1945–1975. Chairman, Senate Foreign Relations Committee, 1959–1974.

Gardiner, Arthur Z.   Head of U.S. Agency for International Development Mission in Saigon, 1959–1963.

Gia Long   Vietnamese Emperor. Original name, Nguyen Anh. From 1788 on he fought against the three Tay-Son brothers, who had divided the country among themselves after ousting the Le kings. By 1802, with French help, he had conquered all of Tonkin, Annam, and Cochin China and became the Emperor Gia Long. He was recognized as such in 1803 by the Chinese, who conferred on the country the name of Vietnam, replacing the previous term, Dai Viet. During his reign, which lasted until 1820, there was a growth of both Chinese and French influence. A palace in Saigon, smaller than the Independence Palace, and used during the 1960s when the larger establishment was under repair from an attempted coup, bore the Emperor's name.

Gilpatric, Roswell   Deputy Secretary of Defense in the Kennedy Administration.

Godley, McMurtrie   American Foreign Service Officer. Ambassador to the Congo, in the Kennedy Administration, later to Laos.

Goodpaster, Andrew   U.S. General. Aide to President Eisenhower. Deputy Commander, Military Assistance Command Vietnam (MACV) under General Abrams. Later Supreme Allied Commander, Europe.

Gougleman, Tucker   Former CIA officer who returned to Vietnam after the fall to rescue South Vietnamese, was captured, and died in prison.

Graham, Daniel   U.S. Lieutenant-General. In 1968 on staff of MACV. Later headed Defense Intelligence Agency.

Haig, Alexander   U.S. General, assistant to Henry Kissinger on National Security Council under President

Nixon, later White House Chief of Staff, Supreme Allied Commander Europe, Secretary of State, 1981–1982.

Hamlet Evaluation System   Technique developed by the CIA in 1964, at request of Secretary of Defense McNamara, for measuring trends in the Vietnamese countryside. A computerized survey, dependent upon a network of observers throughout the provinces, it was based on six categories of security in the rural areas, ranging from Communist controlled to completely secure.

Harkins, Paul D.   U.S. General. First Commander, Military Assistance Command Vietnam (MACV), created in February 1962.

Helms, Richard   Deputy Director for Plans, CIA, under John McCone. Deputy Director CIA, 1965–1966. Director of Central Intelligence, 1966–1973. Ambassador to Iran, 1973–1977.

HES   *See* Hamlet Evaluation System.

Hilsman, Roger   Assistant Secretary of State for Far Eastern Affairs, 1962–1964.

Hinayana   Buddhism as it developed chiefly in Southeast Asia. The term is pejorative and means "Lesser Vehicle," as distinct from Mahayana, "Greater Vehicle." (*See below*). The correct name of this form of Buddhism, used by its followers, is Theravada, "The Way of the Elders."

Hmong   One of the tribes of the mountainous areas of southern China and northern Indochina and Thailand. Predominantly an agricultural people, they traditionally practice spirit and ancestor worship. Formerly referred to as Meo, or Miao, a Lao term meaning "savage." The Hmong who fought against the North Vietnamese are centered in the mountains of northeastern Laos, in the region of Sam Neua. A number of survivors have been settled in the United States.

Ho Nhut Tan   Opposition candidate for the Vietnamese Presidency, 1961.

Hoa Hao   Politico-religious sect, originating in Buddhism

and created around the *bonze* Huynh Phu So about
1939. The name is that of the *bonze*'s native village. The
sect's private army, like that of the Cao Dai (*see above*),
was a threat to the state but was eliminated by Diem in
1956.

Hoang Dinh Tho   South Vietnamese Colonel. Chief of
Quang Tin Province, circa 1970.

Hondas   In this book the reference is to a Japanese-made
motorized scooter, not to the same company's later auto-
mobiles.

Hue   Imperial capital of Vietnam. In South Vietnam Republic, capital of Thua Thien Province.

Hukbalahaps   Communist guerrilla movement in the
Philippines after World War II. Defeated during the
1950s by President Magsaysay with counsel and assistance from Edward Lansdale.

Humphrey, Hubert   U.S. Senator from Minnesota. Vice
President of the United States, 1965–1969, Democratic
Party candidate for President, 1968.

Hunt, Howard   Former CIA employee. While assisting
Republican Party in 1972 election, authored scheme to
discredit President Kennedy by rewriting his role in the
fall of Diem.

Ingersoll, Robert   Ambassador to Japan in the Nixon
Administration, Deputy Secretary of State in the Ford
Administration.

Jacobson, George   Assistant Chief of Staff for CORDS,
MACV, and successor to Colby as Director of CORDS.

Keegan, George   U.S. General. In 1968 on Seventh Air
Force staff. Later Chief of Intelligence of the U.S. Air
Force.

Khe Sanh   Town on east-west Route 9 (running across
Vietnam and Laos to Thailand) just below the DMZ, in
mountains of western Quang Tri Province. Close to
border of Laos, it became battle site in North Vietnamese invasions from their Ho Chi Minh Trail supply
lines.

Khmer   People and language of Cambodia (Kampuchea).

Khmer Rouge   Cambodian Communists, supported by China. Their conquest of Cambodia in 1975, and establishment of their Government under Pol Pot, was followed by forced evacuation of all cities and towns. Until their displacement by a Vietnamese invasion in 1979, the Khmer Rouge killed over one million of their own people.

khoi nghia   "General uprising," an unfulfilled element of Vietnamese Communist doctrine.

Khomeini, Ayatollah   Shiite Imam, in whom Iran's Islamic Constitution, in force since overthrow of the Shah in 1979, reposed supreme religious and temporal authority as *Faghi*.

Khrushchev, Nikita   First Secretary, Soviet Communist Party, 1953–1964. Premier of Soviet Union, 1958–1964.

Kien Hoa   Province in the Mekong Delta, on two of the principal mouths of the Mekong. Known as birthplace of Communist resistance in the Delta.

Kieu Cong Cung   Founder and principal animator of a program tried during Ngo Dinh Diem's early days that sent small teams of civil cadres to the countryside "to eat, sleep, and work with the people," in Col. Edward Lansdale's formulation. Became caught up in campaigns to denounce Communists. Cung died in 1957, and what was left of the program was absorbed by Ngo Dinh Nhu's Can Lao Party.

Kim Van Kieu   *Tale of Kieu*, Vietnamese national epic, written by Nguyen Du in the early 1800s.

Kissinger, Henry   U.S. National Security Adviser, 1969–1975. Secretary of State, 1973–1977.

Komer, Robert W.   CIA analyst on Middle East, brought into National Security Council under Kennedy. Appointed Special Assistant by President Johnson in 1966 to supervise pacification effort in Vietnam. Deputy to Commander MACV, with rank of Ambassador, 1967–1968. Created CORDS. Ambassador to Turkey,

1968–1969. Under Secretary of Defense for Policy, 1977–1981.

Krulak, Victor   General, U.S. Marine Corps. Sent by President Kennedy to investigate situation in Vietnam in 1963. Widely known by nickname "Brute" given him at the U.S. Naval Academy because of his wrestling prowess despite his small size.

Ladejinsky, Wolf   American specialist in land ownership who initiated successful land reform in Japan and Taiwan after World War II. Adviser to Ngo Dinh Diem.

Laird, Melvin   U.S. Congressman. U.S. Secretary of Defense, 1969–1973.

Langley   Community in Northern Virginia in which CIA Headquarters are located.

Lansdale, Edward   U.S. General. As Colonel he achieved prominence through his role as adviser to Philippine President Ramón Magsaysay in suppressing the Hukbalahap (Communist) insurrection after World War II. He was then assigned as adviser to Ngo Dinh Diem in Vietnam in latter's early days, which led to successful consolidation of Diem's power and of the South Vietnamese state. Sent in 1961 by President Kennedy to Vietnam to investigate and report. Returned as pacification adviser to Ambassador Lodge.

Lao   A Tai-speaking people living in various parts of Indochina, founders of the Kingdom of Laos, but also are established in Thailand, Burma, Cambodia, northern Vietnam, and southern China. Also their language (part of the Tai subgroup of the Kadai, or Kam-Tai, language family).

Lao Dong   Vietnamese Workers' Party. Formal name of North Vietnamese Communist party, originally called Indochinese Communist Party.

Laos   Kingdom dating from the fourteenth century and forming one of the three states that made up French Indochina (Cambodia and Vietnam being the other two). Frequent victim of Siamese, Burmese, and Viet-

namese invasions, Laos became a French protectorate in
1893, regaining its independence in 1949. The population is 48 percent Lao, 25 percent Mon-Khmer tribes,
and 27 percent Hmong and other tribes. With the fall of
South Vietnam, Laos fell completely under North Vietnamese influence and was declared a "People's Democratic Republic" in December 1975.

Laotian   Pertaining to the inhabitants of Laos and the
language of the Lao people.

Le Duan   North Vietnamese Politburo member whose
1958 visit to South Vietnam and assessment of conditions there led to the 1959 North Vietnamese decision to
begin war against South Vietnam. After death of Ho
Chi Minh in 1969, succeeded him as leader of North
Vietnam.

Le Duc Tho   Senior North Vietnamese negotiator at the
Paris peace talks among North Vietnam, the United
States, and South Vietnam and the Communist South
Vietnamese "Provisional Government." Tho was the
originator of the proposal to Henry Kissinger that
Thieu simply be assassinated by the United States.

Le Quang Tung   South Vietnamese Colonel. Commander
of South Vietnamese Special Forces. Murdered November 1, 1963, by the generals during the coup against
Ngo Dinh Diem and Ngo Dinh Nhu.

Le Van Kim   South Vietnamese General. Plotter against
Diem.

Le Van Than   South Vietnamese Colonel, chief of Thua
Thien Province, which included Hue and contained the
1st Vietnamese Division and the American 101st Airborne Division. Pressed successful pacification.

LeMay, Curtis   General, United States Air Force, whose
formula for the Vietnamese War was to "Bomb North
Vietnam back into the Stone Age."

Lemnitzer, Lyman   U.S. General, Chairman, Joint Chiefs
of Staff.

Lin Biao   (Lin Piao) 1908–1971. Chinese Communist

military leader, during 1960s heir apparent to Mao Tse-tung and helped lead Cultural Revolution. According to Chinese statements, he plotted against Mao and was killed in an air crash while fleeing.

Luce, Clare Boothe　Playwright, author, editor. U.S. Congresswoman, 1943–1947. U.S. Ambassador to Italy, 1953–1957.

Lyautey, Louis H. G.　1854–1934. Marshal of France, 1921. Served Tonkin, 1894; Madagascar, 1897; Algeria, 1906–1907. Resident-General Morocco 1912, holding it against German intrigues during World War I and inaugurating economic and social development. Minister of War, 1916–1917. Commanded in Riff War, 1925. Author of social and philosophical works. Elected to French Academy, 1912.

MAAG　Military Assistance Advisory Group.

MacArthur, Douglas　1880–1964. U.S. General. Aide to President Theodore Roosevelt. Brigadier-General, World War I, twice wounded. Commandant of West Point, 1919. Chief of Staff of the Army, 1930–1935. Field Marshal, Philippine Army. Commander U.S. Army Forces Philippines, 1941–1942. Commander-in-Chief of Allied Forces Pacific Southwest, 1943. General of the Army, 1944. Commander-in-Chief of Allied Forces Pacific, 1945, of Allied Forces Japan, 1945–1951, of Allied Forces Korea, 1950–1951. Relieved of commands by President Truman, 1951, for unauthorized policy statements.

MACV　Military Assistance Command Vietnam, 1964–1973.

Magsaysay, Ramon　1905–1957. As Secretary of Defense of the Philippines he presided over defeat of the Hukbalahaps, advised by U.S. Colonel Edward Lansdale, who also assisted him in running a campaign for the Presidency in which, in an honest election, he defeated President Quirino. President of the Philippines, 1953–1957. Died in airplane crash.

Mahayana　Buddhism as it developed in Tibet and China.

The form extant in those countries as well as Mongolia and Korea (in Japan, Zen was favored by the *samurai* from the fourteenth century on). The name means "Greater Vehicle" and is used to distinguish from the Theravada (or Hinayana "Lesser Vehicle") Buddhism of Southeast Asia.

Mang Tiet   Canal that passes through the eastern area of Vinh Long Province and links the two principal arms of the Mekong in the Delta.

Mansfield, Michael J.   U.S. Senator from Montana, 1953–1977. Senate Majority Leader, 1961–1977 (longest tenure in Senate history). U.S. Ambassador to Japan, 1977–1989.

Mao Tse-tung   (Mao Zedong) 1893–1976. One of original founders of Chinese Communist Party in 1921, Mao became Chairman in 1935. Famed as theorist of revolution and guerrilla warfare in agrarian economies. Led the Long March, 1934–1936, and, after defeat of Nationalists in 1949, the Chinese People's Republic until his death, following which many of his policies (most notably the Cultural Revolution of 1965–1969), if not his personal standing, were repudiated by his successors.

Marcos, Ferdinand   1917– . President of the Philippines, 1965–1986.

Maryknoll   American Catholic order.

McAfee, Gage   American lawyer, serving with AID Mission in Vietnam, assigned to Phoenix, where he worked on legal standards for that program.

McCloskey, Paul   Republican Congressman from California. During 1971, member of House of Representatives Committee on Government Operations Subcommittee on Foreign Operations and Government Information, which held hearings on assistance programs in Vietnam.

McCloy, John   1894–1989. Assistant Secretary of War during World War II. President of the World Bank. High

Commissioner to Germany, 1949–1953. One of the "wise men" consulted about Vietnam by President Johnson in 1968.

McCone, John American industrialist. Director of Central Intelligence, 1961–1965.

McGarr, Lionel Lieutenant-General, U.S. Army. Head of Military Assistance Advisory Group, Saigon.

McGovern, George 1922– . U.S. Senator from South Dakota, 1963–1981. Democratic Party candidate for the Presidency, 1972.

McManaway, Clayton Chief of Planning, CORDS. Later U.S. Ambassador to Haiti.

Mendenhall, Joseph U.S. Foreign Service Officer. Chief of Political Section, Saigon Embassy, under Ambassador Durbrow. Sent by President Kennedy with General Krulak in 1963 on observation mission to Vietnam.

Montagnards French for "mountain people." Applied in Vietnam to some thirty different tribes of farmers and hunters living in the mountains, most of whom were forced into those areas by the penetration of the Vietnamese along the coastal plains nearly two thousand years ago.

Mounier, Emmanuel 1905–1950. French philosopher and writer, who sought a synthesis between Christianity and socialism. Exponent of "personalism." Influenced thinking of Ngo Dinh Nhu.

Murphy, Robert American Foreign Service Officer. U.S. Special Representative in North Africa, 1940–1943. Political Adviser to Supreme Commander Allied Forces, Germany, 1944–1945.

My Lai Village in Quang Ngai Province, scene of massacre of inhabitants by a platoon of American soldiers.

My-Diem *See* American-Diemists.

Myers, Robert J. Deputy Chief of Far East Division, CIA, 1963–1965.

Nasser, Gamal Abdel 1918–1970. Led Army coup, 1952,

ousting King Farouk. President of Egypt, 1956–1970. Nationalized the Suez Canal, 1956. Obtained Soviet assistance for building Aswan High Dam (completed 1970) after U.S. withdrew. In 1967, his blockade of Israeli port of Eilat brought on third Israeli-Arab War and Egyptian defeat.

National Endowment for Democracy   Private institution created by Act of Congress 1983, governed by Board of Directors drawn from business organizations, organized labor, Democratic and Republican Parties. Receives annual appropriation from Congress. Makes grants to private organizations for the promotion and development of democratic institutions abroad.

NED   Acronym for preceding.

Nghe An   Ho Chi Minh's native province (North Vietnam).

Ngo Dinh Can   Fifth of the six Ngo brothers. Lived simply in Hue, ostensibly taking care of their mother, but was in fact Diem's eyes and ears for Central Vietnam.

Ngo Dinh Diem   Third of the Ngo brothers. Originally a civil servant, he resigned and became leading advocate of independence from the French. Invited by Ho Chi Minh to join him in coalition against French in 1945, Diem refused. In 1950 went to U.S., staying in several Maryknoll seminaries and pressing aim of Vietnamese independence on influential Americans. After 1954 division of Vietnam into North and South, Emperor Bao Dai offered him Prime Ministry. Diem accepted. After achieving control of the Army, he eliminated the Saigon gangsters (Binh Xuyen) and then the private armies of the Cao Dai and Hoa Hao sects. In October 1955, Diem conducted a referendum that ousted Bao Dai and installed him as President of South Vietnam. He then refused all-Vietnam elections foreseen under 1954 Geneva Accords and proceeded to establishment of South Vietnamese state. Murdered November 1, 1963.

Ngo Dinh Khoi   Eldest of the Ngo brothers. Murdered by Communists, 1945.

Ngo Dinh Luyen   Youngest Ngo brother. Nominally Ambassador to London under Diem.

Ngo Dinh Nhu   Fourth of the Ngo brothers. Assistant and counselor to his brother Diem, who considered him indispensable. Creator of strategic hamlets program. Murdered with Diem, November 1, 1963.

Ngo Dinh Nhu, Madame   Wife of preceding. Played prominent role in Government affairs during Diem's Presidency. Widely identified by Americans with comic strip character "The Dragon Lady." Father was Ambassador to Washington. Resigned post in protest at Diem's policies and daughter's statements on Buddhist immolations. After her husband's murder, Madame Nhu lost a daughter in an automobile accident, and her parents were murdered in Washington years later. A brother, charged with the crime, was declared incompetent to stand trial.

Ngo Dinh Thuc   Second of the Ngo brothers. Entered the Catholic priesthood, and became Bishop of Vinh Long, then Archibishop of Hue. First Vietnamese to be consecrated a bishop of the Roman Catholic Church.

Ngo Dzu   South Vietnamese General.

Ngo Quang Truong   South Vietnamese General. Performed outstandingly against the 1972 North Vietnamese Easter offensive.

Ngo Truong Huu   President Diem's Civic Action Minister.

Nguyen Anh   Founder of Vietnamese imperial Nguyen dynasty, 1803–1955. *See* Gia Long.

Nguyen Cao Ky   South Vietnamese General. Commander of Air Force. Vice President of South Vietnam, 1967–1971.

Nguyen Dinh Quat   Opposition candidate for South Vietnamese Presidency, 1961.

Nguyen Dinh Thuan   Diem's Secretary of State for the Presidency.

Nguyen Huu Tho   Leader of Communist South Vietnamese National Liberation Front.

Nguyen Khanh South Vietnamese General. Military aide to Diem. In 1964, seized power and exiled the junta to Dalat. His rule ultimately degenerated into further confusion, and a series of incompetent Prime Ministers from Saigon political circles succeeded him.

Nguyen Ngoc Loan South Vietnamese police commander, caught executing Communist captive, Tet 1968 in famous photo by Eddie Adams of AP.

Nguyen Ngoc Tho Vice President of South Vietnam under Diem.

Nguyen Thi Binh "Foreign Minister" of Communist South Vietnamese Provisional Government. From Kien Hoa Province.

Nguyen Tien Hung Coauthor with Jerrold L. Schecter of *The Palace File*.

Nguyen Van Thieu 1923–. South Vietnamese General. President of South Vietnam, 1967–1975.

Nha Trang Vietnamese port. Capital of Khanh Hoa Province.

Nhan Dan North Vietnamese journal. April 1, 1976, issue published General Van Tien Dung's account of the final North Vietnamese campaign against the South.

Nolting, Frederick E., Jr. American Foreign Service Officer. U.S. Ambassador to South Vietnam, 1961–1963.

Nosovan, Phoumi Laotian General. Leader of royalist forces against Communists and neutralists.

NSC National Security Council. Established by the National Security Act of 1947. Members are the President, the Vice President, the Secretary of State, and the Secretary of Defense. The National Security Adviser heads the staff, and the Director of Central Intelligence and the Chairman of the Joint Chiefs of Staff are advisers to the Council.

nuoc nam Staple fish sauce of Vietnam.

OCO Office of Civilian Coordination of the American Embassy, Saigon. Combined by Robert Komer with military Revolutionary Development Support to make CORDS, organization for integration of pacification campaign.

Osborn, K. Barton   Witness with "sensational" allegations about Phoenix program at July 1971 hearing of Subcommittee on Foreign Operations and Government Information of the House of Representatives Committee on Government Operations.

PARU   Police Aerial Resupply Unit. Element of Thai National Police.

Pathet Lao   Laotian Communist-controlled front group and North Vietnamese political creation to assist in their takeover of Laos.

Patton, George S.   1885–1945. U.S. General, famous for his rapid advances, belligerence, and poetry.

Pau   City in southwestern France. Center for French Army paratroop training.

Pham Ngoc Thao   South Vietnamese Colonel. Chief of Kien Hoa Province. Protégé of Diem but turned against Diem in 1963. Later plotted against Nguyen Khanh. Made coup attempt in 1965, failed, was killed. Brother was North Vietnamese Ambassador to East Germany. Posthumously claimed by North Vietnamese as one of their agents.

Phan Quang Dan   American-educated South Vietnamese doctor and popular Saigon politician, known as "Doctor Dan." Opposed Diem in 1961 Presidential election, was imprisoned. Appointed Minister for refugee resettlement by President Thieu.

Phan Rang   Nguyen Van Thieu's native province.

Phillips, Rufus   Officer, AID Mission, Saigon, in charge of AID support for strategic hamlets program.

Phoenix   Approximate translation of Vietnamese *Phuong Hoang*. One of some fifteen programs under Vietnamese Central Pacification and Development Council (1969–1972), with support from CORDS. Intelligence coordination to identify and combat the secret Viet Cong infrastructure.

Phu Quoc Vietnamese island in the Gulf of Thailand, just off the Cambodian coast.

Phuoc Long Province about seventy-five miles north of Saigon, site of North Vietnamese January 1975 attack from Cambodian bases.

Phuong Hoang *See* Phoenix.

Pleiku Highland province, and its capital, in central South Vietnam, of great strategic importance.

Pol Pot Leader of Khmer Rouge in Cambodia.

Polgar, Thomas Last CIA Station Chief, Saigon.

Potemkin 1739–1791. Plotted against Tsar Peter III to bring Catherine II (the Great) to the throne. Lover and favorite of the Empress. Created Field Marshal, 1784, Commander-in-Chief in second war against Turkey. Governor General of "New Russia" (Ukraine). Colonized southern steppes, annexed Crimea, built Kherson and Sevastopol. Famous for villages constructed of facades only, to show Empress on whirlwind tour the progress achieved. Made Prince of Tauris.

Provincial Reconnaissance Unit Program begun in the mid-1960s to provide forces to province chiefs to seek out guerrillas. As situation improved they were integrated into the National Police, about 1972.

PRU *See* preceding.

Pyle, Alden Graham Greene's *Quiet American.*

Quang Nam Third South Vietnamese province south of the border with North Vietnam. Site of U.S. Marine Headquarters.

Quang Ngai Fifth South Vietnamese province south of the border with North Vietnam. Base for the U.S. Americal Division. Reading from south to north, Quang Ngai, Quang Tin, Quang Nam, Thua Thien (Hue), and Quang Tri Provinces constituted Military Region

1, one of the most exposed of the four into which South Vietnam was divided.

Quang Tin   Fourth South Vietnamese province south of the border with North Vietnam.

Quang Tri   Northernmost province of South Vietnam.

Qui Nhon   Port city, capital of Binh Dinh Province in Central Vietnam. With Hanoi and Haiphong was opened to the French in 1874.

Raborn, William   U.S. Admiral. Director of Central Intelligence, 1965–1966.

Razak, Tun Abdul   Prime Minister of Malaysia, mid-1960s.

RDS   Revolutionary Development Support. U.S. military staff section at MACV. Combined with Embassy OCO (*see* above) by Robert Komer to make CORDS. After Komer's departure (and notwithstanding President Johnson's liking for the "Revolutionary" in RDS, suggested to him by Nguyen Cao Ky), the R in CORDS was changed to "Rural."

Reid, Ogden   U.S. Congressman from New York.

Rhade   South Vietnamese tribe of highlanders (*Montagnards*) located in the highlands of Darlac Province in the region of Ban Me Thuot.

Rhodes, Alexandre de   1591–1660. French Jesuit missionary who successfully romanized written Vietnamese.

Richardson, John   CIA Chief of Station, Saigon, 1962–1963.

Rostow, Walt   Special Assistant to President Johnson.

Rusk, Dean   U.S. Secretary of State, 1961–1969.

San Clemente   President Nixon's California residence. "The Western White House."

Sandino, Augusto Cesar   1893–1934. Nicaraguan guerrilla leader. Waged guerrilla warfare against U.S. Marines, 1927–1932. With withdrawal of U.S. Marines,

1933, Sandino accepted amnesty terms. Assassinated 1934 in Managua on orders of Anastasio Somoza (1896-1956).

Sarit   Thai Marshal and military dictator.

Sauvageot, Jean Andre   U.S. Army Major. Interpreter to and from Vietnamese.

Schecter, Jerrold L.   Coauthor, with Nguyen Tien Hung of *The Palace File*.

Schlesinger, James R.   Director of Central Intelligence, 1973. Secretary of Defense, 1973-1975.

Scotton, Frank   USIS officer in Vietnam, detailed to CORDS.

Scowcroft, Brent   Lieutenant-General, U.S. Air Force. Deputy National Security Adviser under Henry Kissinger, 1974-1975. National Security Adviser, 1975-1977, and 1989-.

SEPES   *Service d'Etudes Politiques et Sociales*. President Diem's intelligence and security service.

Sheehan, Neil   American journalist posted in Vietnam in the early 1960s. Editor, *The Pentagon Papers*. Author of *A Bright Shining Lie: John Paul Vann and America in Vietnam*.

Sihanouk, Prince Norodom   Born 1922. King of Cambodia, 1941-1955. Prime Minister, 1955-1960. Head of State, 1960-1970, 1975-1976. Overthrown by General Lon Nol in 1970, Sihanouk returned as nominal Head of State under the Khmer Rouge. Resigned in 1976 and was kept under house arrest until 1979, when he was allowed to go to the U.N. to call for Vietnamese withdrawal from Cambodia. Then went to China, from where he engaged in moves to bring about Vietnamese withdrawal.

Singlaub, John   U.S. Major General. OSS in World War II. Served on MACV staff. Headed covert operations against North Vietnam.

Somoza, Anastasio   Nicaraguan dictator, in succession to

his brother Luis and father, also Anastasio. Ousted by popular uprising in 1979. Assassinated 1981.

Souvanna Phouma, Prince   Neutralist head of the Laotian Government.

Spellman, Francis Cardinal   1889–1967. Archbishop of New York. Catholic Vicar of the U.S. Armed Forces.

Spirit of Bandung   In 1955, representatives of twenty-eight "non-aligned" nations of Africa and Asia met at Bandung, Indonesia, to denounce colonialism and, with Nehru of India and Sukarno of Indonesia most prominent, to create the neutralist movement of the Third World, i.e., neutral between the First World of the West and the Second World of the Soviet bloc. The separate identity of the Third World and the policy of neutralism constituted the essence of the Spirit of Bandung.

Strategic Hamlets   Program conceived and inaugurated by Ngo Dinh Nhu for the defense of rural South Vietnam against Communist attacks and penetration. Abandoned after Nhu's death.

Sukarno   1901–1970. First President of Indonesia, 1949–1967. With Nehru, he was the chief animator of the Bandung Conference of 1955, which advocated neutralism (*see* Spirit of Bandung). Adopted authoritarian rather than parliamentary rule. In 1966 Indonesian military staved off Communist coup and clipped Sukarno's power, deposing him in 1967.

Sullivan, William   American Foreign Service Officer. Ambassador to Laos. Later Ambassador to Iran.

tache d'huile   French for "spot of oil." Describes Marshal Lyautey's (*see* above) strategy for pacification, i.e., spreading out from secure bases as a spot of oil spreads out on a piece of cloth.

Tammany Hall   Democratic Party political machine of New York City.

Tan Son Nhut   Airport of Saigon.

Tay Ninh   Seat of the spiritual and temporal center of the

Cao Dai sect (*see* Cao Dai). South Vietnamese province and its capital.

Tay-Son Rebellion Popular revolt in Cochin China, 1773, led by three brothers Tay-Son (the name coming from their village), which captured Hue in 1775, Saigon in 1776, and eliminated the Le dynasty in 1789, following which the brothers divided Tonkin, Annam, and Cochin China among them. Tay-Son rule, opposed by the Nguyen and their followers, lasted until 1802 (*see* Gia Long).

Taylor, Maxwell U.S. General. Army Chief of Staff in Eisenhower Administration. Special Adviser for Military Affairs to President Kennedy, 1961. Chairman, Joint Chiefs of Staff, 1961–1964. Ambassador to Vietnam, 1964–1965.

Tet Vietnamese name for lunar new year.

Thich Quang Duc Buddhist monk who publicly set fire to himself in Saigon, 1963.

Tho, Pauline Nguyen Van Member of South Vietnamese parliament for Kien Hoa Province, later Senator. Graduate of Bowdoin College.

Thompson, Sir Robert Deputy Secretary, then Secretary of Defense, of the Federation of Malaya during the 1950s and major architect of that nation's successful elimination of a Communist insurgency.

Tito 1892–1980. Josip Broz. Croat soldier in Austro-Hungarian Army, World War I, captured by Russians in 1915, released by Bolsheviks after Revolution. Organized Yugoslav Communist Party. Led Partisan resistance in Yugoslavia during World War II. Established Communist state, of which he was Prime Minister, 1945–1953, and President, 1953–1980. Successfully broke with Stalin and the Soviet Communist Party in 1948. Became leader of Third World movement.

Tonkin Northernmost of three historical regions of Vietnam, centered about the Red River valley and bordering China in the north, Laos on the west, and Annam on the south. (*See* Annam and Cochin China.)

Tonkin Gulf Incident   Reported encounter between U.S. destroyers and North Vietnamese torpedo boats in July 1964, as a result of which Congress passed a Resolution authorizing the President to take military action to defend U.S. forces and allies in South Vietnam. Repealed in 1970.

Tran Kim Tuyen   President Diem's security and intelligence chief. Director of SEPES (*see* above). After being exiled, plotted with Pham Ngoc Thao (*see* above) against Diem.

Tran Ngoc Chau   South Vietnamese Colonel. Chief of Kien Hoa Province, initiator of rural teams for census. Arrested for not reporting contacts with his North Vietnamese brother.

Tran Thien Khiem   South Vietnamese General. Principal supporter of Nguyen Khanh (*see* above). Later Prime Minister under President Thieu.

Tran Van Don   South Vietnamese General. One of junta that overthrew Diem. Later Senator.

Tran Van Huong   Prime Minister of South Vietnam, 1964–1965 and 1967–1968. Vice President, 1971–1975.

Truehart, William D.   American Foreign Service Officer. Deputy Chief of Mission at Saigon under Ambassador Nolting.

Truong Chinh   North Vietnamese Communist official who destroyed the landowner class in North Vietnam after 1954. Name meaning "Long March."

Truong Dinh Dzu   Former President Southeast Asia Rotary, was opposition candidate for Presidency of South Vietnam, 1961, but withdrew when charged by Diem Government with financial irregularities.

Truong Nhu Tang   Leading Viet Cong. Later fled Vietnam. Charged that Pham Ngoc Thao (*see* above) worked with Communists.

Truong sisters   Leaders of a revolt against Chinese rule in A.D. 40 who committed suicide when defeated.

USIA   United States Information Agency.

USIS   United States Information Service. The USIA's posts and personnel abroad.

USS Vincennes   American cruiser that mistakenly shot down an Iranian passenger plane while on station in the Persian Gulf, 1988.

Van Tien Dung   North Vietnamese General. Commander of victorious 1975 assault on South Vietnam.

Vang Pao   Leader of the Hmong in their CIA-supported struggle against the North Vietnamese. Major, then General, Royal Laotian Army.

Vann, John Paul   Lieutenant Colonel, U.S. Army. Resigned his commission, returned to South Vietnam with AID Mission. Assigned to CORDS, first in the region around Saigon and then in the Delta. In 1971 was named Senior Adviser with authority over all U.S. civilians and military in Military Region II. Held Kontum against the 1972 North Vietnamese Easter offensive. Killed in helicopter crash, 1972.

VCI   Viet Cong Infrastructure. Intelligence target of Phoenix program.

Vientiane   Capital of Laos, located on the Mekong River.

Vietnamization   Name given to practical consequences in Vietnam of the Nixon Doctrine, i.e., withdrawal of American troops and reinforcement of South Vietnamese forces to withstand the North Vietnamese.

Viet Nam Quoc Dan Dang   Remnant of Central Vietnam underground political organization dating from French times.

Viets   The people of Viet Nam (*nam* means "south"; in its first incarnation, about 200 B.C., the Viet kingdom was called Nam Viet). The Viets were formed as a people in neolithic times by the fusion of a number of different ethnic elements, including the Chinese.

Vinh Long   Province, capital of same name, in the Delta, heavily contested with Communists over a long period, but finally fully secured by American and South Vietnamese cooperation.

VNQDD   Acronym for Viet Nam Quoc Dan Dang (*see* above).

Vo Nguyen Giap   North Vietnamese General. Victor of Dien Bien Phu.

Vu Van Mau   South Vietnamese Foreign Minister under Diem, resigned and shaved head as loyal Buddhist, 1963. Later reappeared as "Foreign Minister" for Duong Van Minh at the final collapse of South Vietnam.

Walters, Vernon   U.S. Lieutenant General. Deputy Director of the CIA. Ambassador to U.N.

Warnke, Paul   Lawyer. Assistant Secretary of Defense for International Security Affairs under Clark Clifford.

Westmoreland, William   U.S. General. Commander MACV, 1964–1968.

Weyand, Frederick   U.S. General. Commander U.S. forces, Saigon area, during Tet 1968 offensive.

Williams, "Hanging Sam"   U.S. Lieutenant General. Chief, Military Assistance Advisory Group, Saigon, 1959–1961.

Xay Dung Nong Thon   Rural development program of President Diem. Was absorbed by strategic hamlets program.

Xuan Loc   Site of heroic resistance by South Vietnamese 18th Division to North Vietnamese 1975 juggernaut.

Yalu River   Throughout its length, the Yalu forms the southern three-fifths of the border between North Korea and China (Manchuria).

Yom Kippur War   Attack on Israel by Egypt and Syria, armed by the Soviet Union, on October 6, 1973 (Yom Kippur, most solemn day of the Jewish calendar). Israeli counter attack drove the Syrians back and crossed the Suez Canal. A cease-fire took effect October 24, 1973.

Yunnan   Province in southwest China bordering on North Vietnam, Laos, and Burma. Source of subversive broadcasts to Thailand in 1960s.

Zumwalt, Elmo   U.S. Admiral. Commanded naval forces in Vietnam. Later Chief of Naval Operations.

Appendix D

Hamlet Evaluation
System Results

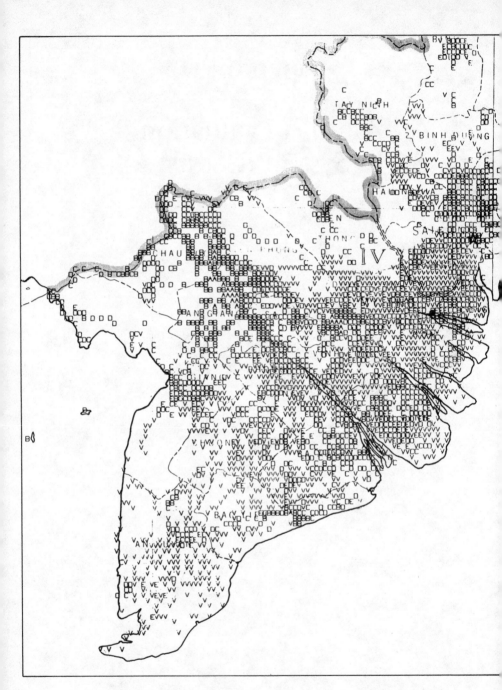

A tactical map of the Mekong Delta for a people's war: this map shows the hamlet evaluation system results for October 1967. The *V*s denote communities judged to be under Viet Cong control, and there are many.

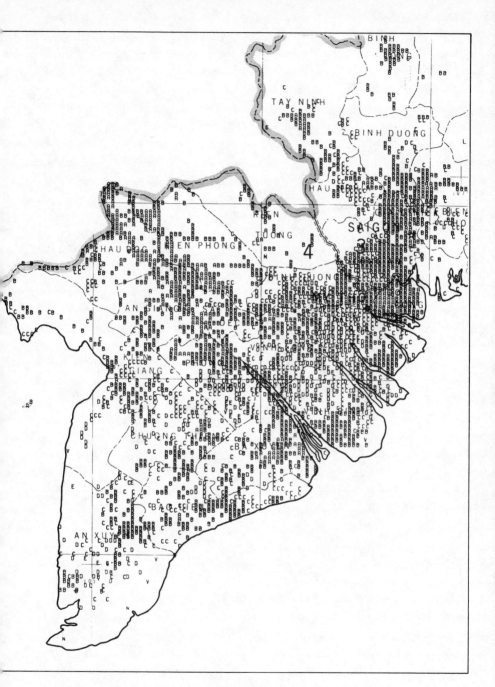

Pacification changes the countryside: this map shows the
hamlet evaluation system results for July 1971. The better
grades of *A*, *B*, and *C* have replaced almost all of the *V*s,
showing how Viet Cong power was replaced by secure
communities.

Index